REX MUNDI
Book One

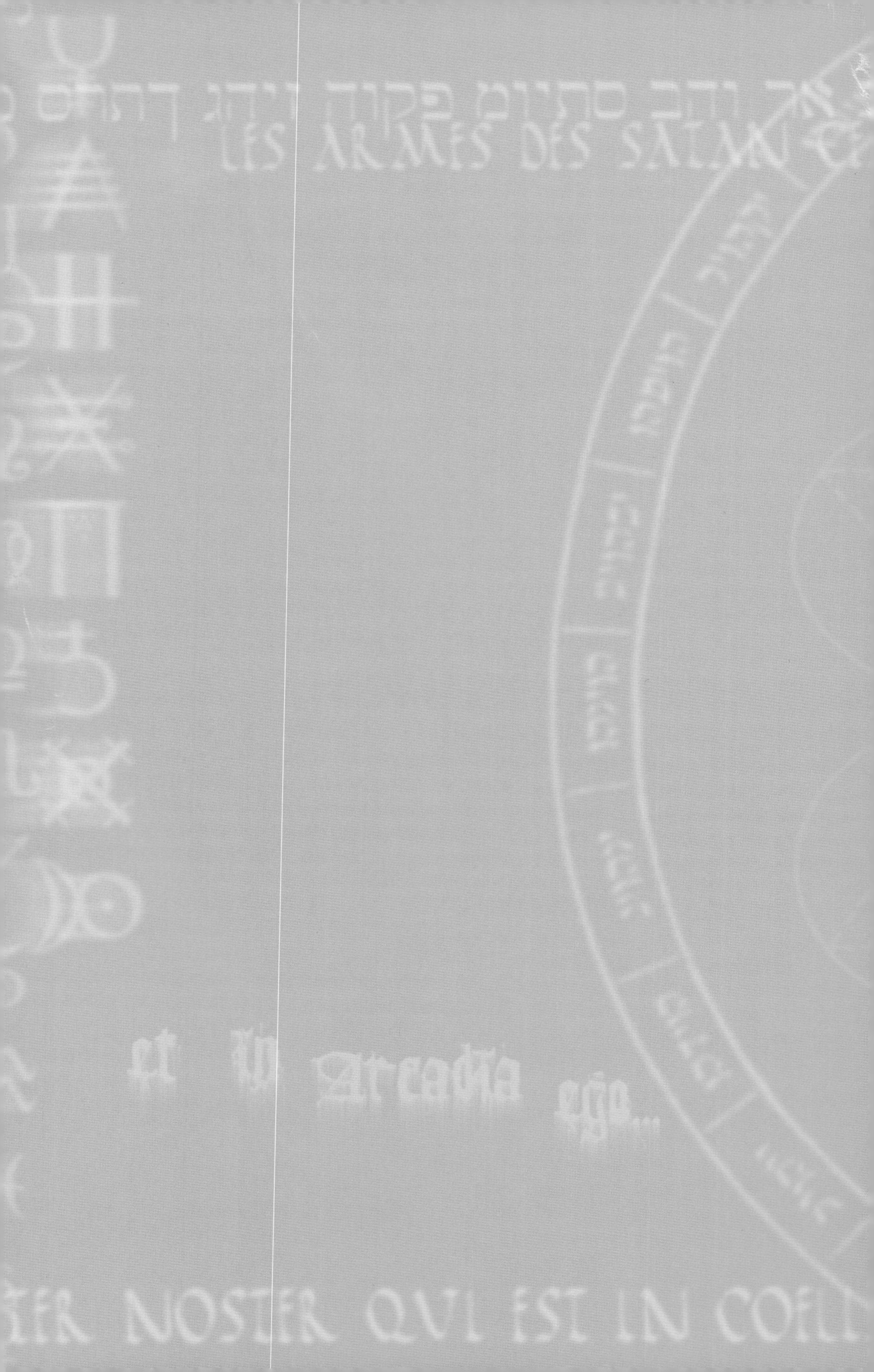
LES ARMES DES SATAN
et in Arcadia ego...
TER NOSTER QVI EST IN COELI

RexMundi

• BOOK ONE •

The Guardian of the Temple

writer ARVID NELSON

artist ERICJ

color artist JEROMY COX

cover artist JUAN FERREYRA

Rex Mundi created by ARVID NELSON and ERICJ

DARK HORSE BOOKS™

publisher
MIKE RICHARDSON

editor
SCOTT ALLIE

assistant editors
MATT DRYER, DAVE MARSHALL, and RYAN JORGENSEN

letterer and newspaper designer
ARVID NELSON

book designer
AMY ARENDTS

art director
LIA RIBACCHI

Special thanks to Jason Hvam.
Archival photographs: Eugène Atget.

REX MUNDI BOOK ONE: THE GUARDIAN OF THE TEMPLE

This volume collects issues zero through five of the comic-book series *Rex Mundi*,
originally published by Image Comics, as well as the webcomic Rex Mundi "Brother
Matthew, Blessed Are the Meek."

Published by
Dark Horse Books
A division of Dark Horse Comics, Inc.
10956 SE Main Street
Milwaukie, OR 97222

darkhorse.com

To find a comics shop in your area, call the Comic Shop Locator
Service toll-free at 1-888-266-4226

First edition: November 2006
ISBN-10: 1-59307-652-5
ISBN-13: 978-1-59307-652-8

10 9 8 7 6 5 4 3 2 1

Printed in China

INTRODUCTION

by Joshua Dysart

I'VE DONE THIS BEFORE. Sung the praises of this book. In fact I've been doing it pretty relentlessly for some time now. I've shouted its virtues from rooftops. I've printed out manifestos. I've bought advertising time during the Super Bowl. I've pimped low and I've pimped high. Again and again I've emphatically made the (possibly exaggerated) claim that *Rex Mundi,* with its literate sensibilities and sweeping scope, is the very future of pulp. I tell all who will listen that the book is a deft mixture of old British Sherlock Holmes films and *Da Vinci Code*-esque promises of buried occult wisdom (for the record, the first *Rex Mundi* predates the above-mentioned bestseller). So as you can see, I've got the shim sham dance down. I've done this before. I've been with it since the beginning.

I first discovered *Rex Mundi* at the Comic-Con International: San Diego, the belly of the American comic-book industry beast. For those who don't know, the convention is a three-hundred-yard-long orgy of pop culture crammed into the ever-expanding San Diego Convention Center (a building that now runs, uninterrupted, along the West Coast from the Mexican border to Malibu). This was some time ago. In 1837 or '38 I think. Arvid Nelson and EricJ's table was a carbuncle clinging desperately to the back wall of the joint, dwarfed on all sides by orgasmic video game displays. The two had a black-and-white first issue of their comic, the zygote of the book you now hold, displayed on the table. The title grabbed me. I'm a sucker for religious esoterica and secret societies and therefore a fan of questionably historical works like *Holy Blood/Holy Grail* and *The Templar Revelation*. It's no wonder that a comic book awash in inky, gaslight goodness and called "King of the World" would catch my attention. But it was the creative team that really snagged me. Arvid was a fierce mind and his capacity to work the pitch for his story—*a search for the Holy Grail in the form of murder mystery that takes place in a Paris where magic is prevalent and the Church has never lost its stranglehold on power*—into a discussion on Chinese matrilineal societies was impressive as hell. Eric, absolute sweetheart that he is, was pouncing from potential customer to potential customer with remarkable enthusiasm, beaming at the accomplishment that he and Arvid had pulled off. They were the kind of creators you instantly trust. I bought the book.

That night, in an effort to wind down from the convention social scene (meaning I was drunk and horny), I decided to flip through *Rex Mundi*. The comic was an admittedly clumsily cobbled together sip of absolute narrative ambition. But despite the raw nature of its execution I was immediately engaged. Eric's environments were truly amazing. His obsessive rendering of every brick and curling piece of wrought iron immediately dragged me down into their world. The rich context made it easy for me to relate to Arvid's protagonist, Master Physician Julien Saunière. It was pretty early into the reading experience that I began to have the kind of vicarious relationship with him that readers are always searching for but rarely find. Together Julien and I lived in claustrophobic rooms, leaning in to listen as old friends hinted at great mysteries. We both began to fill with the rising awareness that we were being pulled into something larger than ourselves . . . and by the time we found the dead hooker eviscerated in that cheap hotel room, both he and I knew we couldn't turn away, knew that it was nothing less than the secrets of the world that were calling to us. And there it was.

Suddenly, I found myself telling everyone I knew about it. I watched Arvid and Eric's storytelling grow in leaps and bounds. Watched them set out to recreate the original material when that black-and-white comic that had zapped me so profoundly just wasn't representative of their craft anymore. During my last days at Image Comics I made sure that those in command were aware of *Rex Mundi*'s existence. And when Arvid and Eric managed to convince them to carry *RM*, I was asked to write the forward to that first collection—this same material you now hold. Like I said . . . I've done this before.

Arvid and Eric eventually parted ways . . . citing that great destroyer of collaborative efforts, "artistic differences." I watched from afar as Arvid struggled to keep Julien on the path. Watched as he found new artists with equally astounding vision. I was able to keep reading because he kept the book coming out. Kept the mystery alive. It is no small feat to continue a personal vision in a world of corporatized art and prefab, fast-food entertainment. I couldn't have done what Arvid has done.

I'm told I even somehow introduced Scott Allie at Dark Horse Comics to *Rex Mundi*. I don't recall doing that, but I'm sure it's true. Scott, as well as being an editor I implicitly trust, is also a writer of wonderfully subtle strength (read *The Devil's Footprints*!). So it's only natural that in my constant *Rex Mundi* PR blitz I would've mentioned it to him once or twice, or shoved Arvid in his face in the middle of some convention whirlwind. And now here we are . . . *Rex Mundi* is the newest gleaming jewel in the Dark Horse crown. King of the world indeed. And here I am, writing this forward all over again, trying as best I can not to repeat the earnest sentiments I carved out the first time around. Looking for new things to say about something I've been talking up for years.

In the interest of full disclosure, though I suppose it's pretty obvious by now, I consider Eric and Arvid to be dear, dear friends. I've driven through the thick of L.A. traffic with Eric (no minor adventure) and stood in a Colorado pumpkin patch with Arvid discussing our fathers. So I do have a personal interest in them as people. But that's not really why I'm stepping up to promote this work yet again. No. I'm doing this for Julien Saunière. I'm doing it because I understand him. Whatever surface motivations Arvid has given the good doctor are all well and fine, but the truth is Julien is a man who fetishizes the search for knowledge. That's what's genuine to him. That's his religious act. With each truth uncovered Julien is building himself a real and lasting soul, a soul free of the taint of lies, and that's worth all the risks in the world. Fact is, if I don't do everything in my power to make sure you have an opportunity to read this book, then Julien, and therefore I, will fail. The tale will remain untold. The secrets of the world will win.

I am bound to this book, and I really do believe that if you give it half a chance, you'll be bound to it too.

Then you can write the next forward.

Peace,
Joshua Dysart
(Writer of *Violent Messiahs*, *Swamp Thing*,
and *Conan and the Midnight God*)

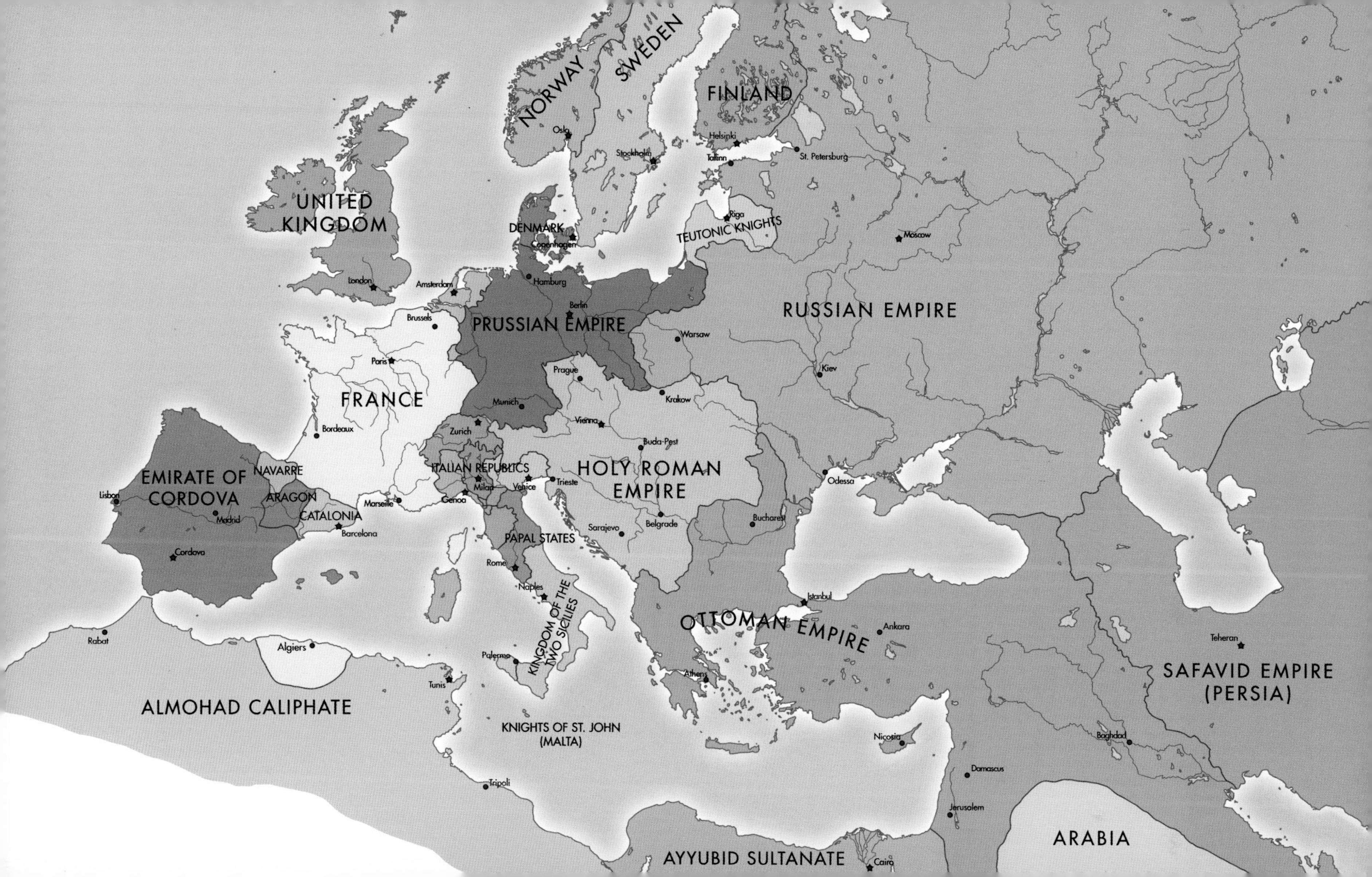
NORWAY
SWEDEN
FINLAND
UNITED KINGDOM
DENMARK
TEUTONIC KNIGHTS
RUSSIAN EMPIRE
PRUSSIAN EMPIRE
FRANCE
HOLY ROMAN EMPIRE
EMIRATE OF CORDOVA
NAVARRE
ARAGON
CATALONIA
ITALIAN REPUBLICS
PAPAL STATES
KINGDOM OF THE TWO SICILIES
OTTOMAN EMPIRE
SAFAVID EMPIRE (PERSIA)
ALMOHAD CALIPHATE
KNIGHTS OF ST. JOHN (MALTA)
ARABIA
AYYUBID SULTANATE
Oslo
Stockholm
Helsinki
Tallinn
St. Petersburg
Riga
Moscow
Copenhagen
Hamburg
Berlin
London
Amsterdam
Brussels
Paris
Warsaw
Prague
Kiev
Krakow
Munich
Vienna
Bordeaux
Zurich
Buda-Pest
Trieste
Venice
Milan
Genoa
Odessa
Lisbon
Madrid
Marseille
Barcelona
Bucharest
Sarajevo
Belgrade
Cordova
Rome
Naples
Istanbul
Ankara
Rabat
Algiers
Palermo
Tunis
Athens
Teheran
Nicosia
Baghdad
Tripoli
Damascus
Jerusalem
Cairo

> "Think not that I am come to send peace on Earth:
> I came not to send peace, but a sword."
>
> —Matthew 10:34

et in arcadia ego...

...TER NOSTER QVI EST IN COELI...

CHAPTER ONE
THE SECRET BENEATH THE CHURCH

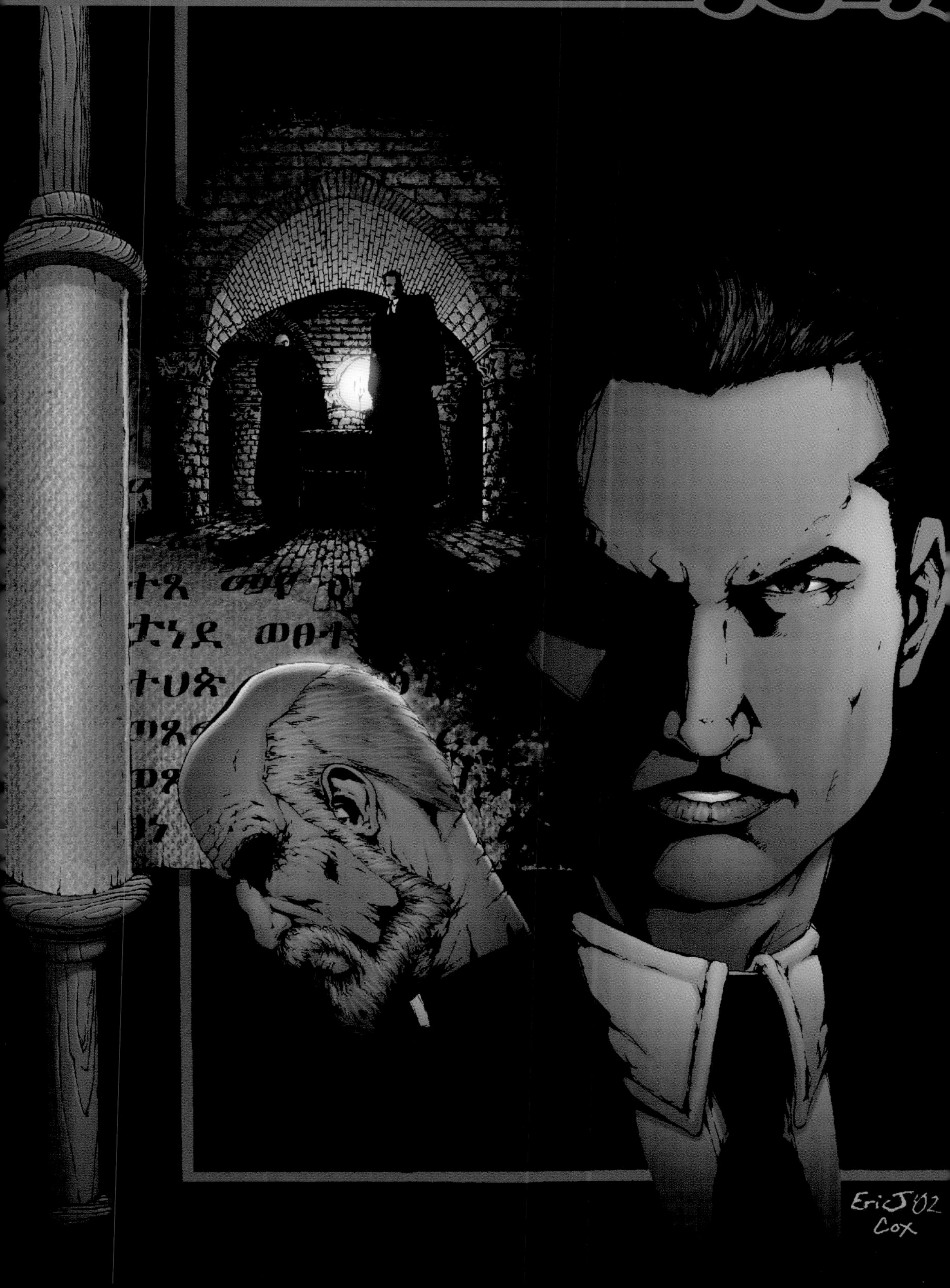

Eric J '02
Cox

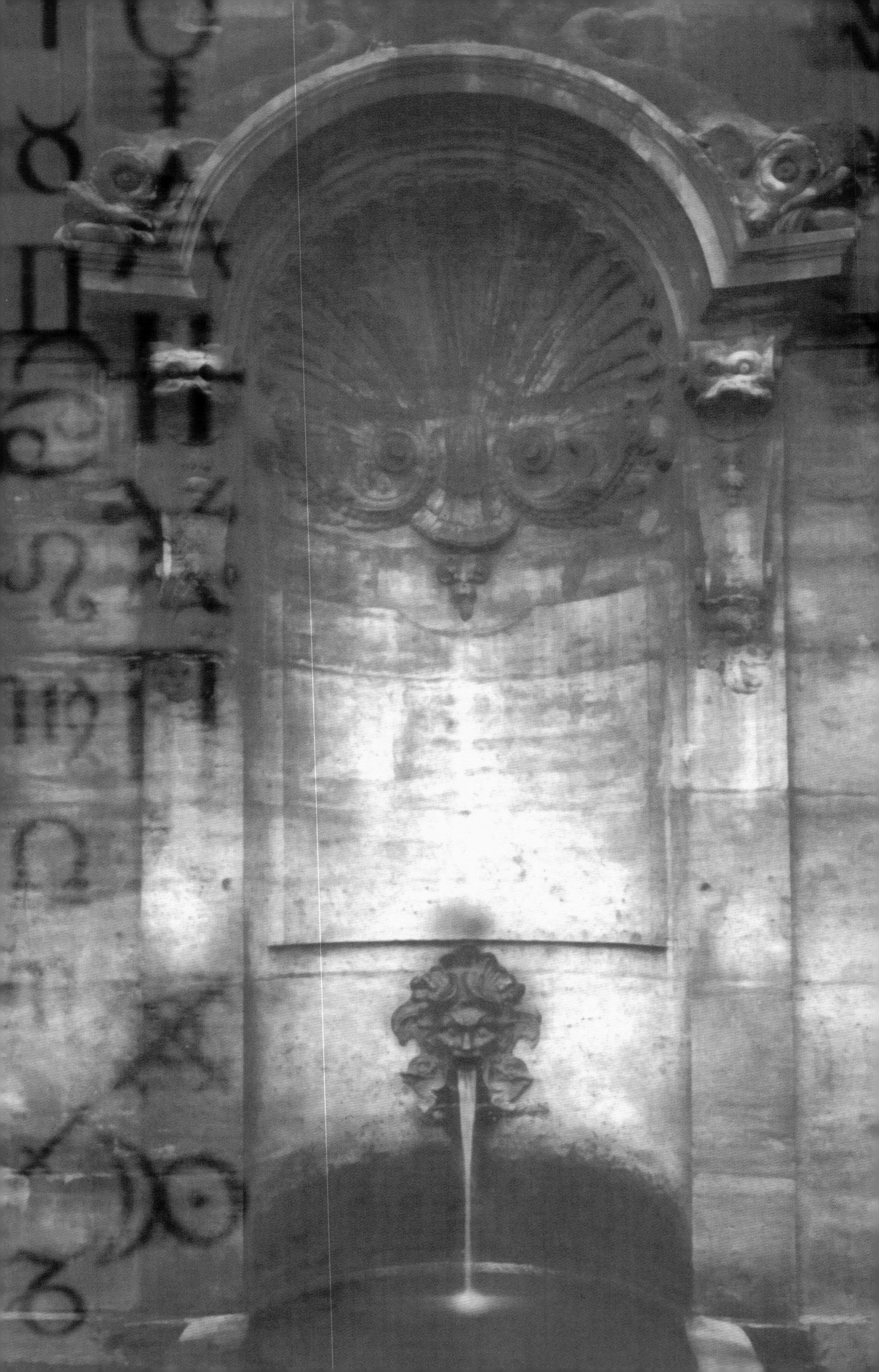

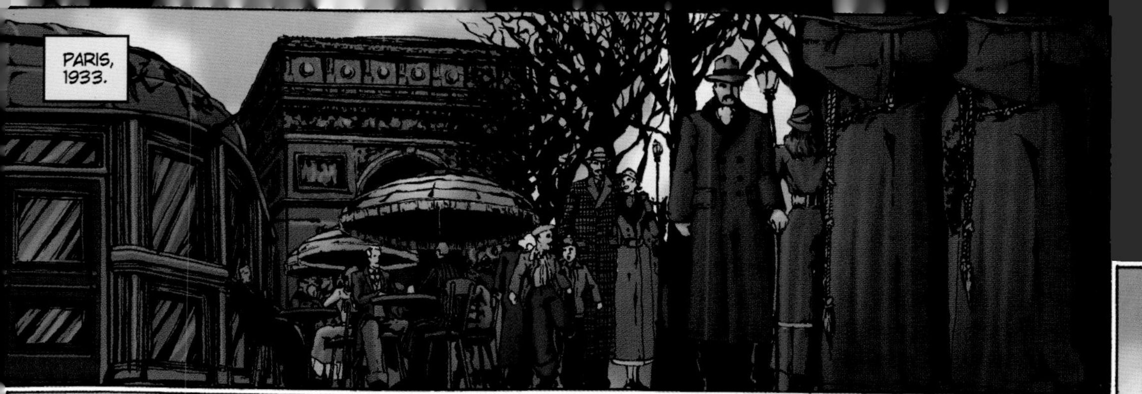
PARIS, 1933.

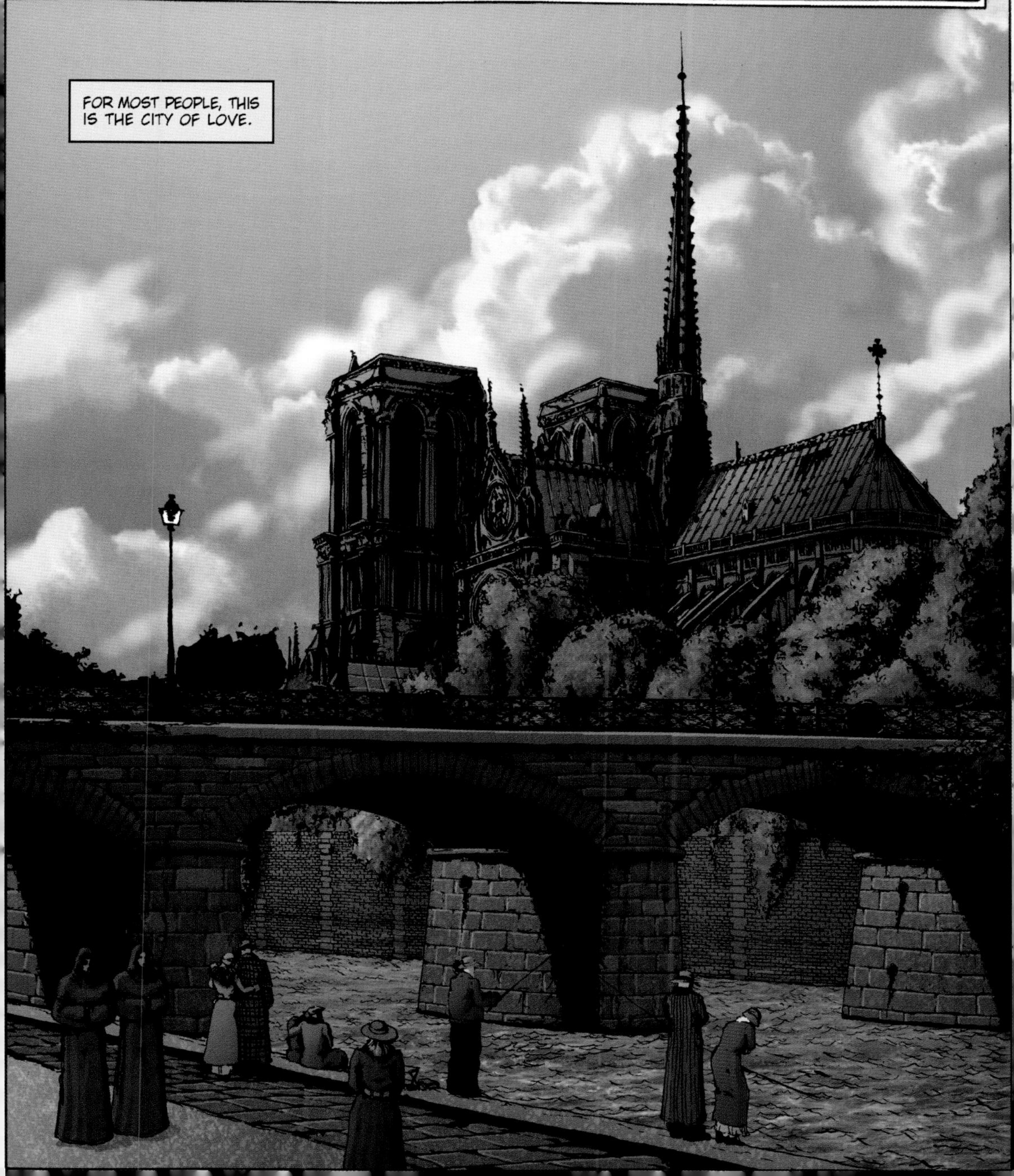
FOR MOST PEOPLE, THIS IS THE CITY OF LOVE.

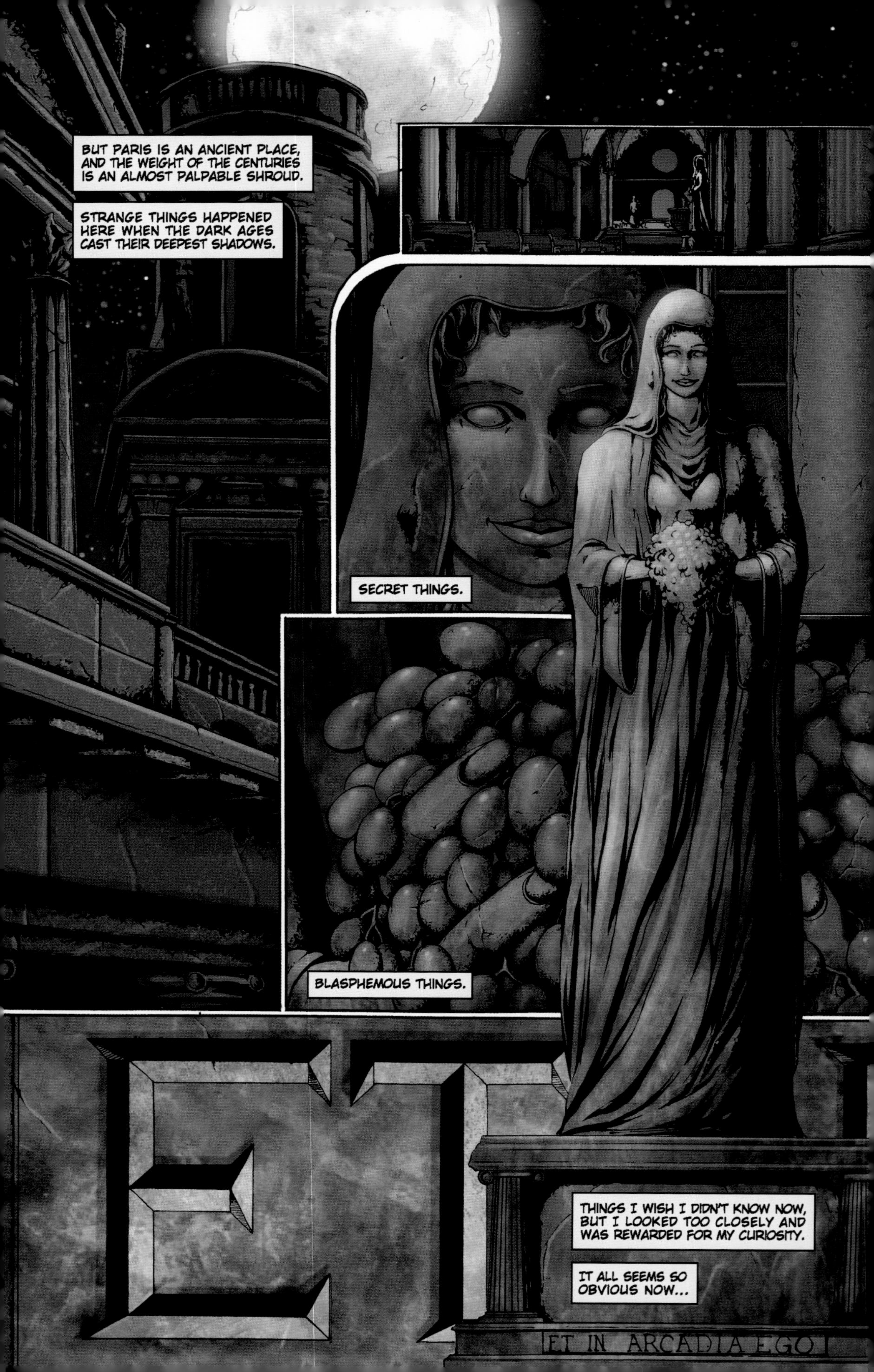
BUT PARIS IS AN ANCIENT PLACE, AND THE WEIGHT OF THE CENTURIES IS AN ALMOST PALPABLE SHROUD.
STRANGE THINGS HAPPENED HERE WHEN THE DARK AGES CAST THEIR DEEPEST SHADOWS.
SECRET THINGS.
BLASPHEMOUS THINGS.
THINGS I WISH I DIDN'T KNOW NOW, BUT I LOOKED TOO CLOSELY AND WAS REWARDED FOR MY CURIOSITY.
IT ALL SEEMS SO OBVIOUS NOW...
ET IN ARCADIA EGO

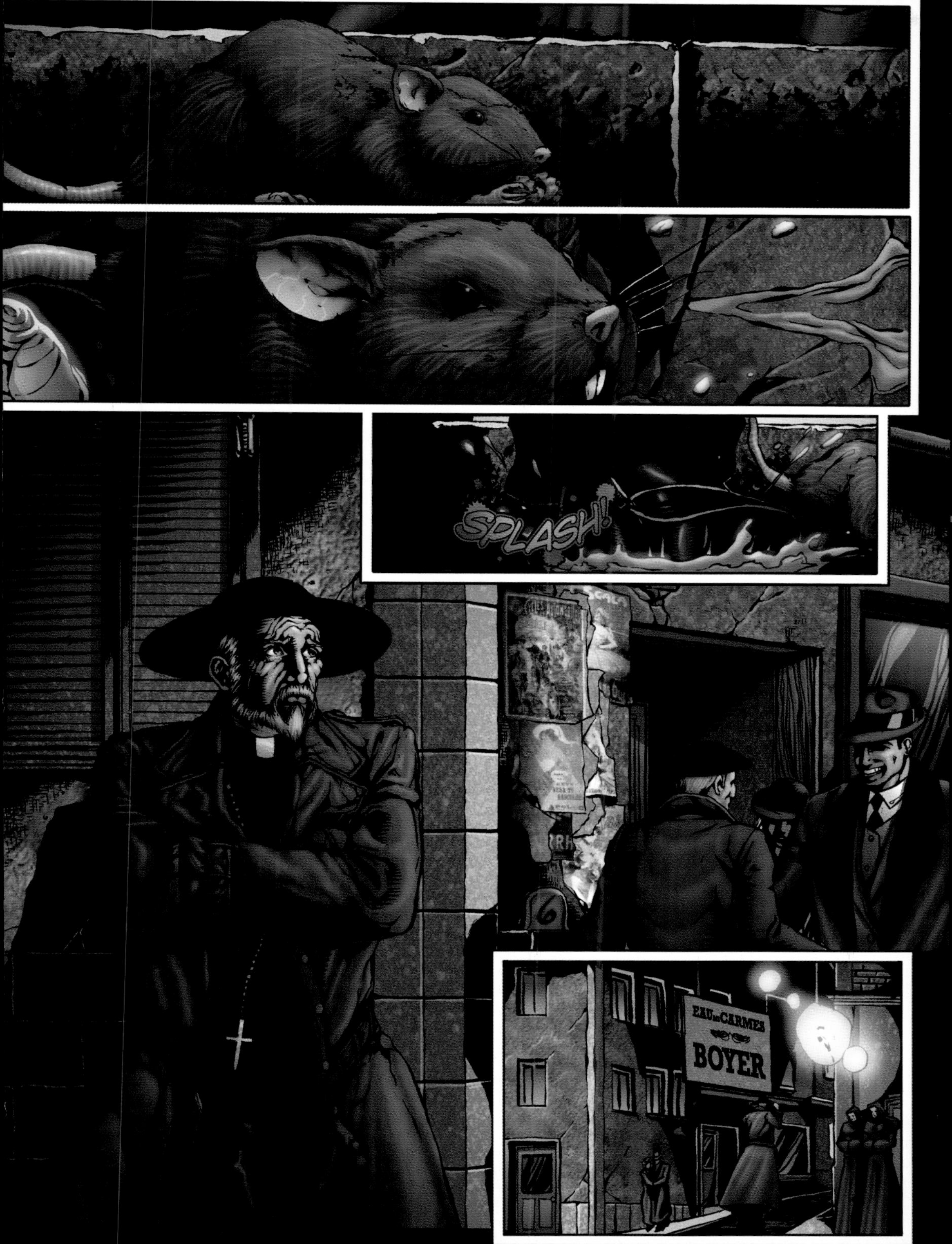

SPLASH!
CARMES
BOYER

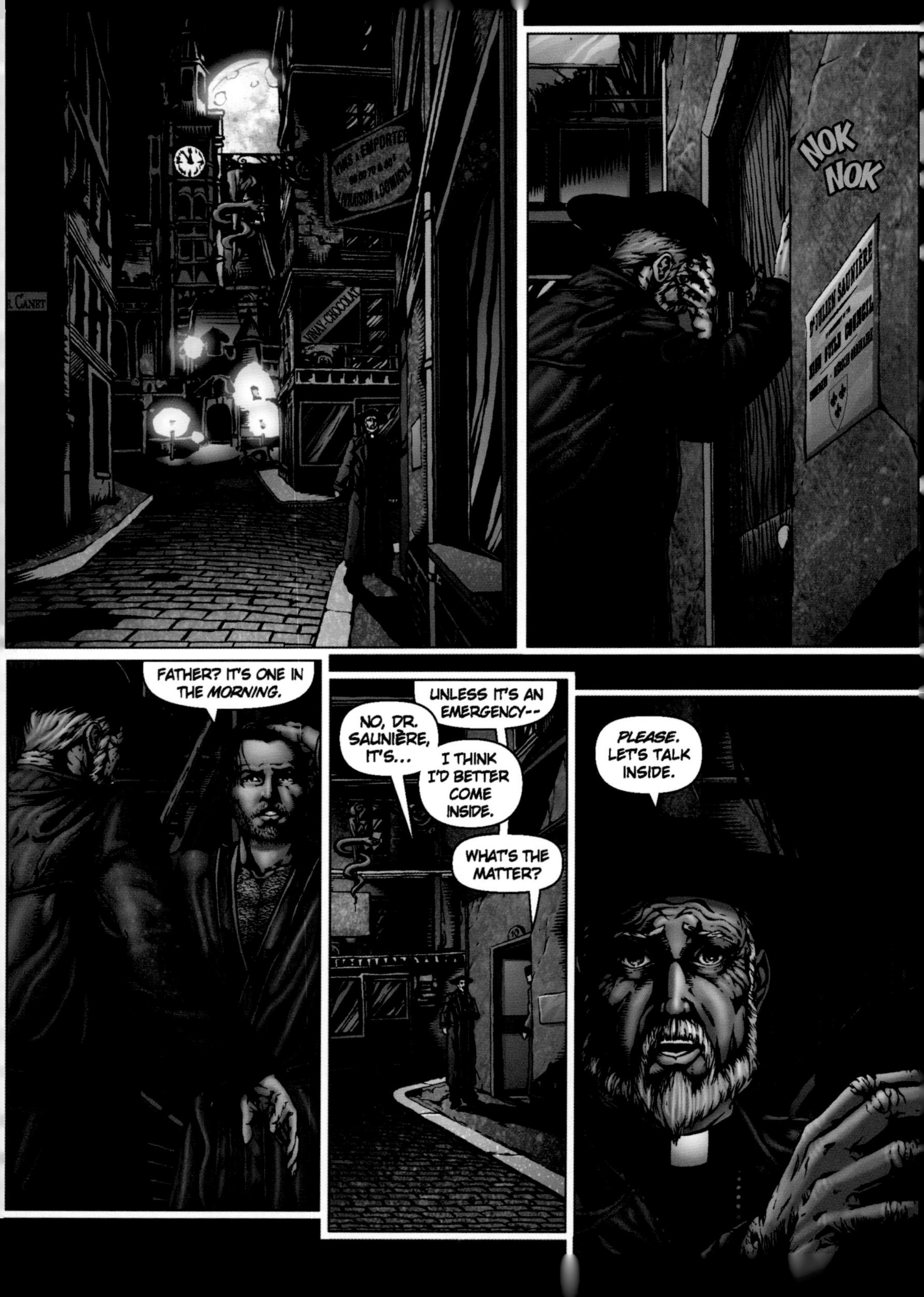
NOK
NOK
FATHER? IT'S ONE IN THE *MORNING*.
UNLESS IT'S AN EMERGENCY--
NO, DR. SAUNIÈRE, IT'S...
I THINK I'D BETTER COME INSIDE.
WHAT'S THE MATTER?
PLEASE. LET'S TALK INSIDE.

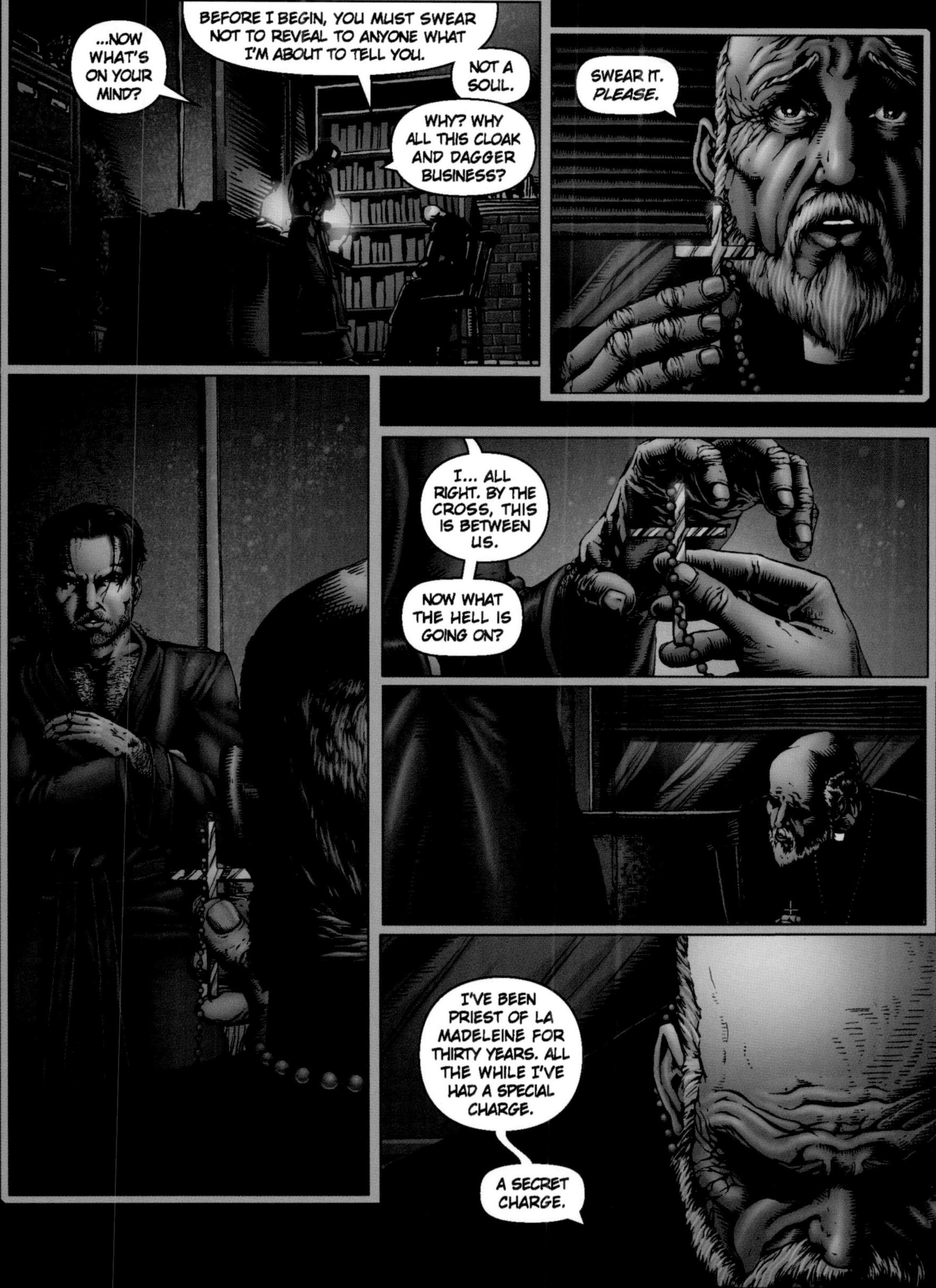
...NOW WHAT'S ON YOUR MIND?
BEFORE I BEGIN, YOU MUST SWEAR NOT TO REVEAL TO ANYONE WHAT I'M ABOUT TO TELL YOU.
NOT A SOUL.
WHY? WHY ALL THIS CLOAK AND DAGGER BUSINESS?
SWEAR IT. *PLEASE.*
I... ALL RIGHT. BY THE CROSS, THIS IS BETWEEN US.
NOW WHAT THE HELL IS GOING ON?
I'VE BEEN PRIEST OF LA MADELEINE FOR THIRTY YEARS. ALL THE WHILE I'VE HAD A SPECIAL CHARGE.
A SECRET CHARGE.

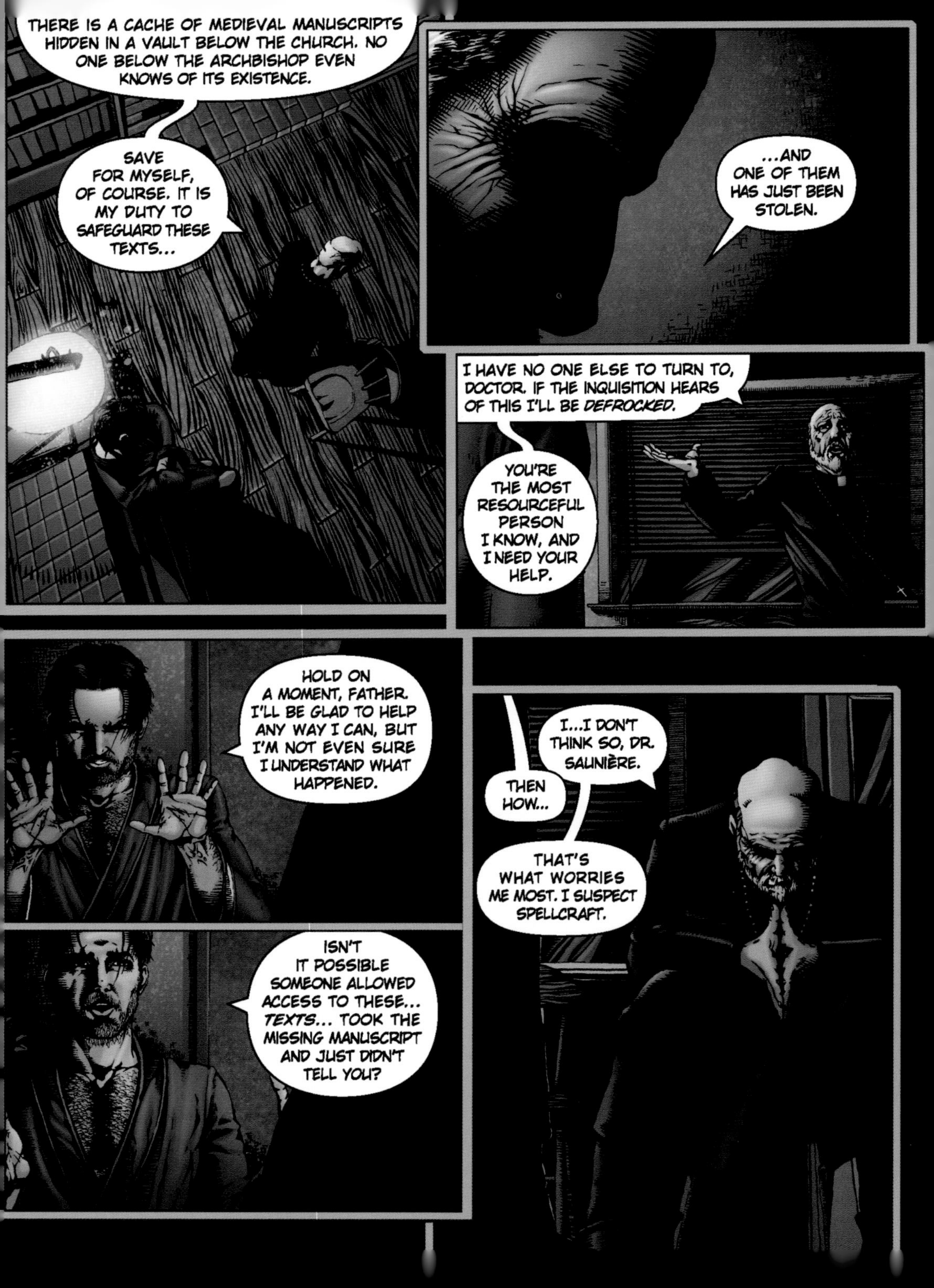
THERE IS A CACHE OF MEDIEVAL MANUSCRIPTS HIDDEN IN A VAULT BELOW THE CHURCH. NO ONE BELOW THE ARCHBISHOP EVEN KNOWS OF ITS EXISTENCE.
SAVE FOR MYSELF, OF COURSE. IT IS MY DUTY TO SAFEGUARD THESE TEXTS...
...AND ONE OF THEM HAS JUST BEEN STOLEN.
I HAVE NO ONE ELSE TO TURN TO, DOCTOR. IF THE INQUISITION HEARS OF THIS I'LL BE *DEFROCKED.*
YOU'RE THE MOST RESOURCEFUL PERSON I KNOW, AND I NEED YOUR HELP.
HOLD ON A MOMENT, FATHER. I'LL BE GLAD TO HELP ANY WAY I CAN, BUT I'M NOT EVEN SURE I UNDERSTAND WHAT HAPPENED.
ISN'T IT POSSIBLE SOMEONE ALLOWED ACCESS TO THESE... *TEXTS*... TOOK THE MISSING MANUSCRIPT AND JUST DIDN'T TELL YOU?
I...I DON'T THINK SO, DR. SAUNIÈRE.
THEN HOW...
THAT'S WHAT WORRIES ME MOST. I SUSPECT SPELLCRAFT.

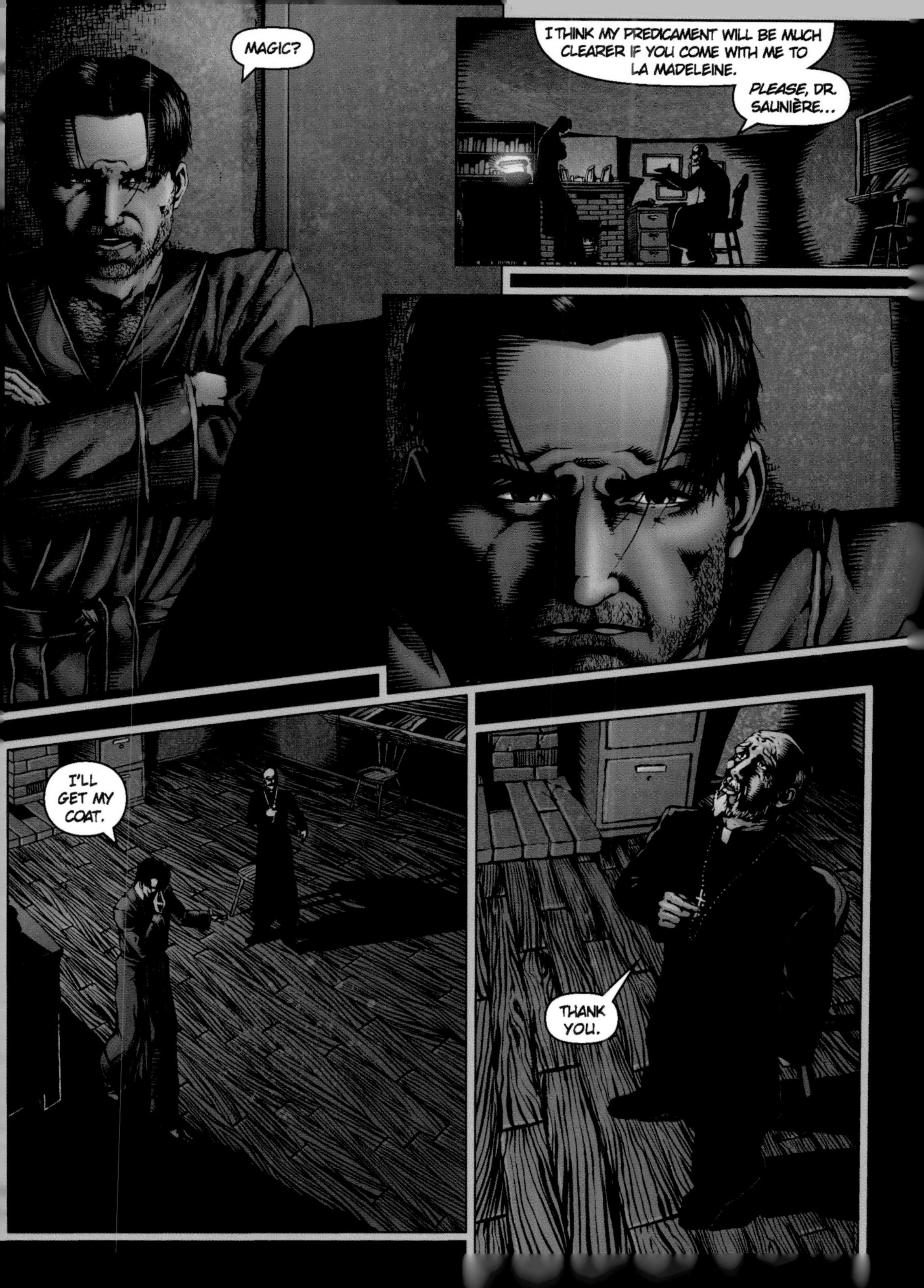
MAGIC?
I THINK MY PREDICAMENT WILL BE MUCH CLEARER IF YOU COME WITH ME TO LA MADELEINE.
PLEASE, DR. SAUNIÈRE...
I'LL GET MY COAT.
THANK YOU.

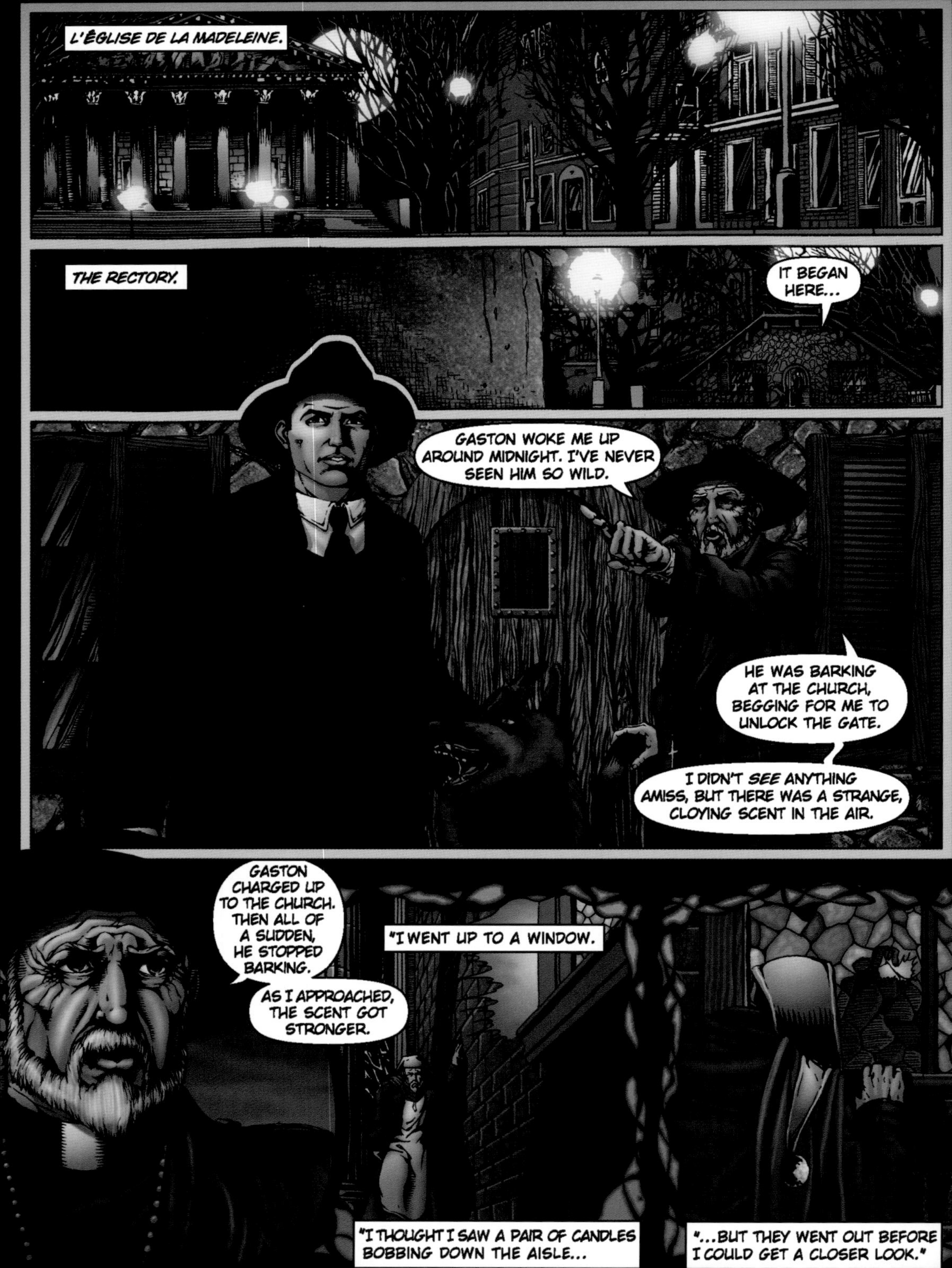
L'ÉGLISE DE LA MADELEINE.
THE RECTORY.
IT BEGAN HERE...
GASTON WOKE ME UP AROUND MIDNIGHT. I'VE NEVER SEEN HIM SO WILD.
HE WAS BARKING AT THE CHURCH, BEGGING FOR ME TO UNLOCK THE GATE.
I DIDN'T SEE ANYTHING AMISS, BUT THERE WAS A STRANGE, CLOYING SCENT IN THE AIR.
GASTON CHARGED UP TO THE CHURCH. THEN ALL OF A SUDDEN, HE STOPPED BARKING.
AS I APPROACHED, THE SCENT GOT STRONGER.
"I WENT UP TO A WINDOW.
"I THOUGHT I SAW A PAIR OF CANDLES BOBBING DOWN THE AISLE...
"...BUT THEY WENT OUT BEFORE I COULD GET A CLOSER LOOK."

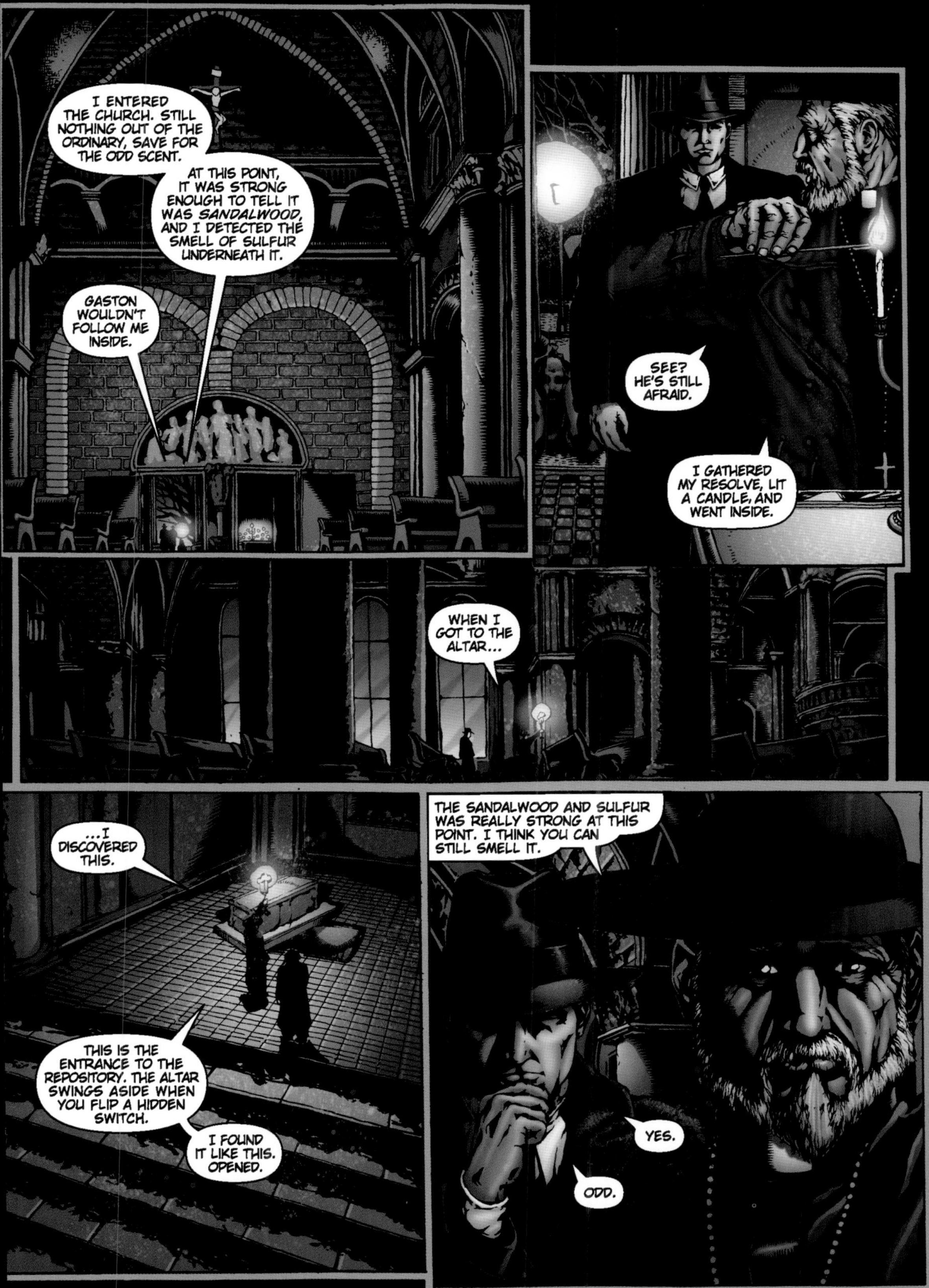
I ENTERED THE CHURCH. STILL NOTHING OUT OF THE ORDINARY, SAVE FOR THE ODD SCENT.
AT THIS POINT, IT WAS STRONG ENOUGH TO TELL IT WAS *SANDALWOOD*, AND I DETECTED THE SMELL OF SULFUR UNDERNEATH IT.
GASTON WOULDN'T FOLLOW ME INSIDE.
SEE? HE'S STILL AFRAID.
I GATHERED MY RESOLVE, LIT A CANDLE, AND WENT INSIDE.
WHEN I GOT TO THE ALTAR...
...I DISCOVERED THIS.
THIS IS THE ENTRANCE TO THE REPOSITORY. THE ALTAR SWINGS ASIDE WHEN YOU FLIP A HIDDEN SWITCH.
I FOUND IT LIKE THIS. OPENED.
THE SANDALWOOD AND SULFUR WAS REALLY STRONG AT THIS POINT. I THINK YOU CAN STILL SMELL IT.
YES.
ODD.

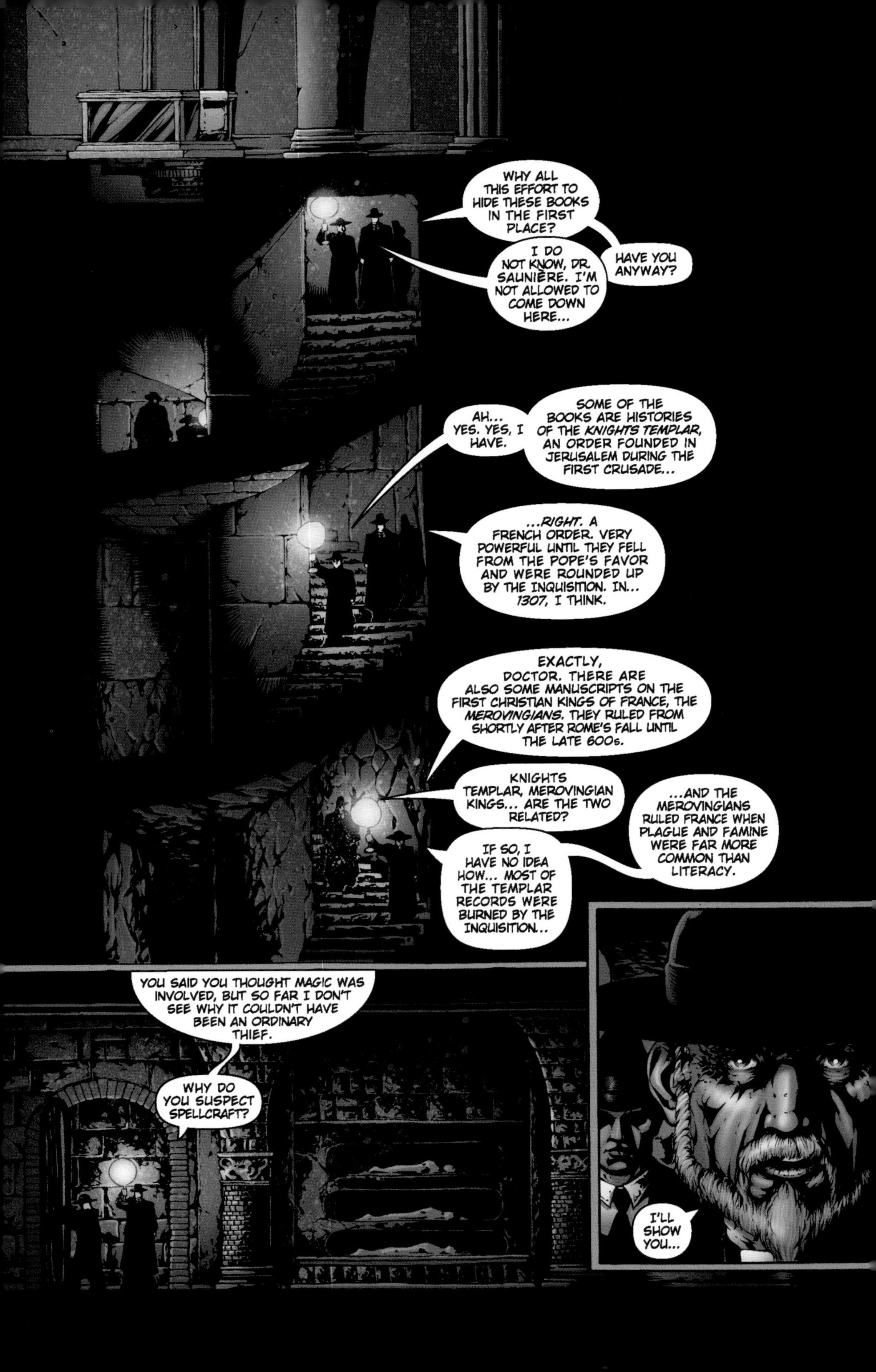
WHY ALL THIS EFFORT TO HIDE THESE BOOKS IN THE FIRST PLACE?
I DO NOT KNOW, DR. SAUNIÈRE. I'M NOT ALLOWED TO COME DOWN HERE...
HAVE YOU ANYWAY?
AH... YES. YES, I HAVE.
SOME OF THE BOOKS ARE HISTORIES OF THE *KNIGHTS TEMPLAR*, AN ORDER FOUNDED IN JERUSALEM DURING THE FIRST CRUSADE...
...*RIGHT*. A FRENCH ORDER. VERY POWERFUL UNTIL THEY FELL FROM THE POPE'S FAVOR AND WERE ROUNDED UP BY THE INQUISITION. IN... *1307*, I THINK.
EXACTLY, DOCTOR. THERE ARE ALSO SOME MANUSCRIPTS ON THE FIRST CHRISTIAN KINGS OF FRANCE, THE *MEROVINGIANS*. THEY RULED FROM SHORTLY AFTER ROME'S FALL UNTIL THE LATE 600s.
KNIGHTS TEMPLAR, MEROVINGIAN KINGS... ARE THE TWO RELATED?
IF SO, I HAVE NO IDEA HOW... MOST OF THE TEMPLAR RECORDS WERE BURNED BY THE INQUISITION...
...AND THE MEROVINGIANS RULED FRANCE WHEN PLAGUE AND FAMINE WERE FAR MORE COMMON THAN LITERACY.
YOU SAID YOU THOUGHT *MAGIC* WAS INVOLVED, BUT SO FAR I DON'T SEE WHY IT COULDN'T HAVE BEEN AN ORDINARY THIEF.
WHY DO YOU SUSPECT SPELLCRAFT?
I'LL SHOW YOU...

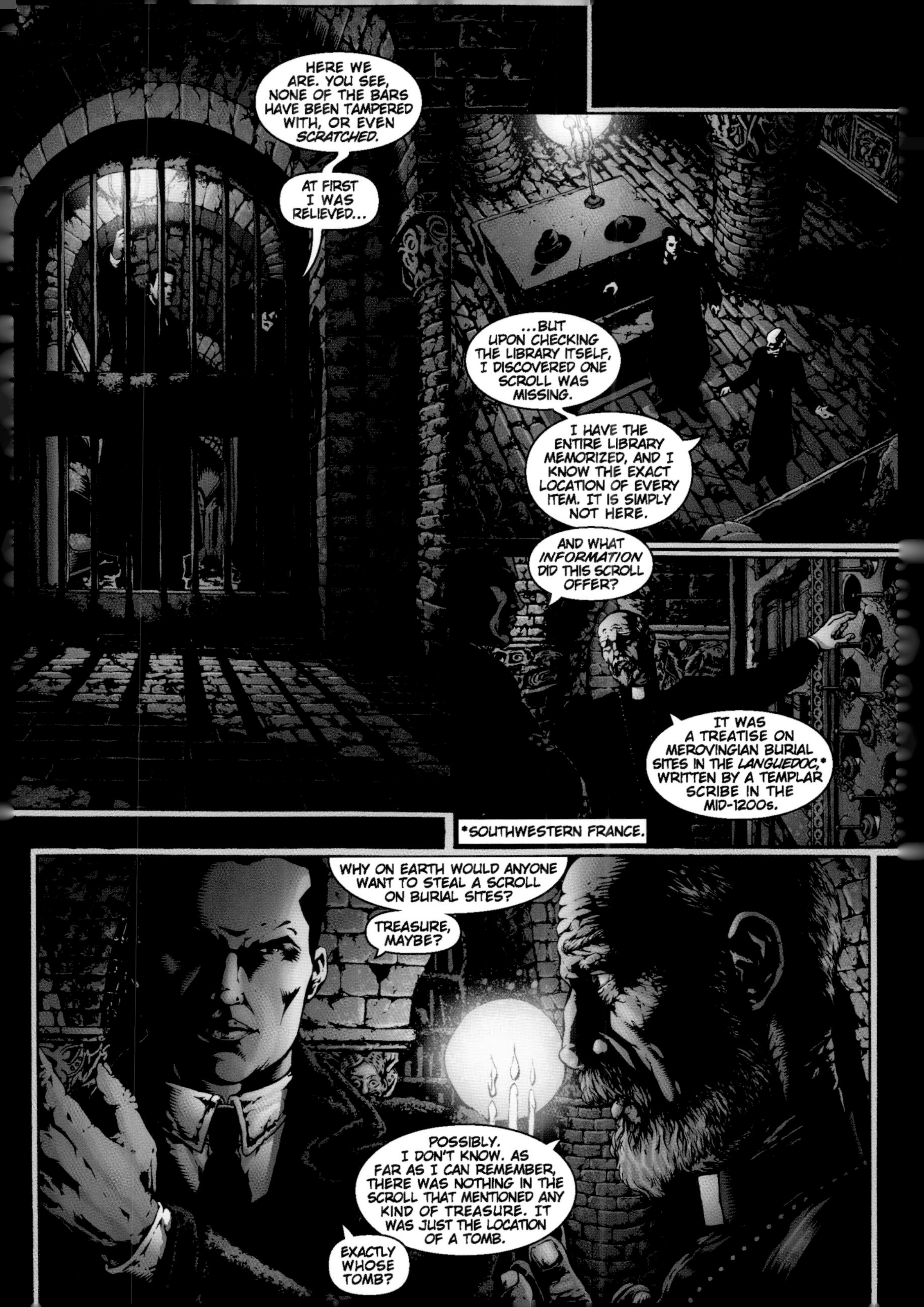
HERE WE ARE. YOU SEE, NONE OF THE BARS HAVE BEEN TAMPERED WITH, OR EVEN *SCRATCHED.*
AT FIRST I WAS RELIEVED...
...BUT UPON CHECKING THE LIBRARY ITSELF, I DISCOVERED ONE SCROLL WAS MISSING.
I HAVE THE ENTIRE LIBRARY MEMORIZED, AND I KNOW THE EXACT LOCATION OF EVERY ITEM. IT IS SIMPLY NOT HERE.
AND WHAT *INFORMATION* DID THIS SCROLL OFFER?
IT WAS A TREATISE ON MEROVINGIAN BURIAL SITES IN THE *LANGUEDOC,** WRITTEN BY A TEMPLAR SCRIBE IN THE MID-1200s.
*SOUTHWESTERN FRANCE.
WHY ON EARTH WOULD ANYONE WANT TO STEAL A SCROLL ON BURIAL SITES?
TREASURE, MAYBE?
POSSIBLY. I DON'T KNOW. AS FAR AS I CAN REMEMBER, THERE WAS NOTHING IN THE SCROLL THAT MENTIONED ANY KIND OF TREASURE. IT WAS JUST THE LOCATION OF A TOMB.
EXACTLY WHOSE TOMB?

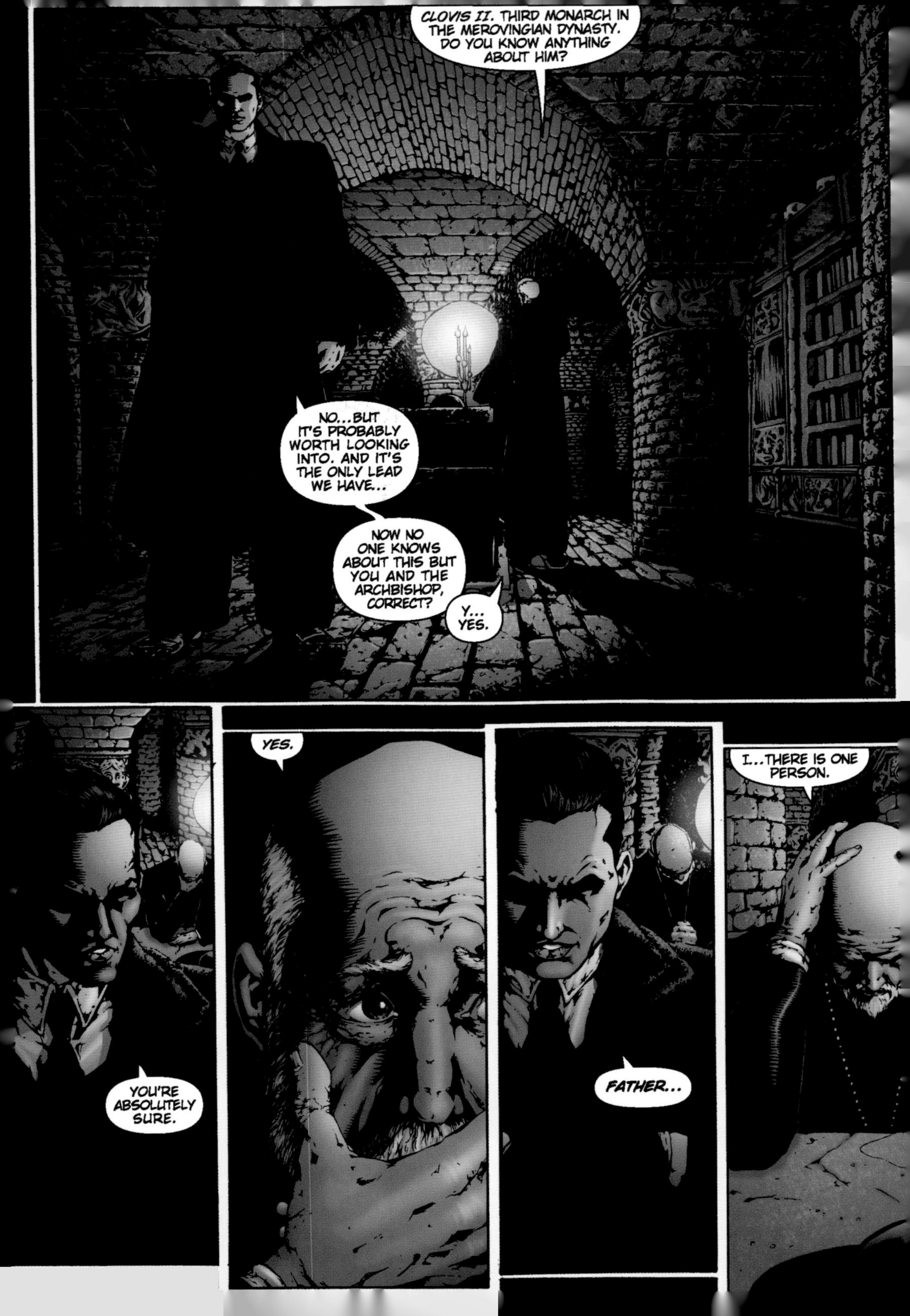
CLOVIS II. THIRD MONARCH IN THE MEROVINGIAN DYNASTY. DO YOU KNOW ANYTHING ABOUT HIM?
NO...BUT IT'S PROBABLY WORTH LOOKING INTO. AND IT'S THE ONLY LEAD WE HAVE...
NOW NO ONE KNOWS ABOUT THIS BUT YOU AND THE ARCHBISHOP, CORRECT?
Y... YES.
YOU'RE ABSOLUTELY SURE.
YES.
FATHER...
I...THERE IS ONE PERSON.

IT'S... HER NAME IS MARIE-CHRISTINE.

FATHER, FORGIVE ME...

GO ON, FATHER.

YOU KNOW I WORK AT A *MAGDALENE** IN THE 13TH ARRONDISSEMENT. SHE CAME THERE ONE NIGHT, SEEKING HELP. SHE LOOKED SO LOST...

WE STARTED TALKING. BEFORE I KNEW IT WE WERE FRIENDS AND THEN...

IT HAPPENED SO FAST...

*HOUSE FOR REFORMED PROSTITUTES.

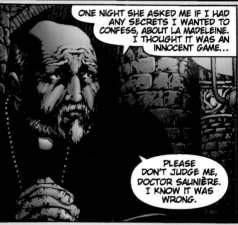

ONE NIGHT SHE ASKED ME IF I HAD ANY SECRETS I WANTED TO CONFESS, ABOUT LA MADELEINE. I THOUGHT IT WAS AN INNOCENT GAME...

PLEASE DON'T JUDGE ME, DOCTOR SAUNIÈRE. I KNOW IT WAS WRONG.

IT WAS WORSE THAN WRONG. IT WAS STUPID.

I KNOW, JULIEN, I KNOW...

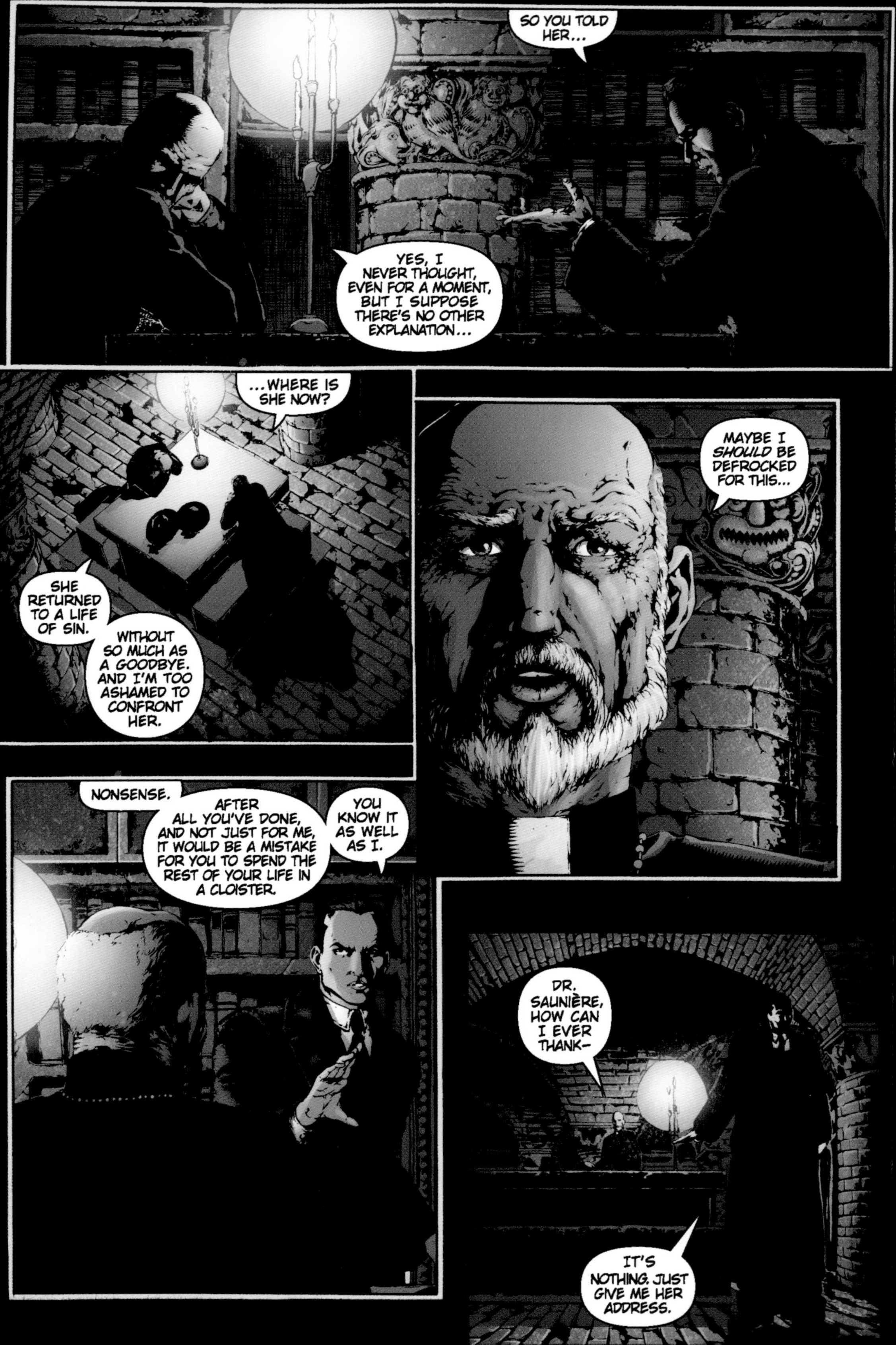
SO YOU TOLD HER...
YES, I NEVER THOUGHT, EVEN FOR A MOMENT, BUT I SUPPOSE THERE'S NO OTHER EXPLANATION...
...WHERE IS SHE NOW?
SHE RETURNED TO A LIFE OF SIN.
WITHOUT SO MUCH AS A GOODBYE. AND I'M TOO ASHAMED TO CONFRONT HER.
MAYBE I *SHOULD* BE DEFROCKED FOR THIS...
NONSENSE.
AFTER ALL YOU'VE DONE, AND NOT JUST FOR ME, IT WOULD BE A MISTAKE FOR YOU TO SPEND THE REST OF YOUR LIFE IN A CLOISTER.
YOU KNOW IT AS WELL AS I.
DR. SAUNIÈRE, HOW CAN I EVER THANK–
IT'S NOTHING. JUST GIVE ME HER ADDRESS.

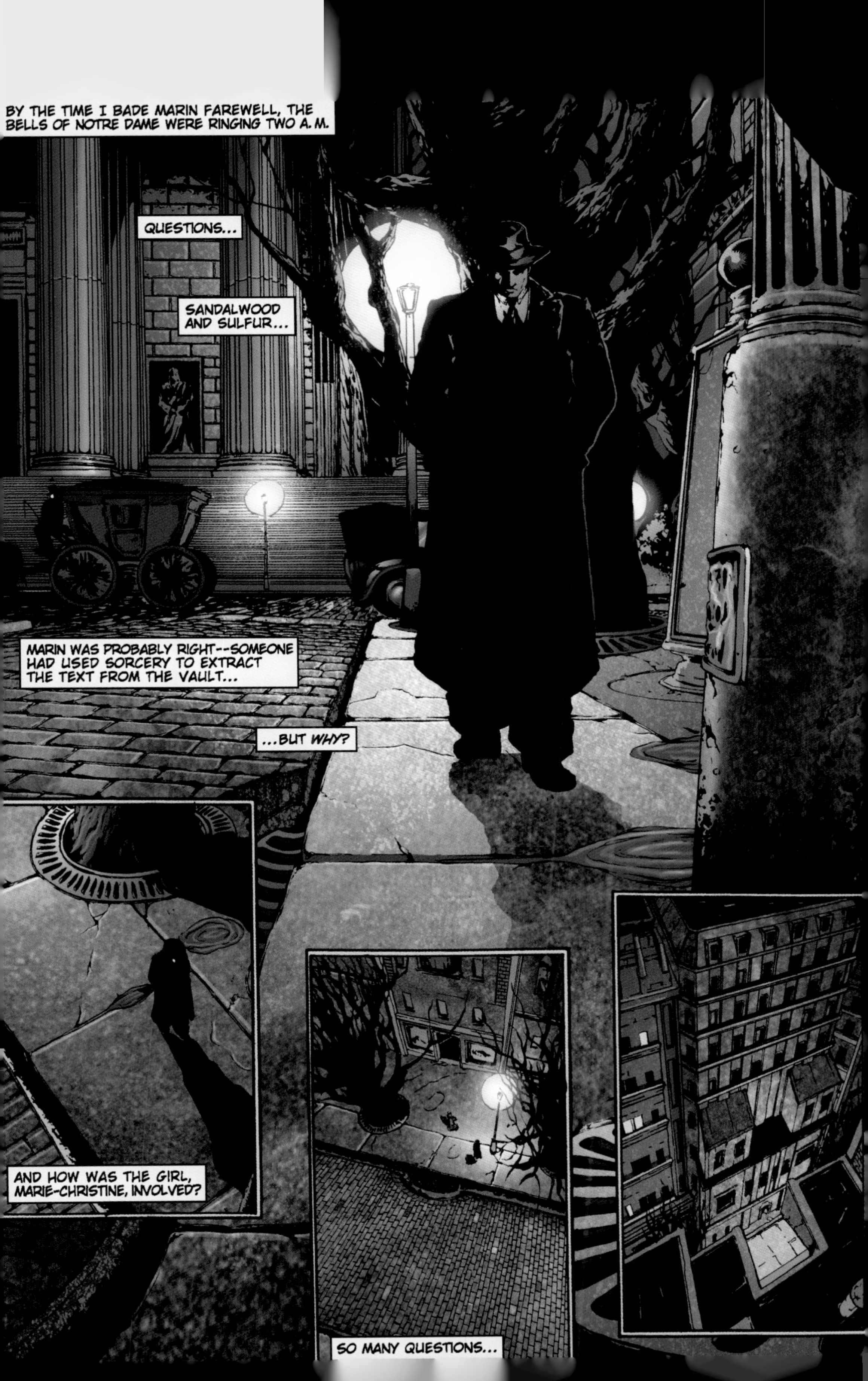
BY THE TIME I BADE MARIN FAREWELL, THE BELLS OF NOTRE DAME WERE RINGING TWO A.M.
QUESTIONS...
SANDALWOOD AND SULFUR...
MARIN WAS PROBABLY RIGHT--SOMEONE HAD USED SORCERY TO EXTRACT THE TEXT FROM THE VAULT...
...BUT *WHY?*
AND HOW WAS THE GIRL, MARIE-CHRISTINE, INVOLVED?
SO MANY QUESTIONS...

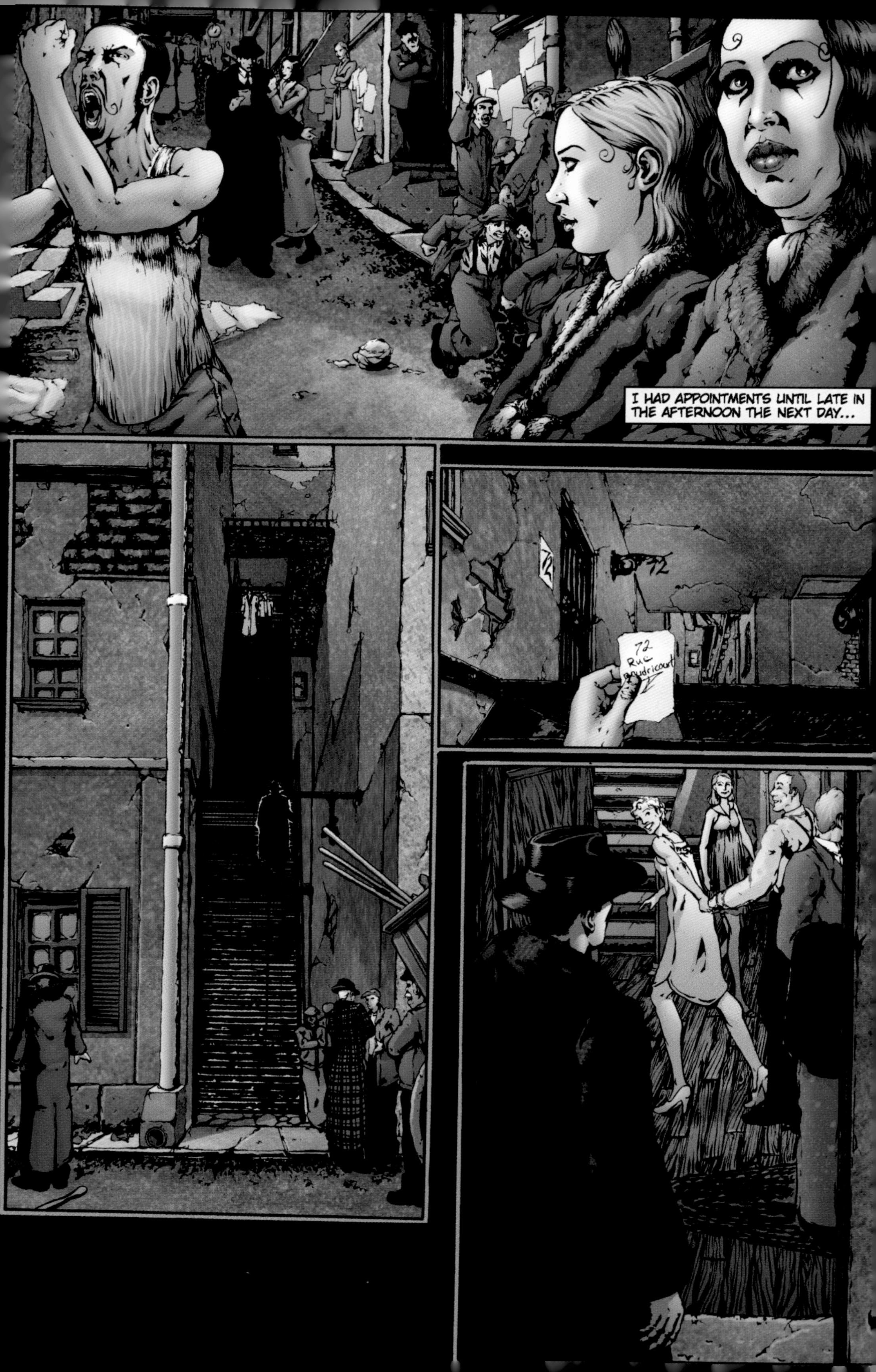
I HAD APPOINTMENTS UNTIL LATE IN THE AFTERNOON THE NEXT DAY...
72
72
72
Rue

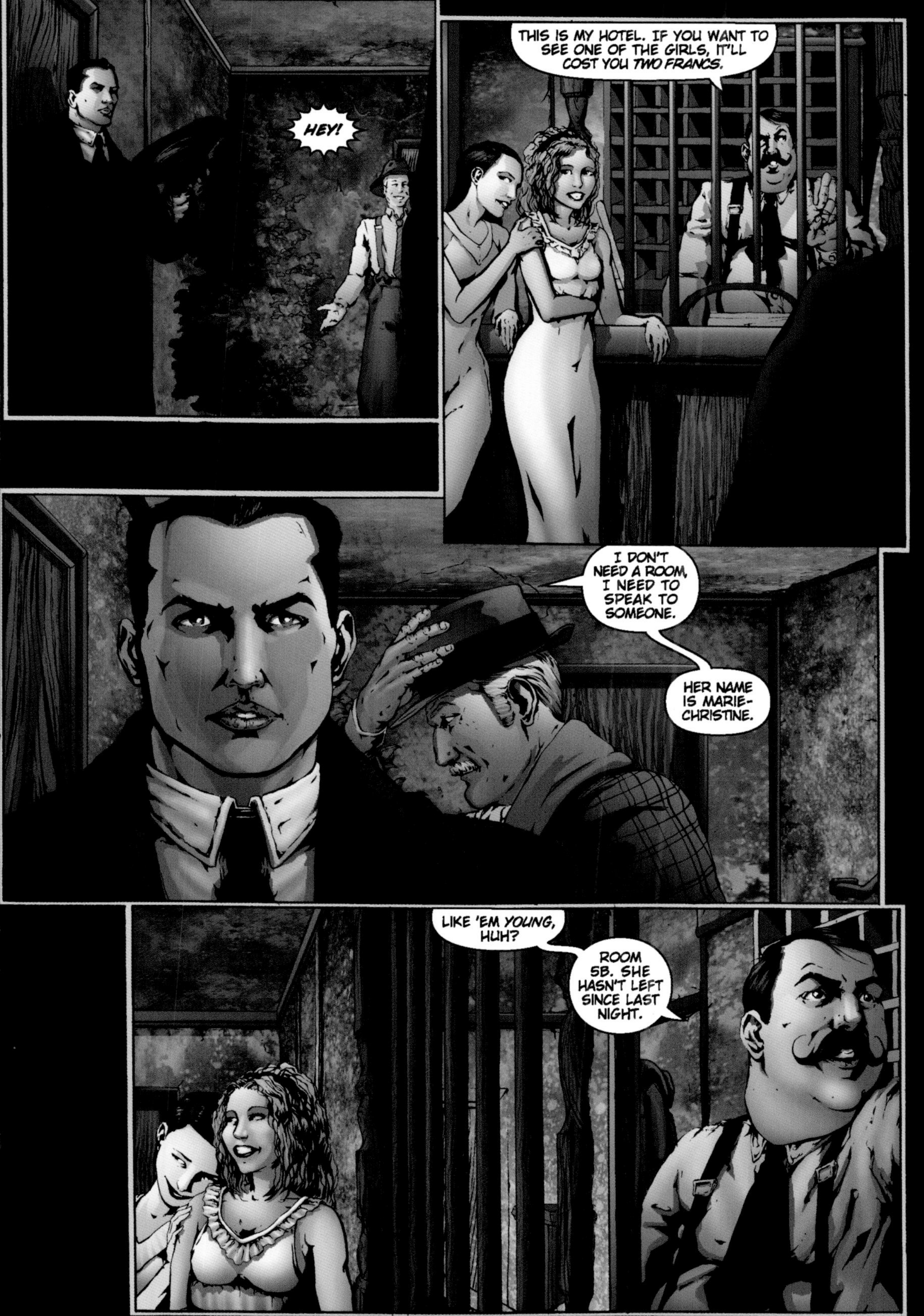
HEY!
THIS IS MY HOTEL. IF YOU WANT TO SEE ONE OF THE GIRLS, IT'LL COST YOU TWO FRANCS.
I DON'T NEED A ROOM, I NEED TO SPEAK TO SOMEONE.
HER NAME IS MARIE-CHRISTINE.
LIKE 'EM YOUNG, HUH?
ROOM 5B. SHE HASN'T LEFT SINCE LAST NIGHT.

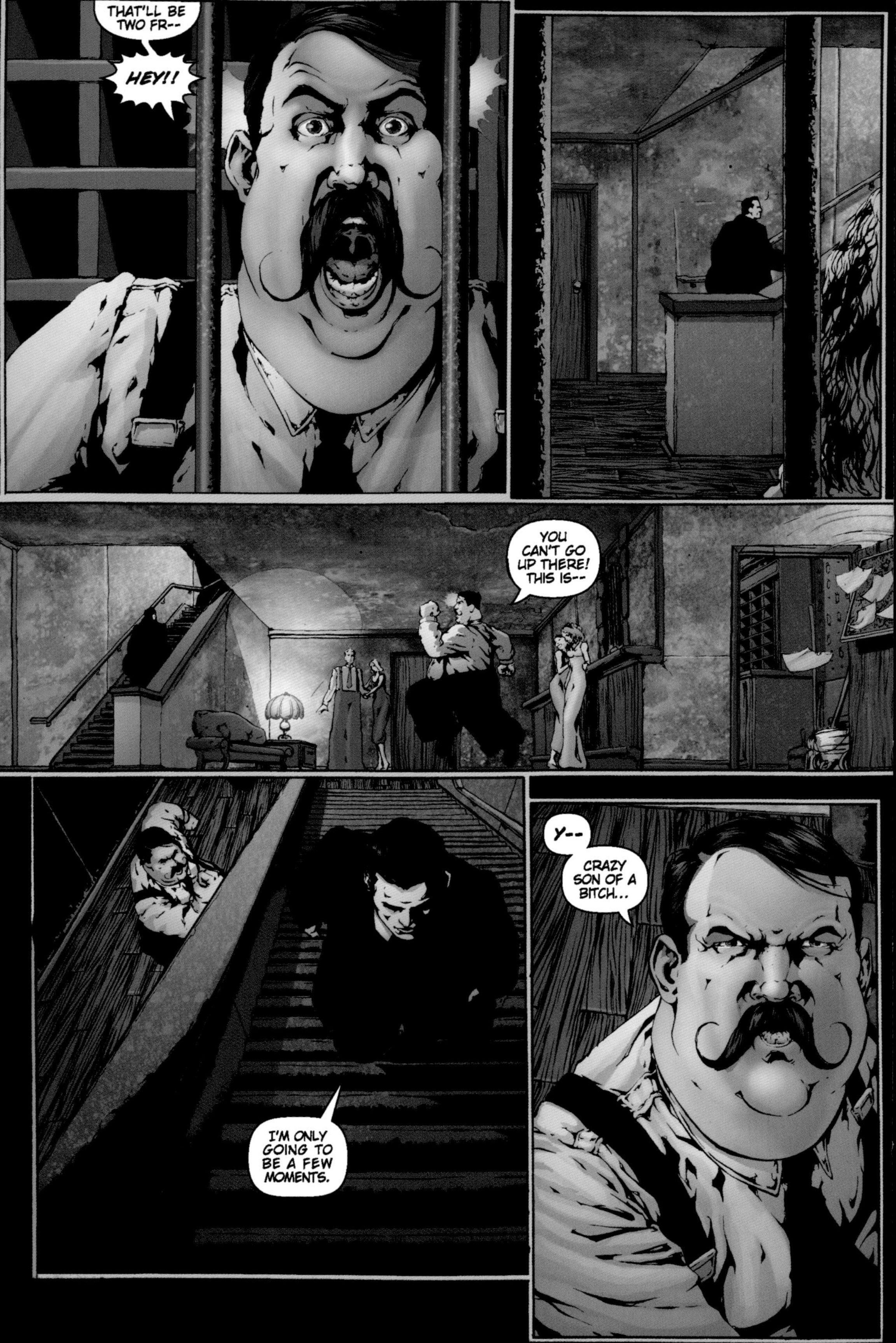
THAT'LL BE TWO FR--
HEY!!
YOU CAN'T GO UP THERE! THIS IS--
I'M ONLY GOING TO BE A FEW MOMENTS.
Y--
CRAZY SON OF A BITCH...

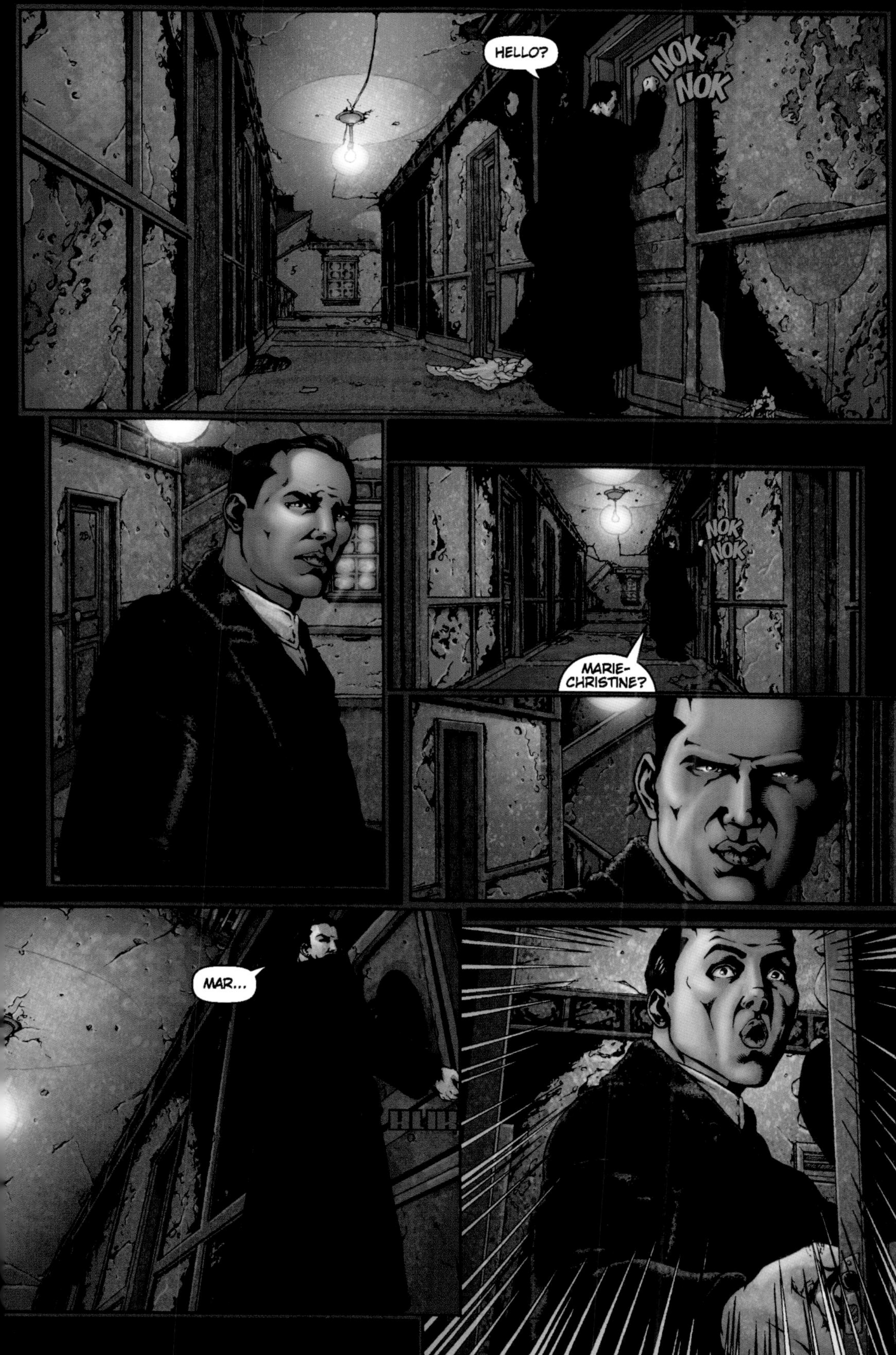
HELLO?
NOK
NOK
NOK
NOK
MARIE-CHRISTINE?
MAR...

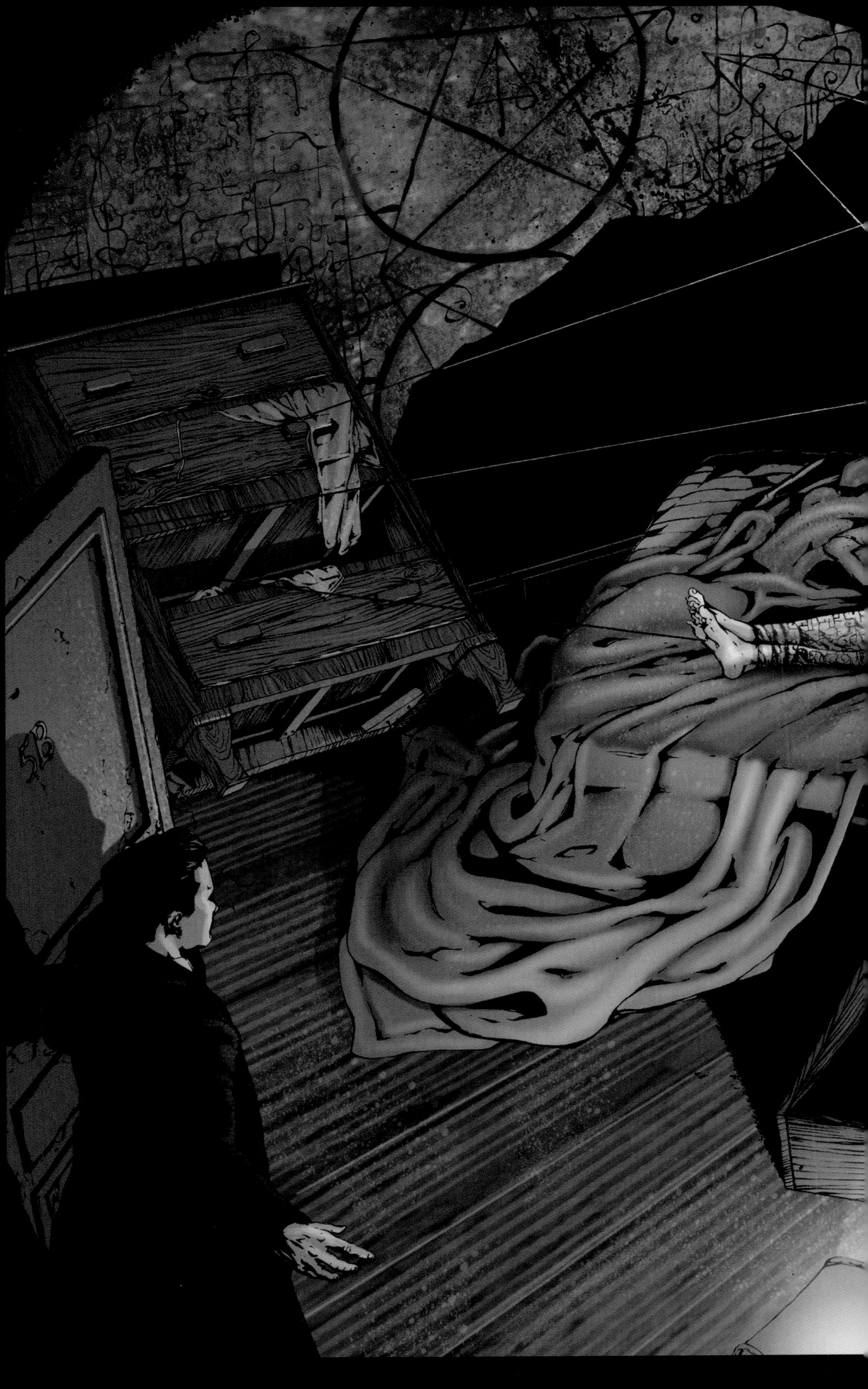

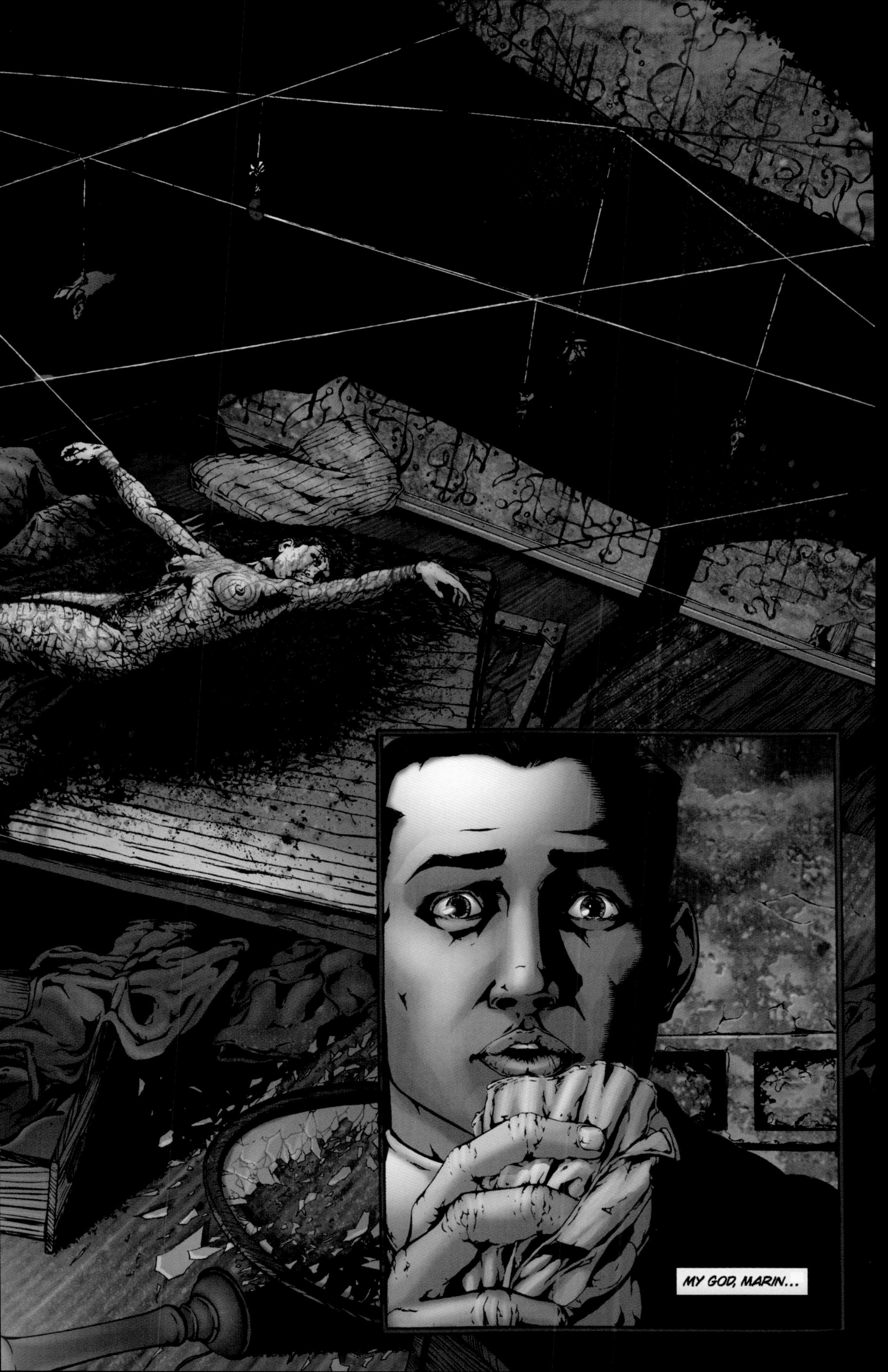
MY GOD, MARIN...

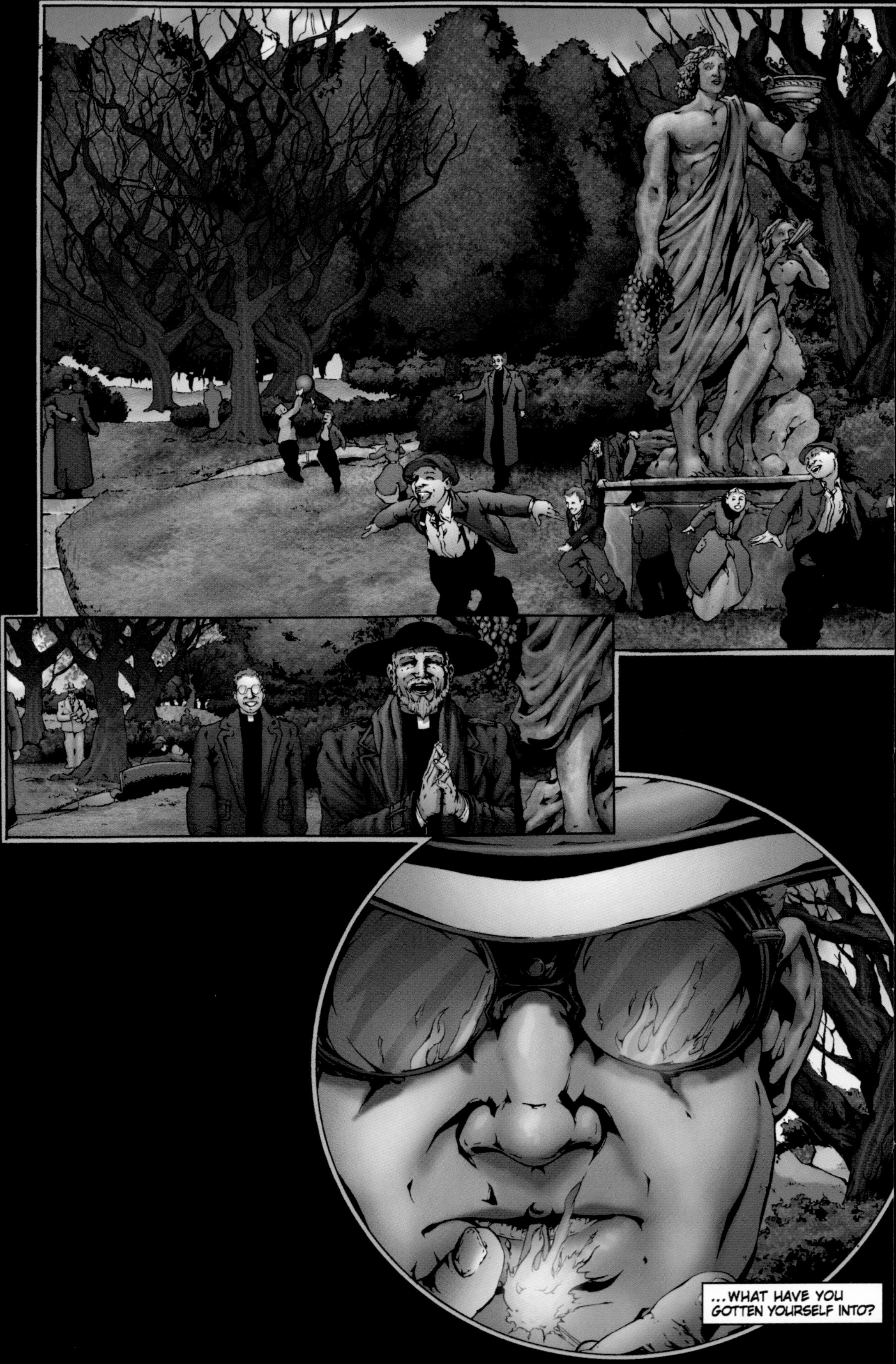
...WHAT HAVE YOU GOTTEN YOURSELF INTO?

Le Journal de la Liberté

Paris's leading anglophone newspaper • vol. 205, no. 95 • Oct. 18, MCMXXXIII

apal seal

Editors in Chief: M. Tait Bergstrom, M. Matthew Pasteris. **Story Editor:** M. Arvid Nelson. **Art Editors:** M. Eric Johnson, M. Jeromy Cox. **Photography Editor:** M. Alex Waldman. **Layout supervisor:** M. William Kartalopoulos. **Editors Emeritus:** M. Clark A. Smith, M. Howard P. Lovecraft, M. Robert E. Howard. Redacted by the Holy Parisian Inquisition under the direction of His Excellency Archbishop Emile-Jean Ireneaux. La Journal de Liberté is printed under the benign auspices of his most puissant majesty KING LOUIS XXII of FRANCE.

✤GOD SAVE THE KING✤

of approval

INQUISITION DECLARES "WAR ON CRIME"

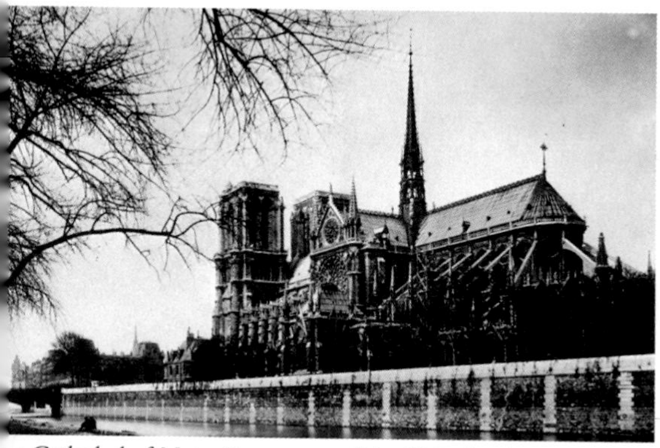

e Cathedral of Notre Dame, seat of the Holy Inquisition in Paris.

Oct. 17th, 4th ème – ›m the dark spires of Notre ›me, Inquisition officials clared a "war on crime" terday, promising Parisian izens a vice-free city within ecade.

"From now on, gangsters practitioners of witchcraft l have no place to hide," His cellency Archbishop Ireneaux l. "Our policy: no tolerance. is is the end."

Responding to critics who m Inquisition tactics are 'utal" and "repressive," Archbishop Ireneaux cited the effectiveness of the Inquisition in rooting out crime.

"What France needs is a moral police force, a spiritual police force," he said. "Who else has the right to police men's souls as well as their actions?"

Indeed, since his appointment as Archbishop of Paris, Ireneaux has made a marked difference in the lives of every Parisian, from street urchins to aristocrats.

"Well, it's a lot safer now, walking down the street at night," said a shopkeeper who spoke on the condition of anonymity. "But let me tell you, I'm just as scared now as I ever was. If the d--n witches don't get you, the Inquisition will."

"Utter nonsense," said Ireneaux. "No God-fearing, law-abiding Christian need be concerned about this initiative. It is our fundamental belief that every citizen of this city who believes in Jesus

Continued on p. A26

AND INQUISITOR MORICANT NAMED HEAD OF NEW TASK FORCE

Oct. 17th, 4th ème – s Excellency Archbishop ›neaux named Grand Inisitor Moricant head of new crime initiative laid t at Notre Dame yesterday ernoon.

Moricant, present at yesday's press conference at ›tre Dame, express gratile to God for being cho-.

"All thanks be unto the rd. I pray fervently that m worthy of this assign›nt," he said.

Moricant is a veteran Inisitor with 15 years exrience behind the mask. takes pride in the direct thodology he employs to nbat crime and heresy.

"Sometimes torture and forcible seizure of property are necessary and desirable methods of law enforcement," he said.

"In fact, these things are vital components of any effective police force's arsenal. And we intend to utilize everything we have in our new crusade."

Little is known about Moricant's past. As with all Inquisitioners, information on his life prior to donning the mask is kept strictly confidential.

"We must be Christlike in our quest to purify our brethren wallowing in sin, estranged from the love of God," Moricant said. "For that reason, we have sacri-

Continued on p. A26

PRUSSIAN MILITARISM: HOW GREAT A THREAT?

Oct. 17th, 7th ème – Emperor Karl-Frederick VII's armed forces grow larger and stronger every day, but debate rages in the Halls as to what is the best course of action for France. What exactly does the Kaiser mean by "restoring the glory of the Reich of Frederick the Great?" Is this a veiled threat to French sovereignty, or is it a reaction to the encroachment of the Ottomans, generally perceived as a threat to European culture?

The debate has been violently polarized by two men, perhaps the two most powerful men in France beneath the King.

Charles Martel, His Majesty's Mayor of the Court, consistently advocates clemency and conciliation.

"If we lighten our tone, the Prussians will lighten theirs. It's that simple. A lot of what's going on in Prussia right now is a direct result of the fiery speeches being made in the Hall of the Sword," Martel said.

Martel refers most directly to the Duke of Lorraine, expected to be voted the Master of the Sword following a vote taking place later this

Continued on p. A26

DUKE OF ORLEANS APPOINTED OTTOMAN EMISSARY

Oct 18th, 7th ème – The Hall of the Sword nominated Phillipe Berenger Verlaine, Duke of Orleans, as Ambassador to the Ottoman Empire. Orleans is also His Majesty King Louis XXII's first choice, and the vote is expected to clear the Hall of the Robe next week.

Orleans is noted for his conciliatory stance toward Islam, and this plays a large part in why he was chosen by the King.

His Excellency the Duke said he was "honored" by the appointment. Responding to critics who claim he is "too soft," he said he would not "roll over for the Sheik."

"I will stand firm for French culture, make no mistake," he said.

The Duke himself, in a short acceptance speech he gave outside the Hall of the Sword yesterday afternoon, brought up the issue of the political and military stability of the Holy Roman Empire.

"We have got to make it clear, perfectly clear, that we-

Continued on p. A5

OTTOMANS WARY

Ottoman officials were less enthusiastic about the appointment.

"His Majesty Suleiman II has grave concerns about this latest appointment," The Honorable Ali Al-Faddiq, Ottoman Ambassador to Fra-

Continued on p. A14

INSIDE:

THE PARISIAN'S GUIDE TO SORCERY

There is perhaps no phenomenon as captivating to the human mind as sorcery. Nor is there a topic more subject to misinterpretation and obfuscation. This guide attempts to clear up some of the mystery surrounding occult arts, but, due to the subject matter, the authors did most of their research undercover, obtaining interviews only under the strictest confidence. ***Le Journal de la Liberté,*** *therefore, cannot make any claims as to the accuracy of the information presented below.*

MAGIC IN EVERYDAY LIFE

The subject of sorcery is as fascinating as it is frustrating. "Occult" is derived from the Latin "occultus," meaning "hidden," and no word could better describe practitioners of the esoteric arts. Rumors, disinformation and half truths are plentiful, while facts, if they can be verified, are scarce.

Although it is estimated that one out of every ten people claim to "have knowledge or access to knowledge regarding occult arts," the actual figure reported by the Guild of Sorcerers is closer to one in one hundred.

The Guild itself propagates the mystery, only offering its services to individuals who can prove their ancestors have secured Guild contracts in the past, effectively closing off the vast majority of the population from access.

Moreover, the Guild does not have an open recruitment policy, and how apprentice sorcerers are chosen is completely unknown.

"We just keep to ourselves. It's advantageous, because there are a lot of misconceptions about what we do," a member of the Guild, who spoke on the condition of anonymity, said.

Much of this reluctance to go public may be due to the Church's position on sorcery.

"For most people sorcery is a quick path to damnation," said Brother Eustache of the Parisian Inquisition. "If you are a known unlicensed sorcerer, we're watching you very closely. If you are not a known unlicensed sorcerer, we will find you."

Practicing sorcery without a Guild license is considered witchcraft by the Inquisition and is punishable by death. Yet this does not dampen a widespread interest in magic.

"There are definitely a significant amount of people out there who practice sorcery without a Guild license," said our source within the Guild.

Where do the these rogue magicians gain their knowledge? The answer isn't clear to anyone.

"It's quite possible there are failed Guild sorcerers out there making fast money by teaching the craft illicitly," said one source within the Guild. "Our standards are extremely rigorous. A lot of people almost make it, but not quite, and that can engender a lot of bitterness."

"A lot of people almost make it, but not quite, and that can engender a lot of bitterness."

"We believe Satanic cults have a lot to do with the proliferance of occult magic," said Brother Eustache.

MAGIC IN THEORY

So what makes magic work? The answer to this question is extremely complex, based on the Judeo-Christian tradition of *Cabalah,* a mystical school of thought based on revelatory interpretations of the books of Old Testament.

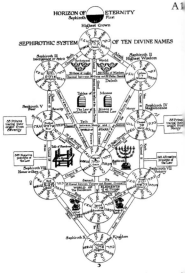

As above, so below: woodcut of a cabalist exploring the secrets of heaven and earth.

Two of the most important books of cabalistic literature, virtual textbooks for any aspiring sorcerer, are the *Zohar,* "The Book of Splendor," and the *Sepher Yetzirah,* "The Book of Formation." It is not certain when these texts were written, but historians believe they were collected around 200 years after the death of Christ.

"Of course, the actual teachings are much older," said our source within the Sorcerers' Guild. Indeed, Jews hold that the Sepher Yetzirah was penned by none other than Abraham himself.

Sorcerers claim these two books are the product of "divine revelation," that the authors, whoever they were, received their knowledge directly from God.

According to the principles laid out in these books, God Himself was not directly responsible for the creation of the universe. Rather, He manifested Himself in ten "Sephirah," (singular: Sephiroth) which then effected the actual task of creation. "Sephiroth," our source informed us, is a complicated term.

"'Sephiroth' doesn't translate well into English. It means a lot of things. 'Archangel,' 'process' 'demiurgic entity' and 'ray' are all perfectly acceptable meanings," he said.

These Sephirah each contributed to the creation of the universe in a unique way. Exactly how our source would not say.

"A good magician never reveals his tricks," he said with a wry smile.

He did go on to describe the Sephirah as "interacting with each other to create mystical gateways and channels of power.

"The channels between the Sephirah are the source of all magical power," said our source. "It's a relational system. Alone, the Sephirah are nothing. It is only in their relationships with each other that they are meaningful."

Knowing how to tap into these channels of power be-

HORIZON OF
ETERNITY
SEPHIROTHIC SYSTEM
OF TEN DIVINE NAMES
Highest Crown
Sephiroth II
Highest Wisdom
Sephiroth III
Sephiroth V
Sephiroth IV
Sephiroth VIII
Sephiroth VII
Sephiroth X
Kingdom

The Sephirothic Tree of Life: According to cab lists, God manifested Himself in ten "Sephira from which all creation ensued.

tween the Sephirah is t key to the sorcerer's pow Sorcerers do so by looki inward. Literally.

"There are ten ener centers in the human bo also called Sephirah," s our source. "Knowing wh these are, and how to acc the energy stored within, critical to spell casting. Wh the bible says man is creat in God's image, that's litera true. Your body is a map the universe. Your body i code for the secrets of God

Our source refused comment any further, th leaving us with more qu tions than answers. Exac how does one tap into t Sephira? Where on the bo are they located? What the exact "connections" b tween them, and how do th function?

There are other rumo about the Guild of Sorc ers that remain equally u answerable. It is rumo sorcerers ritually tattoo locations of the sephi onto their bodies as a sort guide or meditation aid.

Indeed, our source w gloves to the interview, a took particular care not to move his necktie or unb ton his collar, although was unseasonably warm. V it to conceal tattoos, or because he caught cold eas How had he become a sorc er in the first place, and w secrets had he learned dur his apprenticeship? As w most questions concern spellcraft, it's anyone's gu save for the sorcerers.

CHAPTER TWO
UNEXPECTED VISITORS

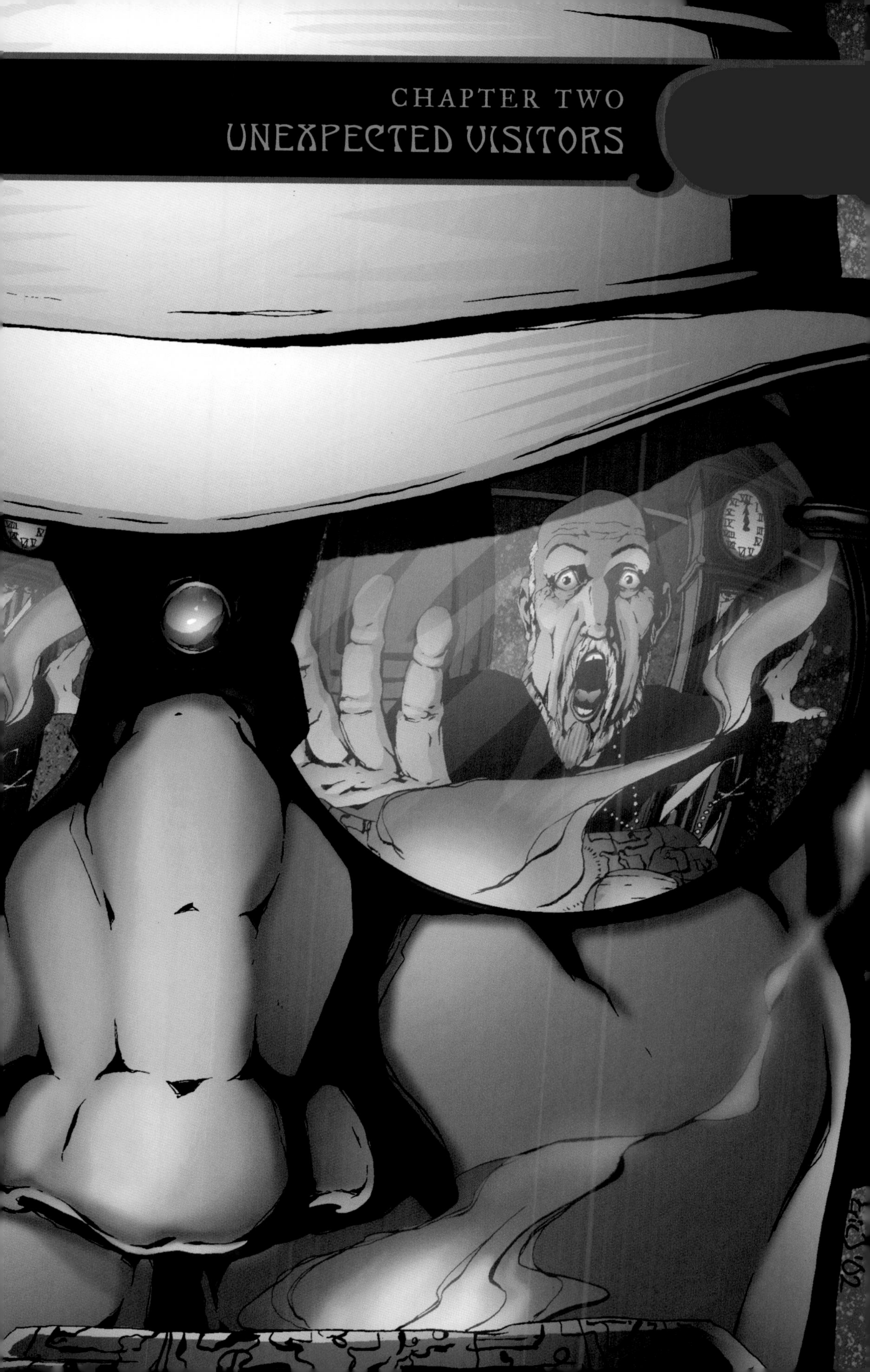

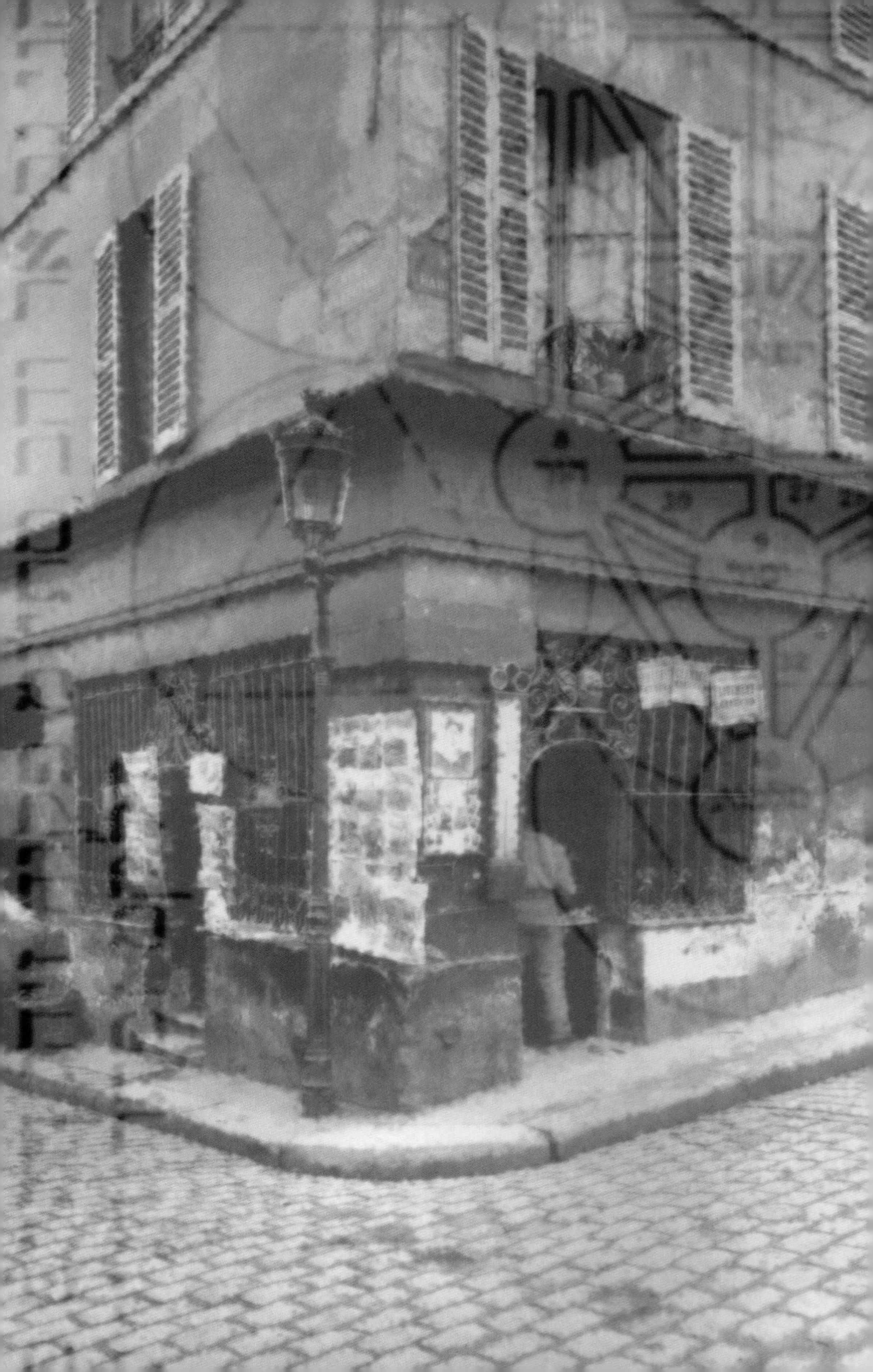

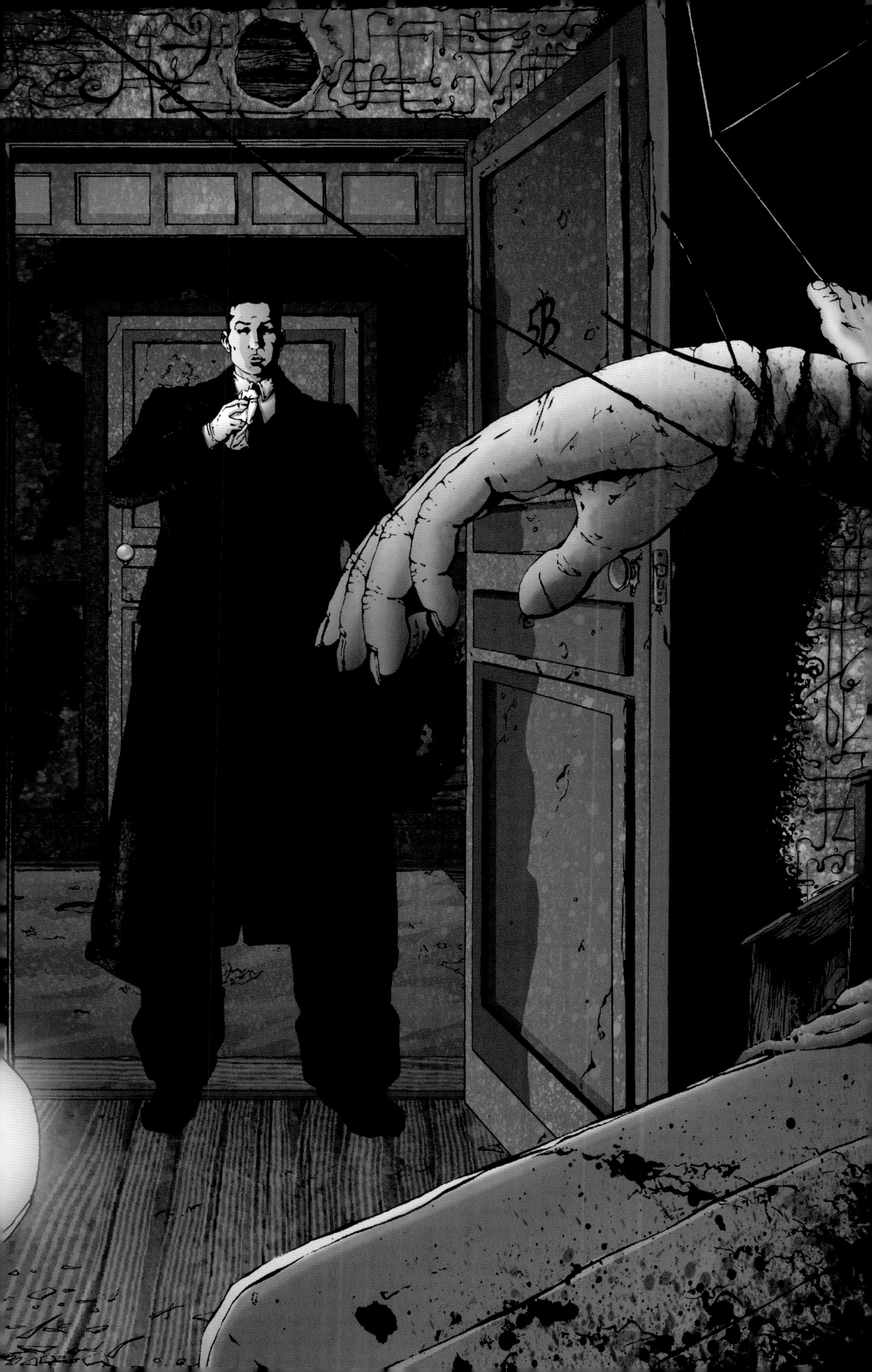

I TRIED NOT TO LOOK AT HER EYES. I HAD SEEN DEAD BODIES BEFORE WHILE AT THE GUILD UNIVERSITY...

...BUT THIS WASN'T A MEDICAL CADAVER.

THE BLOOD WAS PARTIALLY CONGEALED AND RIGOR MORTIS HAD SET IN.

SO SHE HAD DIED MORE THAN EIGHT HOURS AGO.

SEVERE LACERATIONS AND CONTUSIONS AROUND HER WRISTS WHERE SHE HAD BEEN TIED DOWN.

THE AMOUNT OF BLOOD INDICATED HER HEART HAD BEEN PUMPING WHEN THIS HAPPENED.

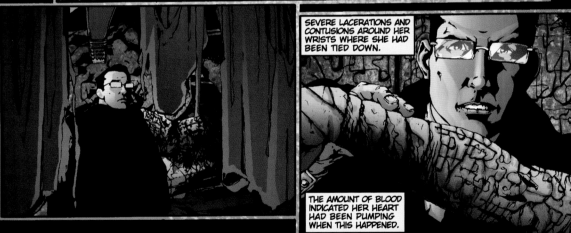

SHE HAD BEEN CONSCIOUS DURING THE WHOLE THING.

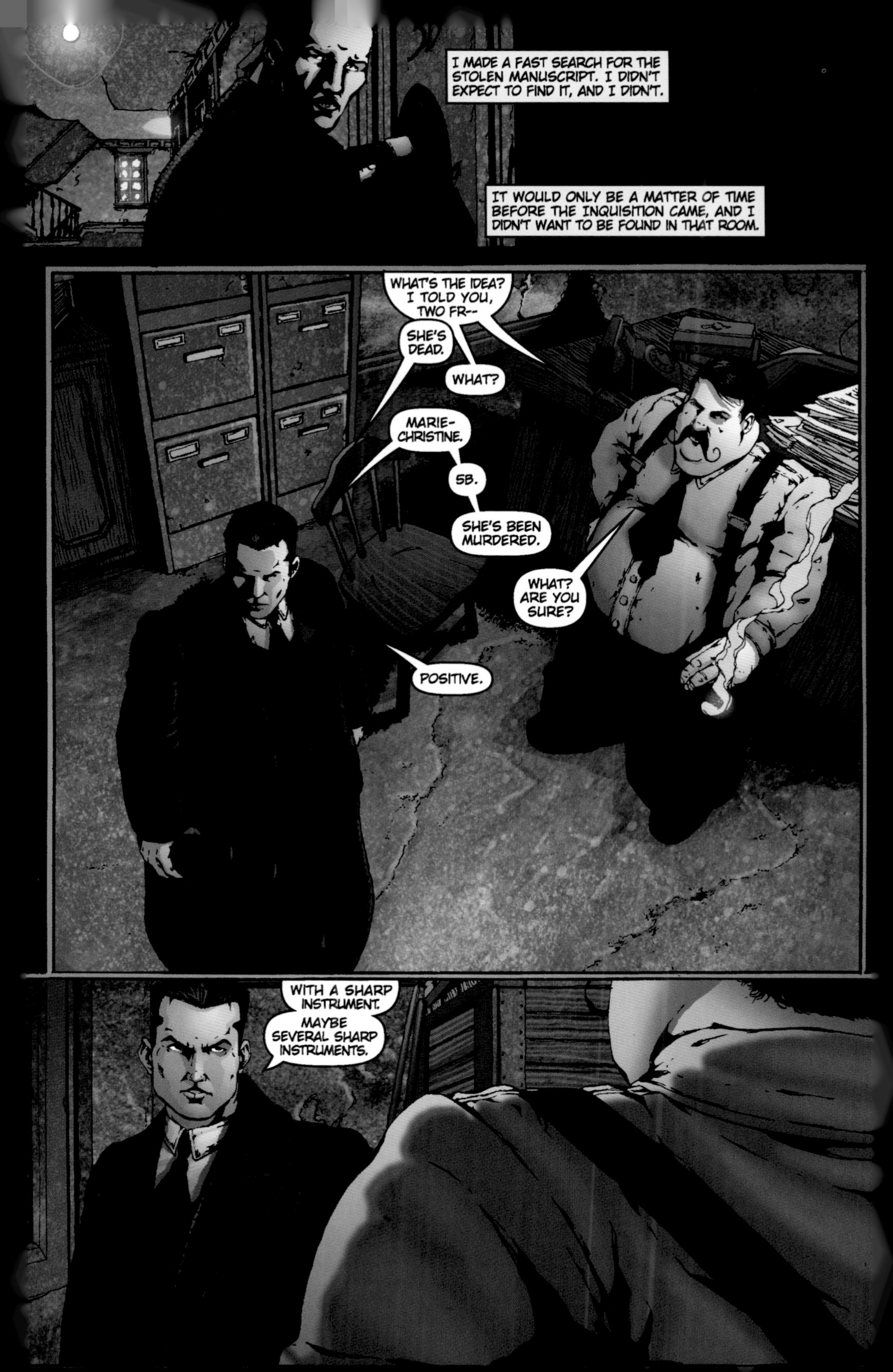
I MADE A FAST SEARCH FOR THE STOLEN MANUSCRIPT. I DIDN'T EXPECT TO FIND IT, AND I DIDN'T.
IT WOULD ONLY BE A MATTER OF TIME BEFORE THE INQUISITION CAME, AND I DIDN'T WANT TO BE FOUND IN THAT ROOM.
WHAT'S THE IDEA? I TOLD YOU, TWO FR--
SHE'S DEAD.
WHAT?
MARIE-CHRISTINE.
5B.
SHE'S BEEN MURDERED.
WHAT? ARE YOU SURE?
POSITIVE.
WITH A SHARP INSTRUMENT.
MAYBE SEVERAL SHARP INSTRUMENTS.

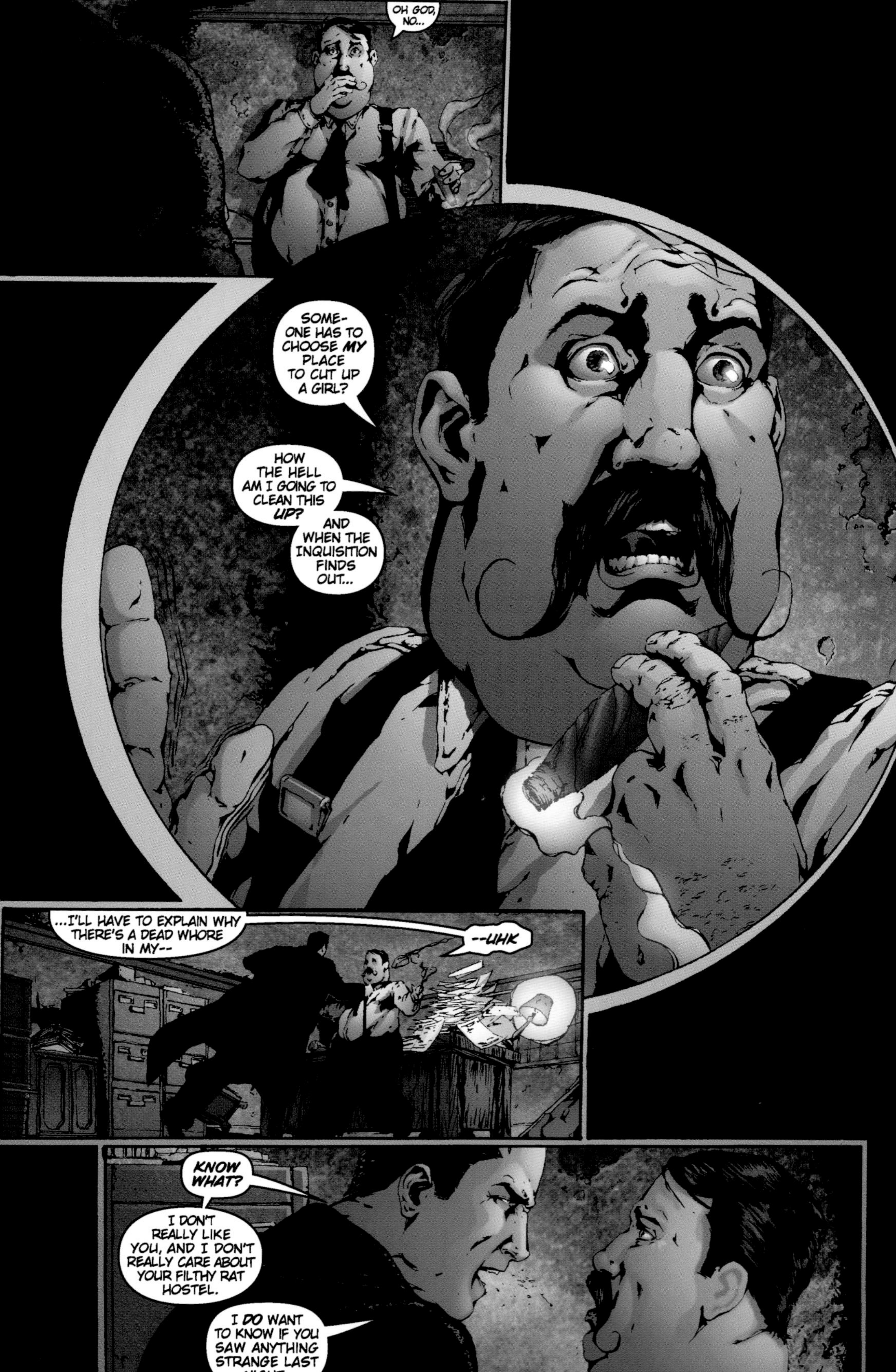
OH GOD, NO...
SOME-ONE HAS TO CHOOSE **MY** PLACE TO CUT UP A GIRL?
HOW THE HELL AM I GOING TO CLEAN THIS **UP?**
AND WHEN THE INQUISITION FINDS OUT...
...I'LL HAVE TO EXPLAIN WHY THERE'S A DEAD WHORE IN MY--
--UHK
KNOW WHAT?
I DON'T REALLY LIKE YOU, AND I DON'T REALLY CARE ABOUT YOUR FILTHY RAT HOSTEL.
I **DO** WANT TO KNOW IF YOU SAW ANYTHING STRANGE LAST

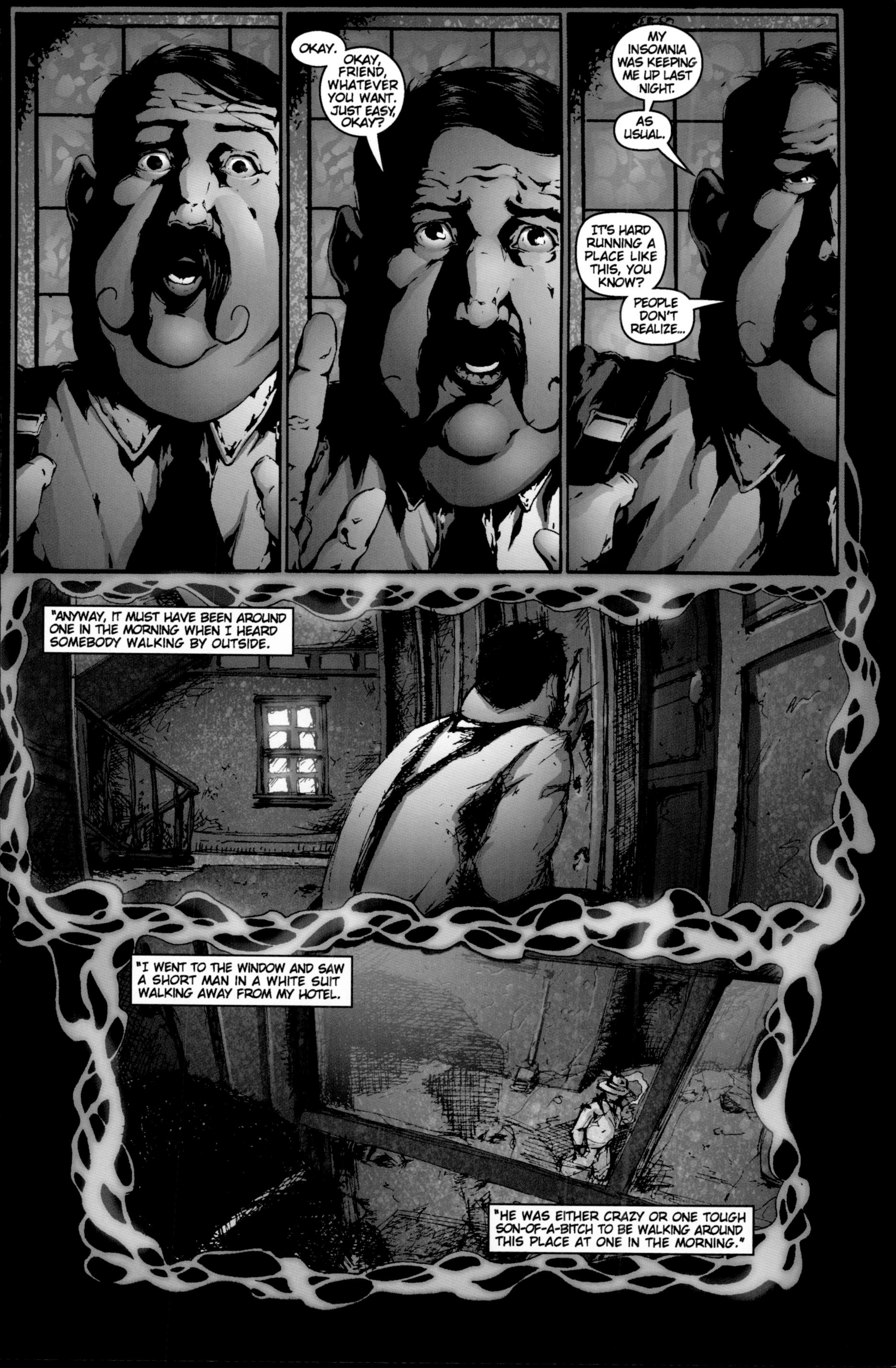
OKAY.
OKAY, FRIEND, WHATEVER YOU WANT. JUST EASY, OKAY?
MY INSOMNIA WAS KEEPING ME UP LAST NIGHT.
AS USUAL.
IT'S HARD RUNNING A PLACE LIKE THIS, YOU KNOW?
PEOPLE DON'T REALIZE...
"ANYWAY, IT MUST HAVE BEEN AROUND ONE IN THE MORNING WHEN I HEARD SOMEBODY WALKING BY OUTSIDE.
"I WENT TO THE WINDOW AND SAW A SHORT MAN IN A WHITE SUIT WALKING AWAY FROM MY HOTEL.
"HE WAS EITHER CRAZY OR ONE TOUGH SON-OF-A-BITCH TO BE WALKING AROUND THIS PLACE AT ONE IN THE MORNING."

THAT'S ALL I SAW, I SWEAR.

AND YOU, WERE YOU MARIE-CHRISTINE'S... PROCURER?

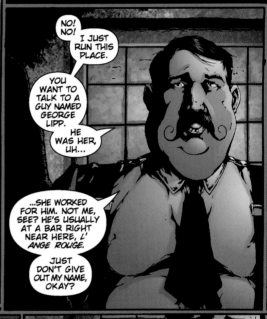

NO! NO!

I JUST RUN THIS PLACE.

YOU WANT TO TALK TO A GUY NAMED GEORGE LIPP.

HE WAS HER, UH...

...SHE WORKED FOR HIM. NOT ME, SEE? HE'S USUALLY AT A BAR RIGHT NEAR HERE, L' ANGE ROUGE.

JUST DON'T GIVE OUT MY NAME, OKAY?

I WON'T. HERE ARE YOUR TWO FRANCS.

HEY, THANKS!

CRAZY SON OF A BITCH...

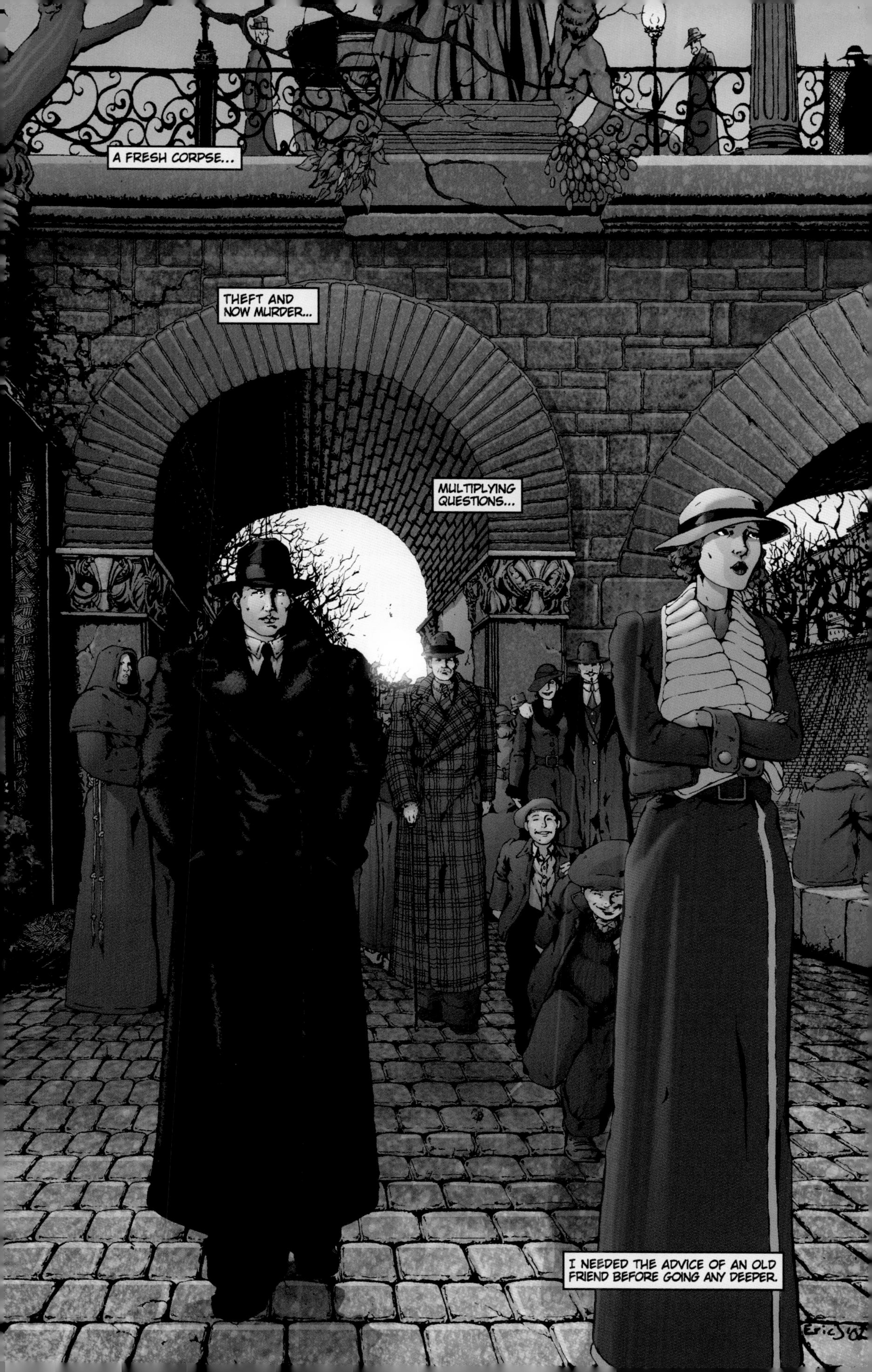
A FRESH CORPSE...
THEFT AND NOW MURDER...
MULTIPLYING QUESTIONS...
I NEEDED THE ADVICE OF AN OLD FRIEND BEFORE GOING ANY DEEPER.

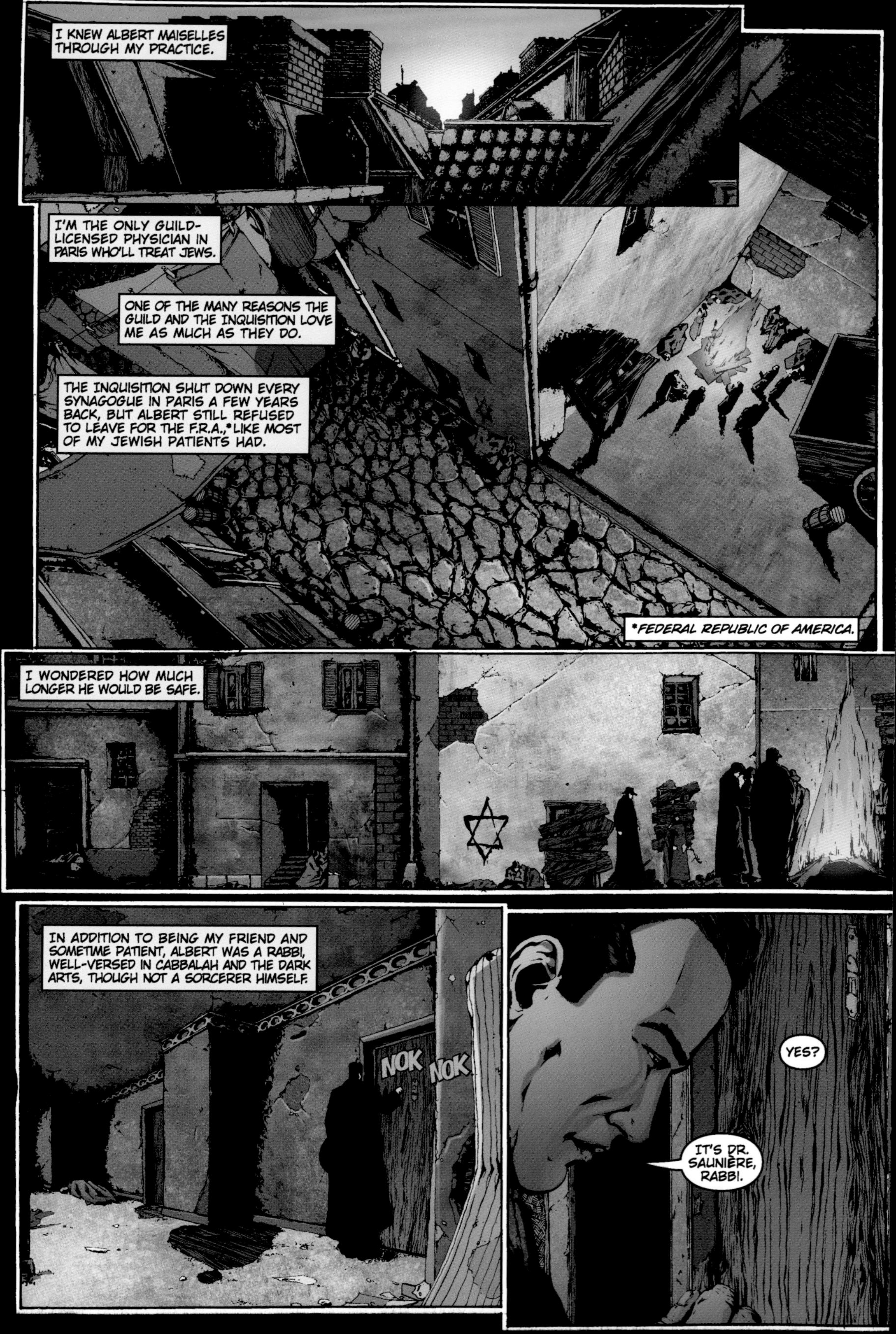
I KNEW ALBERT MAISELLES THROUGH MY PRACTICE.
I'M THE ONLY GUILD-LICENSED PHYSICIAN IN PARIS WHO'LL TREAT JEWS.
ONE OF THE MANY REASONS THE GUILD AND THE INQUISITION LOVE ME AS MUCH AS THEY DO.
THE INQUISITION SHUT DOWN EVERY SYNAGOGUE IN PARIS A FEW YEARS BACK, BUT ALBERT STILL REFUSED TO LEAVE FOR THE F.R.A.,* LIKE MOST OF MY JEWISH PATIENTS HAD.
*FEDERAL REPUBLIC OF AMERICA.
I WONDERED HOW MUCH LONGER HE WOULD BE SAFE.
IN ADDITION TO BEING MY FRIEND AND SOMETIME PATIENT, ALBERT WAS A RABBI, WELL-VERSED IN CABBALAH AND THE DARK ARTS, THOUGH NOT A SORCERER HIMSELF.
NOK
NOK
YES?
IT'S DR. SAUNIÈRE, RABBI.

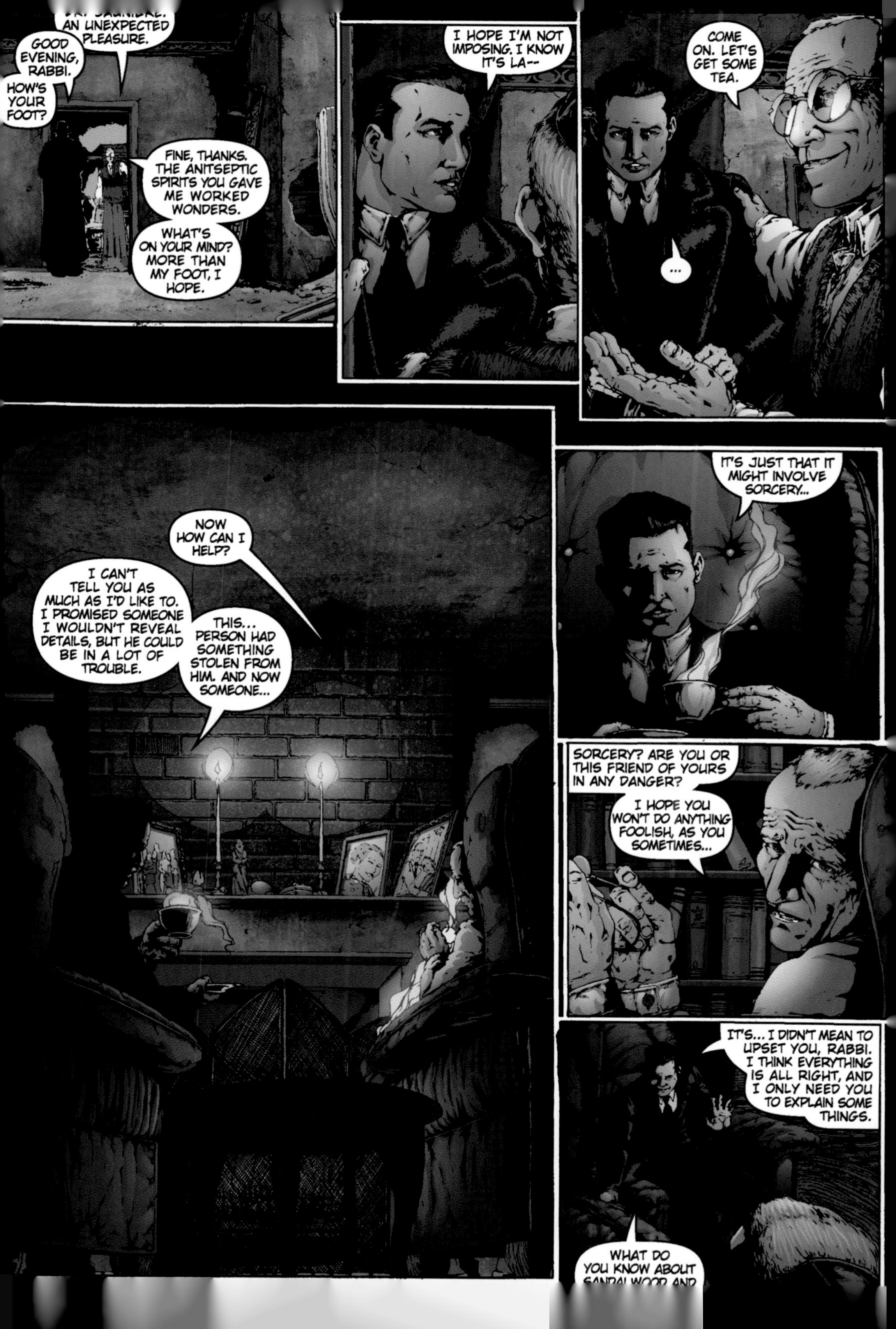
AN UNEXPECTED PLEASURE.
GOOD EVENING, RABBI.
HOW'S YOUR FOOT?
FINE, THANKS. THE ANITSEPTIC SPIRITS YOU GAVE ME WORKED WONDERS.
WHAT'S ON YOUR MIND? MORE THAN MY FOOT, I HOPE.
I HOPE I'M NOT IMPOSING. I KNOW IT'S LA--
COME ON. LET'S GET SOME TEA.
...
NOW HOW CAN I HELP?
I CAN'T TELL YOU AS MUCH AS I'D LIKE TO. I PROMISED SOMEONE I WOULDN'T REVEAL DETAILS, BUT HE COULD BE IN A LOT OF TROUBLE.
THIS... PERSON HAD SOMETHING STOLEN FROM HIM. AND NOW SOMEONE...
IT'S JUST THAT IT MIGHT INVOLVE SORCERY...
SORCERY? ARE YOU OR THIS FRIEND OF YOURS IN ANY DANGER?
I HOPE YOU WON'T DO ANYTHING FOOLISH, AS YOU SOMETIMES...
IT'S... I DIDN'T MEAN TO UPSET YOU, RABBI. I THINK EVERYTHING IS ALL RIGHT, AND I ONLY NEED YOU TO EXPLAIN SOME THINGS.
WHAT DO YOU KNOW ABOUT

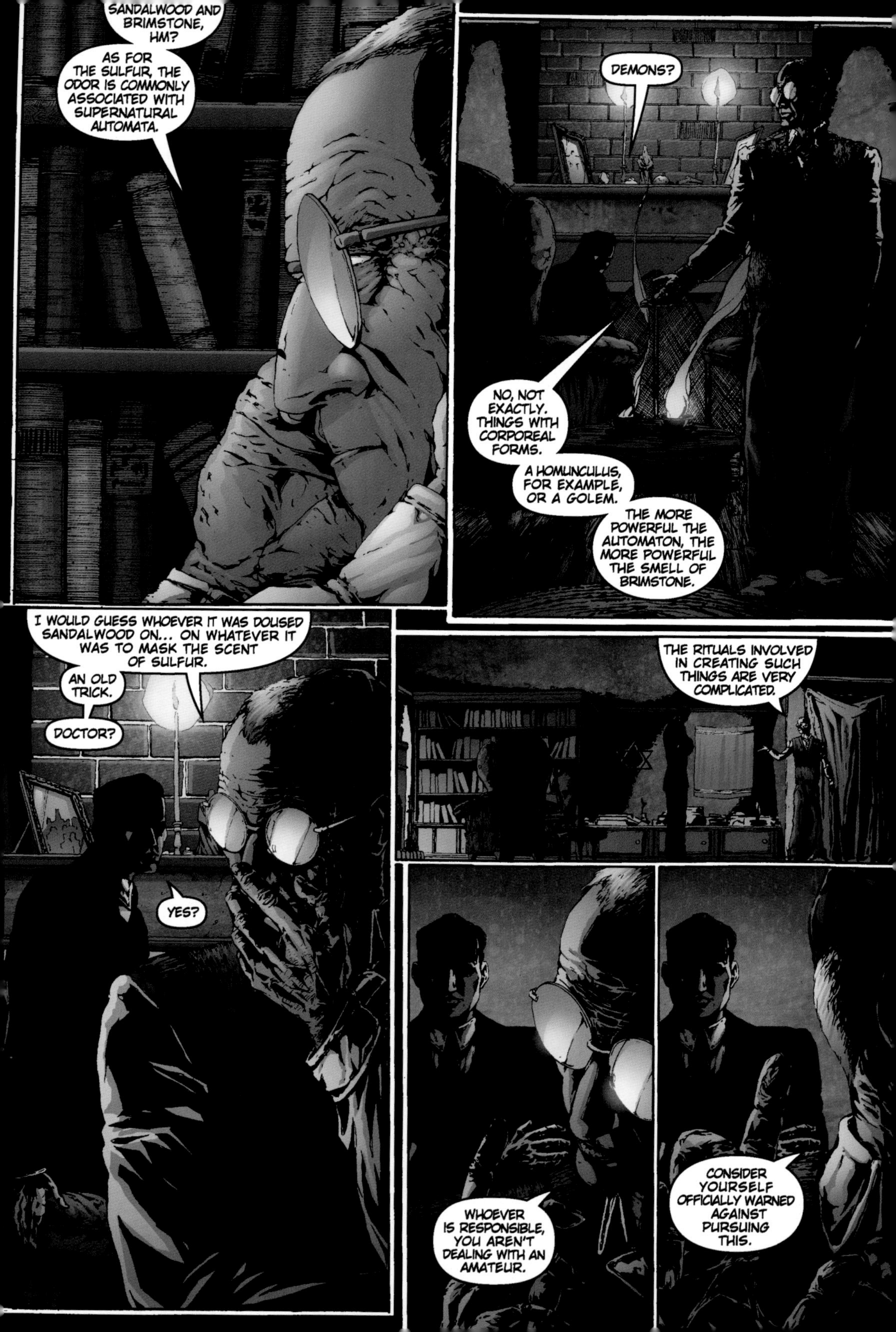
SANDALWOOD AND BRIMSTONE, HM?
AS FOR THE SULFUR, THE ODOR IS COMMONLY ASSOCIATED WITH SUPERNATURAL AUTOMATA.
DEMONS?
NO, NOT EXACTLY. THINGS WITH CORPOREAL FORMS.
A HOMUNCULUS, FOR EXAMPLE, OR A GOLEM.
THE MORE POWERFUL THE AUTOMATON, THE MORE POWERFUL THE SMELL OF BRIMSTONE.
I WOULD GUESS WHOEVER IT WAS DOUSED SANDALWOOD ON... ON WHATEVER IT WAS TO MASK THE SCENT OF SULFUR.
AN OLD TRICK.
DOCTOR?
YES?
THE RITUALS INVOLVED IN CREATING SUCH THINGS ARE VERY COMPLICATED.
WHOEVER IS RESPONSIBLE, YOU AREN'T DEALING WITH AN AMATEUR.
CONSIDER YOURSELF OFFICIALLY WARNED AGAINST PURSUING THIS.

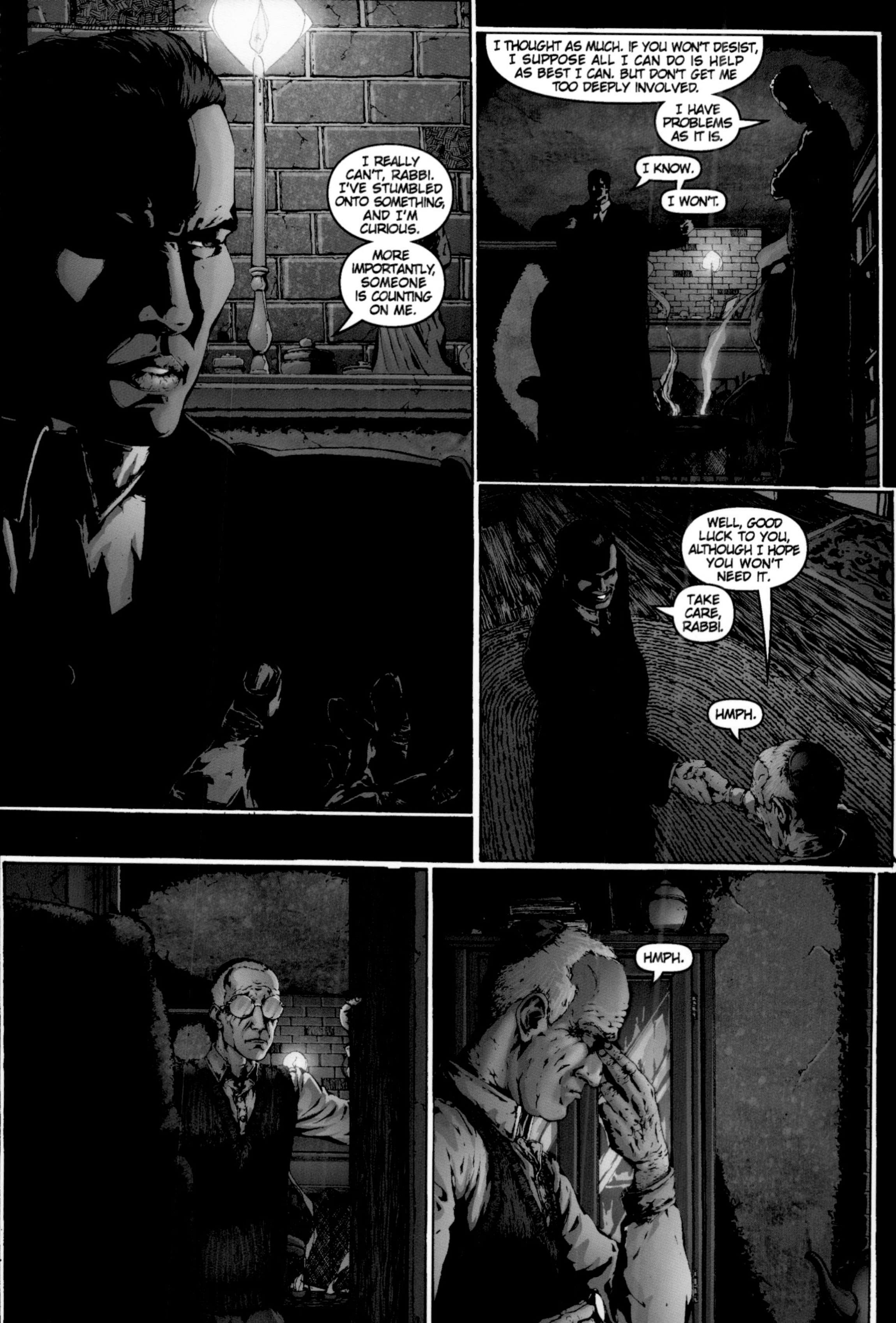
I REALLY CAN'T, RABBI. I'VE STUMBLED ONTO SOMETHING, AND I'M CURIOUS.
MORE IMPORTANTLY, SOMEONE IS COUNTING ON ME.
I THOUGHT AS MUCH. IF YOU WON'T DESIST, I SUPPOSE ALL I CAN DO IS HELP AS BEST I CAN. BUT DON'T GET ME TOO DEEPLY INVOLVED.
I HAVE PROBLEMS AS IT IS.
I KNOW.
I WON'T.
WELL, GOOD LUCK TO YOU, ALTHOUGH I HOPE YOU WON'T NEED IT.
TAKE CARE, RABBI.
HMPH.
HMPH.

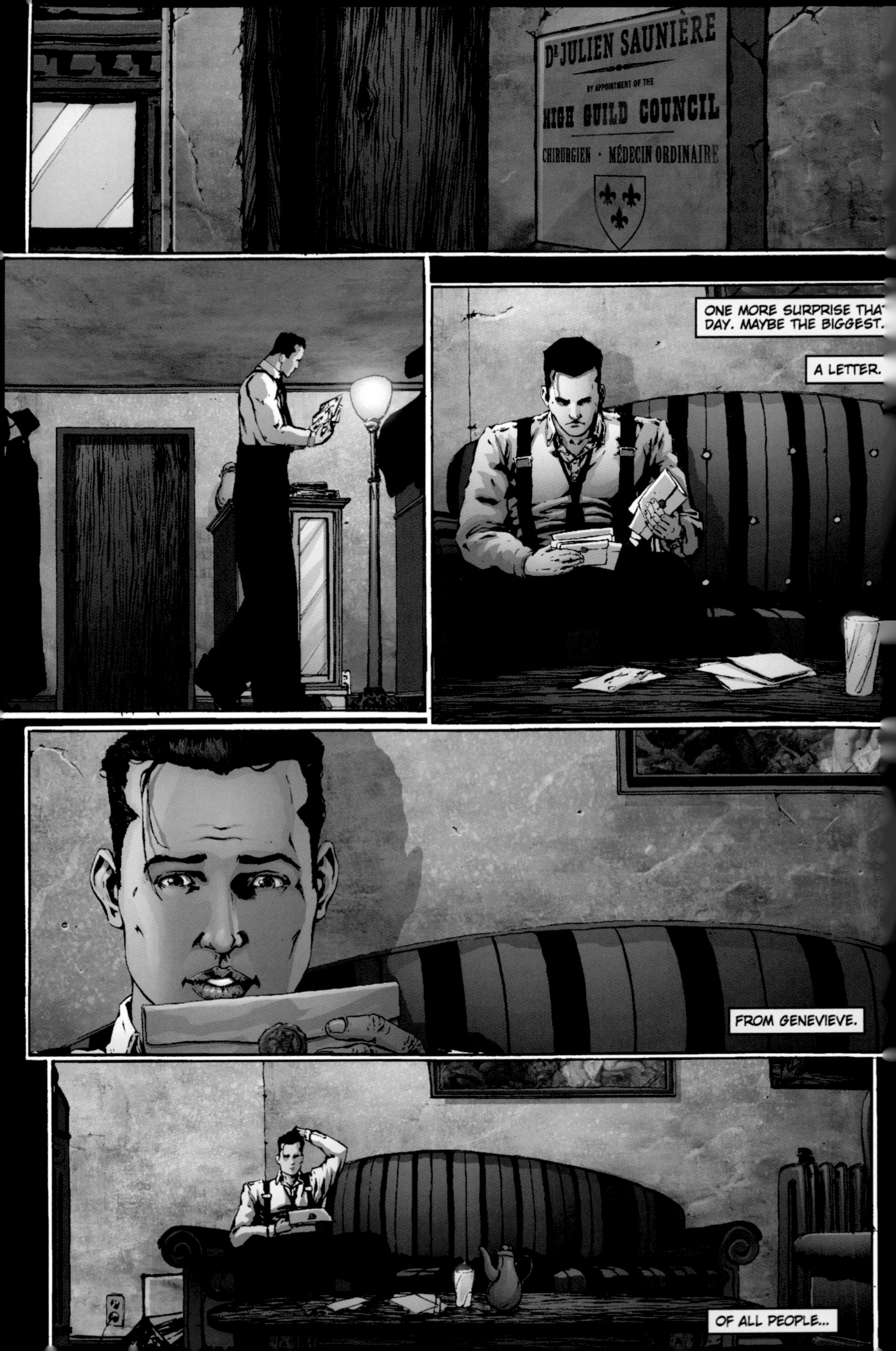
Dr JULIEN SAUNIÈRE
BY APPOINTMENT OF THE
HIGH GUILD COUNCIL
CHIRURGIEN · MÉDECIN ORDINAIRE
ONE MORE SURPRISE THAT DAY. MAYBE THE BIGGEST.
A LETTER.
FROM GENEVIEVE.
OF ALL PEOPLE...

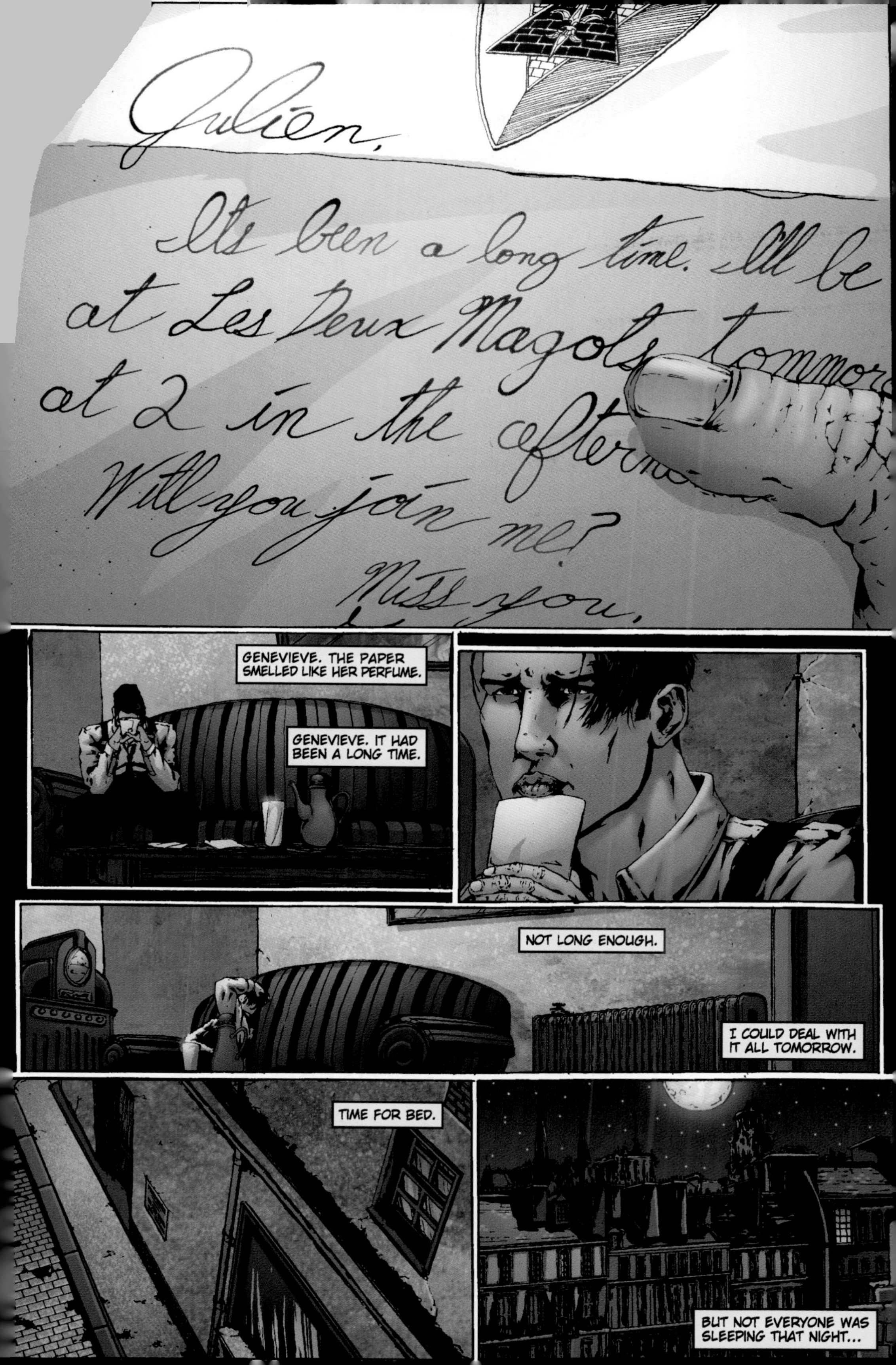

Julien,
Its been a long time. Ill be
at Les Deux Magots tommor
at 2 in the aftern
Will you join me?
Miss you,
GENEVIEVE. THE PAPER SMELLED LIKE HER PERFUME.
GENEVIEVE. IT HAD BEEN A LONG TIME.
NOT LONG ENOUGH.
I COULD DEAL WITH IT ALL TOMORROW.
TIME FOR BED.
BUT NOT EVERYONE WAS SLEEPING THAT NIGHT...

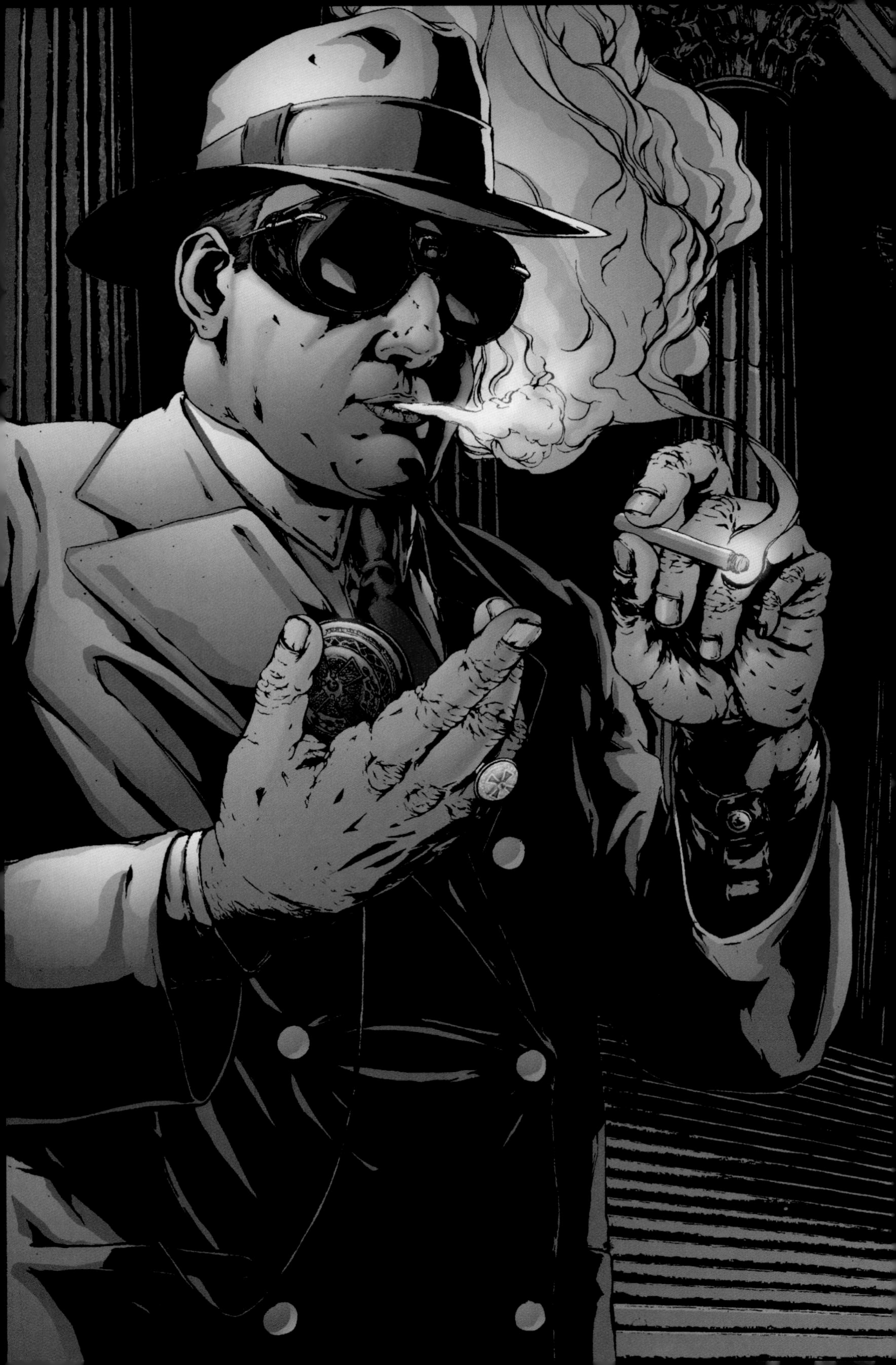

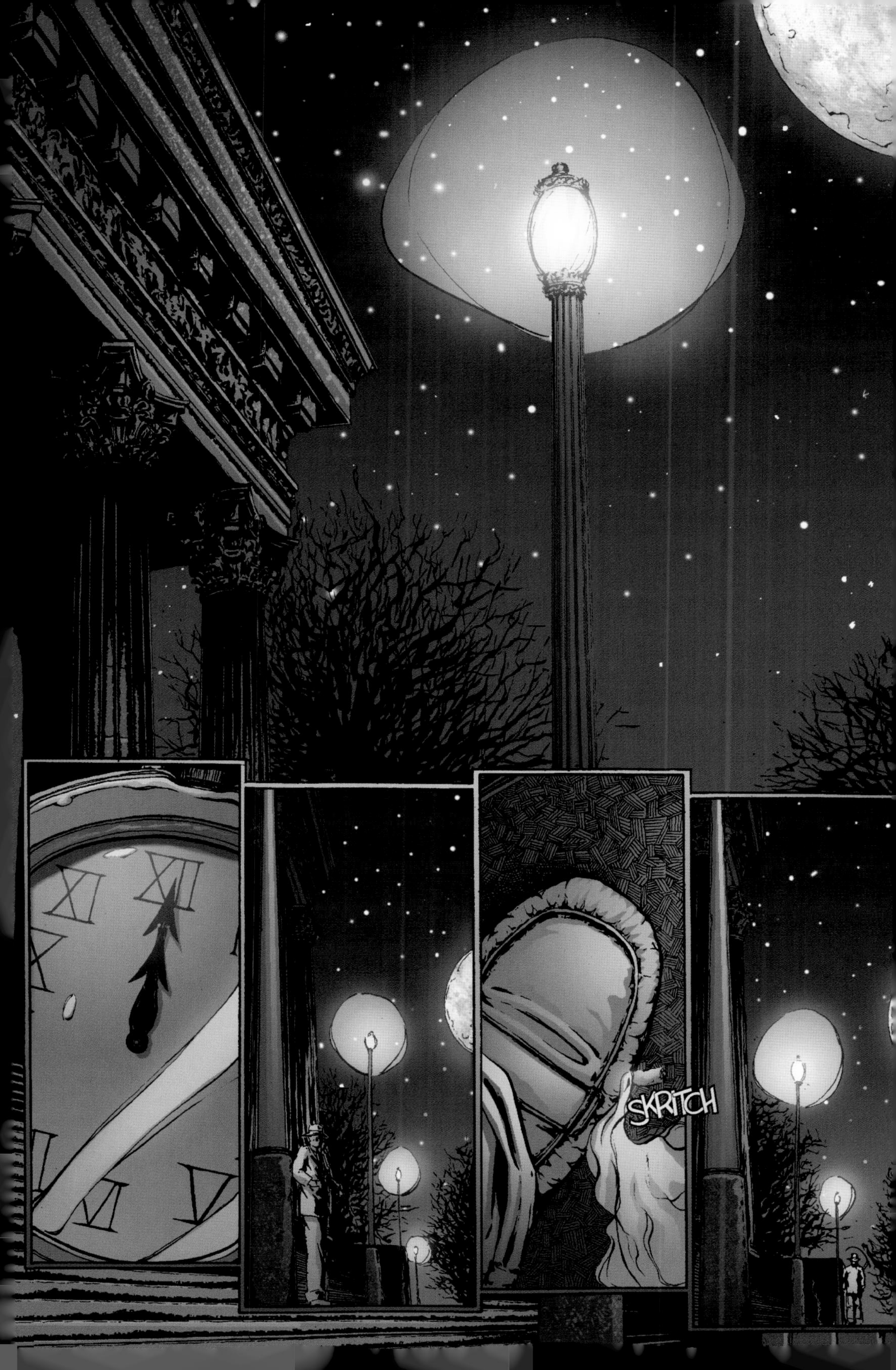
SKRITCH

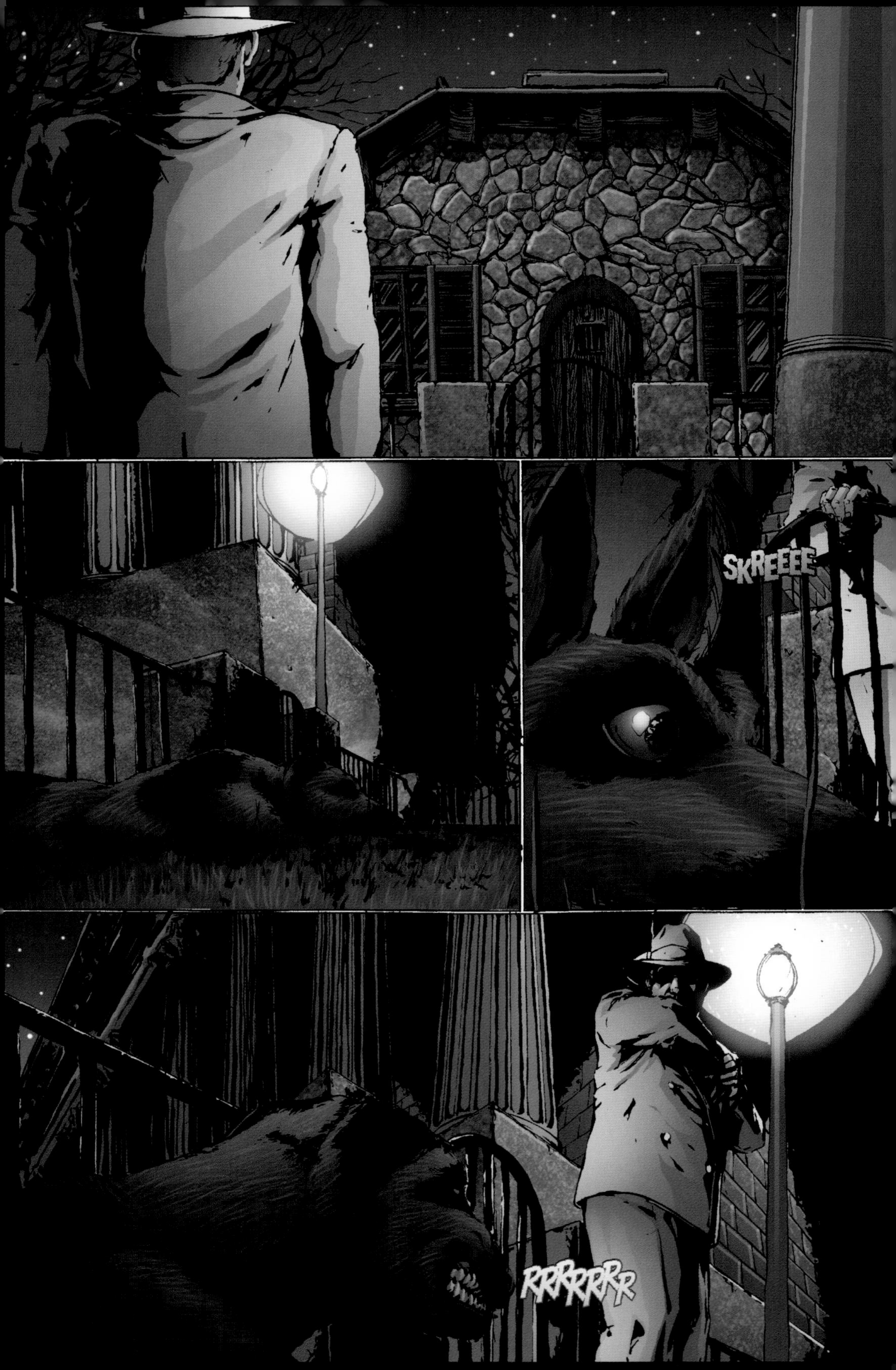
SKREEEE
RRRRRRRR

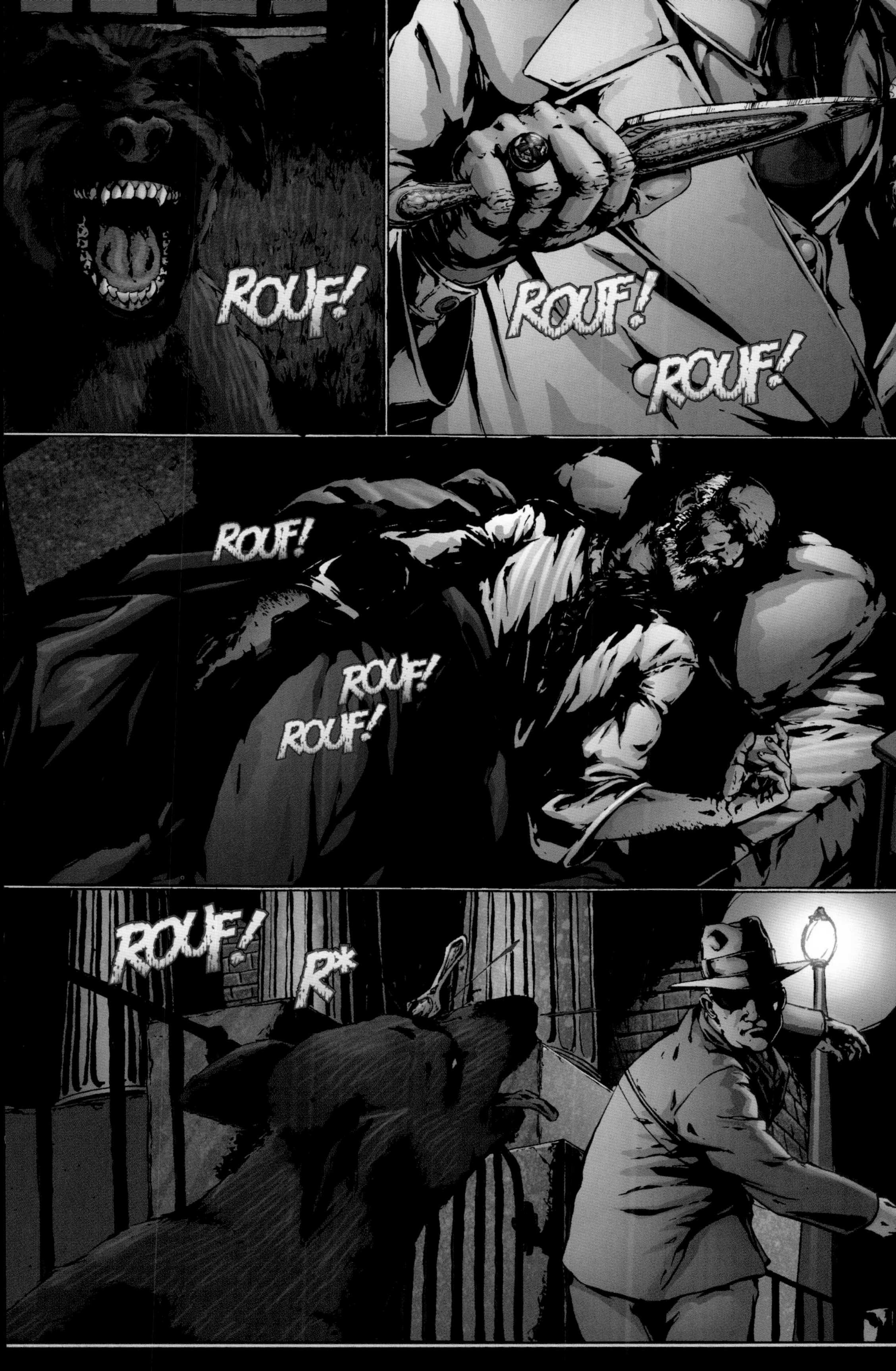
ROUF!
ROUF!
ROUF!
ROUF!
ROUF!
ROUF!
ROUF!
R*

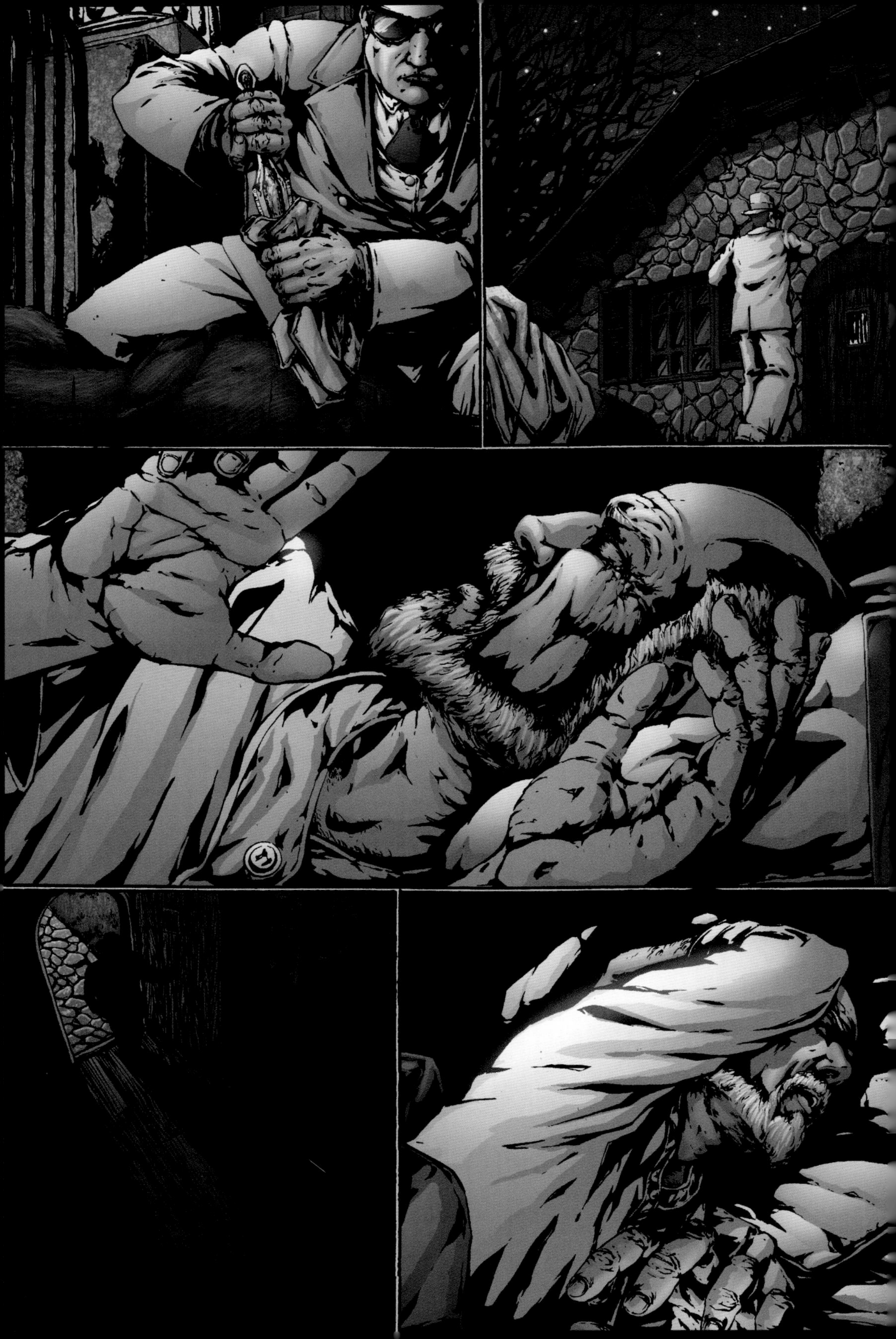

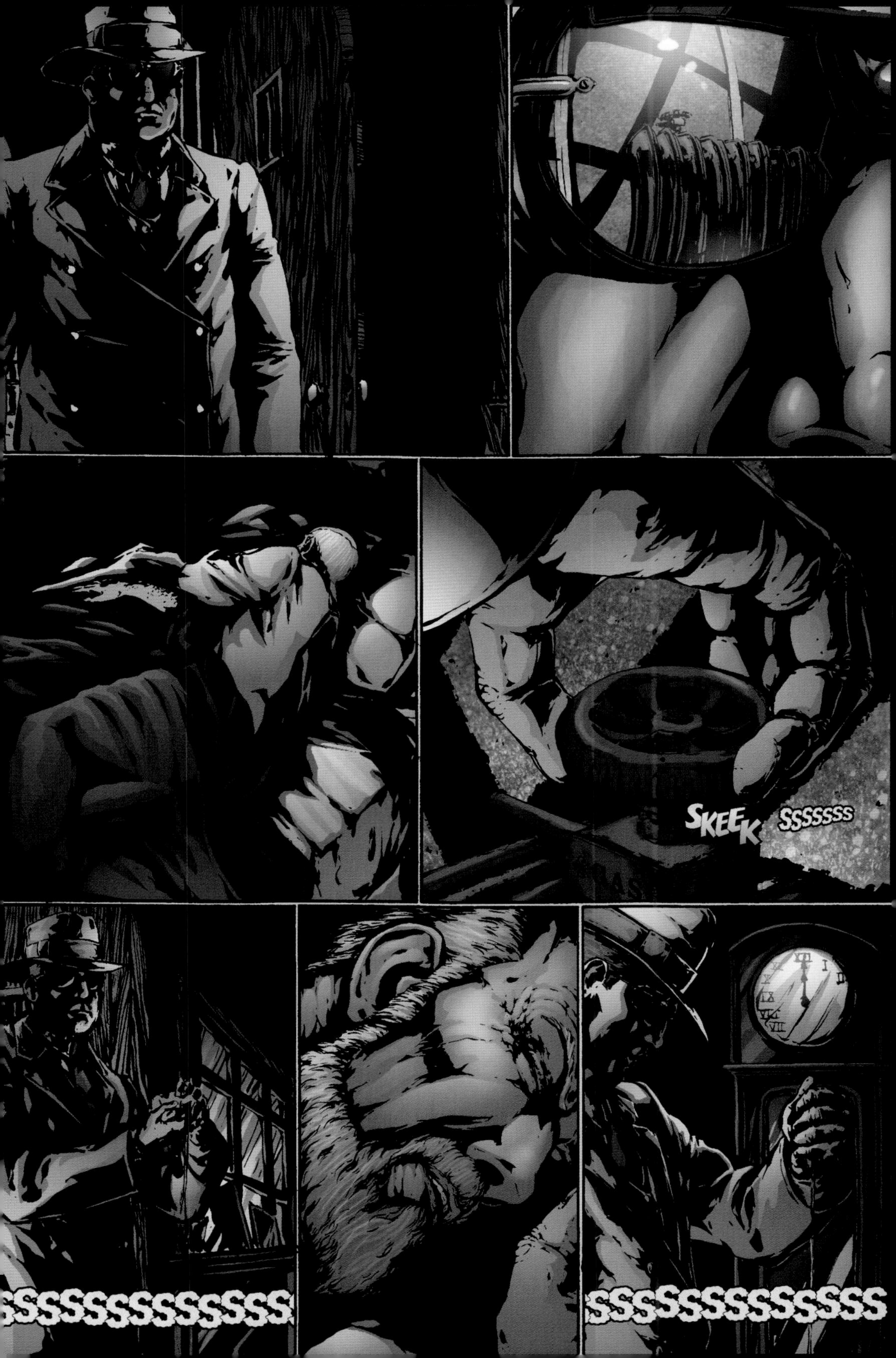
SKEEK
SSSSSS
SSSSSSSSSSSSSS
SSSSSSSSSSSSSSS

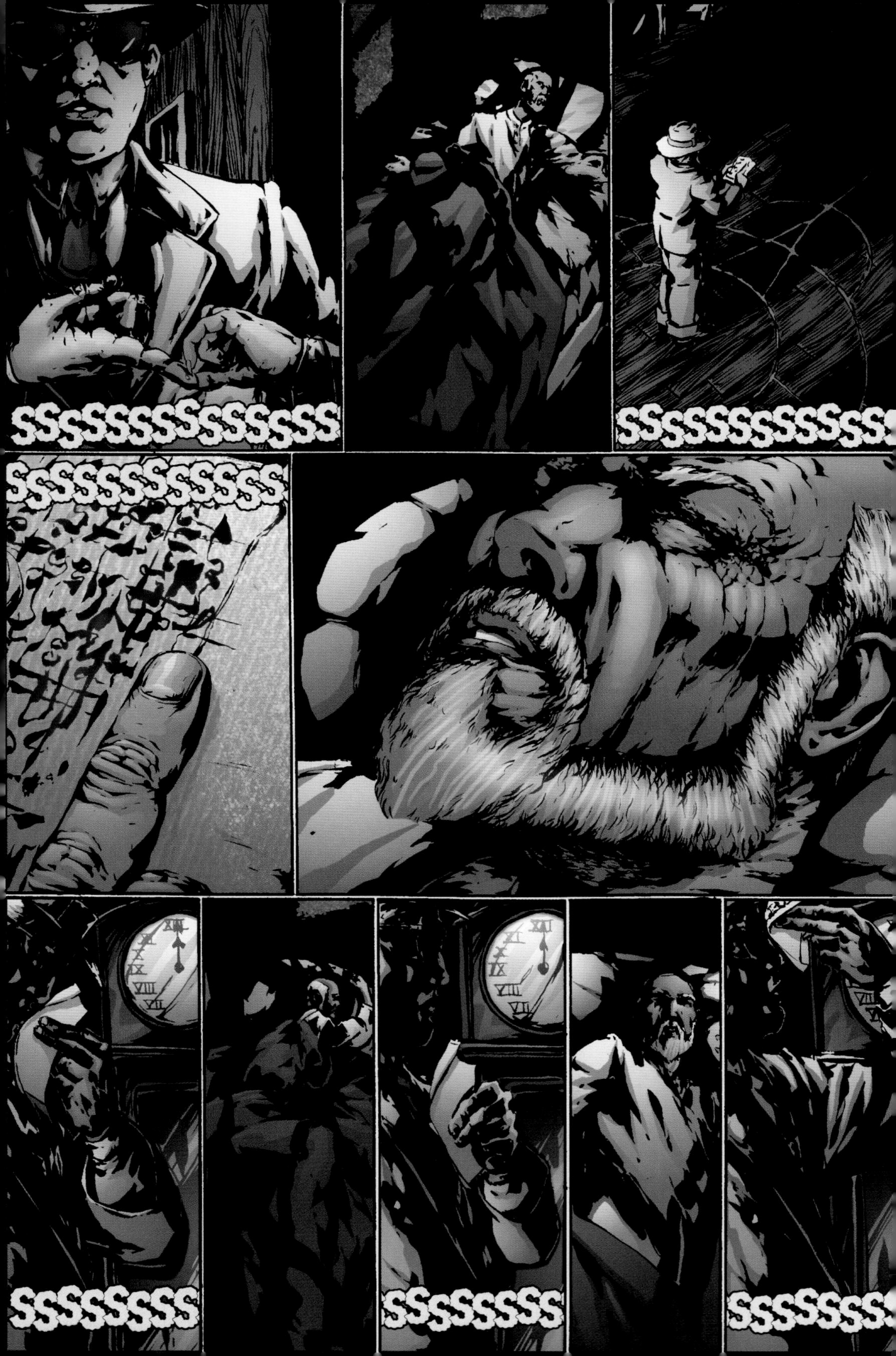
SSSSSSSSSSSSSS
SSSSSSSSSSSSSS
SSSSSSSSSSSSS
SSSSSSSS
SSSSSSSS
SSSSSSSS

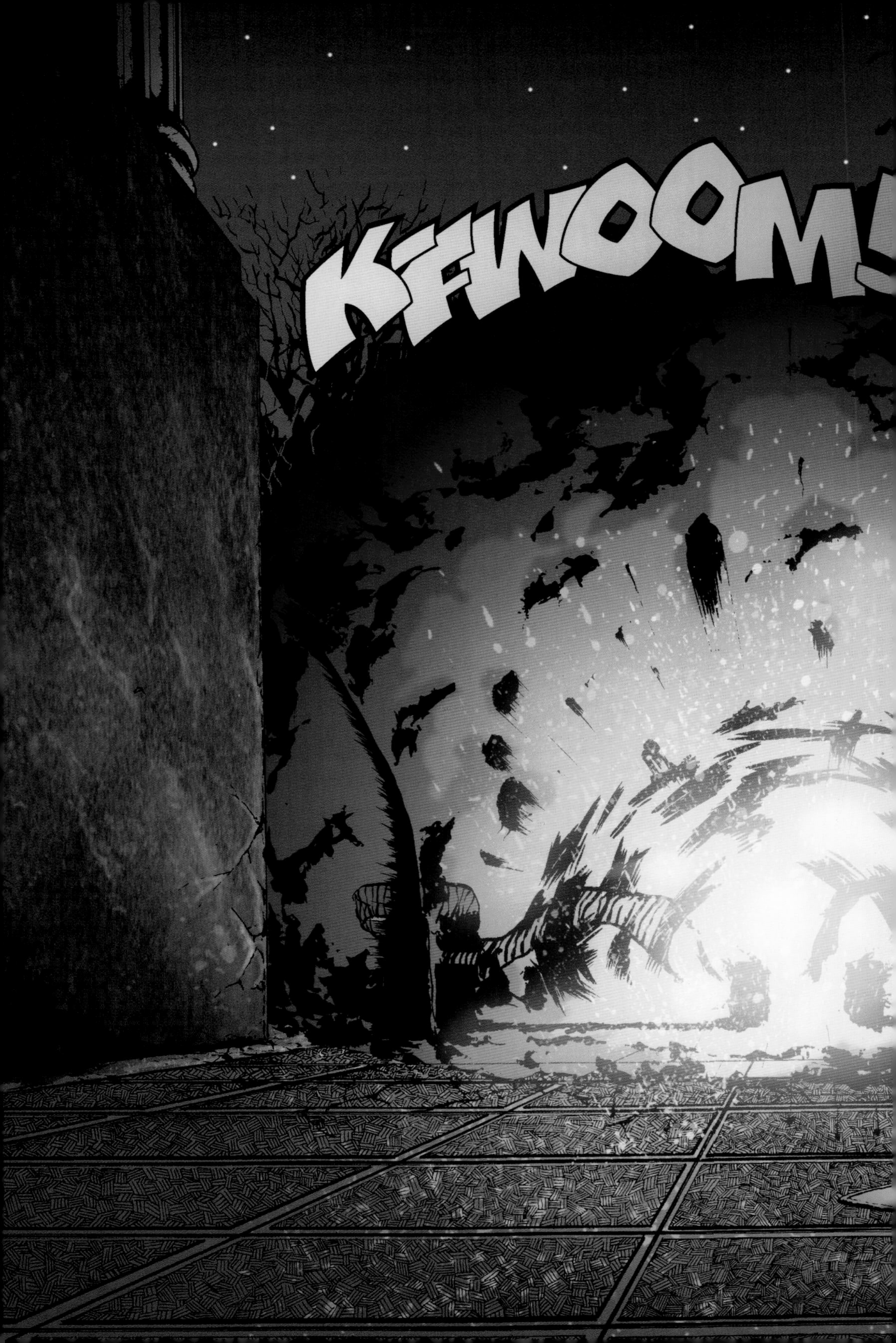
K'FWOOM!

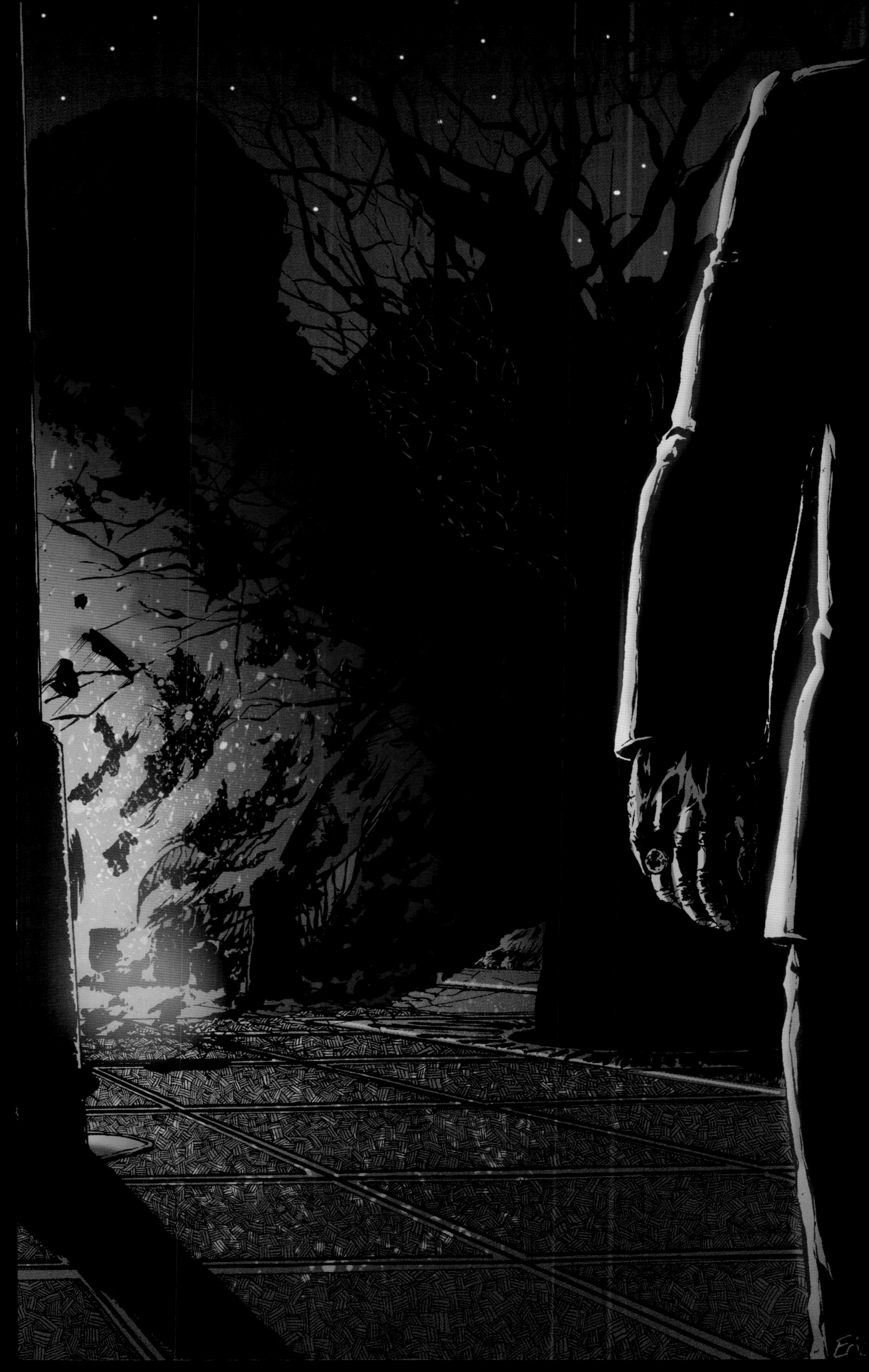

Le Journal de la Liberté

Paris's leading anglophone newspaper • vol. 205, no. 96 • Oct. 19, MCMXXXIII

Editors in Chief: M. Tait Bergstrom, M. Matthew Pasteris. **Story Editor:** M. Arvid Nelson. **Art Editors:** M. EricJ, M. Jeromy Cox. **Photography Editor:** M. Alex Waldman. **Layout Supervisor:** M. William Kartalopoulos. **Editors Emeritus:** M. Clark A. Smith, M. Howard P. Lovecraft, M. Robert E. Howard. Redacted by the Holy Parisian Inquisition under the direction of His Excellency Archbishop Emile-Jean Ireneaux. Le Journal de Liberté is printed under the benign auspices of his most puissant majesty KING LOUIS XXII of FRANCE.

papal seal ✦ God Save the King ✦ *of approv*

Ottoman Officials Cite Concern Over "Escalating Economic Tension"

Ottoman officials today said they had "grave concerns" about new economic legislation passed into law earlier this year.

The new policies, which go into effect next January, provide what French policy makers have called "necessary and fair" tariffs and regulations on imported goods, with the aim of "making French goods competitive with imports."

The Ministry of State proposed the legislation, which was unanimously approved by both the Hall of the Sword and the Hall of the Robe.

But the measure is receiving mounting resistance abroad.

The Hon. Ali Al-Faddiq, ambassador to France of the Ottoman Empire, expressed what he called "grave concern" on the part of the Sheik.

"There is very little these new economic measures can do to improve France's relationship with the Ottoman Empire," the ambassador said. "We view these new tariffs as an attempt to undermine the stability of our principalities. France's new trade laws are only escalating economic tension in Europe and Near Asia."

French officials defended the decision.

"We simply cannot allow foreign economic policy to undermine the sale of French goods. It is our belief that the new measures
continued on p. A14

Bonjour! M. Desjardin and his daughter take advantage of yesterday's unseasonable warmth. Photo: Eugene Atget, staff photographer

PRACTICE OF ILLICIT SORCERY ON THE RISE

Last year reported incidents of magically assisted theft and murder increased by nearly 12 percent. Officials called the increase "disturbing."

While the use of sorcery is not illegal, it is strongly discouraged by the Vatican. The use of sorcery to perpetrate a crime is considered an act of witchcraft and is punishable by death.

Even so, practitioners of the occult arts seem more and more inclined to use their skills for sinister aims.

"This is a major concern of ours," said an ecclesiastical official who wished to remain unnamed. "The increase in magically assisted crimes is a trend occurring throughout Europe, not just in France."

The illegal use of magic has been linked to organized crime.

"We're not looking at random occurrences here," said Jacques Berthold, Lieutenant in the Royal Parisian Gendarmerie. "The perpetrators responsible for this increase know what they are doing. These are professionals, not just apprentice conjurers out for kicks."

The Guild of Sorcerers denounced the crimes.

"We find these acts deplorable and a vulgar misuse of our art," said Emelie Peguy, Master Sorcerer. "Whoever is causing this mayhem doesn't have a guild license, and we are offering the Gendarmerie and the Inquisition our fullest support in apprehending suspects accused of such crimes."

Other officials noted that the decentralized, secretive nature of sorcerous education makes the pro-
continued on page B3

HALL OF THE SWORD MEETS IN TWO DAYS

The biannual Congress of the Hall of the Sword takes place two days, and a record number Sword members are expected attend. The focus of the Congress is expected to be foreign policy.

"Prussian militarism is going to be high on our agenda," said Phillipe Verlaine, Duke of Orleans. "As is the new threat posed by the Ottomans."

Orleans's comments reflect the concerns of many of the members of the Hall of the Sword over the militarization of the Prussian economy.

"We, Prussia, and the Holy Roman Empire are the only real powers on the continent aside from Russia," Dominic Fontaine, Duke of Normandy, said. "The mobilization of the Prussian economy, coupled with the fiery speeches being made by the Kaiser, are alarming."

The Hall of the Sword is the most powerful legislative body in France, save for the King himself. The only requisite for membership is a title of nobility extending back to the crusades.

Members of the Sword are expected to rally behind David Louis Plantard, The duke of Lorraine, for the unveiling of a "s
continued on p. A

Young Streetwalker Slain in Apartment

13th Arrondissement – A young woman believed to be a prostitute was murdered in her room late last morning.

The neighborhood in which her body was found is familiar to Inquisitors as a hive of vice.

"This young, fallen woman's death is clearly the result of organized crime," Inquisitor Renant, an investigator on the scene, said. "We pray for her poor, fallen soul and commend her to God."

He refused to comment further on her case.

The corpse was discovered by the young woman's landlord. Our reporters were not allowed to speak to him due to an Inquisitional injunction placed on case a half hour after the body was discovered. The injunction essentially closes the case to public scrutiny.

Such a measure is unusual and not generally applied to crime occurring outside the ecclesiastical community. His excellency the Archbishop was unavailable for comment.

Local residents did not seem overly concerned by the death.

"This is a dangerous part of town," said a nearby resident who asked not to be named. "Girls get cut up all the time. I hate to say it, but it's not much of a surprise for anyone who lives around here."

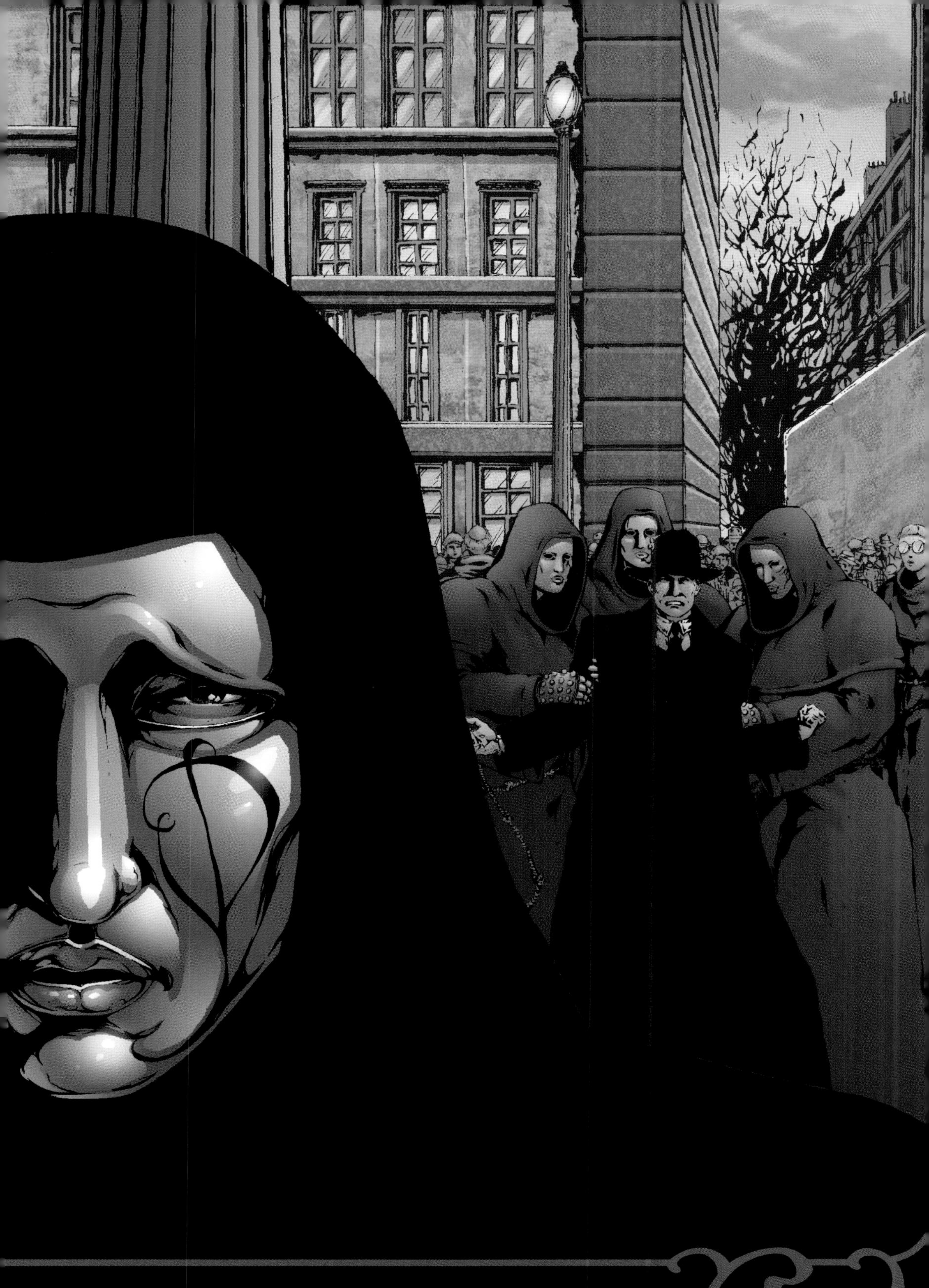

CHAPTER THREE
AN OLD FLAME

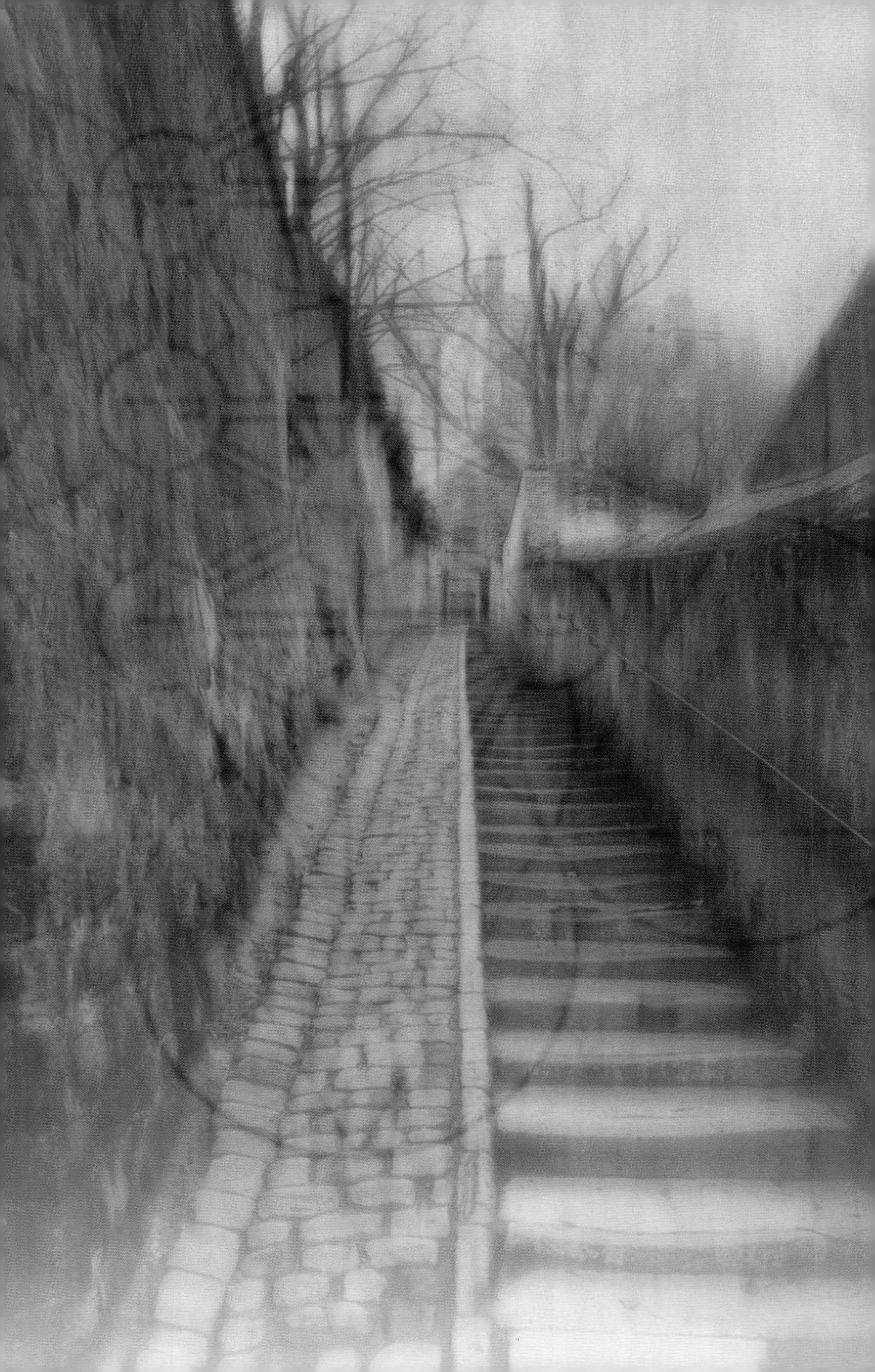

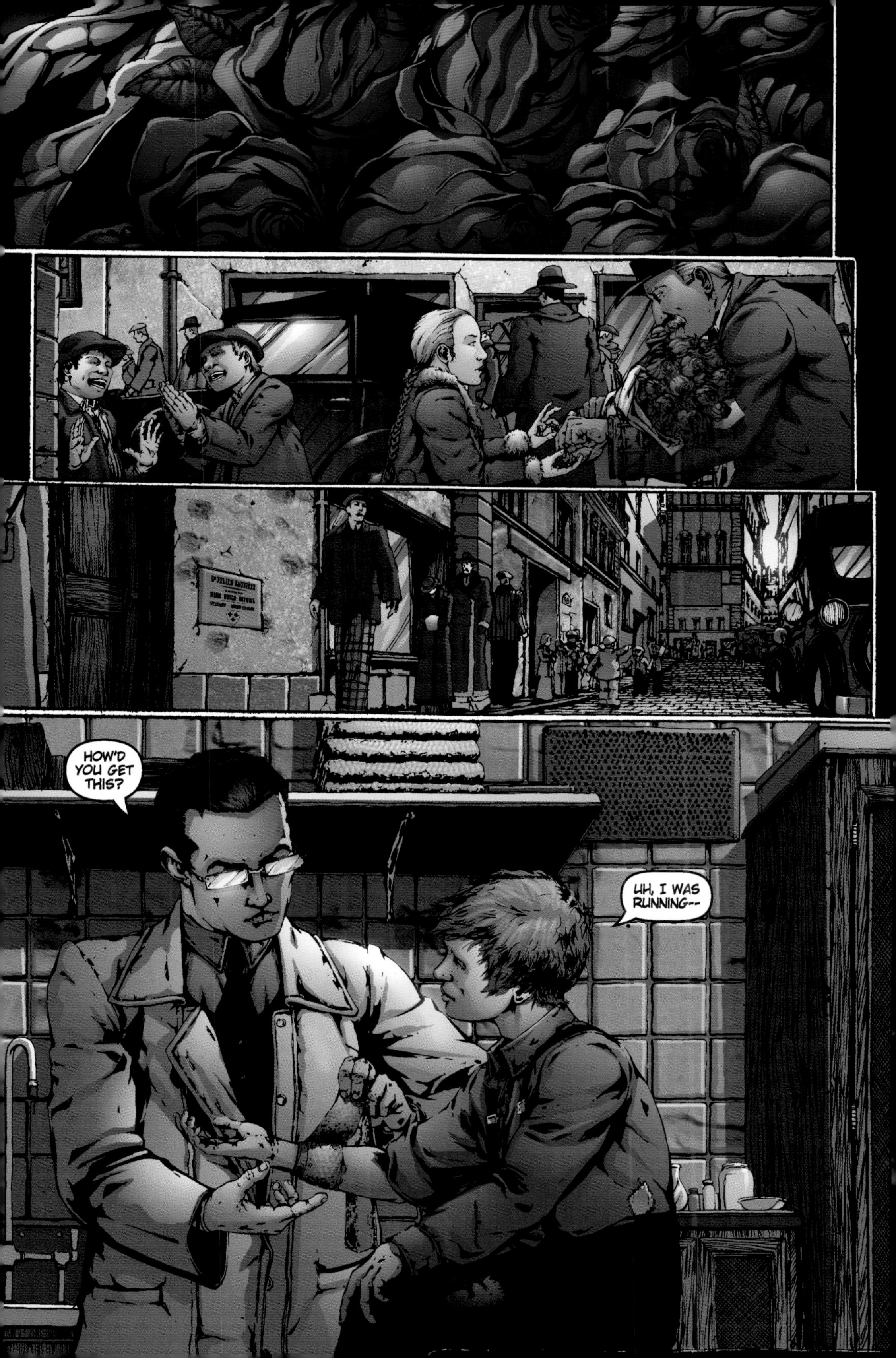
HOW'D YOU GET THIS?
UH, I WAS RUNNING--

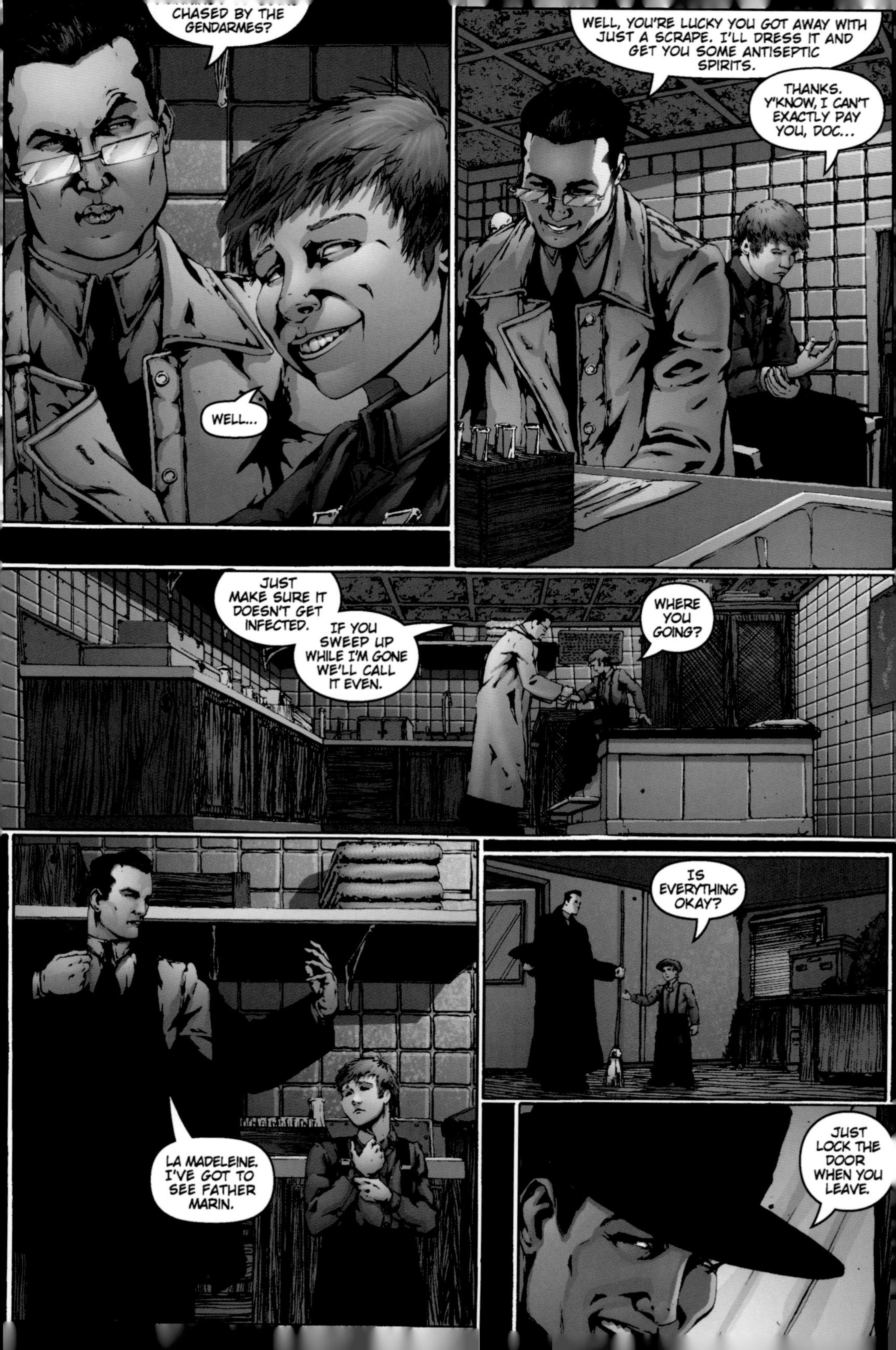
CHASED BY THE GENDARMES?
WELL...
WELL, YOU'RE LUCKY YOU GOT AWAY WITH JUST A SCRAPE. I'LL DRESS IT AND GET YOU SOME ANTISEPTIC SPIRITS.
THANKS. Y'KNOW, I CAN'T EXACTLY PAY YOU, DOC...
JUST MAKE SURE IT DOESN'T GET INFECTED.
IF YOU SWEEP UP WHILE I'M GONE WE'LL CALL IT EVEN.
WHERE YOU GOING?
LA MADELEINE. I'VE GOT TO SEE FATHER MARIN.
IS EVERYTHING OKAY?
JUST LOCK THE DOOR WHEN YOU LEAVE.

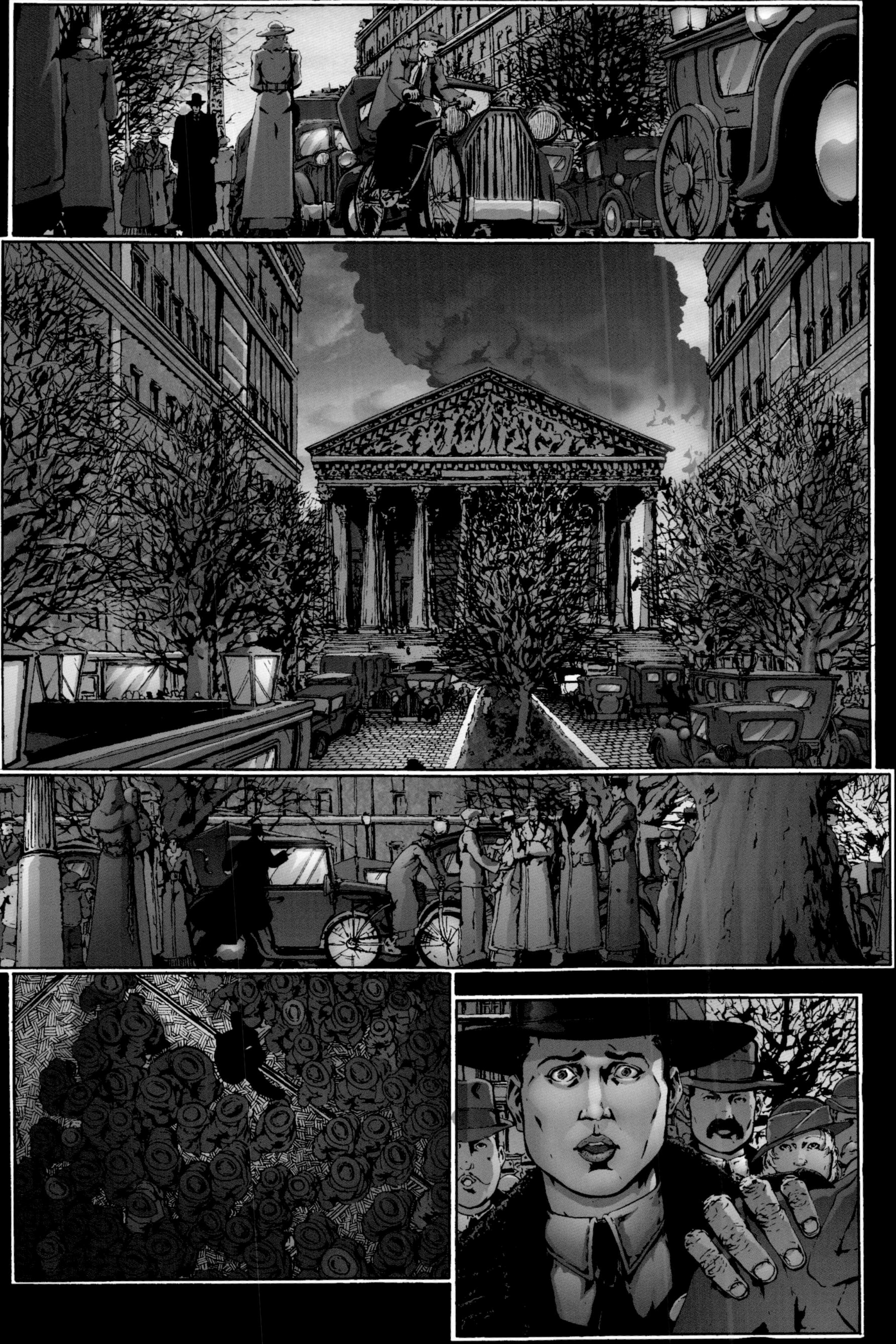

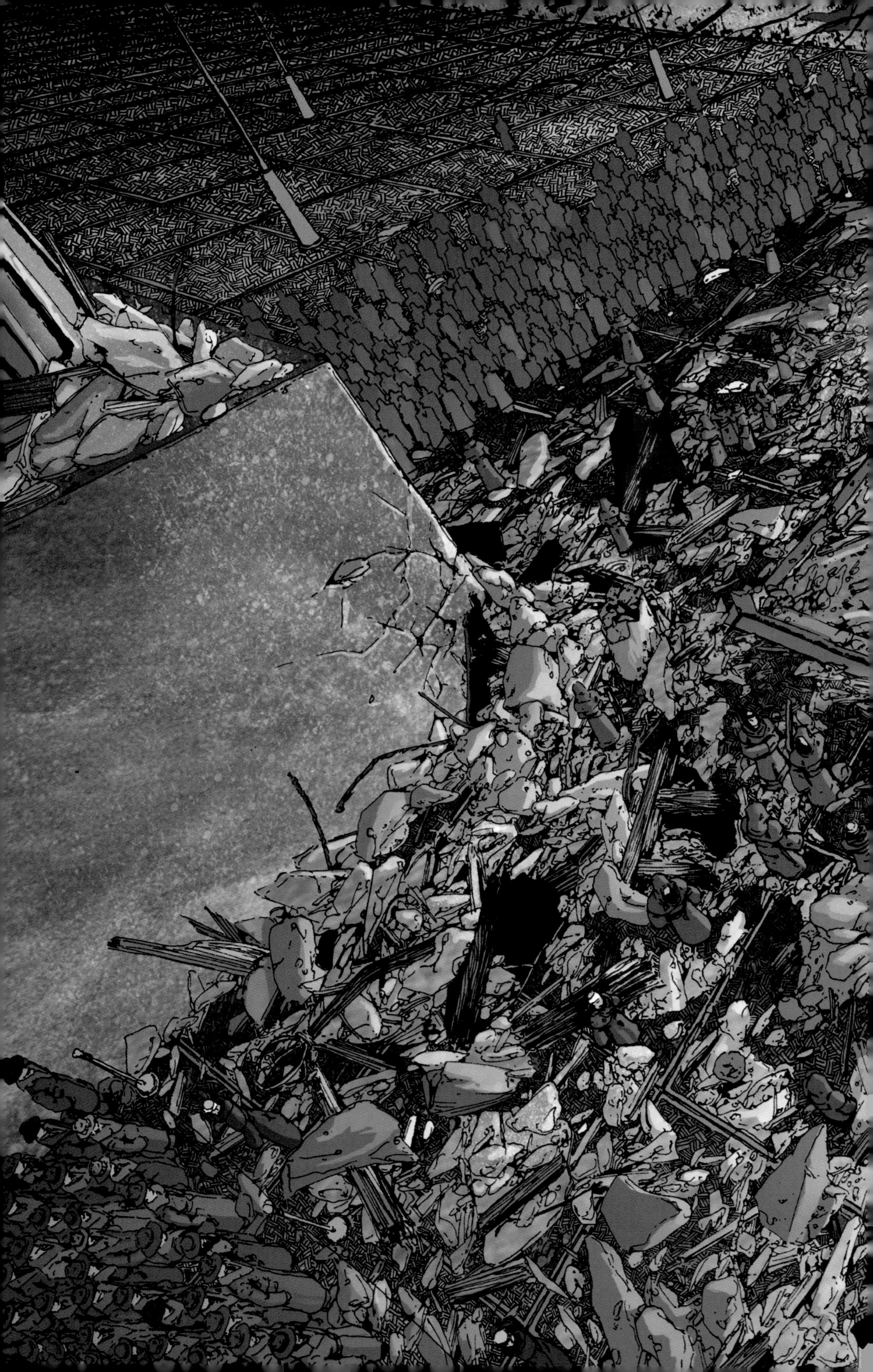

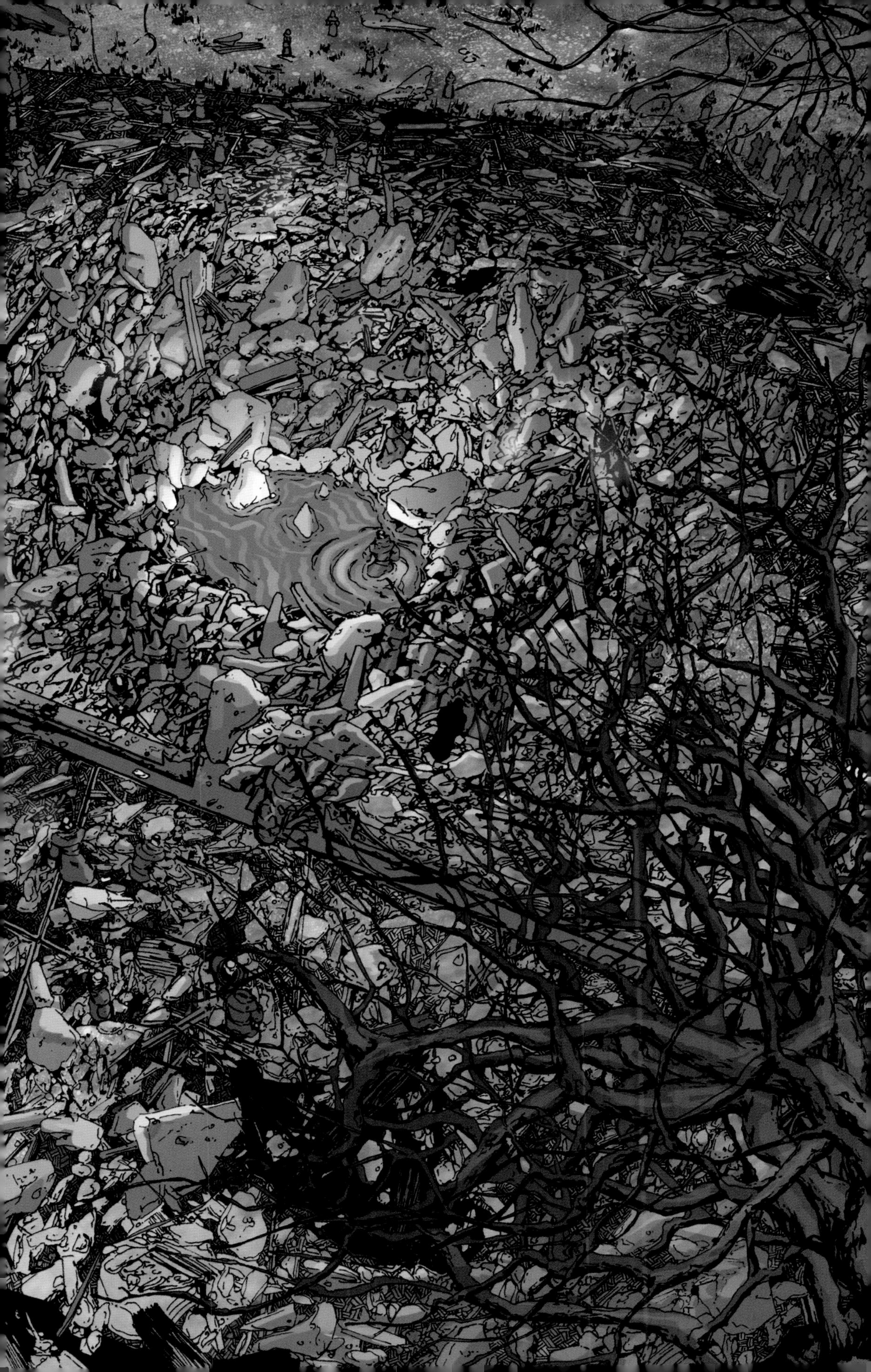

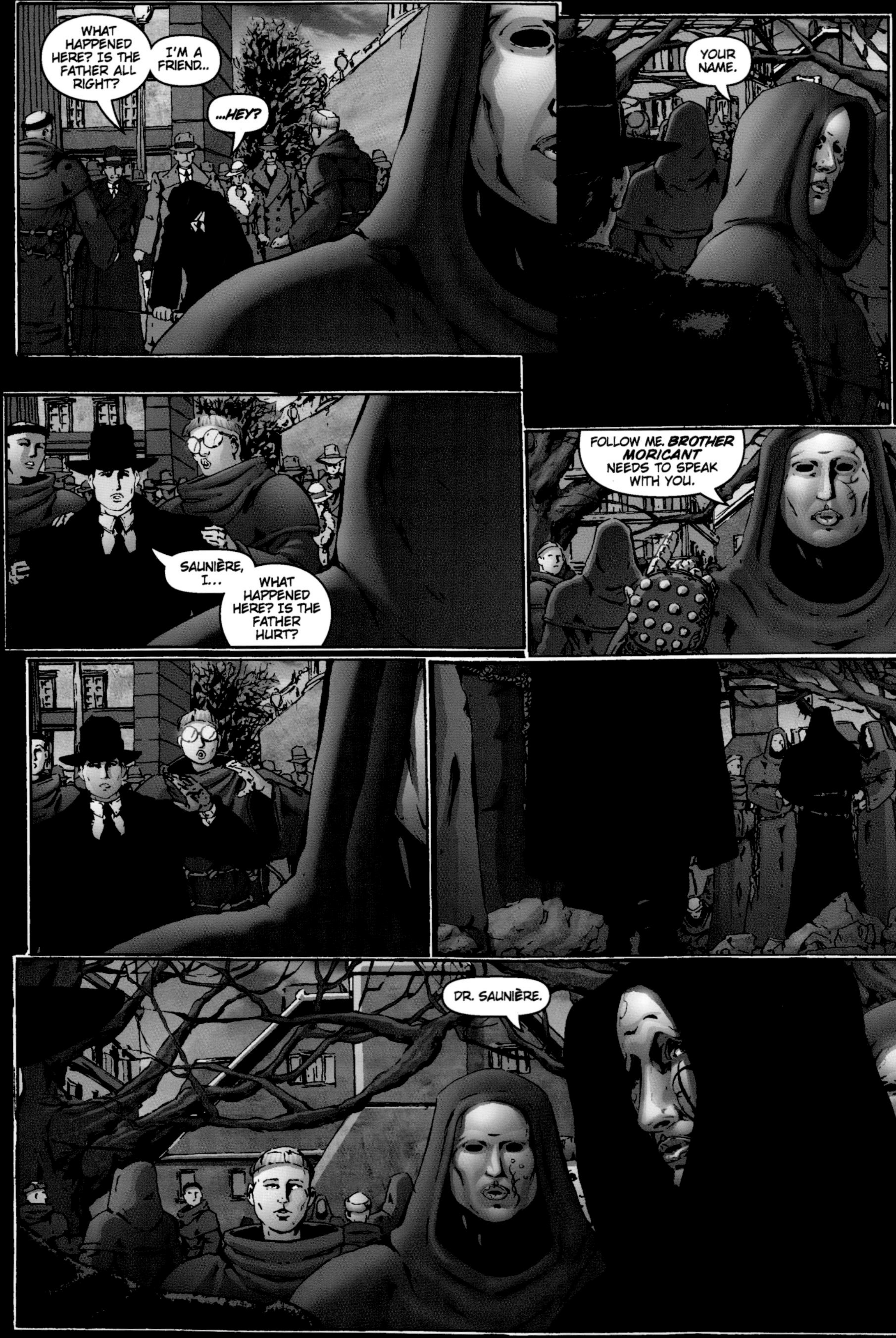
WHAT HAPPENED HERE? IS THE FATHER ALL RIGHT?
I'M A FRIEND...
...HEY?
YOUR NAME.
SAUNIÈRE, I...
WHAT HAPPENED HERE? IS THE FATHER HURT?
FOLLOW ME. BROTHER MORICANT NEEDS TO SPEAK WITH YOU.
DR. SAUNIÈRE.

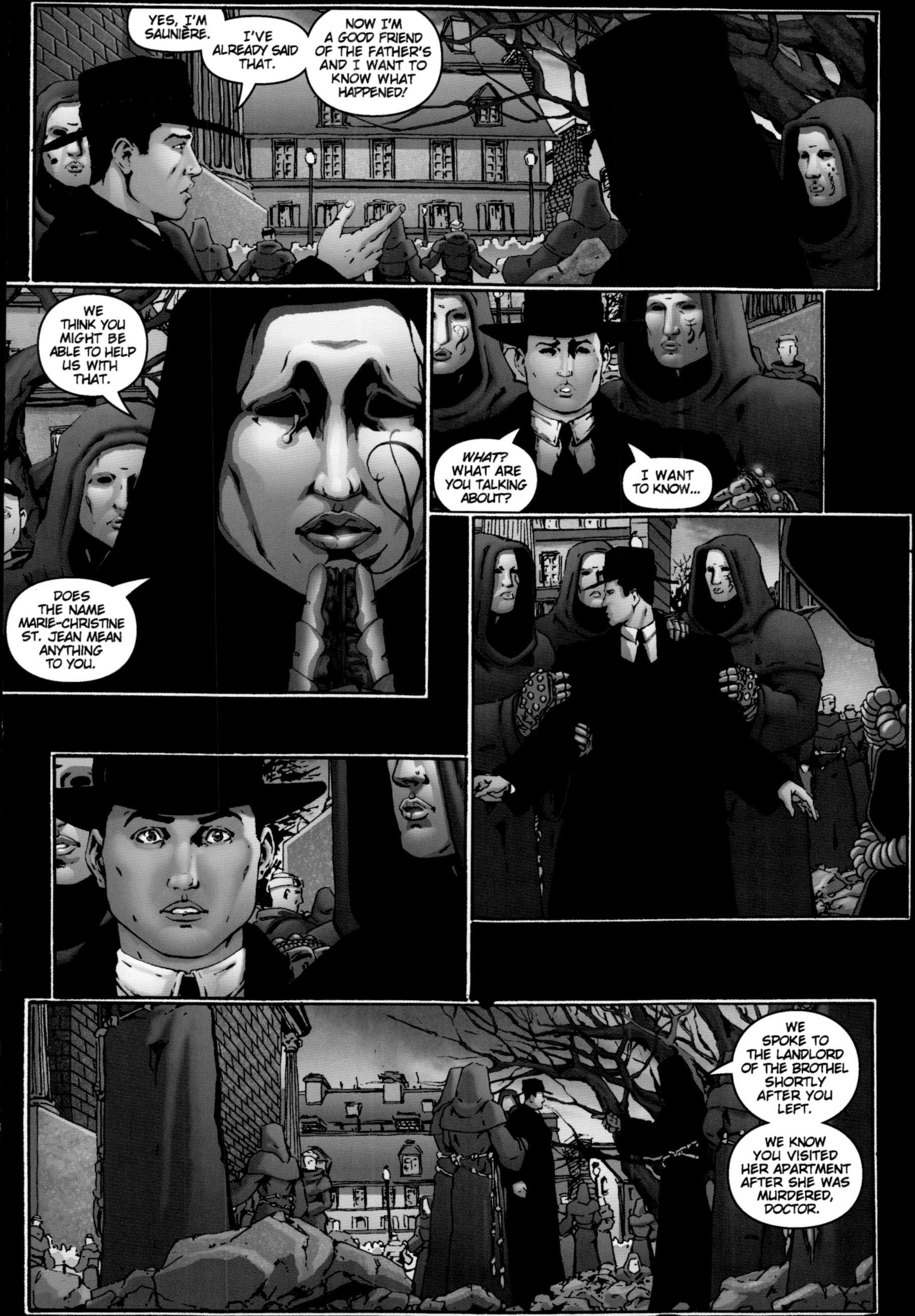

YES, I'M SAUNIÈRE.
I'VE ALREADY SAID THAT.
NOW I'M A GOOD FRIEND OF THE FATHER'S AND I WANT TO KNOW WHAT HAPPENED!
WE THINK YOU MIGHT BE ABLE TO HELP US WITH THAT.
DOES THE NAME MARIE-CHRISTINE ST. JEAN MEAN ANYTHING TO YOU.
WHAT? WHAT ARE YOU TALKING ABOUT?
I WANT TO KNOW...
WE SPOKE TO THE LANDLORD OF THE BROTHEL SHORTLY AFTER YOU LEFT.
WE KNOW YOU VISITED HER APARTMENT AFTER SHE WAS MURDERED, DOCTOR.

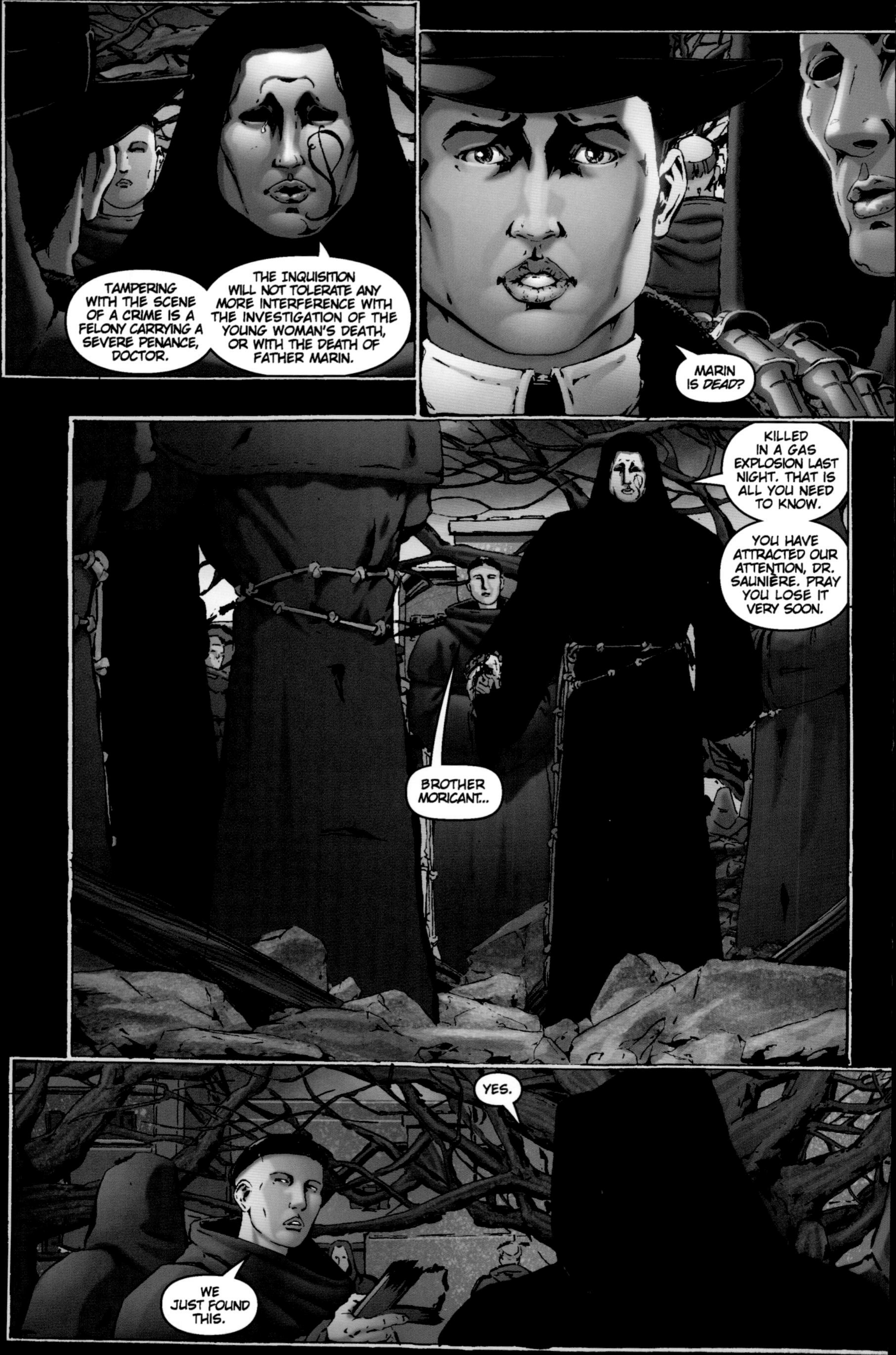
TAMPERING WITH THE SCENE OF A CRIME IS A FELONY CARRYING A SEVERE PENANCE, DOCTOR.
THE INQUISITION WILL NOT TOLERATE ANY MORE INTERFERENCE WITH THE INVESTIGATION OF THE YOUNG WOMAN'S DEATH, OR WITH THE DEATH OF FATHER MARIN.
MARIN IS *DEAD?*
KILLED IN A GAS EXPLOSION LAST NIGHT. THAT IS ALL YOU NEED TO KNOW.
YOU HAVE ATTRACTED OUR ATTENTION, DR. SAUNIÈRE. PRAY YOU LOSE IT VERY SOON.
BROTHER MORICANT...
YES.
WE JUST FOUND THIS.

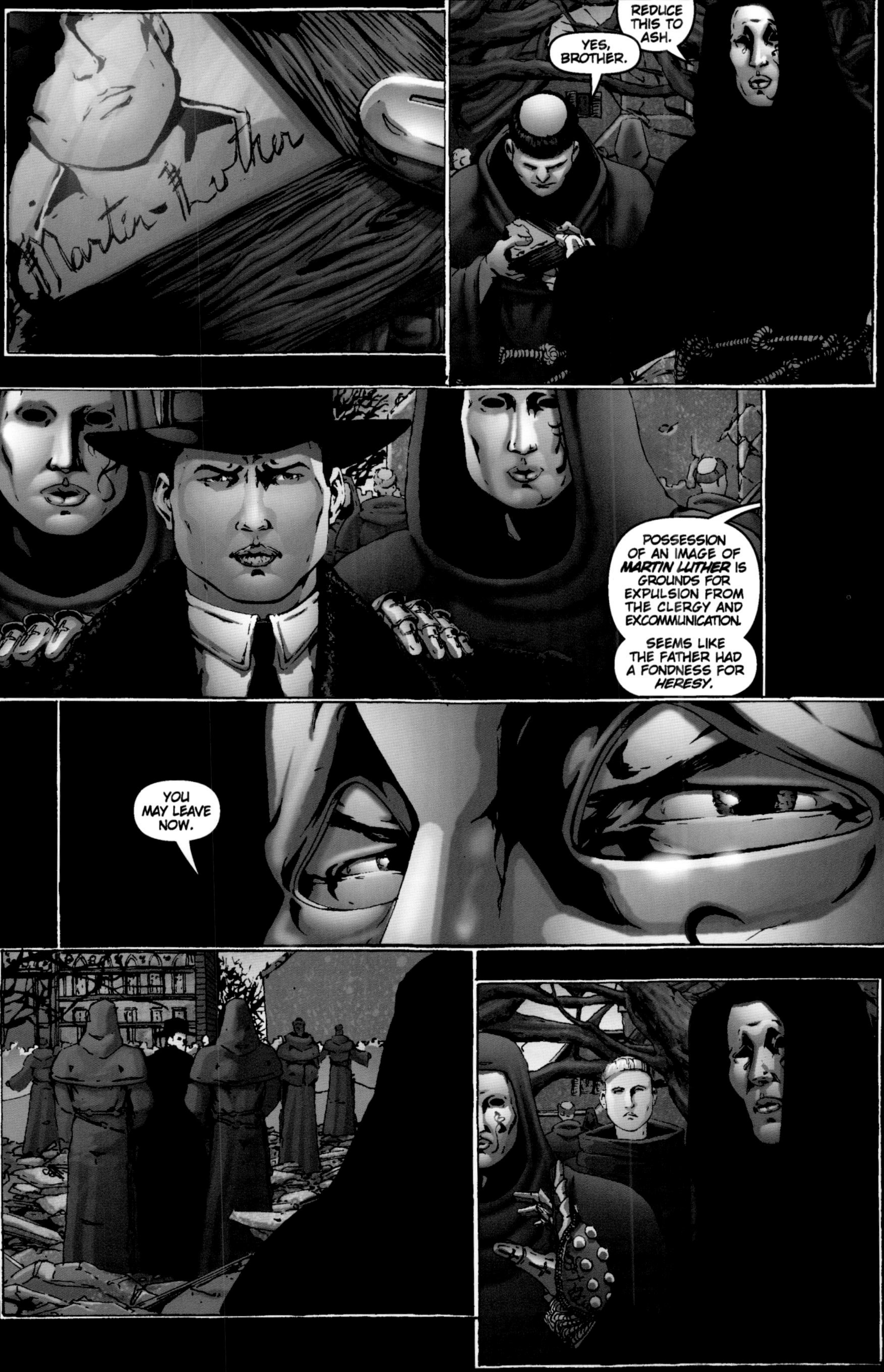
Martin-Luther
REDUCE THIS TO ASH.
YES, BROTHER.
POSSESSION OF AN IMAGE OF MARTIN LUTHER IS GROUNDS FOR EXPULSION FROM THE CLERGY AND EXCOMMUNICATION.
SEEMS LIKE THE FATHER HAD A FONDNESS FOR HERESY.
YOU MAY LEAVE NOW.

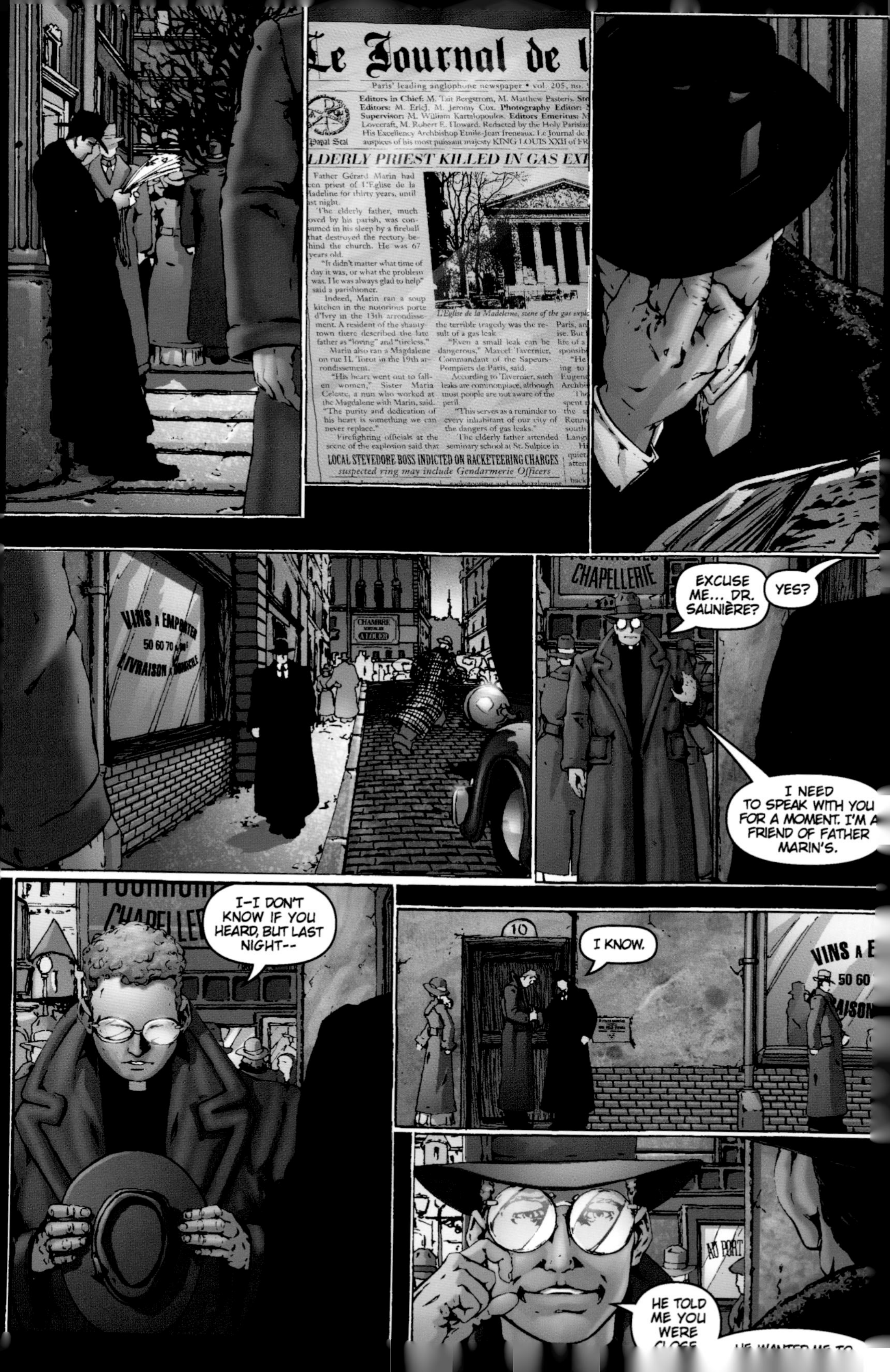
Le Journal de
Paris' leading anglophone newspaper • vol. 205, no.
Editors in Chief: M. Tait Bergstrom, M. Matthew Pasteris.
Editors: M. EricJ, M. Jeromy Cox. Photography Editor:
Supervisor: M. William Kartalopoulos. Editors Emeritus:
Lovecraft, M. Robert E. Howard. Redacted by the Holy Parisian
His Excellency Archbishop Emile-Jean Ireneaux. Le Journal de
auspices of his most puissant majesty KING LOUIS XXII of FR
Papal Seal
LDERLY PRIEST KILLED IN GAS EX
Father Gérard Marin had een priest of L'Eglise de la adeline for thirty years, until st night.
The elderly father, much oved by his parish, was consumed in his sleep by a fireball that destroyed the rectory behind the church. He was 67 years old.
"It didn't matter what time of day it was, or what the problem was. He was always glad to help" said a parishioner.
Indeed, Marin ran a soup kitchen in the notorious porte d'Ivry in the 13th arrondissement. A resident of the shantytown there described the late father as "loving" and "tireless."
Marin also ran a Magdalene on rue H. Torot in the 19th arrondissement.
"His heart went out to fallen women," Sister Maria Celeste, a nun who worked at the Magdalene with Marin, said. "The purity and dedication of his heart is something we can never replace."
Firefighting officials at the scene of the explosion said that the terrible tragedy was the result of a gas leak.
"Even a small leak can be dangerous," Marcel Tavernier, Commandant of the Sapeurs-Pompiers de Paris, said.
According to Tavernier, such leaks are commonplace, although most people are not aware of the peril.
"This serves as a reminder to every inhabitant of our city of the dangers of gas leaks."
The elderly father attended seminary school at St. Sulpice in
L'Eglise de la Madeleine, scene of the gas expl
LOCAL STEVEDORE BOSS INDICTED ON RACKETEERING CHARGES
suspected ring may include Gendarmerie Officers
VINS A EMPORTER
CHAMBRE
A LOUER
CHAPELLERIE
EXCUSE ME... DR. SAUNIÈRE?
YES?
I NEED TO SPEAK WITH YOU FOR A MOMENT. I'M A FRIEND OF FATHER MARIN'S.
I-I DON'T KNOW IF YOU HEARD, BUT LAST NIGHT--
10
I KNOW.
NO PORT
HE TOLD ME YOU WERE

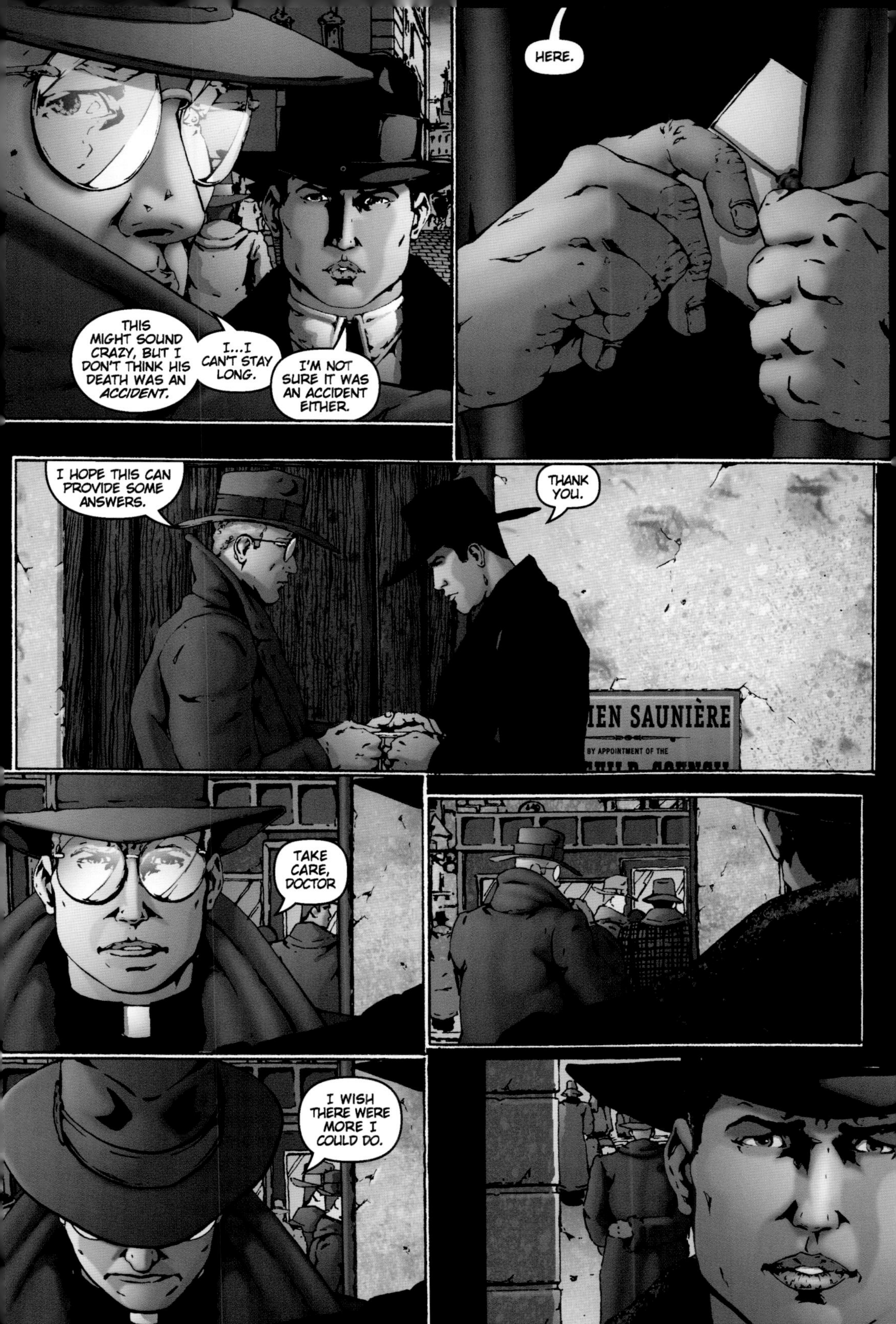
THIS MIGHT SOUND CRAZY, BUT I DON'T THINK HIS DEATH WAS AN *ACCIDENT.*
I...I CAN'T STAY LONG.
I'M NOT SURE IT WAS AN ACCIDENT EITHER.
HERE.
I HOPE THIS CAN PROVIDE SOME ANSWERS.
THANK YOU.
MIEN SAUNIÈRE
BY APPOINTMENT OF THE
TAKE CARE, DOCTOR
I WISH THERE WERE MORE I COULD DO.

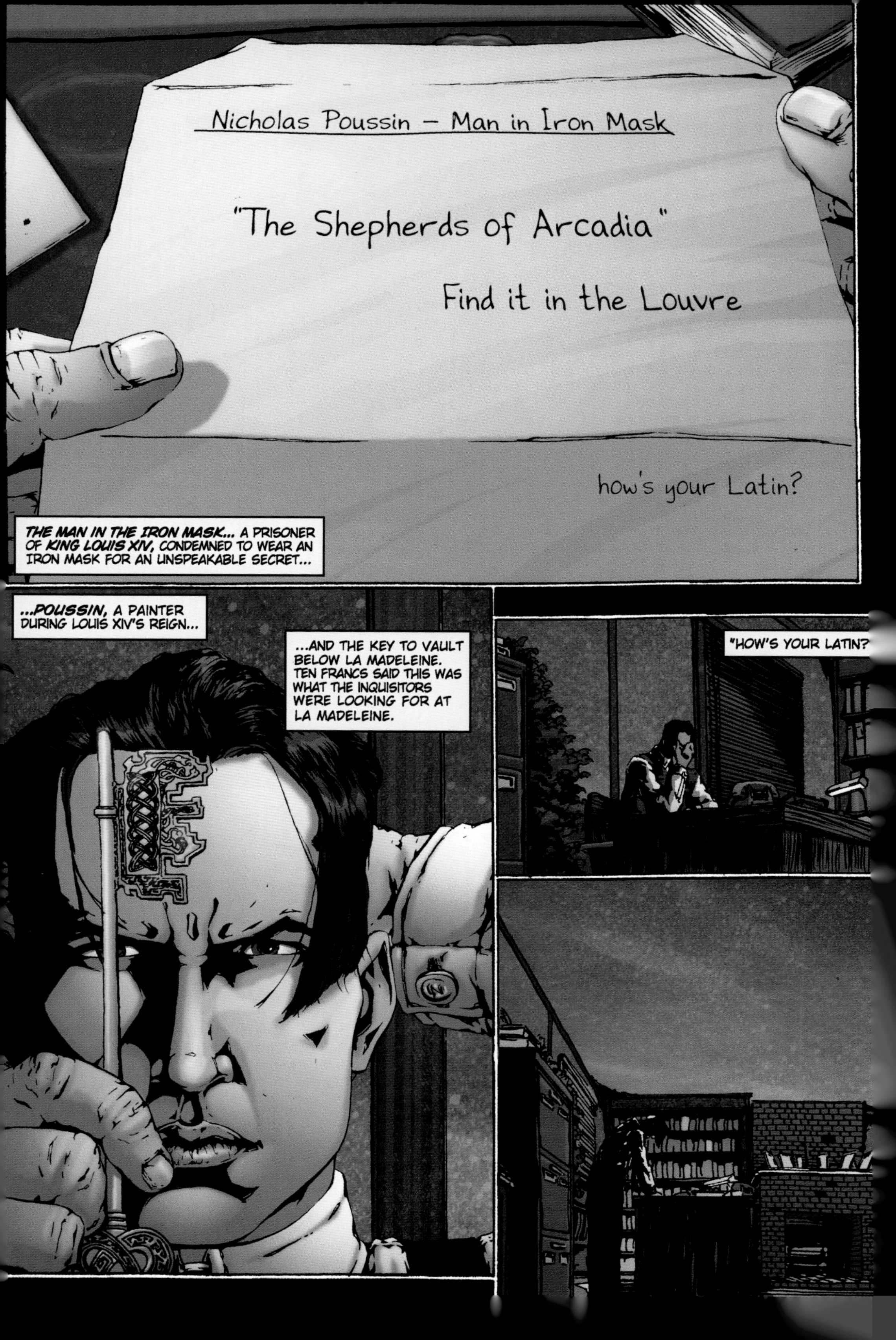
Nicholas Poussin – Man in Iron Mask
"The Shepherds of Arcadia"
Find it in the Louvre
how's your Latin?
THE MAN IN THE IRON MASK... A PRISONER OF KING LOUIS XIV, CONDEMNED TO WEAR AN IRON MASK FOR AN UNSPEAKABLE SECRET...
...POUSSIN, A PAINTER DURING LOUIS XIV'S REIGN...
...AND THE KEY TO VAULT BELOW LA MADELEINE. TEN FRANCS SAID THIS WAS WHAT THE INQUISITORS WERE LOOKING FOR AT LA MADELEINE.
"HOW'S YOUR LATIN?

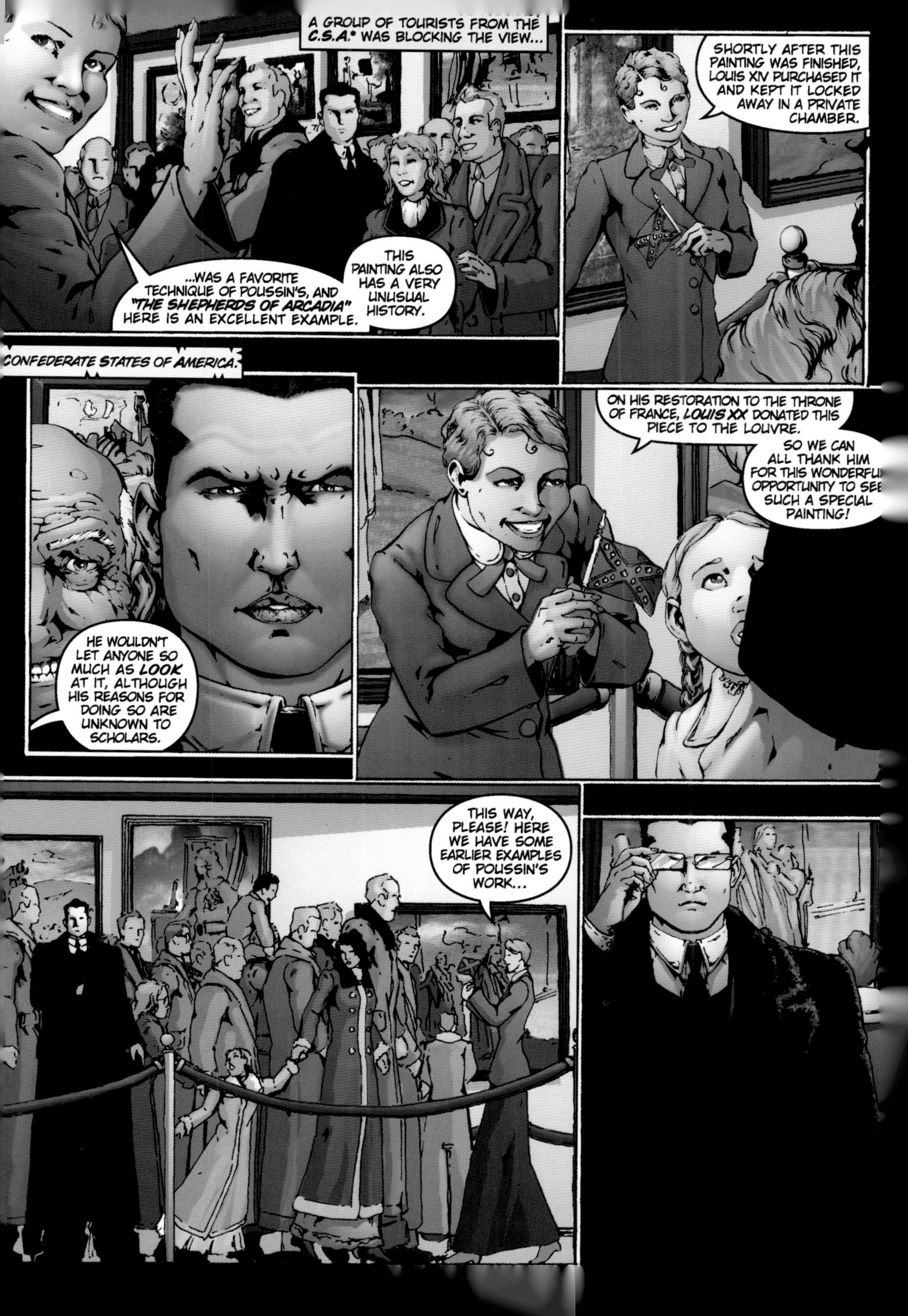
A GROUP OF TOURISTS FROM THE C.S.A.* WAS BLOCKING THE VIEW...
...WAS A FAVORITE TECHNIQUE OF POUSSIN'S, AND "THE SHEPHERDS OF ARCADIA" HERE IS AN EXCELLENT EXAMPLE.
THIS PAINTING ALSO HAS A VERY UNUSUAL HISTORY.
SHORTLY AFTER THIS PAINTING WAS FINISHED, LOUIS XIV PURCHASED IT AND KEPT IT LOCKED AWAY IN A PRIVATE CHAMBER.
*CONFEDERATE STATES OF AMERICA.
HE WOULDN'T LET ANYONE SO MUCH AS LOOK AT IT, ALTHOUGH HIS REASONS FOR DOING SO ARE UNKNOWN TO SCHOLARS.
ON HIS RESTORATION TO THE THRONE OF FRANCE, LOUIS XX DONATED THIS PIECE TO THE LOUVRE.
SO WE CAN ALL THANK HIM FOR THIS WONDERFUL OPPORTUNITY TO SEE SUCH A SPECIAL PAINTING!
THIS WAY, PLEASE! HERE WE HAVE SOME EARLIER EXAMPLES OF POUSSIN'S WORK...

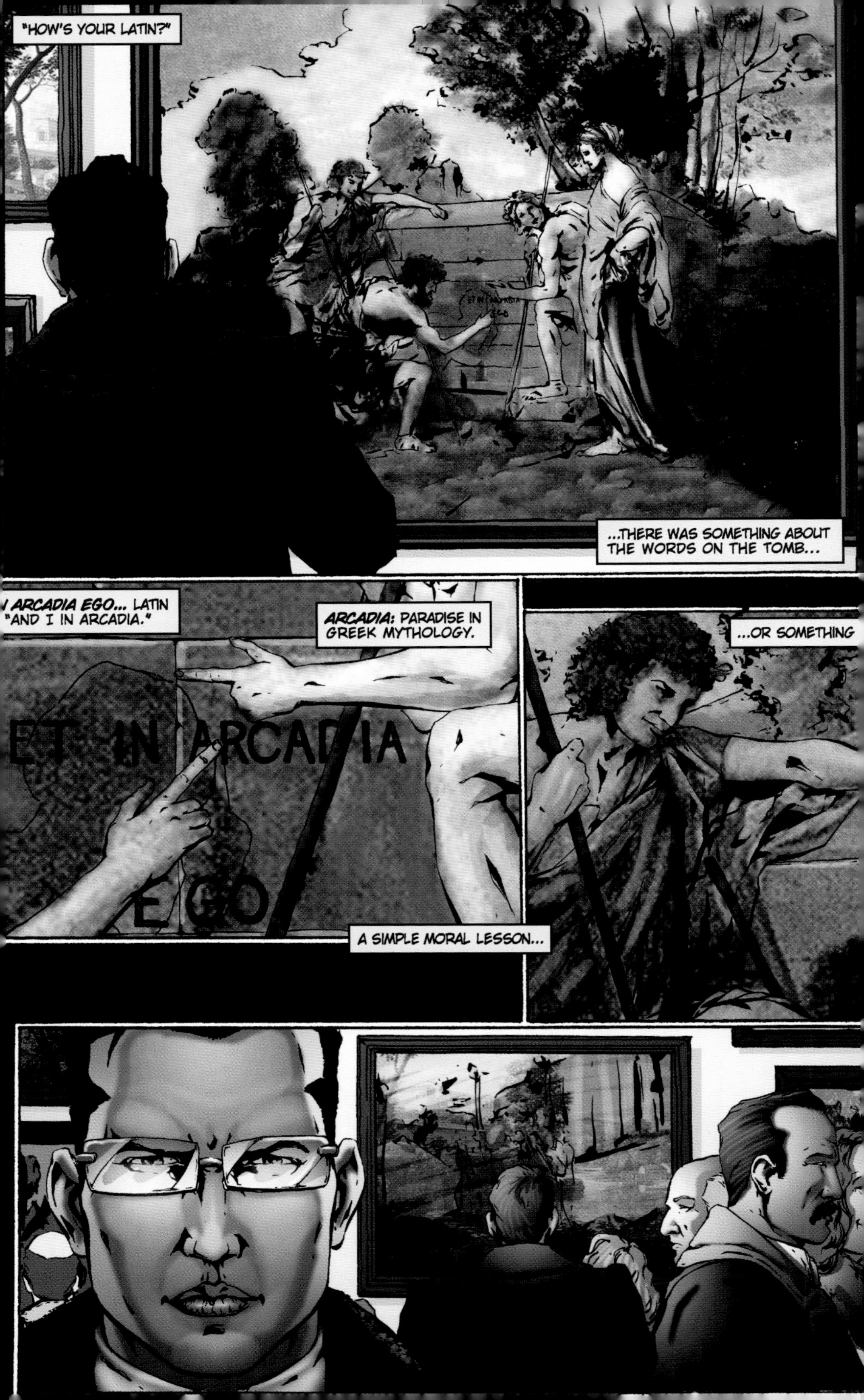
"HOW'S YOUR LATIN?"
...THERE WAS SOMETHING ABOUT THE WORDS ON THE TOMB...
ARCADIA EGO... LATIN "AND I IN ARCADIA."
ARCADIA: PARADISE IN GREEK MYTHOLOGY.
A SIMPLE MORAL LESSON...
...OR SOMETHING
ET IN ARCADIA
EGO

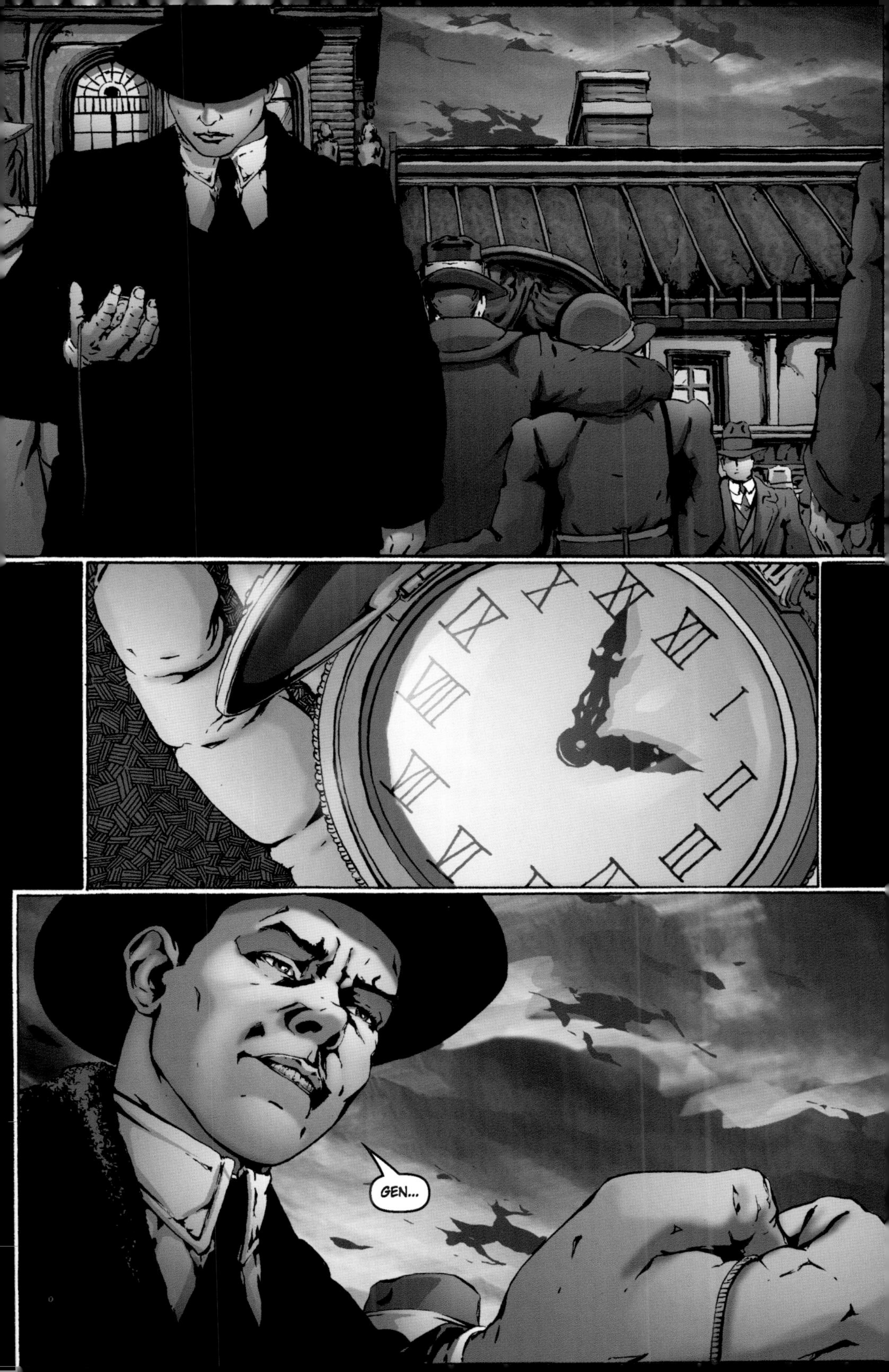
GEN...

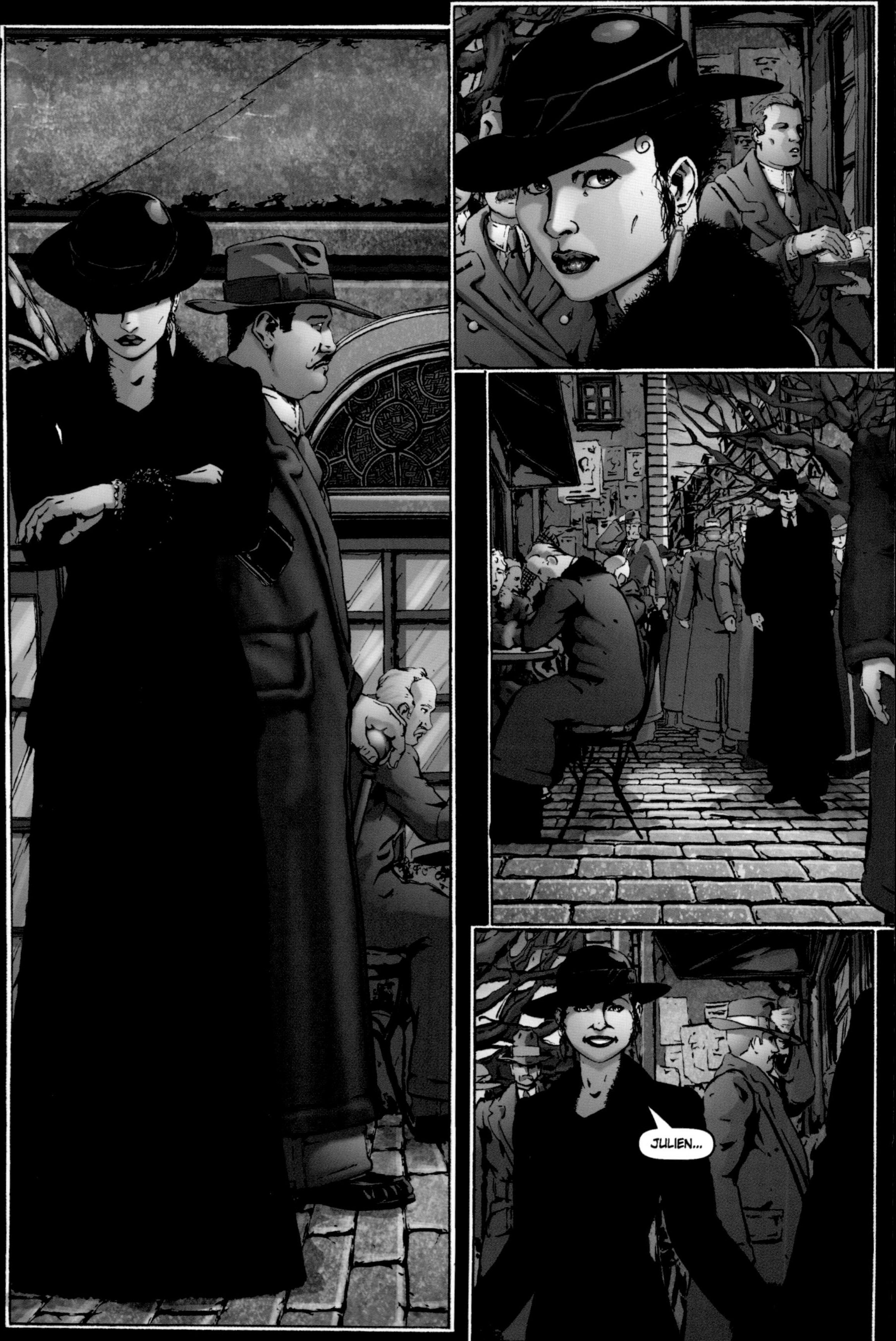
JULIEN...

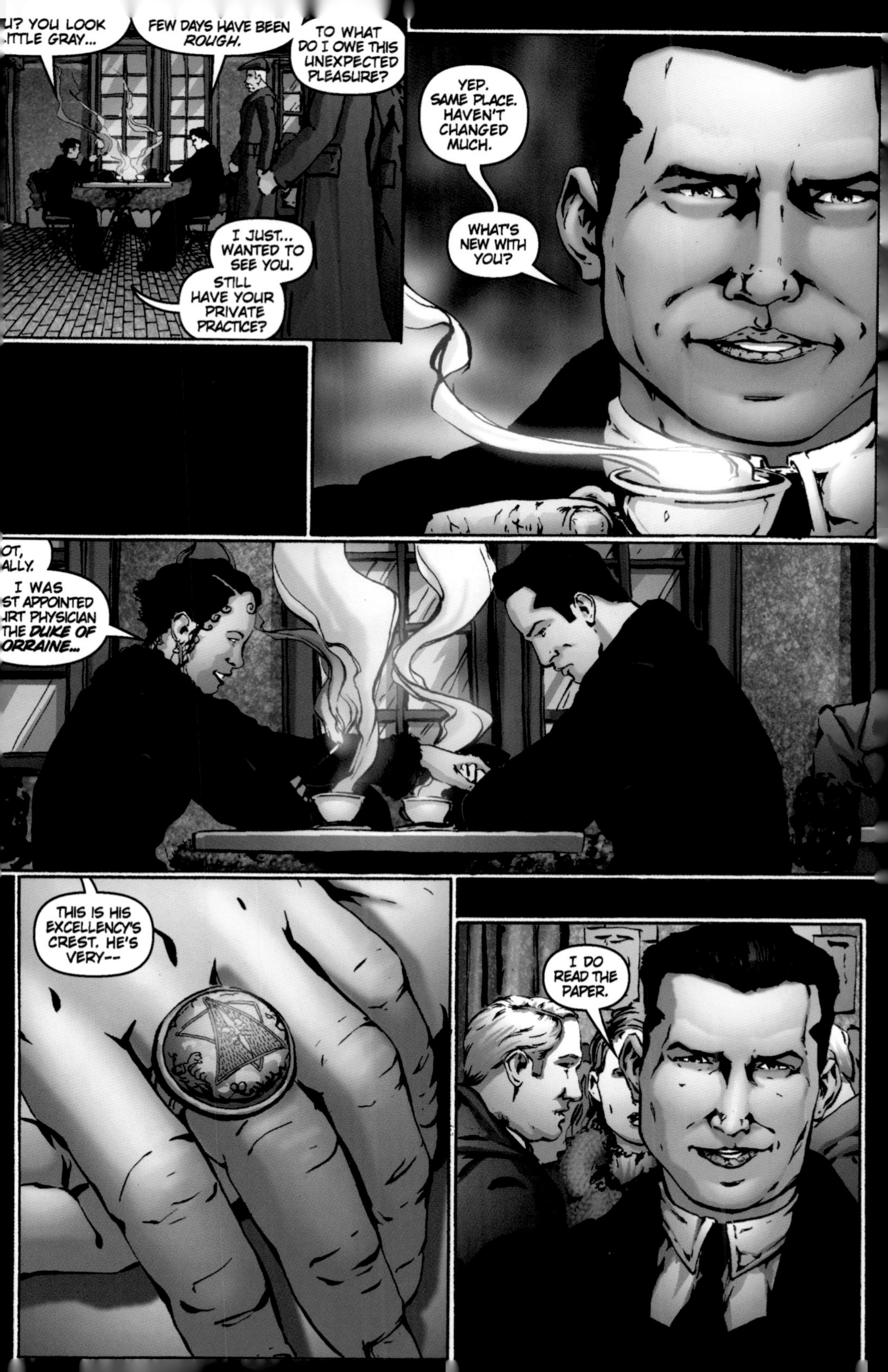

U? YOU LOOK
ITTLE GRAY...
FEW DAYS HAVE BEEN *ROUGH.*
TO WHAT DO I OWE THIS UNEXPECTED PLEASURE?
I JUST... WANTED TO SEE YOU.
STILL HAVE YOUR PRIVATE PRACTICE?
YEP. SAME PLACE. HAVEN'T CHANGED MUCH.
WHAT'S NEW WITH YOU?
OT,
ALLY.
I WAS
ST APPOINTED
RT PHYSICIAN
THE *DUKE OF*
ORRAINE...
THIS IS HIS EXCELLENCY'S CREST. HE'S VERY--
I DO READ THE PAPER.

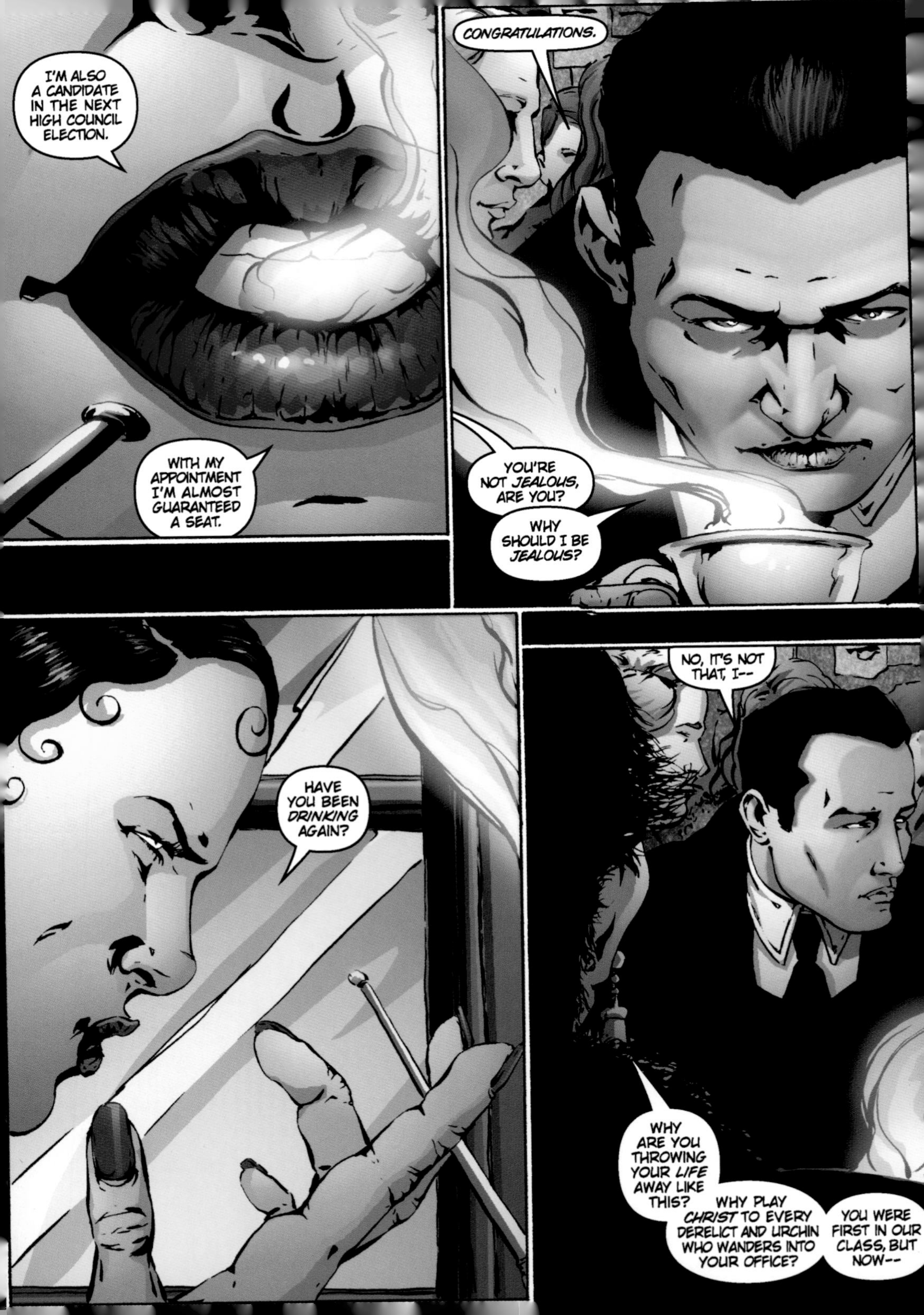
I'M ALSO A CANDIDATE IN THE NEXT HIGH COUNCIL ELECTION.
WITH MY APPOINTMENT I'M ALMOST GUARANTEED A SEAT.
CONGRATULATIONS.
YOU'RE NOT JEALOUS, ARE YOU?
WHY SHOULD I BE JEALOUS?
HAVE YOU BEEN DRINKING AGAIN?
NO, IT'S NOT THAT, I--
WHY ARE YOU THROWING YOUR LIFE AWAY LIKE THIS?
WHY PLAY CHRIST TO EVERY DERELICT AND URCHIN WHO WANDERS INTO YOUR OFFICE?
YOU WERE FIRST IN OUR CLASS, BUT NOW--

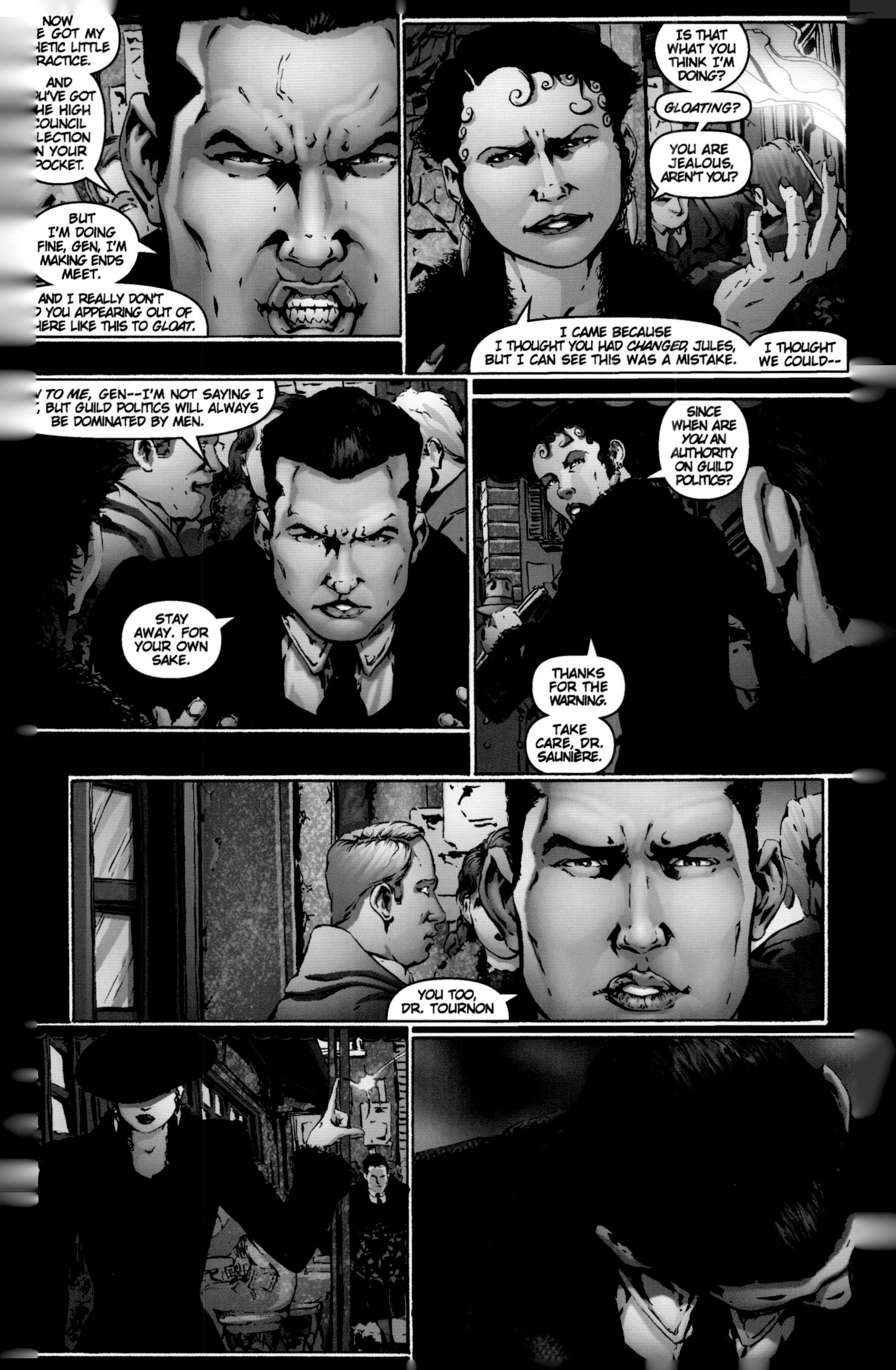
NOW
E GOT MY
HETIC LITTLE
RACTICE.
AND
U'VE GOT
HE HIGH
COUNCIL
LECTION
N YOUR
POCKET.
BUT I'M DOING FINE, GEN, I'M MAKING ENDS MEET.
AND I REALLY DON'T
D YOU APPEARING OUT OF
HERE LIKE THIS TO GLOAT.
IS THAT WHAT YOU THINK I'M DOING?
GLOATING?
YOU ARE JEALOUS, AREN'T YOU?
I CAME BECAUSE I THOUGHT YOU HAD CHANGED, JULES, BUT I CAN SEE THIS WAS A MISTAKE.
I THOUGHT WE COULD--
TO ME, GEN--I'M NOT SAYING I
, BUT GUILD POLITICS WILL ALWAYS
BE DOMINATED BY MEN.
STAY AWAY. FOR YOUR OWN SAKE.
SINCE WHEN ARE YOU AN AUTHORITY ON GUILD POLITICS?
THANKS FOR THE WARNING.
TAKE CARE, DR. SAUNIÈRE.
YOU TOO, DR. TOURNON

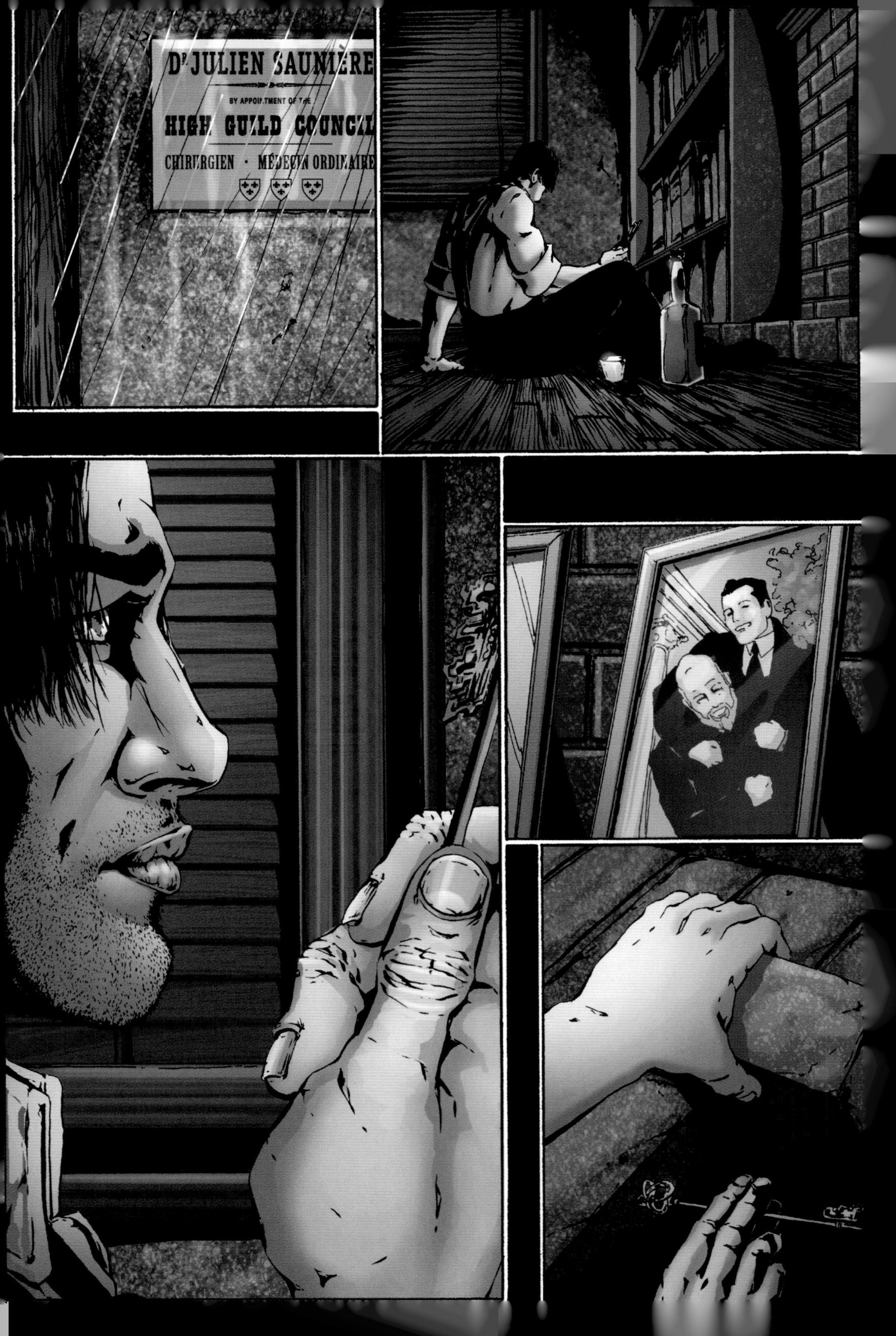
Dr JULIEN SAUNIÈRE
BY APPOINTMENT OF THE
HIGH GUILD COUNCIL
CHIRURGIEN · MÉDECIN ORDINAIRE

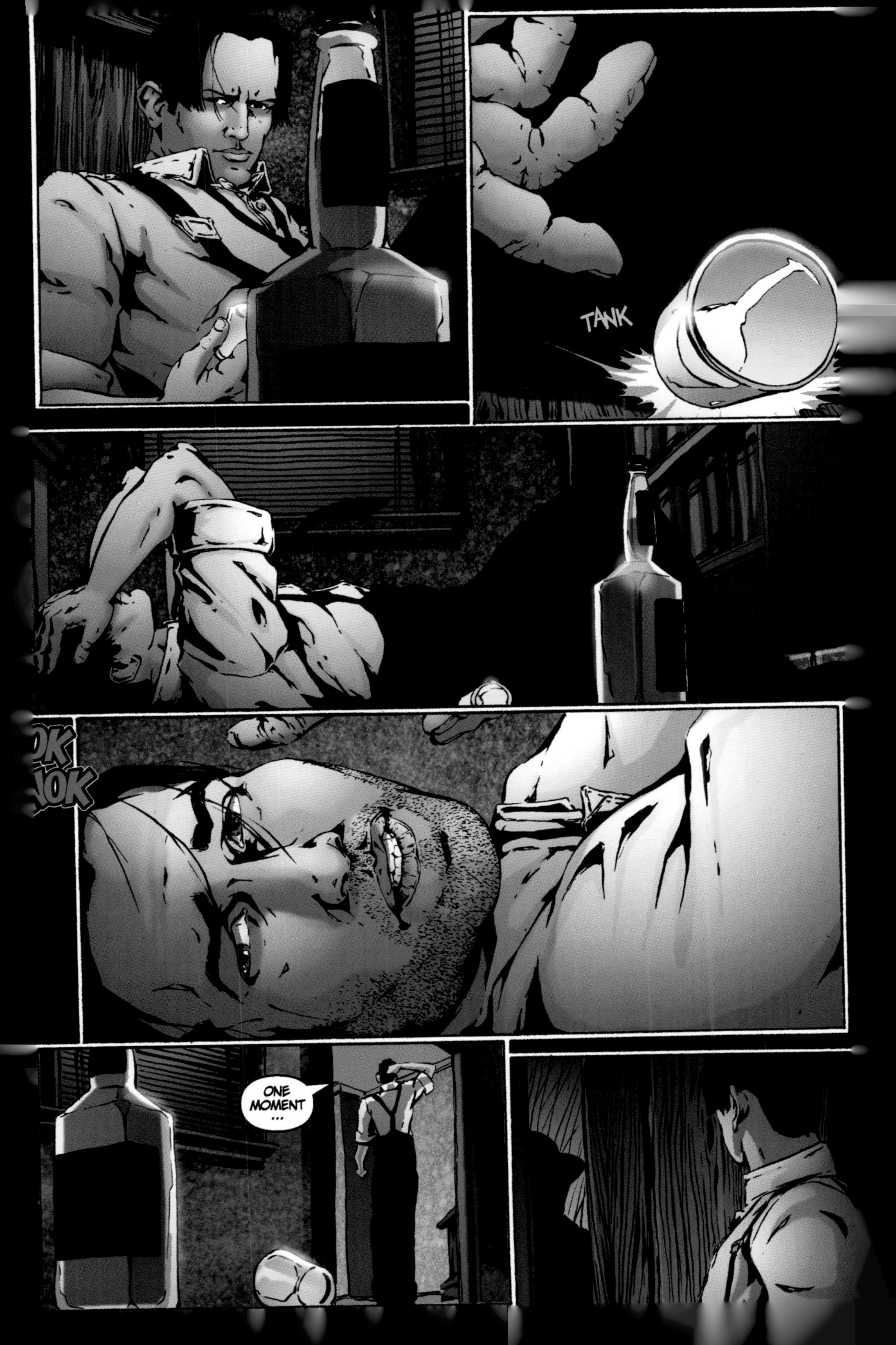
TANK
OK
NOK
ONE MOMENT ...

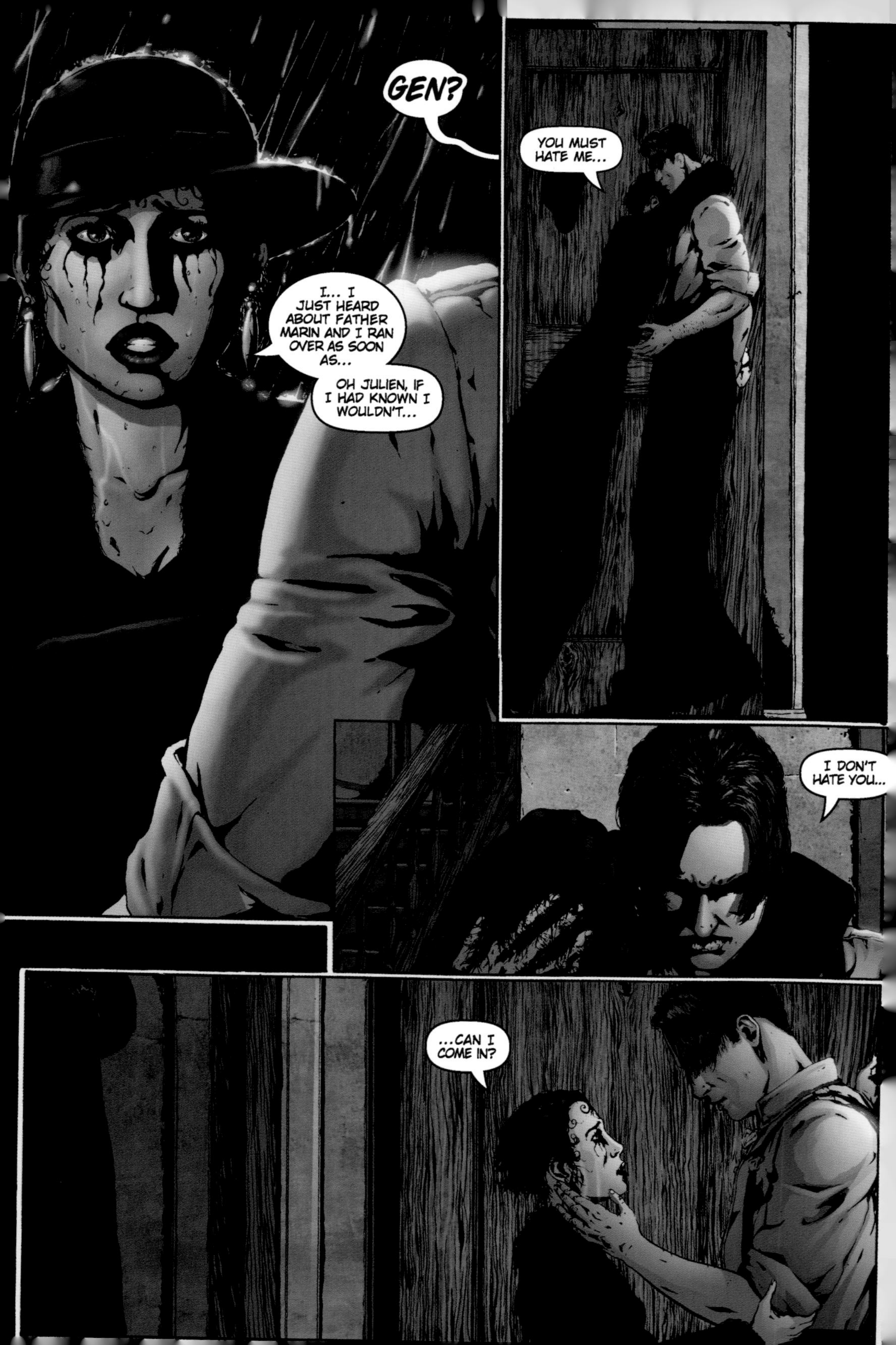
GEN?
I... I JUST HEARD ABOUT FATHER MARIN AND I RAN OVER AS SOON AS...
OH JULIEN, IF I HAD KNOWN I WOULDN'T...
YOU MUST HATE ME...
I DON'T HATE YOU...
...CAN I COME IN?

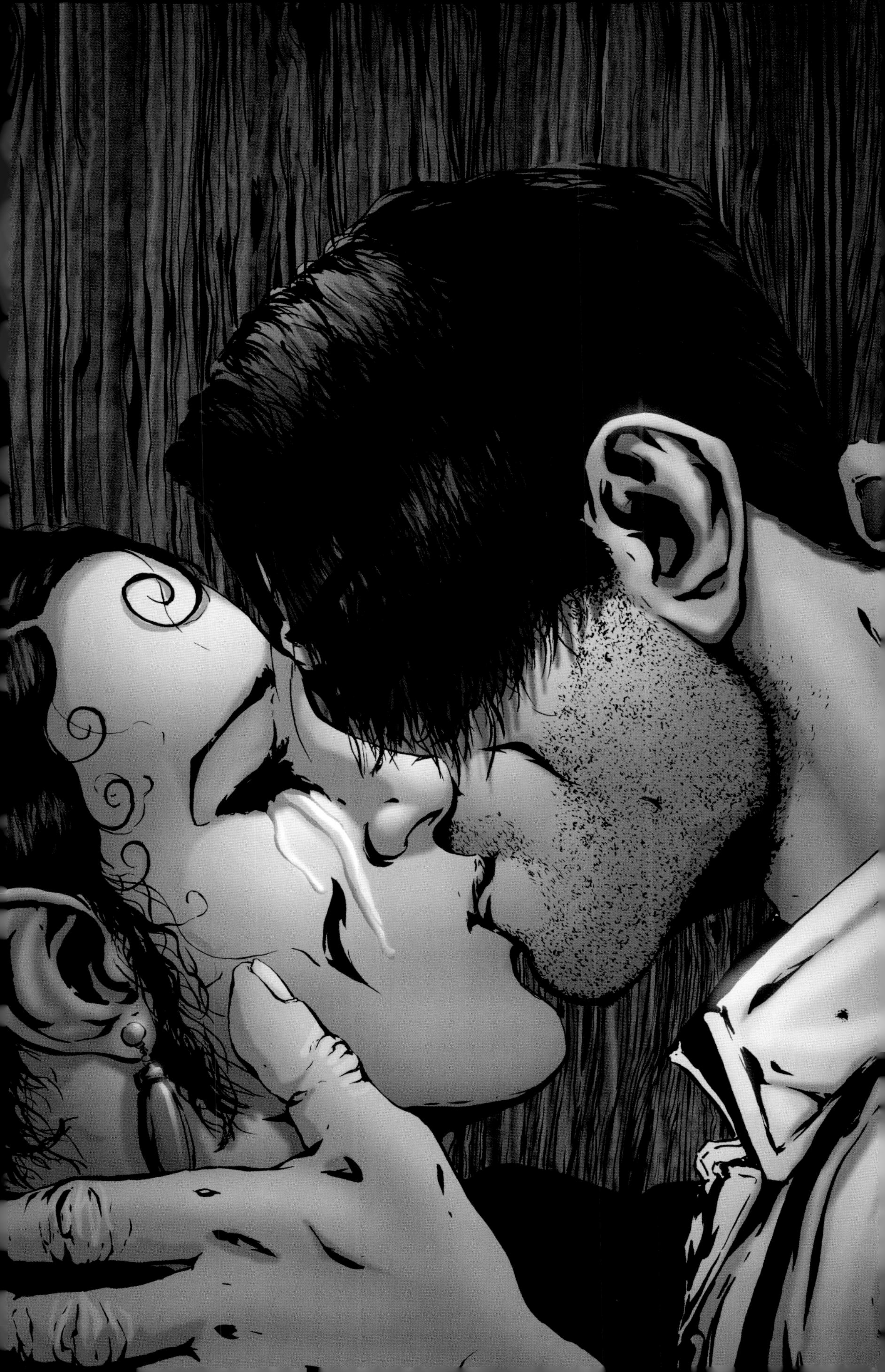

Le Journal de la Liberté

Paris's leading anglophone newspaper • vol. 205, no. 97 • Oct. 20, MCMXXXIII

Editors in Chief: M. Tait Bergstrom, M. Matthew Pasteris. **Story Editor:** M. Arvid Nelson. **Art Editors:** M. EricJ, M. Jeromy Cox. **Photography Editor:** M. Alexander Waldman. **Layout Supervisor:** M. William Kartalopoulos. **Editors Emeritus:** M. Clark A. Smith, M. Howard P. Lovecraft, M. Robert E. Howard. Redacted by the Holy Parisian Inquisition under the direction of His Excellency Archbishop Emile-Jean Ireneaux. Le Journal de Liberté is printed under the benign auspices of his most puissant majesty KING LOUIS XXII of FRANCE. GOD SAVE THE KING.

Papal Seal

of Approva

ELDERLY PRIEST KILLED IN GAS EXPLOSION

Father Gérard Marin was priest of L'Église de la Madeline for thirty years, until last night.

The elderly father, much loved by his parish, was consumed in his sleep by a fireball that destroyed the rectory behind the church. He was 67 years old.

"He was always glad to help" said a parishioner. "It didn't matter what time of day it was, or what the problem was."

Indeed, Marin, a Jesuit, ran a soup kitchen in the notorious porte d'Ivry in the 13th Arrondissement. A resident of the shanty-town there described the late father as "loving" and "tireless."

Marin also ran a Magdalene on rue H. Torot in the 19th arrondissement.

"His heart went out to fallen women," Sister Maria Celeste, a nun who worked at the Magdalene with Marin, said. "The purity and dedication of his heart is something we can never replace."

Firefighting officials at the scene of the explosion said that the terrible tragedy was the result of a gas leak.

L'Église de la Madeleine, scene of the gas explosion early this morning

"Even a small leak can be dangerous," Marcel Tavernier, Commandant of the Sapeurs-Pompiers de Paris, said.

According to Tavernier, such leaks are commonplace, although most people are not aware of the peril.

"This serves as a reminder to every inhabitant of our city of the dangers of gas leaks."

The elderly father attended seminary school at St. Sulpice in Paris, and showed much promise. But he preferred the simple life of a parish priest to the responsibilities of a bishop.

"He was truly content tending to a local parish," H.E. Eugene Ireneaux, The Archbishop of Sens, said.

Though born in Paris, Marin spent most of his early years in the small, rustic parish of Rennes-le-Chateau, located south of Carcassone in the Languedoc region.

His days there were spent in quiet contemplation and dutiful attendance to his parishioners.

Later, Marin was transferred back to Paris, where he served until his death.

"Father Marin had unique abilities that made him an invaluable asset to the Church," said Archbishop Ireneaux. "His love for Christ was excelled only by his intellect. In his special mission in Paris, he demonstrated a pro-
Continued on page B2

LOCAL STEVEDORE BOSS INDICTED ON RACKETEERING CHARGES
suspected ring may include Gendarmerie Officers

The Inquisition announced the arrest of a senior member of the Guild of Stevedores late yesterday afternoon. The arrest comes on the heels of a new Inquisitional initiative aimed at reducing organized crime in Paris.

Jean-Marc Péclet, Grand Master of the Guild of Stevedores, was indicted yesterday afternoon on charges of racketeering and em-

bezzlement of Guild funds.

The Stevedores' Guild, responsible for the transportation and storage of all goods in France, is the largest guild both in terms of membership and in terms of its revenues.

The Guild is also reputed to have ties to organized crime.

"This is no surprise to anyone who works on the quays," said a small business owner in the largely Stevedores-controlled canal districts in the 19th arrondissement.

But what surprised many was the announcement by Inquisition officials that more arrests could be expected, and that members of the Parisian gendarmerie could be included in the indictments.

"We have reason to believe members of the Parisian Gendarm-
Continued on page B1

Wine Tasting Festival Begins This Evening

His Majesty Louis XXII is expected to be in attendance at this year's Vigne d'Or festival.

"His Majesty is a gourmand in the classic sense of the word, and he has done much to ensure the preservation of our greatest national treasure: our wines," said Royal Sommelier Academy member Jean-Christian Gastin.

The festival is the most prestigious in France. The finest sommaliers will be tasting wines from
Continued on page E1

Indochinese Governor Pledges "Reconciliation" to Indigenous Population

Following the suppression of rebellion in the Colonial Territory of Indochina earlier this week, French officials have pledged a policy of reconstruction and rehabilitation to the denizens of the troubled colony.

"Now is a time for reconciliation and peace," said Le Maréchal, the royal colonial governor of Indochina.

The French crown has pledged its support for this new initiative, but also issued a warning.

"It is His Majesty's avowed policy not to tolerate sedition of any kind. France has a rightful claim to Indochina, and the crown will deal with further resistance from local populations the way it has in the past."

Indeed, the suppression of rebellion is an intrinsic part of colonial governance, according to many sources in the Halls and in Versailles.

"There will be more rebellion in the future, I guarantee it," said a member of The Hall of the Robe who wished to remain anonymous. "It becomes a simple question of economics: is the cost of colonization offset by the material wealth generated by the colony? In the case of Indochina, the answer must be 'yes.'"

In fact, Indochina has become a proving ground for French military commanders.

His Lordship the Duke of Lorraine made a name for himself early on in his political career suppressing a revolt swiftly, efficiently, and with what he himself refers to as "the sternest measures."

In fact, following The Duke's campaigns, the colony remained passive for over a decade.

The recent unrest leads many to believe a firmer hand is what's needed to keep the colony productive.

"Lorraine's Indochinese campaigns have shown brute force
Continued on page A

E JOURNAL SPECIAL: A LOOK INSIDE THE GUILDS

uilds are associations of craftsmen dedicated to the profession of a common trade. It is illegal for anyone but a licensed guild master to perform a specialized craft, so virtually all goods and skilled services in Christendom are produced by the guilds. A guild can range in size from several dozen people to several ndred thousand. Some guilds, such as the Guild of Sorcerers, are so secretive that no knows their true size. Guilds are the cornerstone of our economy, but eir workings are mysterious to many. Guild officials claim this secrecy ensures quality standards, but it has also led to mistrust and suspicion by crown and ter. Godfroi Beaumont, a high guild master from the Guild of Stonemasons, consented to talk about the guilds and their place in Christian society, to reveal Le Journal readers some of the mysterious workings of these powerful, multinational corporate entities.

The origin of the guilds exnds into the murky depths of edieval history. No one knows actly how or why these venerle organizations were created. me scholars say they were rmed by kings to collect taxes, d others believe ey were formed downtrodden aftsmen for protion.

"It's all a complicated balancing act."

"Guilds have olved considerably since the mble early days," Beaumont d. "While still bound by the ll of kings, guilds today are ultinational organizations with eir own internal laws and contutions. We are obliged to y taxes, but our multinational aracter makes us difficult for dividual monarchs to control.

"Kings, of course, will always ve the right to put tariffs on ported goods, and they will ways have the right to tax uild products and services," d Beaumont. "But they have consider their treatment of any ild very carefully, because we n always shift tax-generating sinesses to other kingdoms. nd guilds that have a poor putation will find it difficult to nduct business anywhere. It's a complicated balancing act."

Prerequisites for memberip vary from guild to guild. embership in certain guilds is reditary, while membership others, such as the Guild of ysicians, is based solely on e merit of the applicant. Some ilds will let anyone join so ng as the candidate is young ough.

"It's really up to each particular ild. One guild's policies have ry little to do with another's," eaumont said.

Still, there are some practices d organizational structures that e identical in virtually every ild.

First of all, every Guild memer, whether a Stevedore or an ccountant, must follow the me career path.

A guild initiate starts his career an *apprentice*. The apprenticeship enerally lasts for about seven ears.

"Everyone enters the Guild the same place: the bottom," eaumont said. "Even the highest members started out as lowly apprentices. No exceptions."

Seven years as an apprentice can be a very long time indeed.

"All the dangerous, unpleasant jobs are given to apprentices. It feels like forever sometimes. But you learn and you move on," Beaumont said.

Once a member completes the apprenticeship he becomes a *journeyman*. The journeyman period also lasts seven years, and it is during this period that guild members are initiated into the practice of their craft.

"Fourteen years might sound like a long time, but there is no substitute for experience," Beaumont said. "Besides, the apprenticeship often starts quite young, at eleven or twelve and in some cases even younger."

Finally, guild members become certified *masters*, and are allowed to open up shops or perform services for remuneration on behalf of the guild.

For most the guild career path ends here. There are, however, two more guild ranks, *high master* and *grandmaster*.

Each guild has one or more grandmasters, who act as chief executives. "The grandmaster is the father of the guild. He directs strategy from on high. It's often someone with a lot of experience and a history of exceptional service."

"Fourteen years might sound like a long time, but there is no substitute for experience."

The *high masters* work under the grandmaster to steer guild policy. They do not practice the craft of their guild; they are executive administrators.

Compared to a life of constant labor as a regular master, the life of a high master is one of privilege and prestige. But before one can become a high master, one must be elected to the High Guild Council.

The High Guild Council exists to arbitrate inter-guild disputes. As new technologies become available, so do inevitable conflicts between guilds over who has jurisdiction over what new skill. Sometimes advances even lead to the formation of a new guild

The number of seats any guild has on the High Guild Council corresponds to how many members a guild has. The more members, the more council seats. Some guilds, such as the Guild of Sorcerers, exert a disproportionate influence due to the highly specialized nature of their craft.

Seats on the High Council are a coveted sign of prestige for guild members. A seat advances one's status from Master to High Master. Every seven years each guild elects its representatives by a vote by all a guild's masters.

The fact that the High Council meetings—convened in Zurich once a year and during emergencies—are closed to outsiders is just one example of the many ways guilds conceal their inner workings.

Indeed, Beaumont declined any further discussion about the High Guild Council or the inner workings of the Guild of Stonemasons.

"Over the centuries, we have learned to guard the mysteries of our craft very closely," he said. "This is the only way we can ensure high quality standards."

This secrecy surrounding the guilds has led to repeated clashes between guild, church and state. The Bishop of York has even denounced the guilds as "organized crime," and the Imperial Exchequer of the Prussian Empire has compared the High Masters unfavorably to "brigands and extortionists."

Beaumont says guilds are among the largest benefactors of the Church, and he said that if guilds were more open, governments would actually see dramatic declines in tax revenues.

"It is vitally important to the economies of Christiandom that our trade secrets remain secrets. The only way for a monarchy to collect taxes off trade is through a system of strict control," he said.

"We are the most productiove sector of the economy. With guilds, everyone wins."

⚜

SANA
NOCE

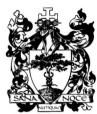

The Guild of Physicians

LUCET ET LUCEBIT

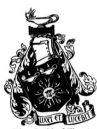

The Guild of Illuminists

IN LUCE MUNDUS

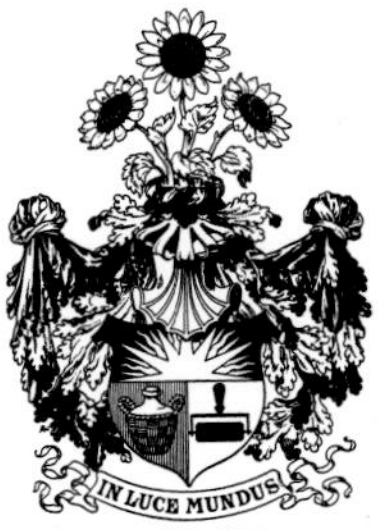

The Guild of Daguerrotypists

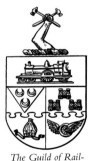

The Guild of Railway Workers

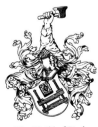

The Guild of Bookbinders

LES ARMES DES SAIN...

et in Arcadia ego...

...ER NOSTER QVI EST IN COELI...

CHAPTER FOUR

THE ARCHBISHOP AND THE PIMP

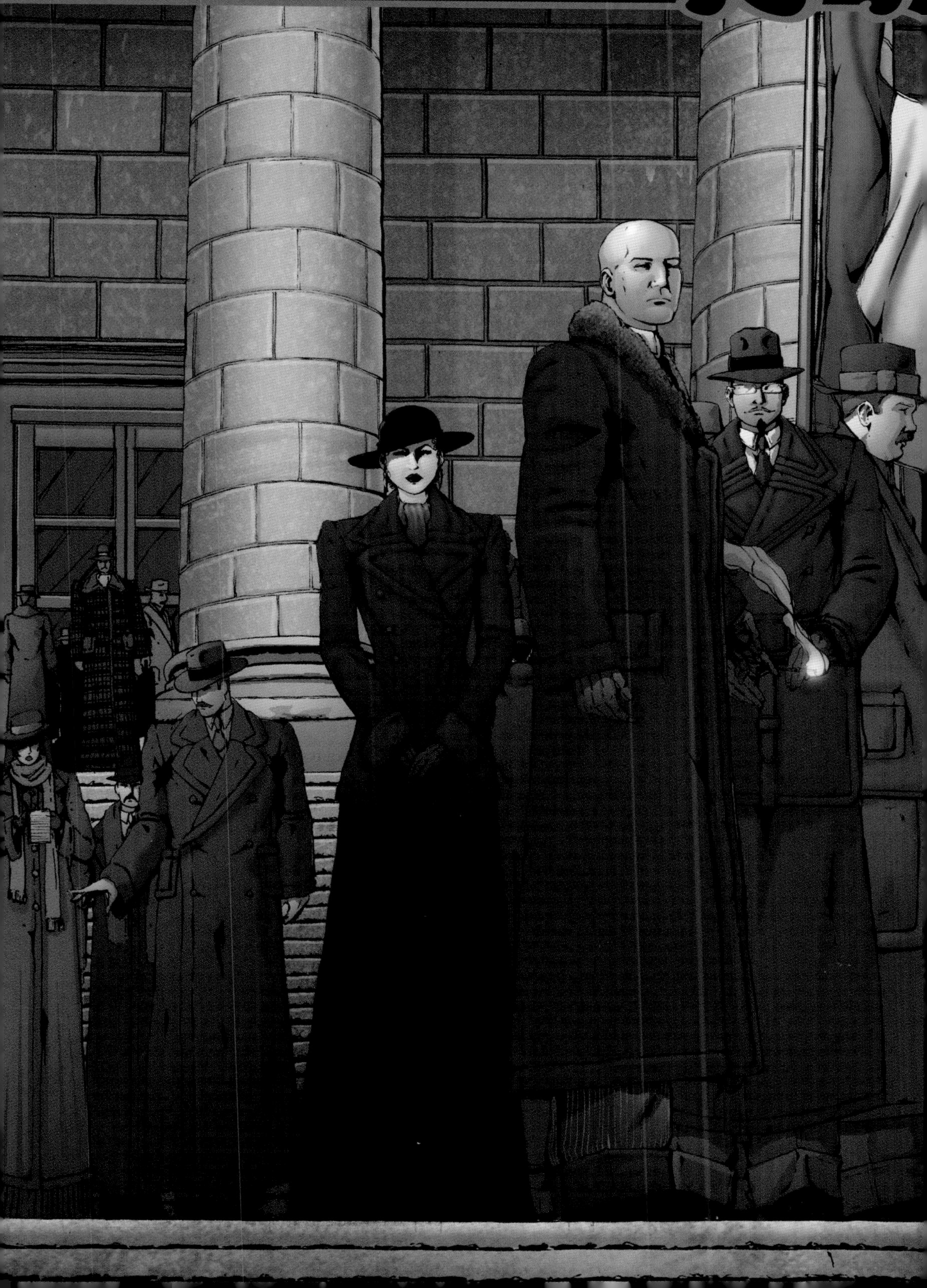

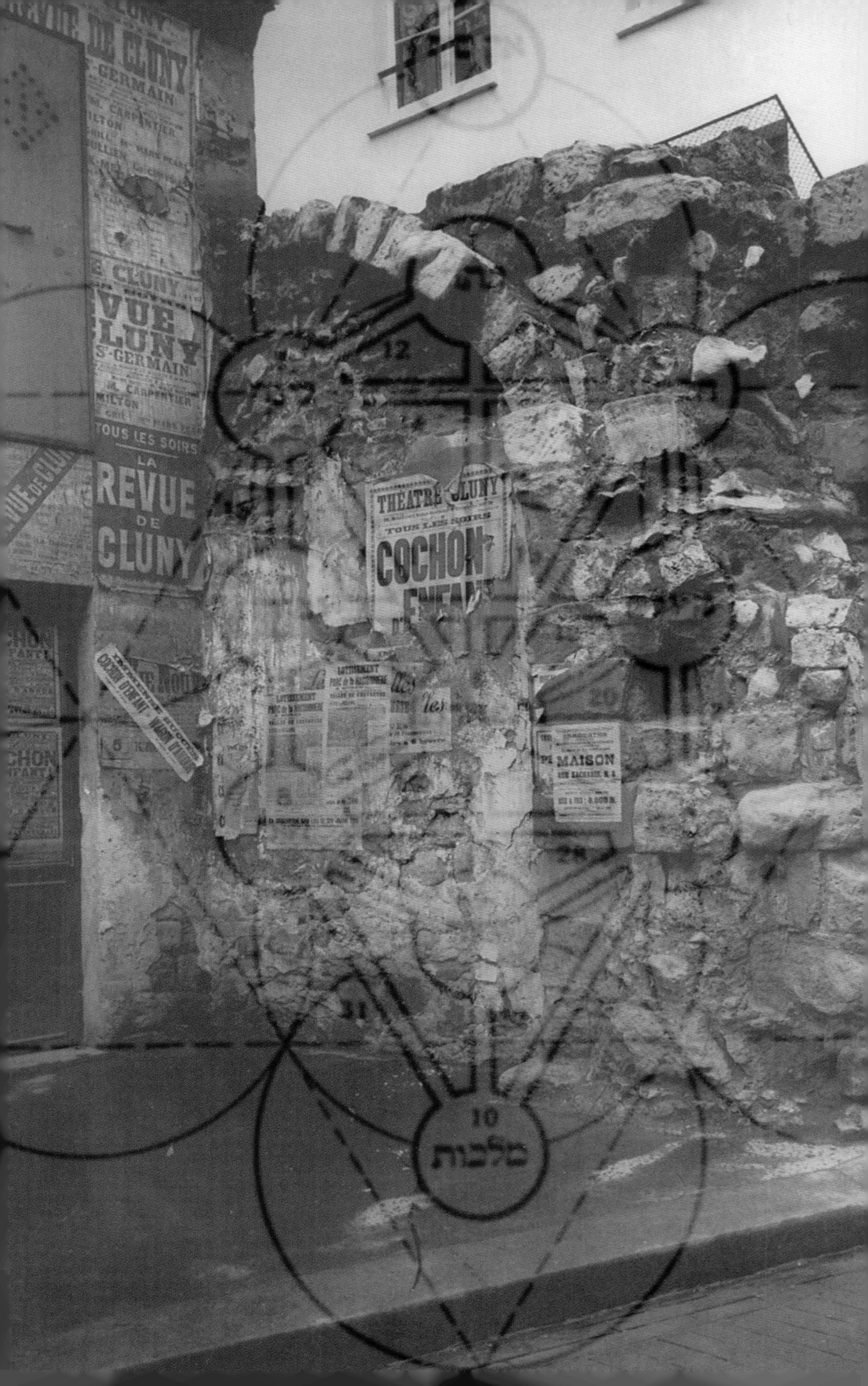

DE CLUNY
S^T-GERMAIN
VUE
LUNY
S^T-GERMAIN
TOUS LES SOIRS
LA
REVUE
DE
CLUNY
THEATRE CLUNY
TOUS LES SOIRS
COCHON
MAISON
12
31
10
מלכות

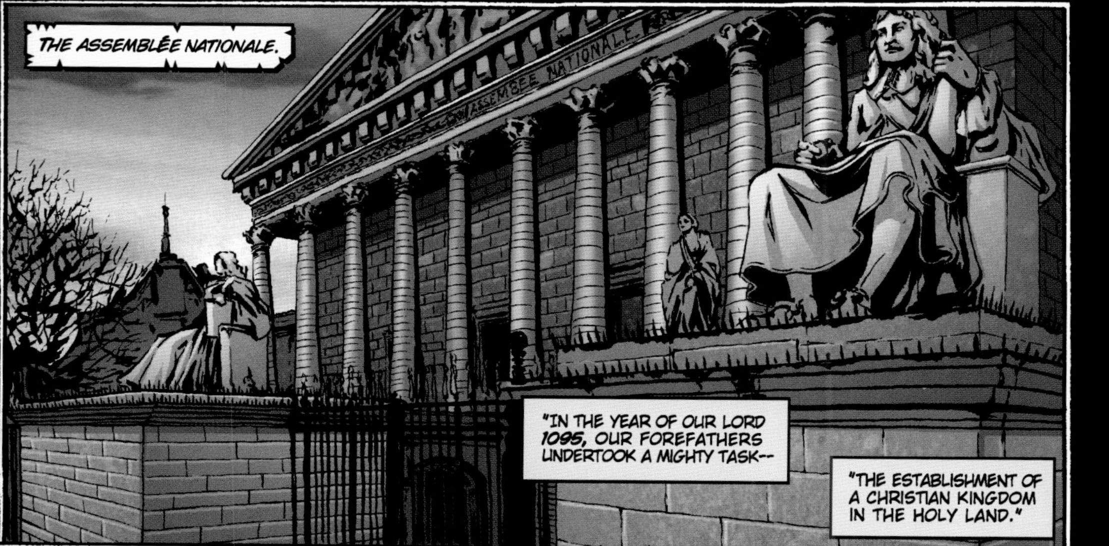
THE ASSEMBLÉE NATIONALE.
ASSEMBLÉE NATIONALE
"IN THE YEAR OF OUR LORD 1095, OUR FOREFATHERS UNDERTOOK A MIGHTY TASK--
"THE ESTABLISHMENT OF A CHRISTIAN KINGDOM IN THE HOLY LAND."

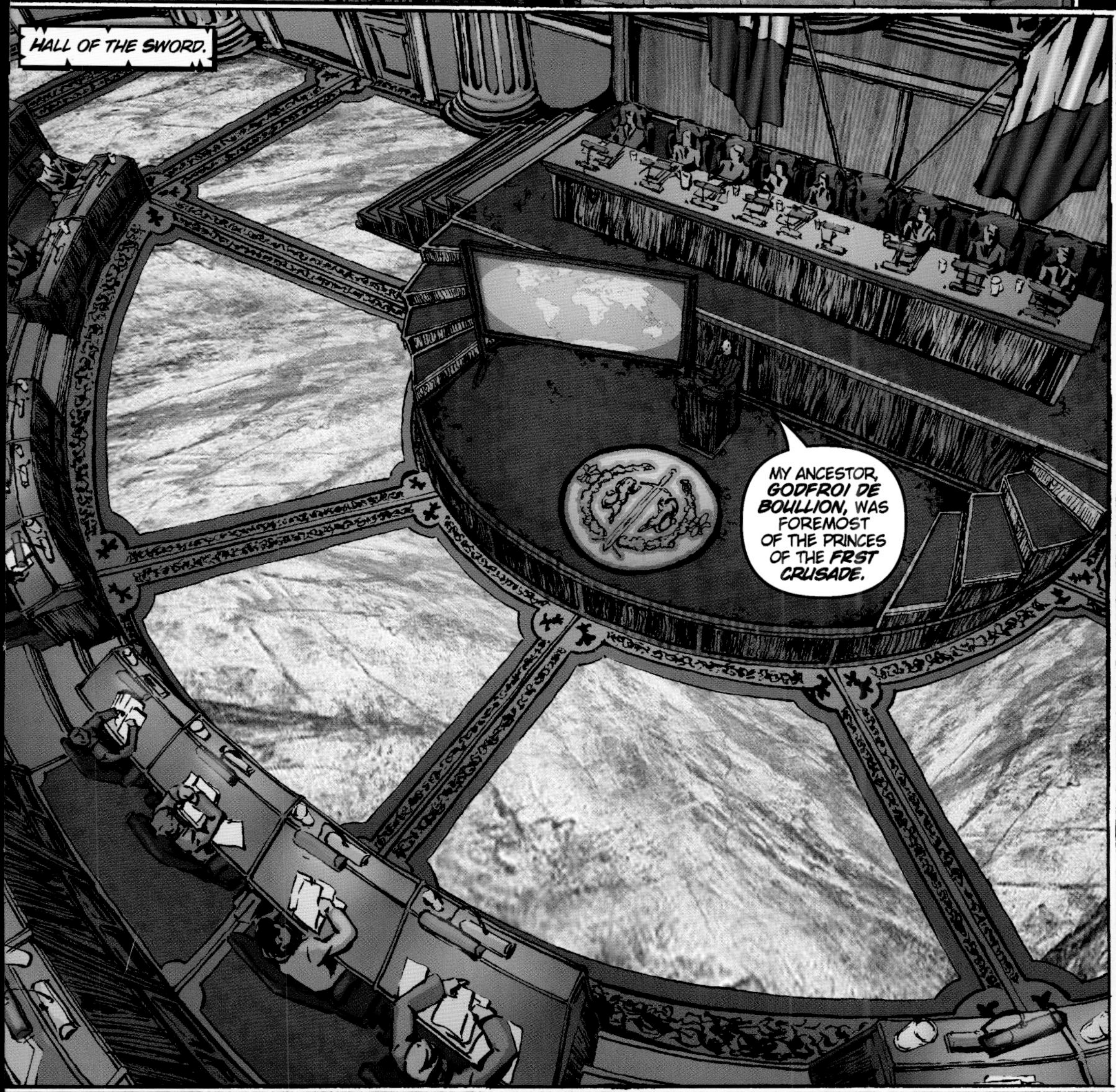
HALL OF THE SWORD.
MY ANCESTOR, GODFROI DE BOULLION, WAS FOREMOST OF THE PRINCES OF THE FRST CRUSADE.

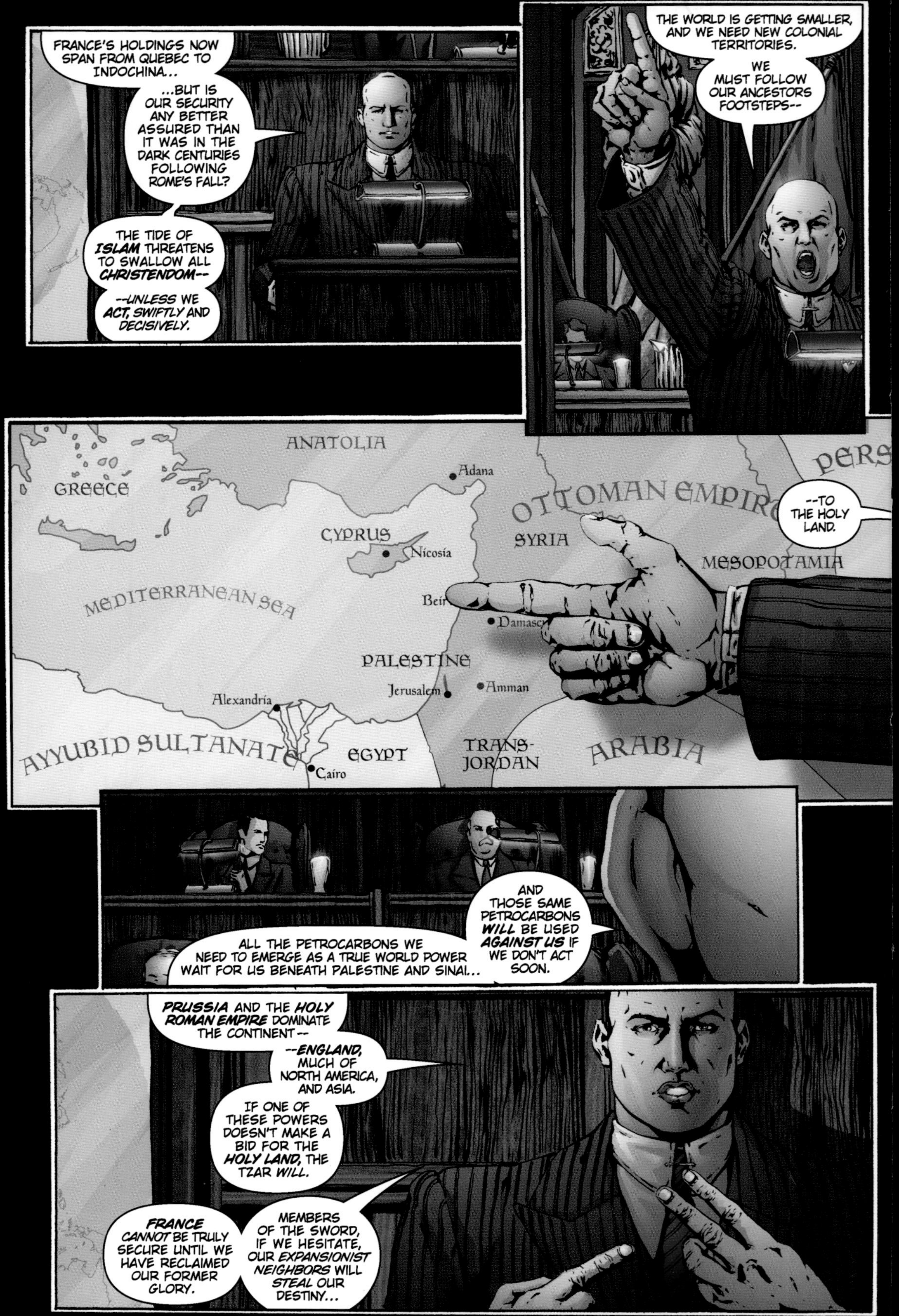

FRANCE'S HOLDINGS NOW SPAN FROM QUEBEC TO INDOCHINA...
...BUT IS OUR SECURITY ANY BETTER ASSURED THAN IT WAS IN THE DARK CENTURIES FOLLOWING ROME'S FALL?
THE TIDE OF ISLAM THREATENS TO SWALLOW ALL CHRISTENDOM--
--UNLESS WE ACT, SWIFTLY AND DECISIVELY.
THE WORLD IS GETTING SMALLER, AND WE NEED NEW COLONIAL TERRITORIES.
WE MUST FOLLOW OUR ANCESTORS FOOTSTEPS--
--TO THE HOLY LAND.
ANATOLIA
GREECE
Adana
OTTOMAN EMPIRE
PERS
CYPRUS
Nicosia
SYRIA
MESOPOTAMIA
MEDITERRANEAN SEA
Beir
Damasc
PALESTINE
Jerusalem
Amman
Alexandria
AYYUBID SULTANATE
EGYPT
Cairo
TRANS-JORDAN
ARABIA
ALL THE PETROCARBONS WE NEED TO EMERGE AS A TRUE WORLD POWER WAIT FOR US BENEATH PALESTINE AND SINAI...
AND THOSE SAME PETROCARBONS WILL BE USED AGAINST US IF WE DON'T ACT SOON.
PRUSSIA AND THE HOLY ROMAN EMPIRE DOMINATE THE CONTINENT--
--ENGLAND, MUCH OF NORTH AMERICA, AND ASIA.
IF ONE OF THESE POWERS DOESN'T MAKE A BID FOR THE HOLY LAND, THE TZAR WILL.
MEMBERS OF THE SWORD, IF WE HESITATE, OUR EXPANSIONIST NEIGHBORS WILL STEAL OUR DESTINY...
FRANCE CANNOT BE TRULY SECURE UNTIL WE HAVE RECLAIMED OUR FORMER GLORY.

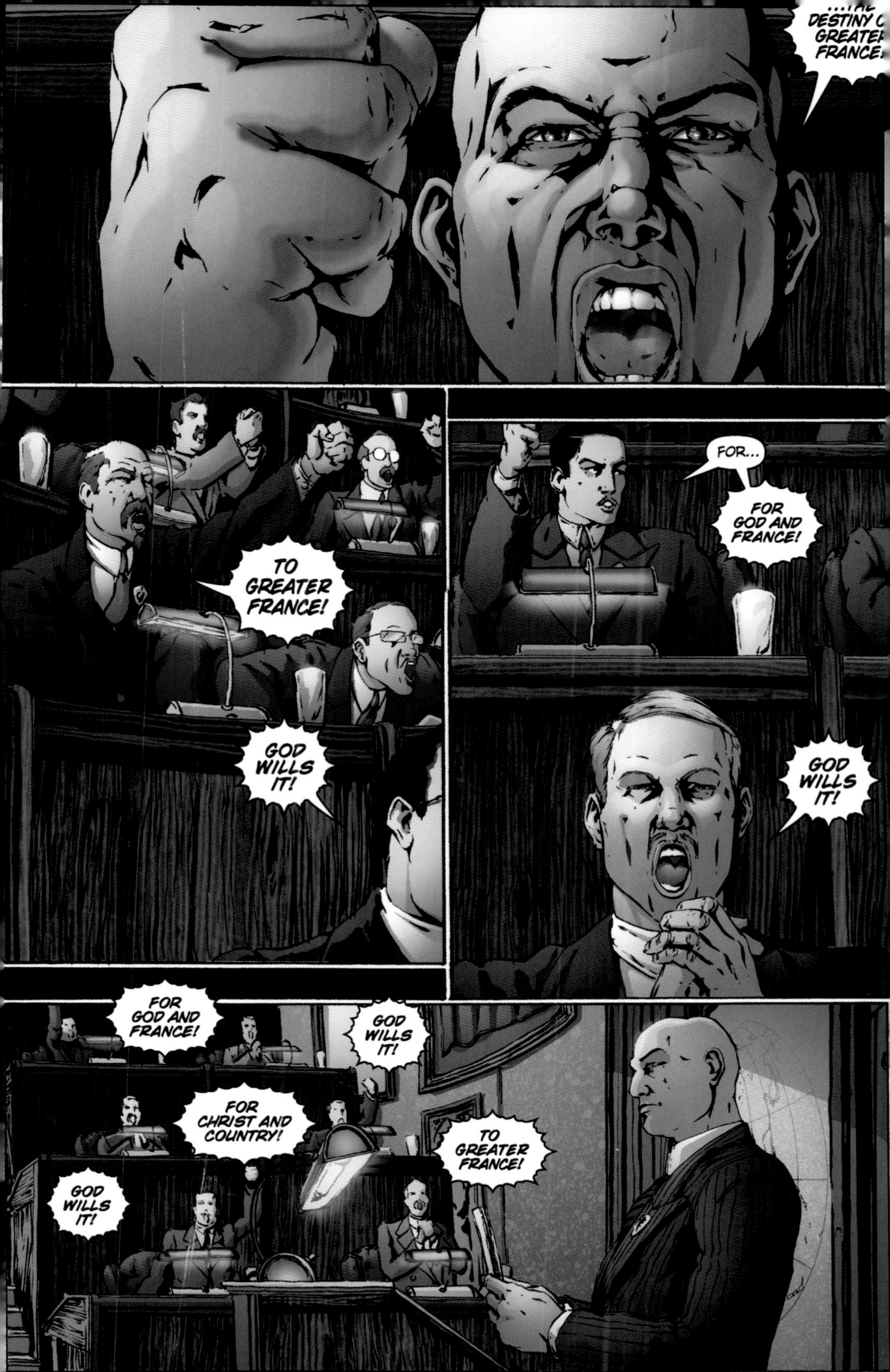

DESTINY O
GREATER
FRANCE!
TO GREATER FRANCE!
GOD WILLS IT!
FOR...
FOR GOD AND FRANCE!
GOD WILLS IT!
FOR GOD AND FRANCE!
GOD WILLS IT!
FOR CHRIST AND COUNTRY!
TO GREATER FRANCE!
GOD WILLS IT!

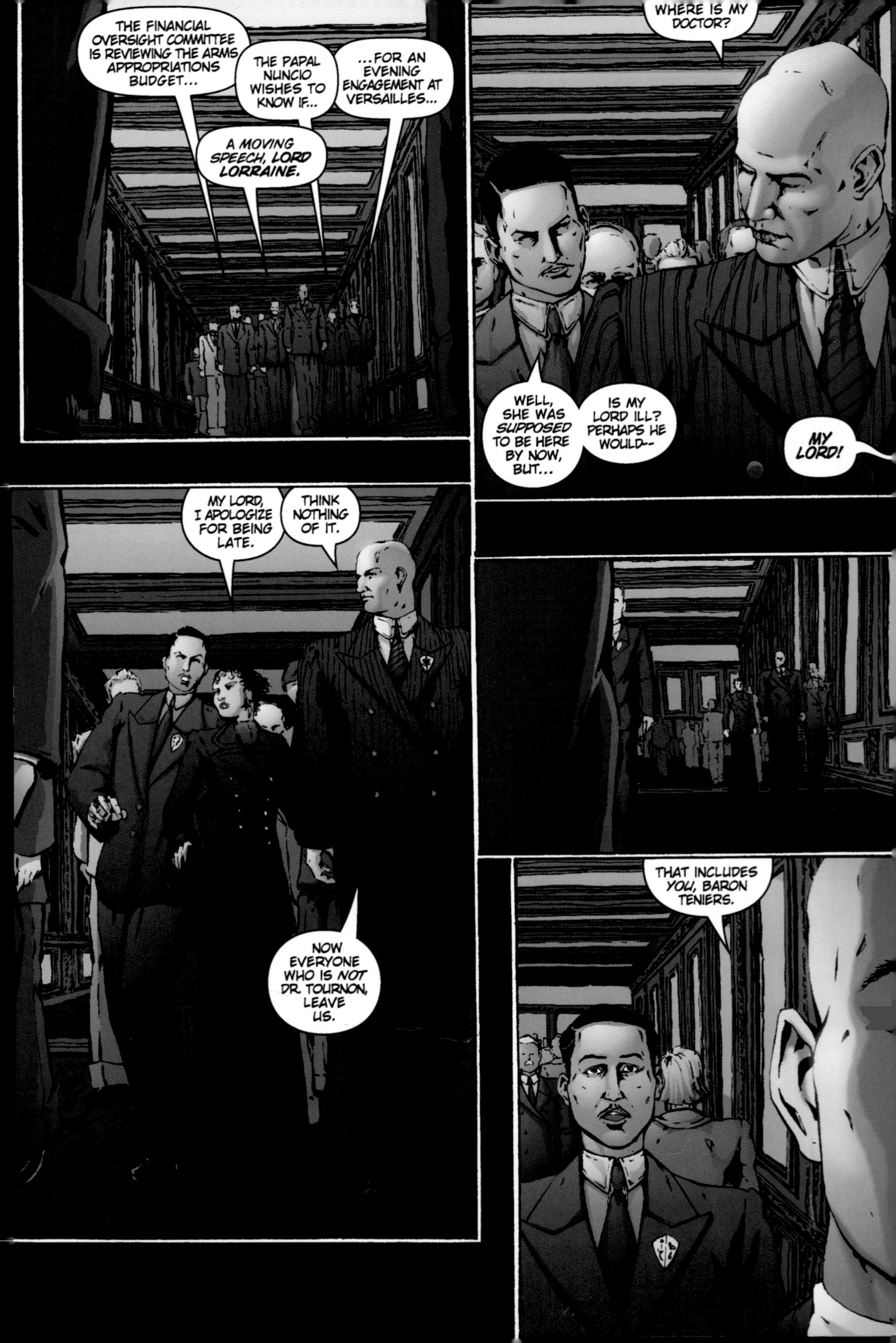
THE FINANCIAL OVERSIGHT COMMITTEE IS REVIEWING THE ARMS APPROPRIATIONS BUDGET...
THE PAPAL NUNCIO WISHES TO KNOW IF...
...FOR AN EVENING ENGAGEMENT AT VERSAILLES...
A MOVING SPEECH, LORD LORRAINE.
WHERE IS MY DOCTOR?
WELL, SHE WAS SUPPOSED TO BE HERE BY NOW, BUT...
IS MY LORD ILL? PERHAPS HE WOULD--
MY LORD!
MY LORD, I APOLOGIZE FOR BEING LATE.
THINK NOTHING OF IT.
NOW EVERYONE WHO IS NOT DR. TOURNON, LEAVE US.
THAT INCLUDES YOU, BARON TENIERS.

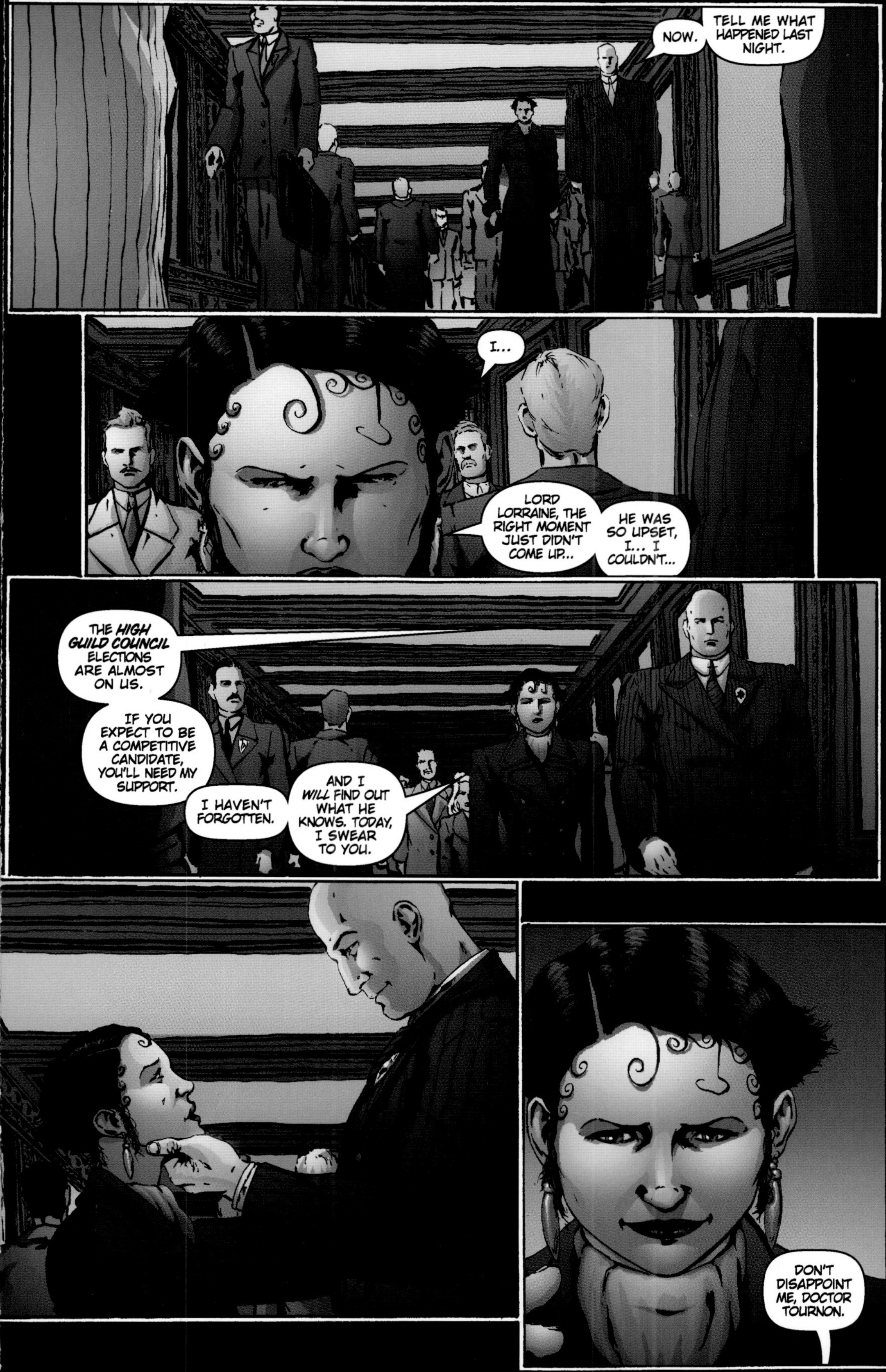
NOW.
TELL ME WHAT HAPPENED LAST NIGHT.
I...
LORD LORRAINE, THE RIGHT MOMENT JUST DIDN'T COME UP...
HE WAS SO UPSET, I... I COULDN'T...
THE *HIGH GUILD COUNCIL* ELECTIONS ARE ALMOST ON US.
IF YOU EXPECT TO BE A COMPETITIVE CANDIDATE, YOU'LL NEED MY SUPPORT.
I HAVEN'T FORGOTTEN.
AND I *WILL* FIND OUT WHAT HE KNOWS. TODAY, I SWEAR TO YOU.
DON'T DISAPPOINT ME, DOCTOR TOURNON.

Dr JULIEN SAUNIÈRE

BY APPOINTMENT OF THE

HIGH GUILD COUNCIL

CHIRURGIEN · MÉDECIN ORDINAIRE

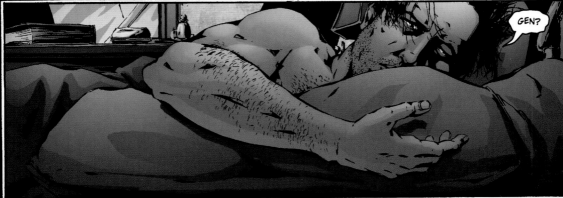

GEN?

DR. SAUNIÈRE.

THE ARCHBISHOP WANTS TO SEE YOU.

GET DRESSED.

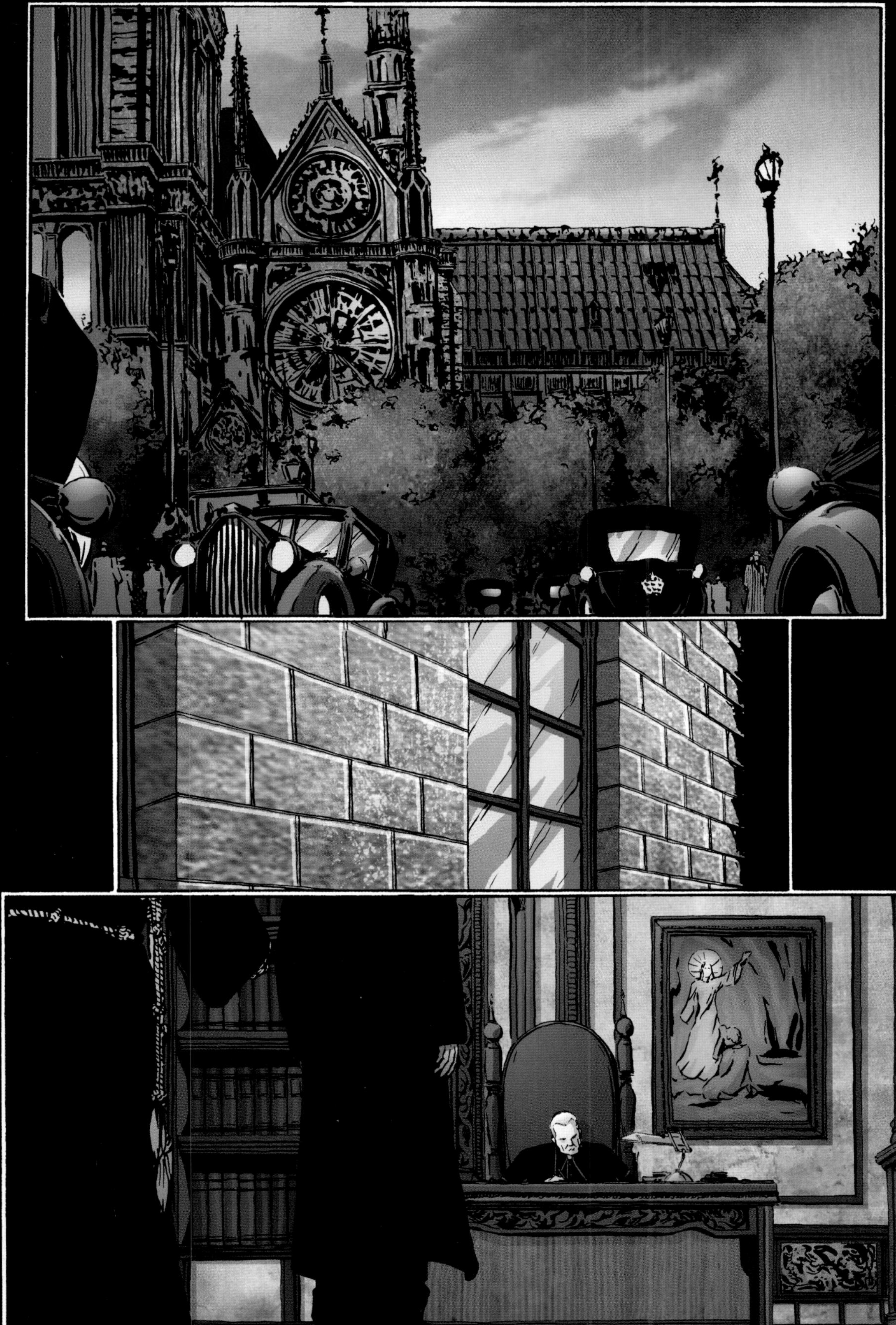

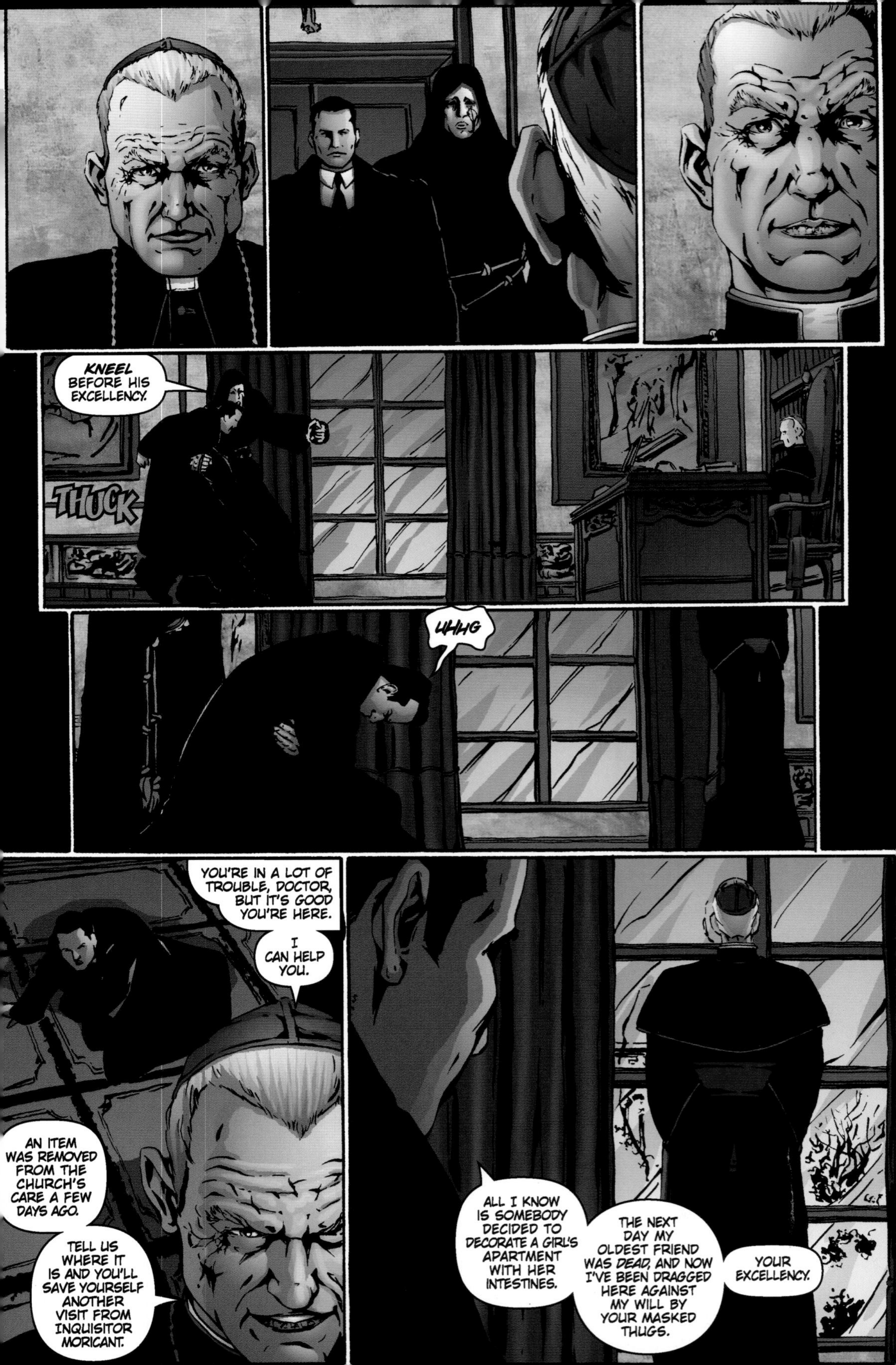
KNEEL BEFORE HIS EXCELLENCY.
THUCK
UHHG
YOU'RE IN A LOT OF TROUBLE, DOCTOR, BUT IT'S GOOD YOU'RE HERE.
I CAN HELP YOU.
AN ITEM WAS REMOVED FROM THE CHURCH'S CARE A FEW DAYS AGO.
TELL US WHERE IT IS AND YOU'LL SAVE YOURSELF ANOTHER VISIT FROM INQUISITOR MORICANT.
ALL I KNOW IS SOMEBODY DECIDED TO DECORATE A GIRL'S APARTMENT WITH HER INTESTINES.
THE NEXT DAY MY OLDEST FRIEND WAS DEAD, AND NOW I'VE BEEN DRAGGED HERE AGAINST MY WILL BY YOUR MASKED THUGS.
YOUR EXCELLENCY.

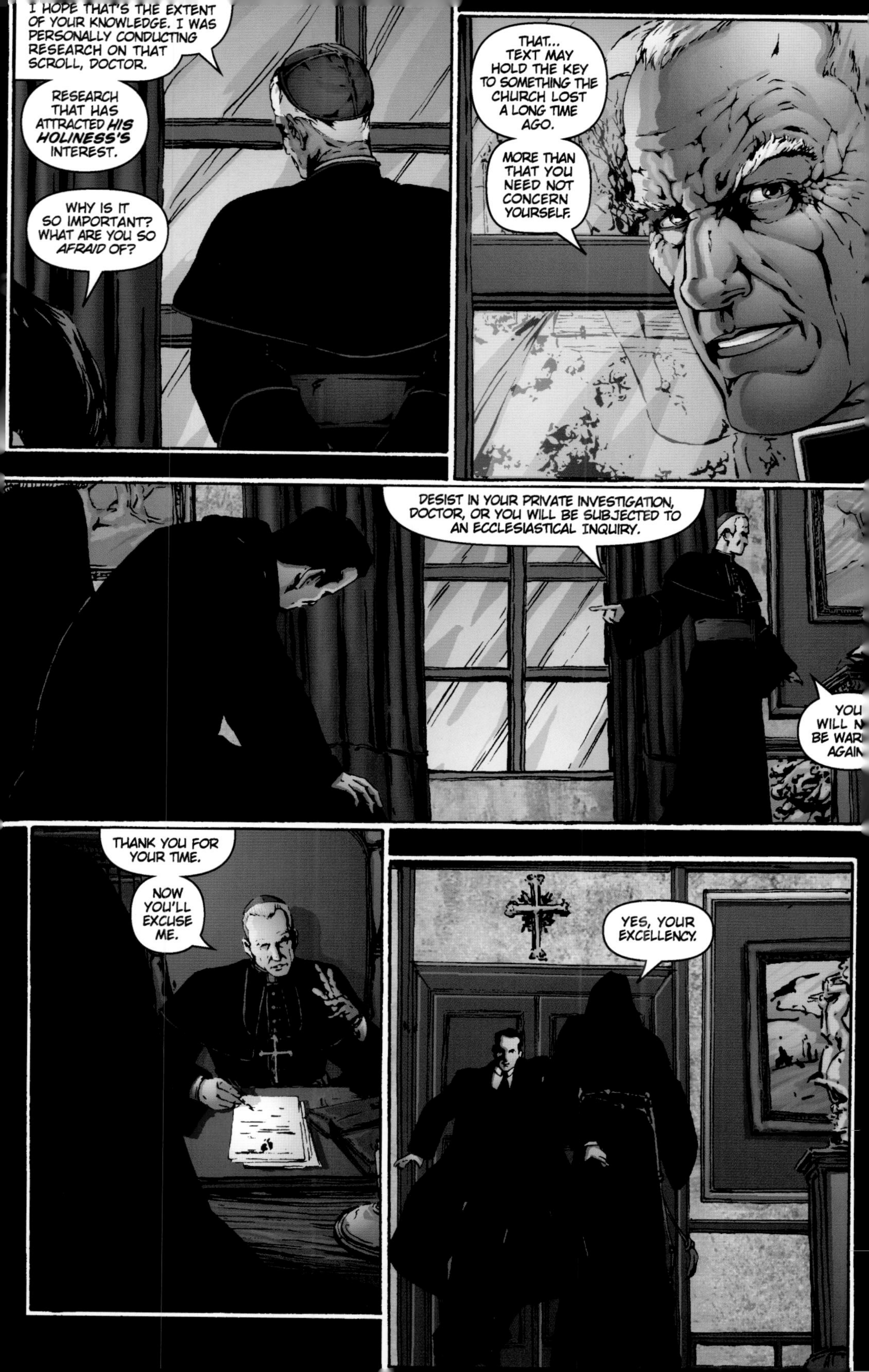
I HOPE THAT'S THE EXTENT OF YOUR KNOWLEDGE. I WAS PERSONALLY CONDUCTING RESEARCH ON THAT SCROLL, DOCTOR.
RESEARCH THAT HAS ATTRACTED *HIS HOLINESS'S* INTEREST.
WHY IS IT SO IMPORTANT? WHAT ARE YOU SO *AFRAID* OF?
THAT... TEXT MAY HOLD THE KEY TO SOMETHING THE CHURCH LOST A LONG TIME AGO.
MORE THAN THAT YOU NEED NOT CONCERN YOURSELF.
DESIST IN YOUR PRIVATE INVESTIGATION, DOCTOR, OR YOU WILL BE SUBJECTED TO AN ECCLESIASTICAL INQUIRY.
THANK YOU FOR YOUR TIME.
NOW YOU'LL EXCUSE ME.
YES, YOUR EXCELLENCY.

JULIEN!

GOD, WHAT *HAPPENED*? I JUST CAME FROM YOUR PRACTICE...

YOUR NEIGHBORS SAID YOU [WENT] WITH AN INQUISITOR, [SO] I CAME HERE...

YEAH. ROUGHED ME UP A LITTLE BIT.

ARE YOU OKAY? DID--

COME ON. I LIVE NEAR HERE.

WELL, THERE DOESN'T SEEM TO BE ANY HEMORRHAGING...

DOES THIS HURT?

YES.

YOU SURE LEFT IN A HURRY THIS MORNING.

I HAD TO BE SOMEWHERE...

OH, JULIEN, I'M JUST GLAD YOU'RE SAFE.

WHAT'S GOING ON? DOES IT INVOLVE FATHER MARIN?

YEAH.

IT DOES.

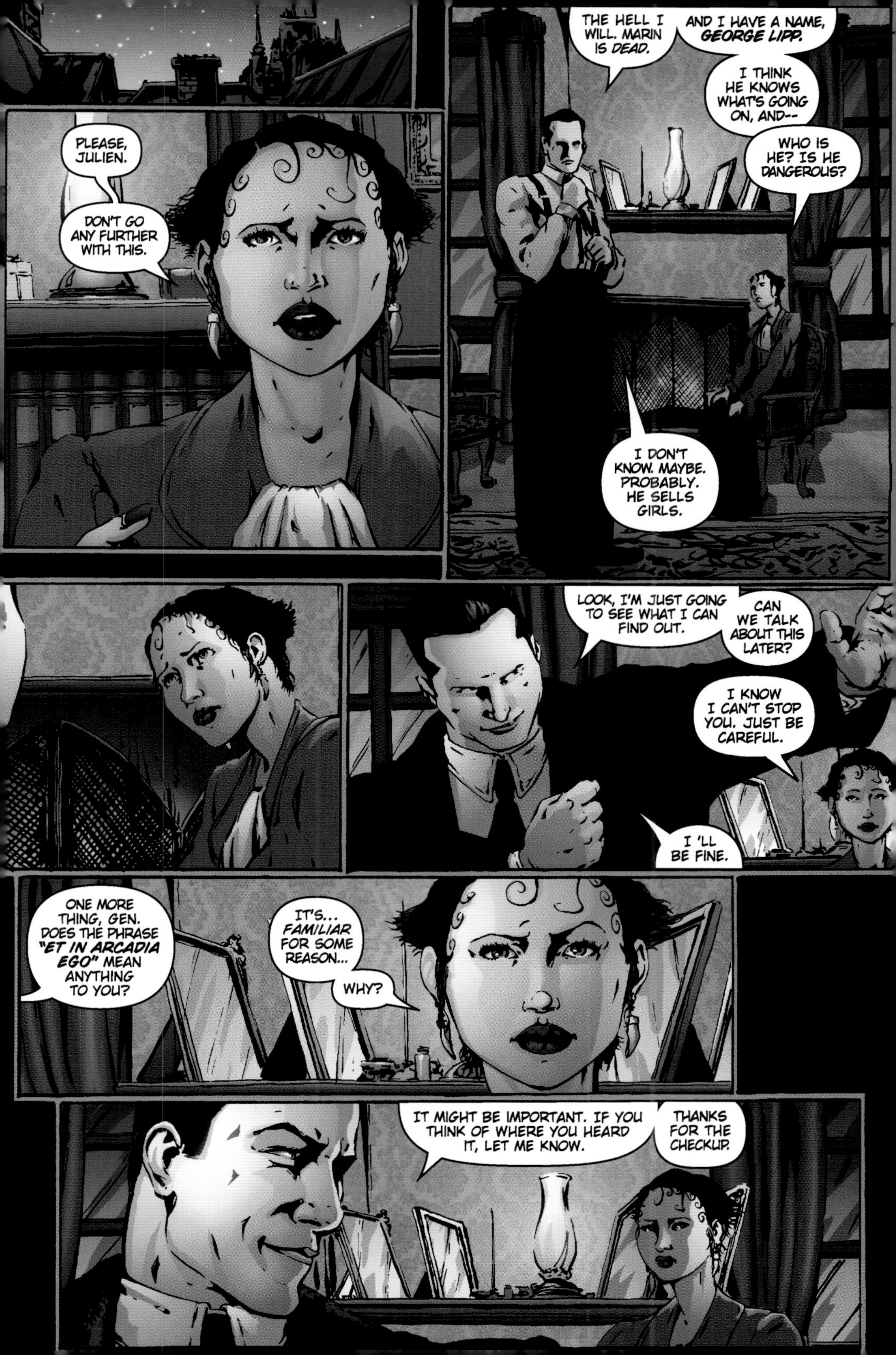
PLEASE, JULIEN.
DON'T GO ANY FURTHER WITH THIS.
THE HELL I WILL. MARIN IS *DEAD.*
AND I HAVE A NAME, ***GEORGE LIPP.***
I THINK HE KNOWS WHAT'S GOING ON, AND--
WHO IS HE? IS HE DANGEROUS?
I DON'T KNOW. MAYBE. PROBABLY. HE SELLS GIRLS.
LOOK, I'M JUST GOING TO SEE WHAT I CAN FIND OUT.
CAN WE TALK ABOUT THIS LATER?
I KNOW I CAN'T STOP YOU. JUST BE CAREFUL.
I'LL BE FINE.
ONE MORE THING, GEN. DOES THE PHRASE ***"ET IN ARCADIA EGO"*** MEAN ANYTHING TO YOU?
IT'S... *FAMILIAR* FOR SOME REASON...
WHY?
IT MIGHT BE IMPORTANT. IF YOU THINK OF WHERE YOU HEARD IT, LET ME KNOW.
THANKS FOR THE CHECKUP.

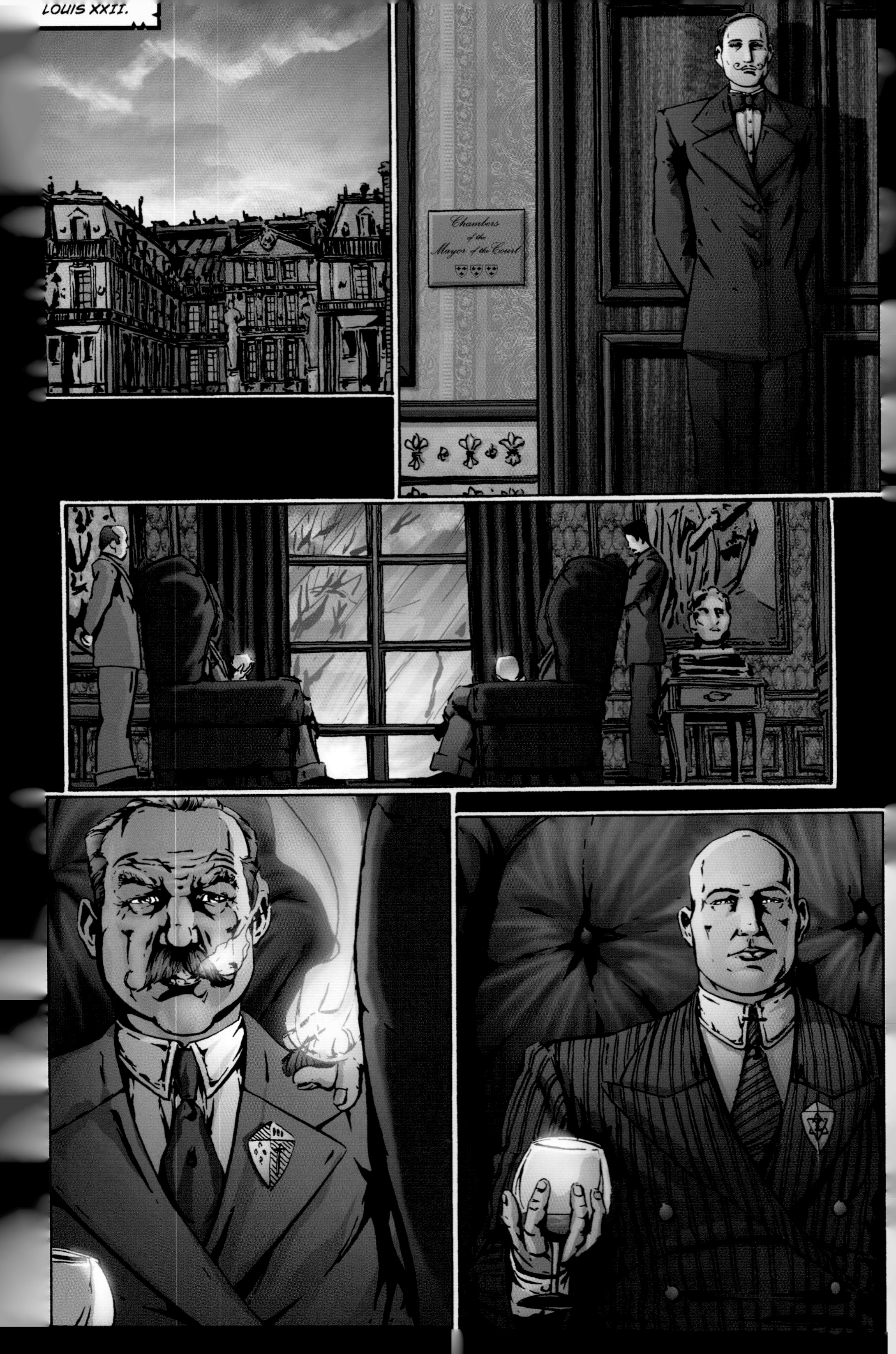
LOUIS XXII.
Chambers of the Mayor of the Court

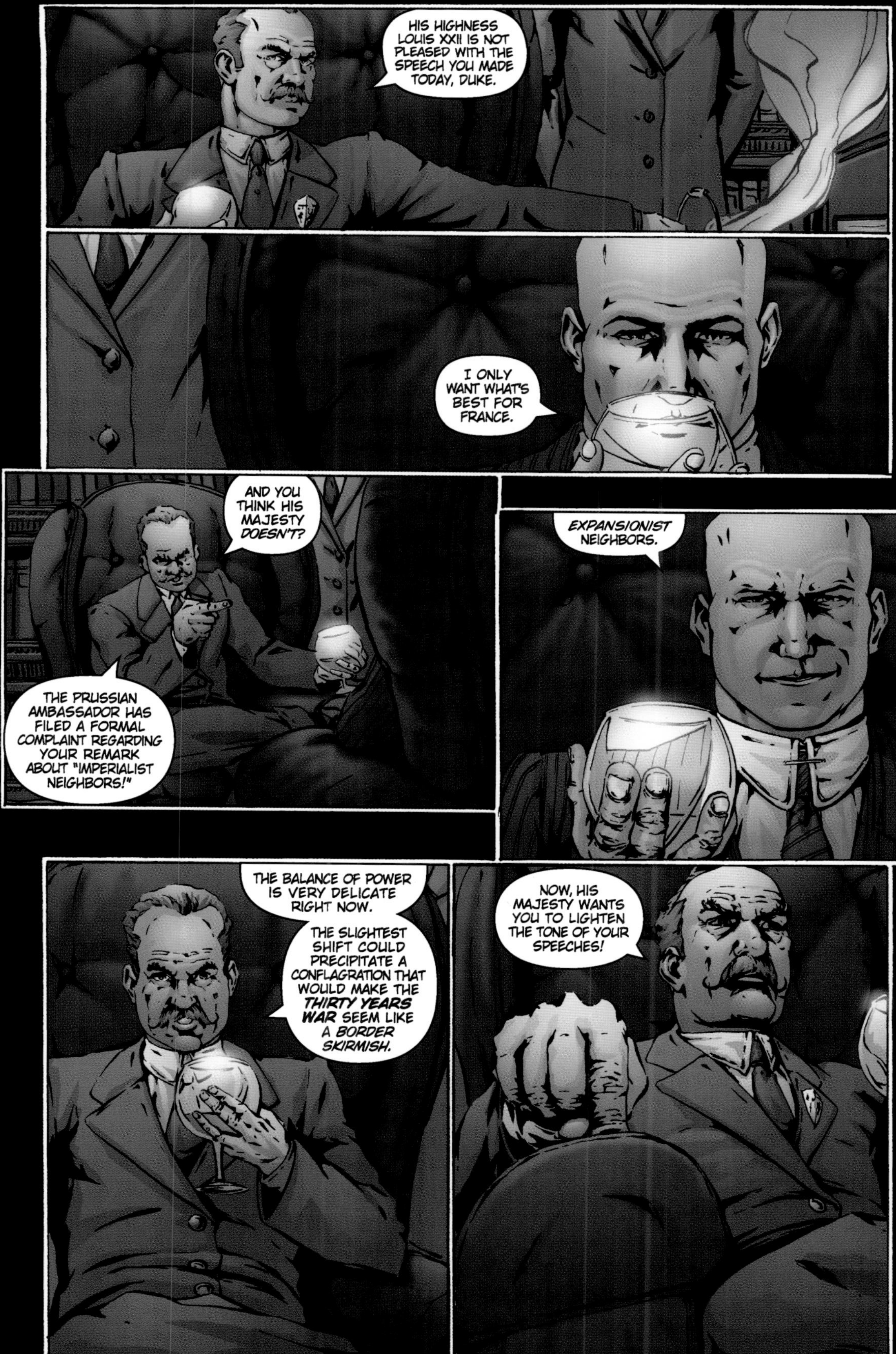
HIS HIGHNESS LOUIS XXII IS NOT PLEASED WITH THE SPEECH YOU MADE TODAY, DUKE.
I ONLY WANT WHAT'S BEST FOR FRANCE.
AND YOU THINK HIS MAJESTY *DOESN'T*?
THE PRUSSIAN AMBASSADOR HAS FILED A FORMAL COMPLAINT REGARDING YOUR REMARK ABOUT "IMPERIALIST NEIGHBORS!"
EXPANSIONIST NEIGHBORS.
THE BALANCE OF POWER IS VERY DELICATE RIGHT NOW.
THE SLIGHTEST SHIFT COULD PRECIPITATE A CONFLAGRATION THAT WOULD MAKE THE ***THIRTY YEARS WAR*** SEEM LIKE A *BORDER SKIRMISH*.
NOW, HIS MAJESTY WANTS YOU TO LIGHTEN THE TONE OF YOUR SPEECHES!

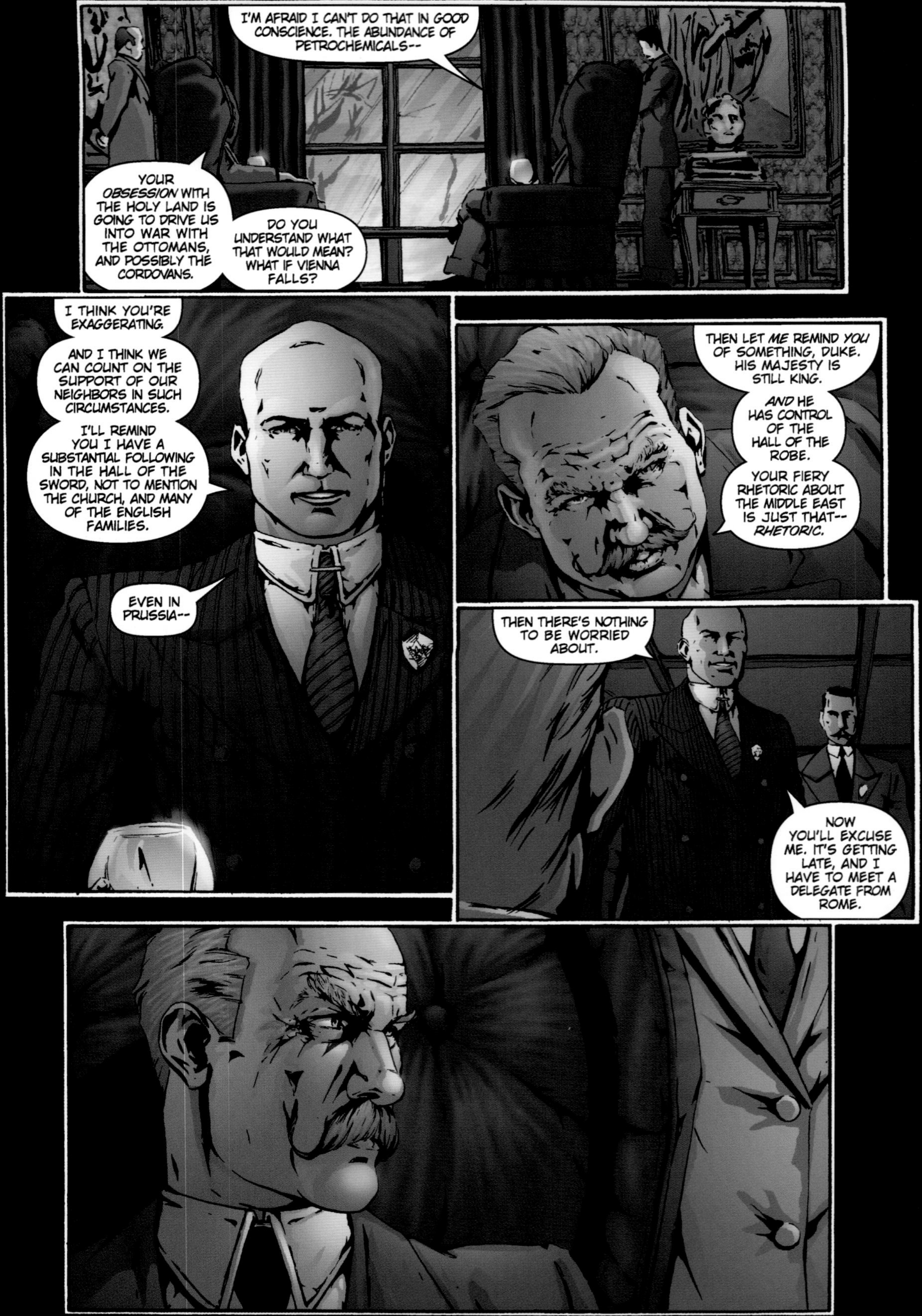
I'M AFRAID I CAN'T DO THAT IN GOOD CONSCIENCE. THE ABUNDANCE OF PETROCHEMICALS--
YOUR *OBSESSION* WITH THE HOLY LAND IS GOING TO DRIVE US INTO WAR WITH THE OTTOMANS, AND POSSIBLY THE CORDOVANS.
DO YOU UNDERSTAND WHAT THAT WOULD MEAN? WHAT IF VIENNA FALLS?
I THINK YOU'RE EXAGGERATING.
AND I THINK WE CAN COUNT ON THE SUPPORT OF OUR NEIGHBORS IN SUCH CIRCUMSTANCES.
I'LL REMIND YOU I HAVE A SUBSTANTIAL FOLLOWING IN THE HALL OF THE SWORD, NOT TO MENTION THE CHURCH, AND MANY OF THE ENGLISH FAMILIES.
EVEN IN PRUSSIA--
THEN LET *ME* REMIND *YOU* OF SOMETHING, DUKE. HIS MAJESTY IS STILL KING.
AND HE HAS CONTROL OF THE HALL OF THE ROBE.
YOUR FIERY RHETORIC ABOUT THE MIDDLE EAST IS JUST THAT-- *RHETORIC.*
THEN THERE'S NOTHING TO BE WORRIED ABOUT.
NOW YOU'LL EXCUSE ME. IT'S GETTING LATE, AND I HAVE TO MEET A DELEGATE FROM ROME.

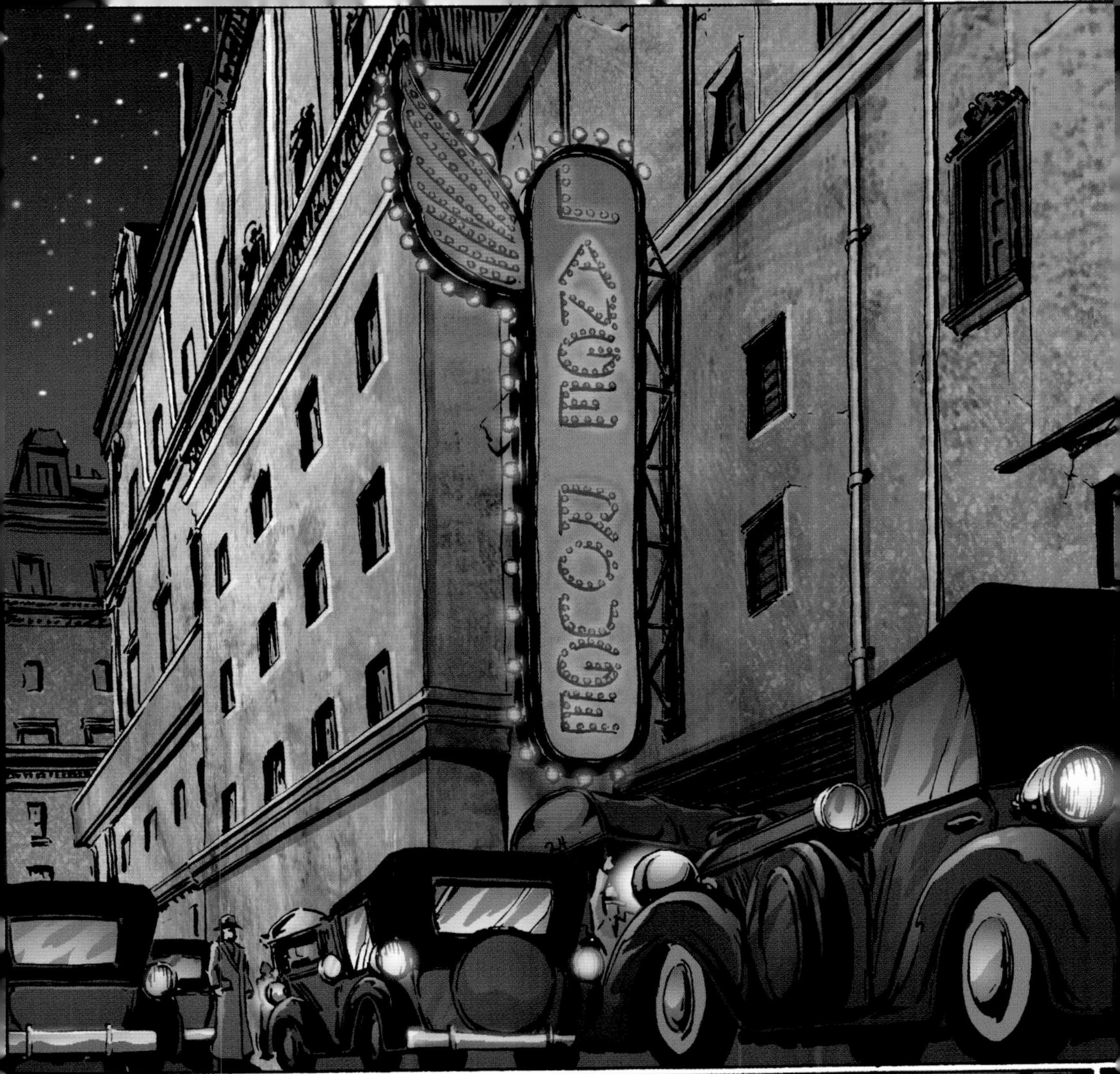
LANGE
ROUGE

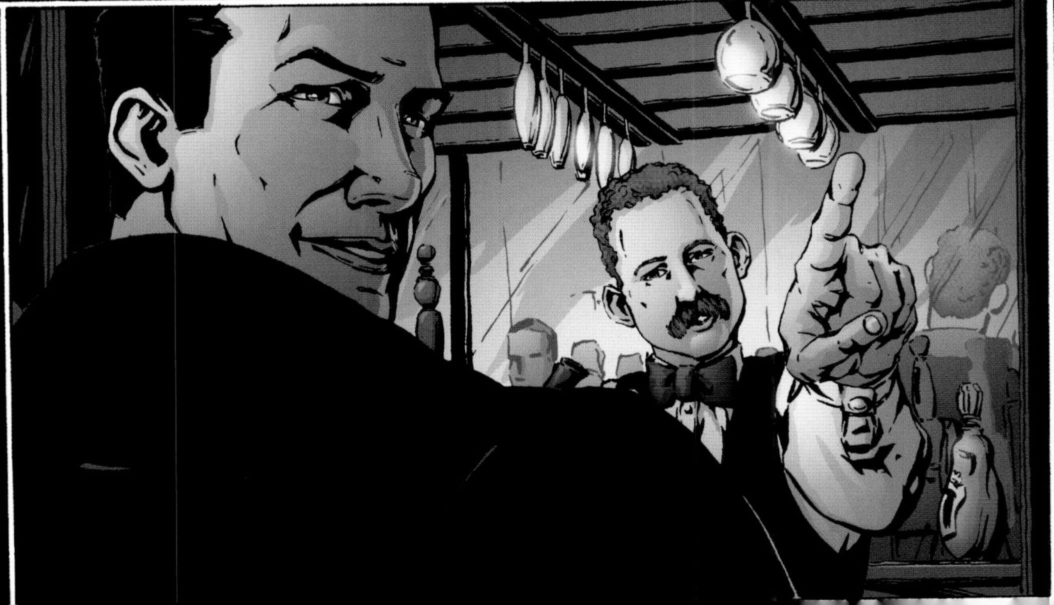

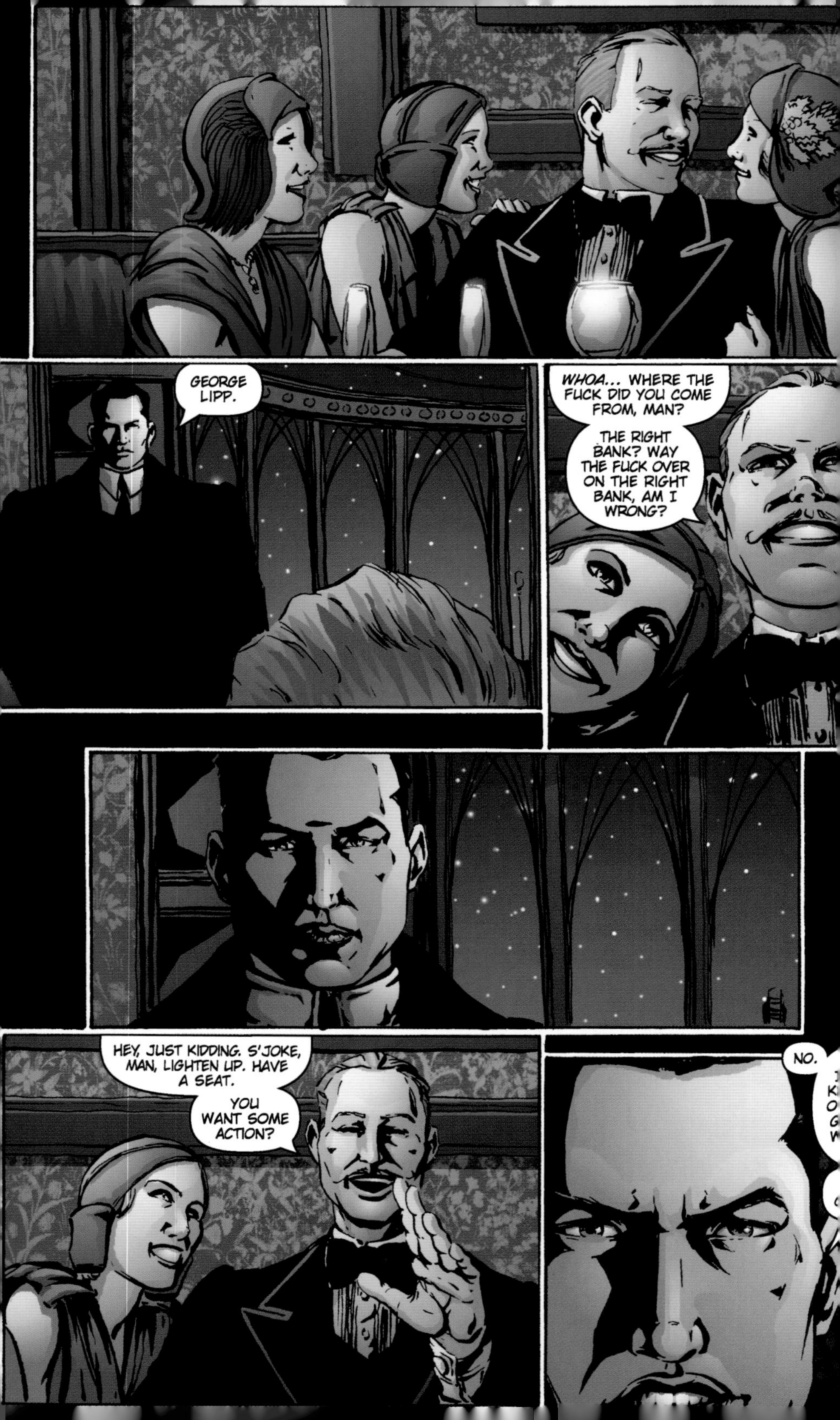
GEORGE LIPP.
WHOA... WHERE THE FUCK DID YOU COME FROM, MAN?
THE RIGHT BANK? WAY THE FUCK OVER ON THE RIGHT BANK, AM I WRONG?
HEY, JUST KIDDING. S'JOKE, MAN, LIGHTEN UP. HAVE A SEAT.
YOU WANT SOME ACTION?
NO.

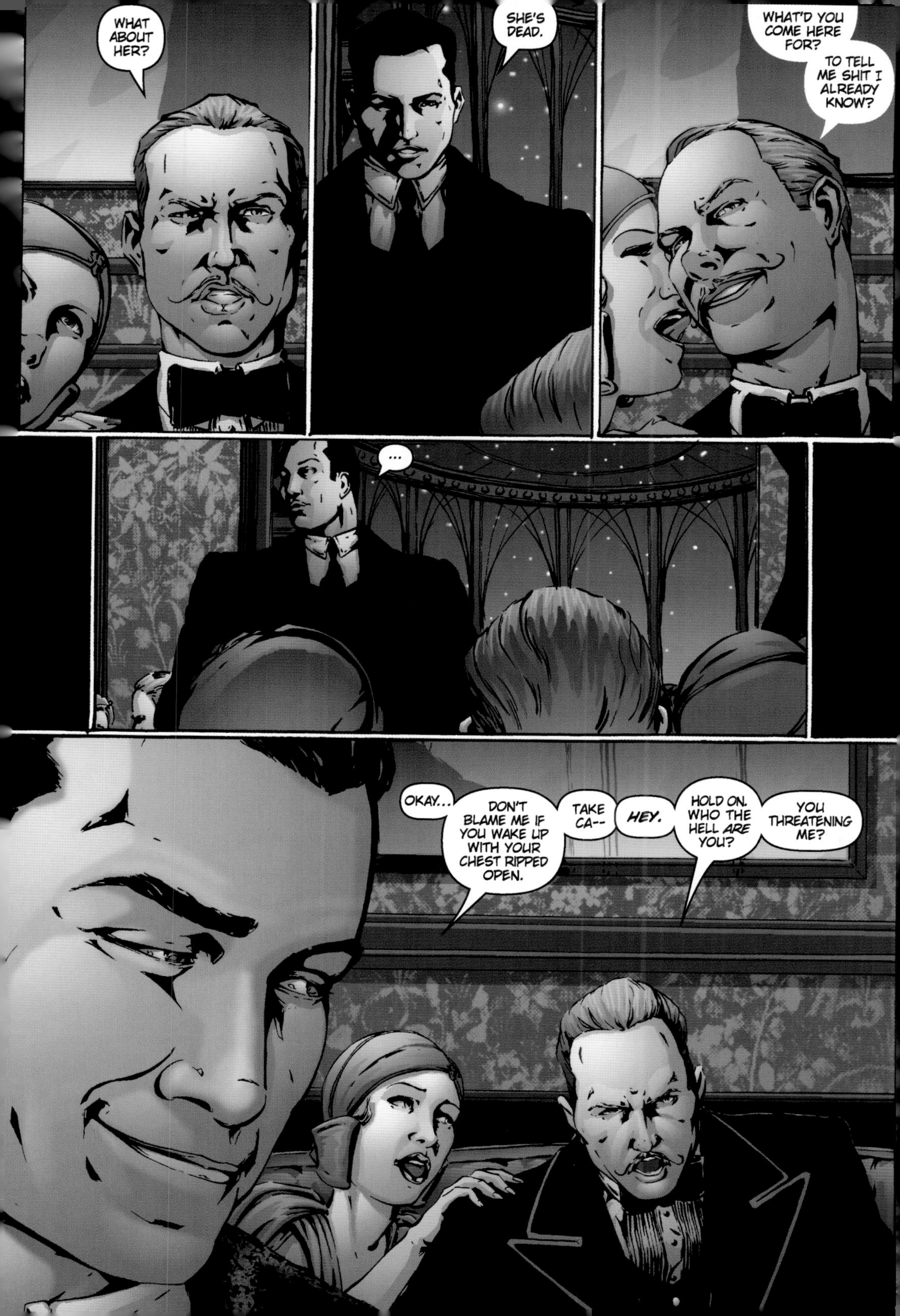
WHAT ABOUT HER?
SHE'S DEAD.
WHAT'D YOU COME HERE FOR?
TO TELL ME SHIT I ALREADY KNOW?
...
OKAY...
DON'T BLAME ME IF YOU WAKE UP WITH YOUR CHEST RIPPED OPEN.
TAKE CA--
HEY.
HOLD ON. WHO THE HELL *ARE* YOU?
YOU THREATENING ME?

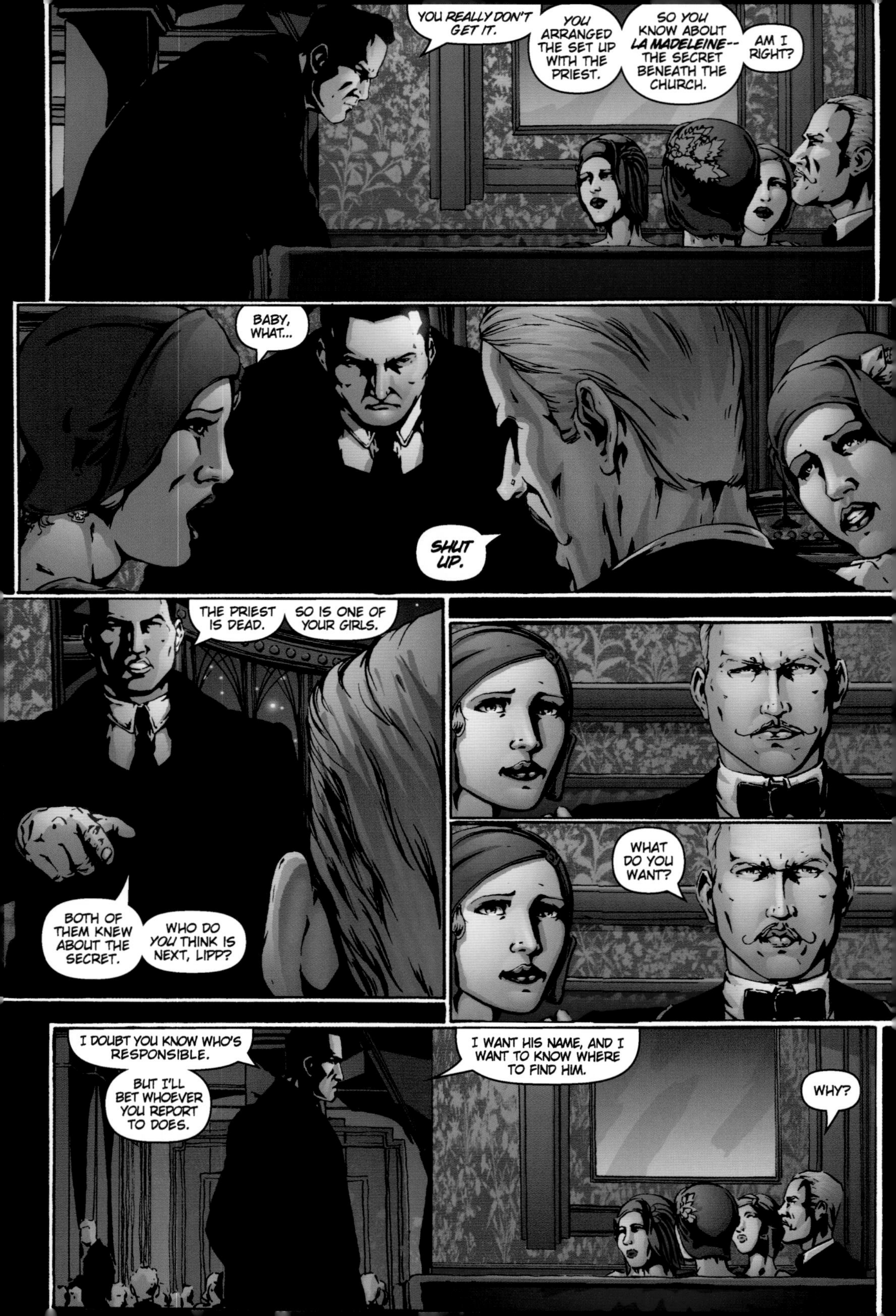
YOU REALLY DON'T GET IT.
YOU ARRANGED THE SET UP WITH THE PRIEST.
SO YOU KNOW ABOUT LA MADELEINE-- THE SECRET BENEATH THE CHURCH.
AM I RIGHT?
BABY, WHAT...
SHUT UP.
THE PRIEST IS DEAD.
SO IS ONE OF YOUR GIRLS.
BOTH OF THEM KNEW ABOUT THE SECRET.
WHO DO YOU THINK IS NEXT, LIPP?
WHAT DO YOU WANT?
I DOUBT YOU KNOW WHO'S RESPONSIBLE.
BUT I'LL BET WHOEVER YOU REPORT TO DOES.
I WANT HIS NAME, AND I WANT TO KNOW WHERE TO FIND HIM.
WHY?

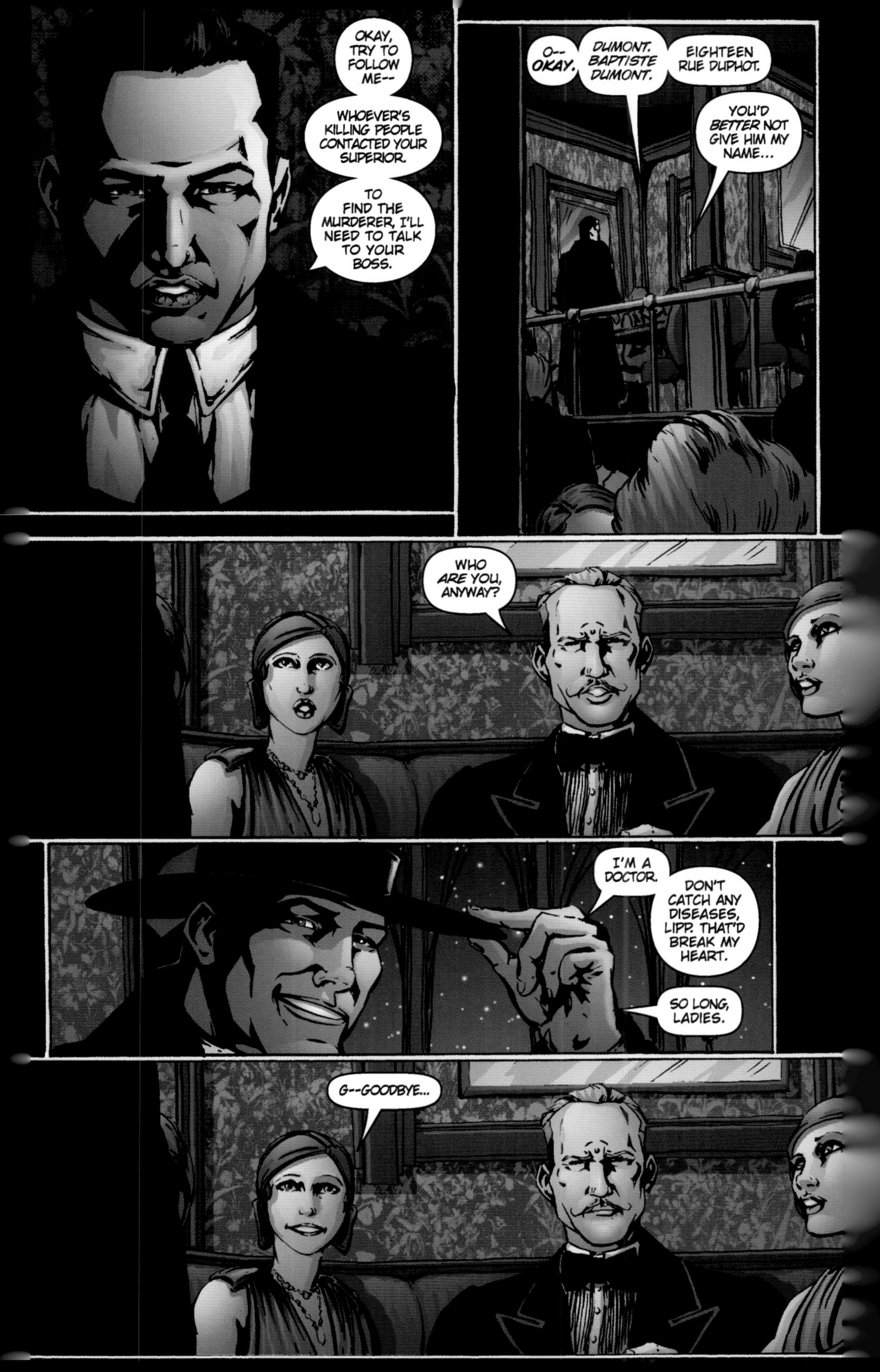
OKAY, TRY TO FOLLOW ME--
WHOEVER'S KILLING PEOPLE CONTACTED YOUR SUPERIOR.
TO FIND THE MURDERER, I'LL NEED TO TALK TO YOUR BOSS.
O-- OKAY.
DUMONT. BAPTISTE DUMONT.
EIGHTEEN RUE DUPHOT.
YOU'D BETTER NOT GIVE HIM MY NAME...
WHO ARE YOU, ANYWAY?
I'M A DOCTOR.
DON'T CATCH ANY DISEASES, LIPP. THAT'D BREAK MY HEART.
SO LONG, LADIES.
G--GOODBYE...

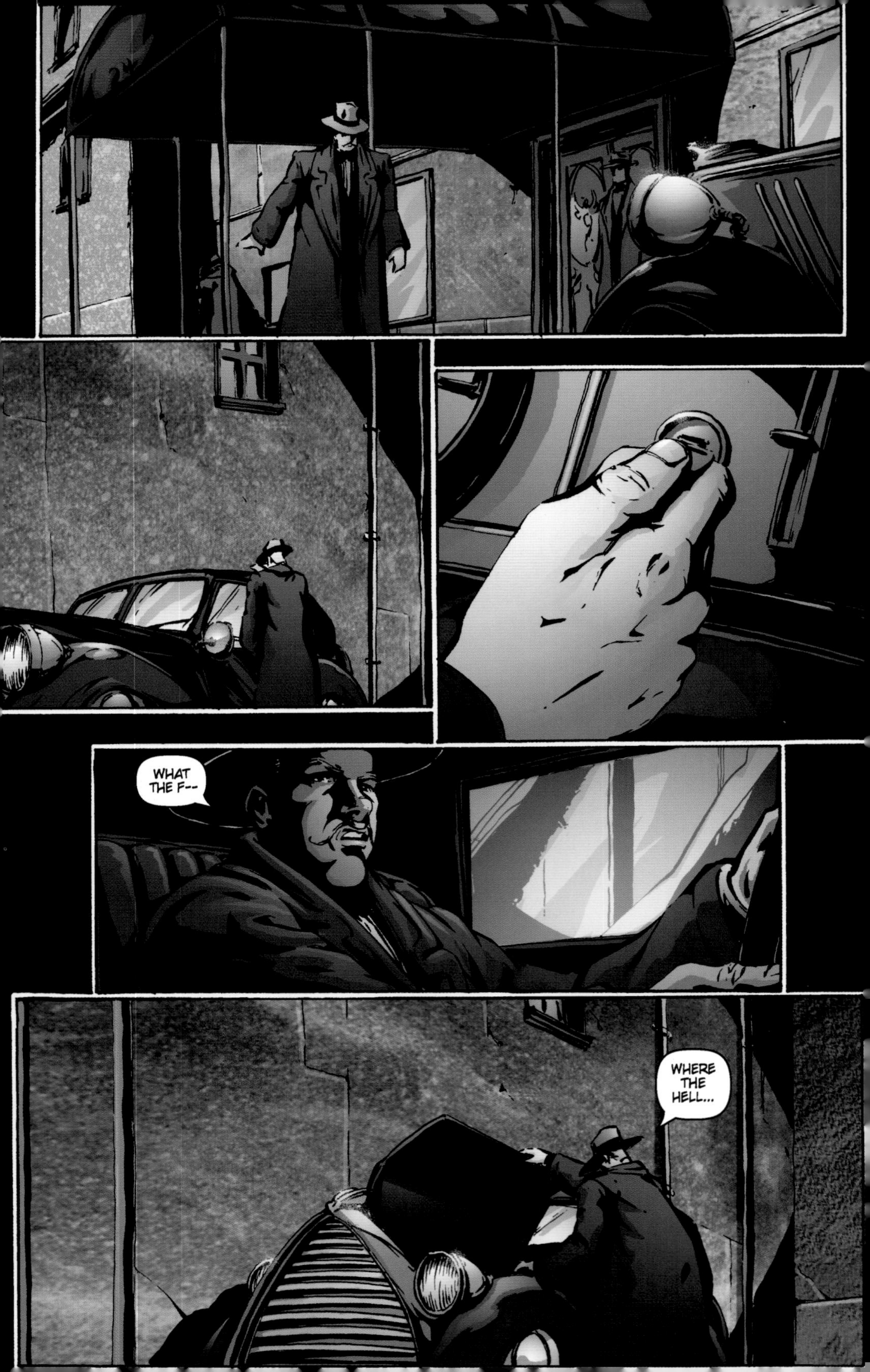
WHAT THE F--
WHERE THE HELL...

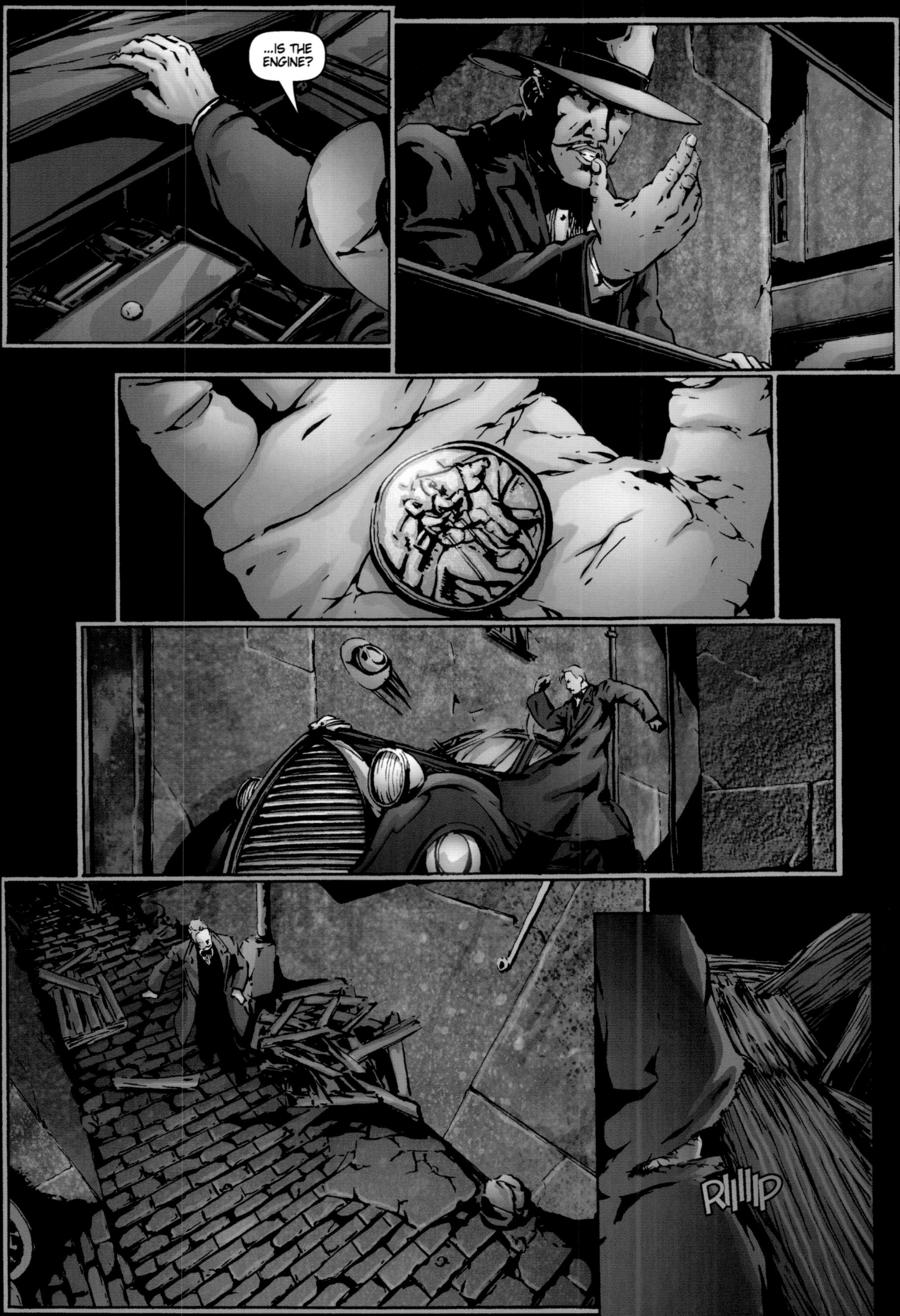
...IS THE ENGINE?
RIIIIP

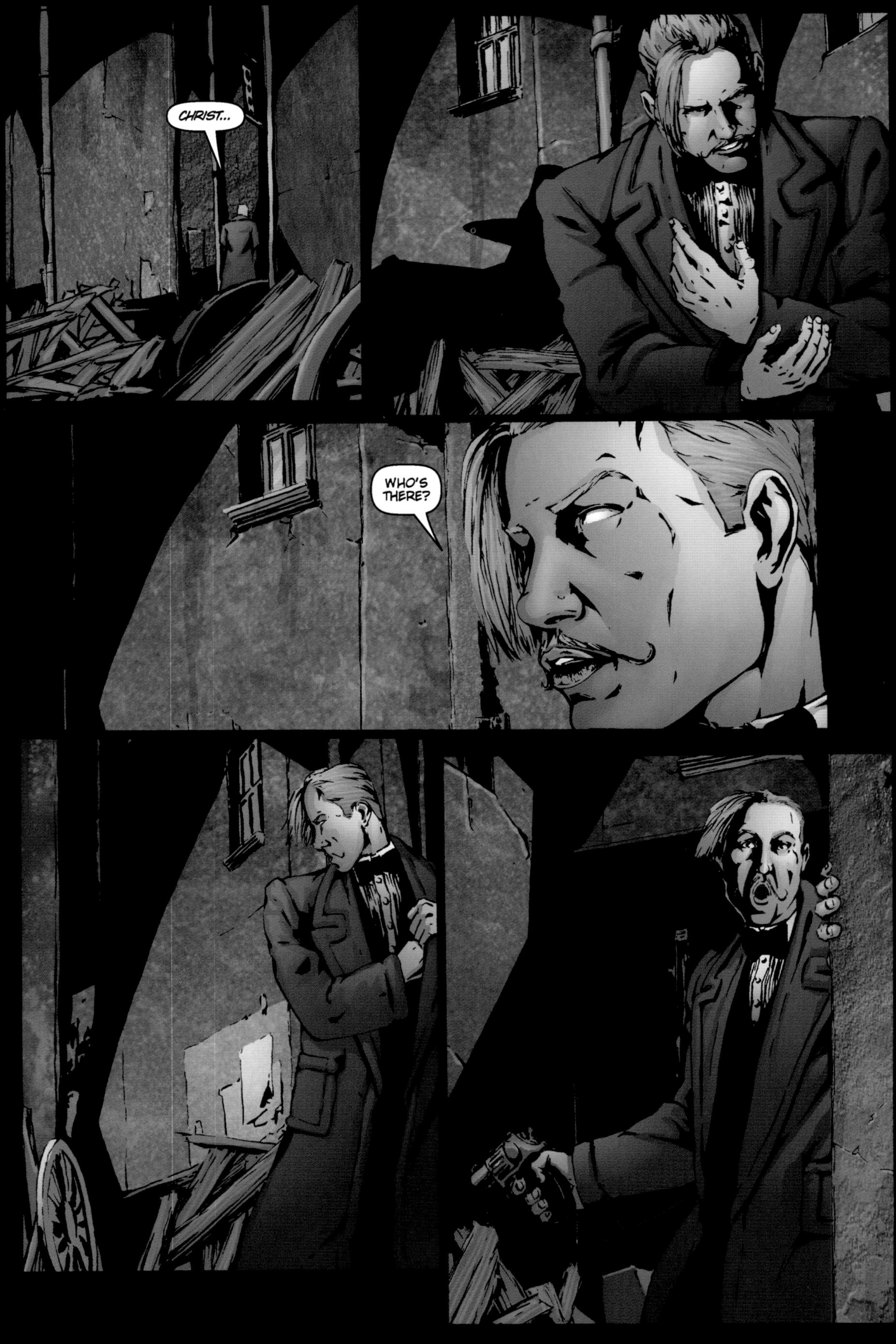
CHRIST...
WHO'S THERE?

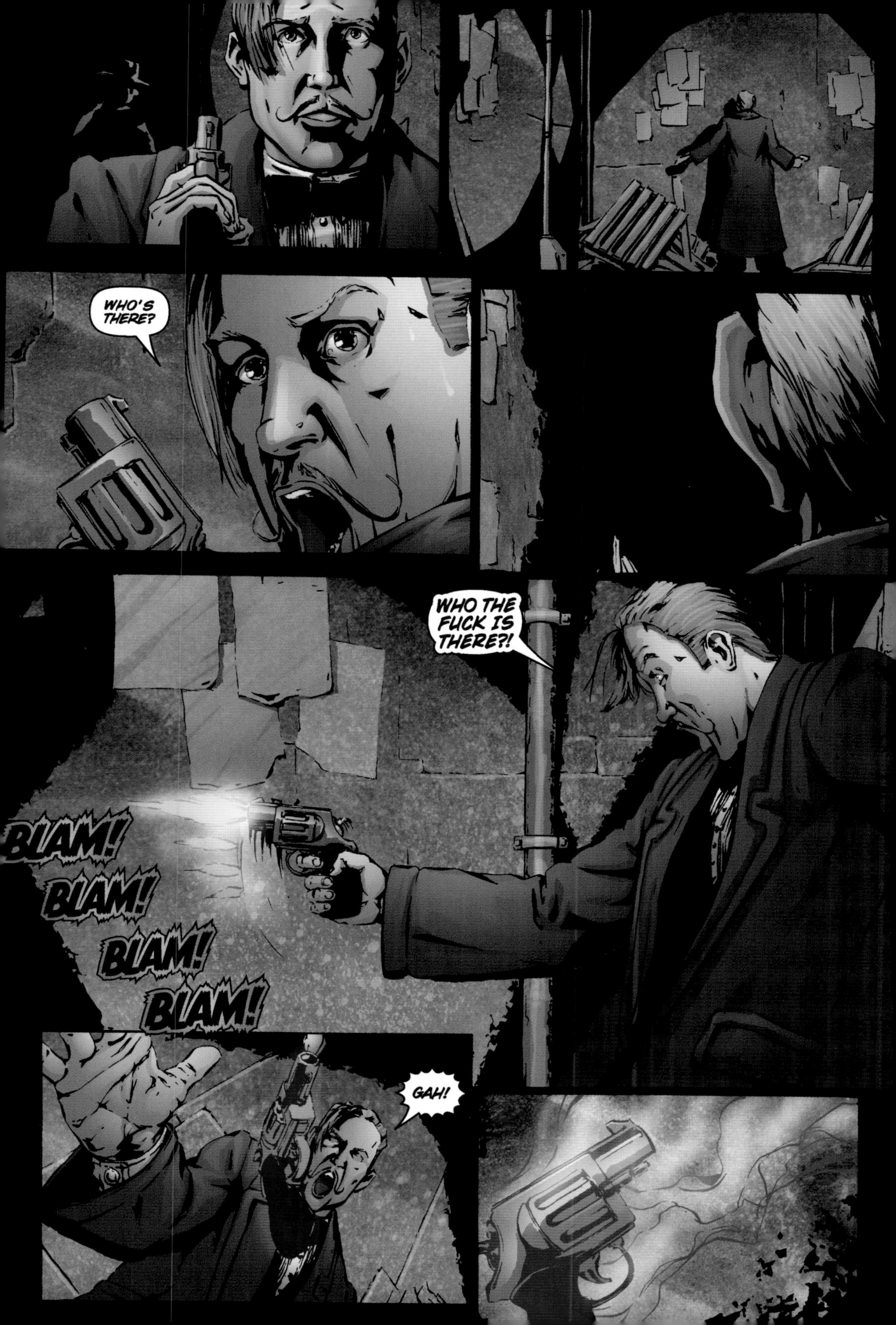
WHO'S THERE?
WHO THE FUCK IS THERE?!
BLAM!
BLAM!
BLAM!
BLAM!
GAH!

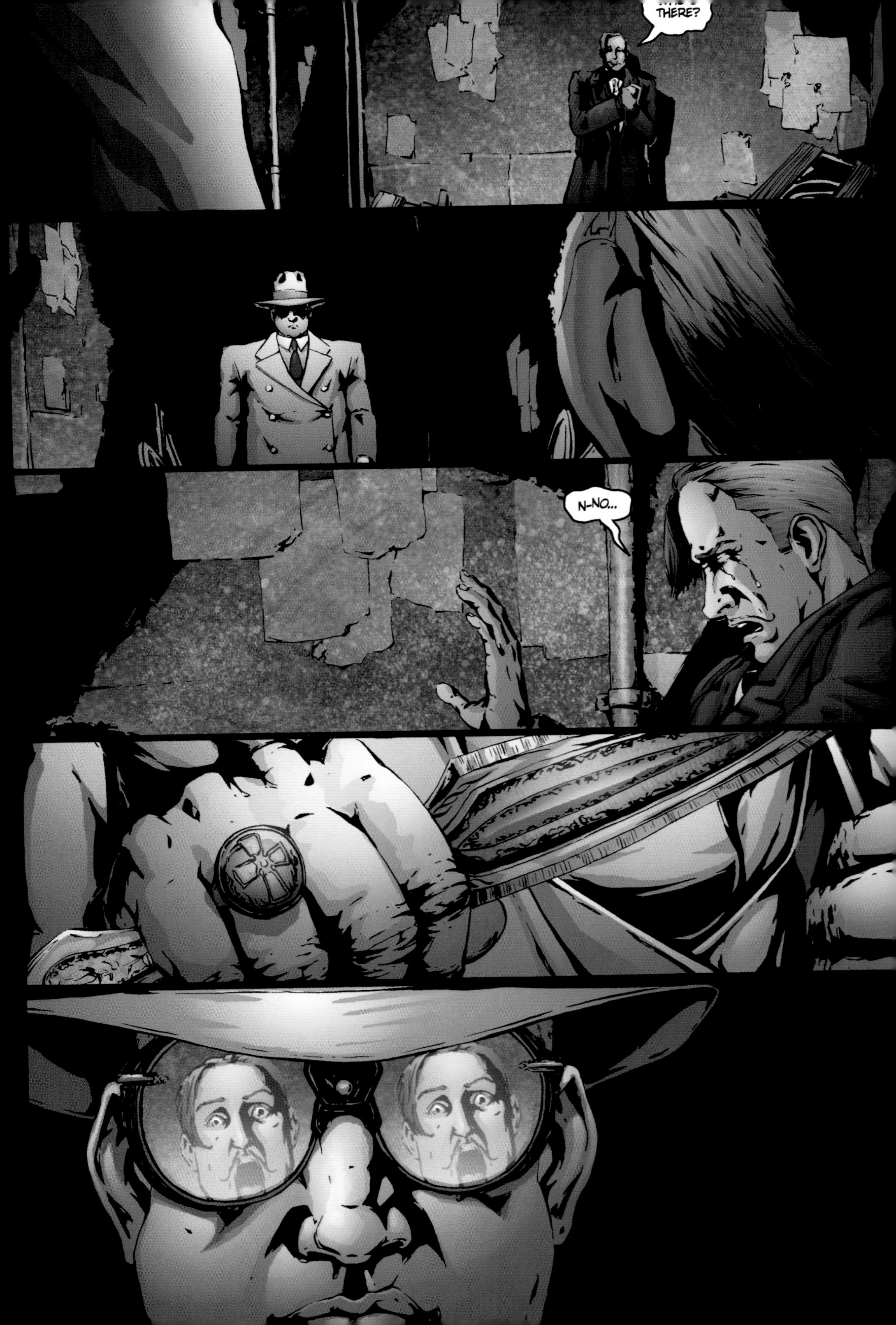
THERE?
N-NO...

Le Journal de la Liberté

Paris's leading anglophone newspaper • vol. 205, no. 98 • Oct. 21, MCMXXXIII

Papal Seal

Editors in Chief: M. Tait Bergstrom, M. Matthew Pasteris. **Story Editor:** M. Arvid Nelson. **Art Editors:** M. EricJ, M. Jeromy Cox. **Photography Editor:** M. Alexander Waldman. **Layout Supervisor:** M. William Kartalopoulos. **Editors Emeritus:** M. Clark A. Smith, M. Howard P. Lovecraft, M. Robert E. Howard. Redacted by the Holy Inquisition under the direction of His Excellency Archbishop Emile-Jean Ireneaux. Le Journal de Liberté is printed under the benign auspices of his most puissant majesty KING LOUIS XXII of FRANCE. GOD SAVE THE KING.

of Approval

Senegalese "Ship of Horrors" of Confederate Origin - English Navy

A slave ship apprehended by the English Navy off the coast of Senegal yesterday is owned by a slave-trading company in the Confederate States of America, according to English naval officials.

Although the boat was boarded in international waters, its scheduled itinerary was between Dakar, Senegal, and Charleston, South Carolina, neither of which is a British possession.

The ship's itinerary presents diplomatic "issues," according to the French Foreign Ministry.

So far there has been no official comment by the French Crown, but King Louis XXII is not expected to intervene.

British officials have insisted the ship will not return to the CSA with its human cargo.

"The Queen has made it very clear that any slaving vessel apprehended by the English Navy will be destroyed, and its human cargo returned to its country of origin," Captain Reginald Henderson of the *HMS Indefatigable*, the vessel responsible for the boarding, said.

"The conditions aboard are utterly abominable. I have never seen human beings kept in such a state of abject wretchedness. It is a ship of horrors."

Although the English Navy helped protract the American Civil War into a brutal stalemate seventy years ago, relations between the Confederate States of America and England have since cooled dramatically.

Confederate States President Huey Long expressed his "indignation and outrage" at the seizure, claiming the vessel was engaged

continued on page A15

INQUISITORS RAID OPIUM DEN

Two cenobites wounded in shootout with dope fiends

Two inquisitors were wounded early this morning in a daring raid on a drug den in the 19th Arrondissement. Their wounds were not critical, and neither man needed hospitalization.

"We are relieved that none of our agents were seriously wounded," Archbishop Eugène Ireneaux said. "Raids like this always pose a risk to our operatives."

Gendarmerie officers supporting the inquisitors gunned down ten drug dealers in the fusillade. Seven of the men were pronounced dead on the scene by Dr. Antoine Laborde, forensic attaché of the Guild of Physicians. The other three are in critical condition at the Convent of St. Barbara in Montmartre.

Eighteen more were arrested and are in the custody of the church.

According to Inquisition officials, the arrests and seizure of the drug-producing facility represents a victory for "the forces of righteousness and order" in Paris.

"This was a major production and distribution center for a large part of the 19th Arrondissement," Inquisitor Legris, chief inquisitor for the investigation, said. "This is much more than a sting operation involving low-level dealers on the street. We went straight to the top here."

The operation was the product of a nine-month joint operation by the Royal Gendarmerie and the Holy Inquisition. Gendarmerie and Inquisition officials alike hailed the raid as a "sterling example" of how secular and ecclesiastical law enforcement agencies can work together.

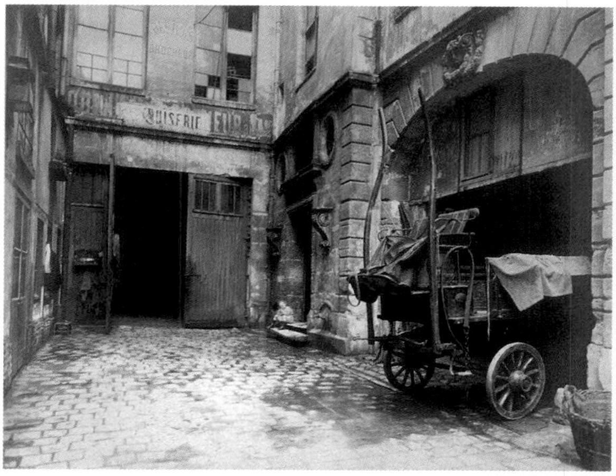

UISERIE

Scene of the "deplorable bed of iniquity." Eugène Atget, staff photographer

"We were very pleased by the cooperation from the Gendarmerie in this matter," Legris said. Gendarmerie officials seized on the opportunity to demonstrate the effectiveness of secular law enforcement.

"A lot of people have been criticizing the effectiveness of the [Royal Gendarmerie] in the past few days," Lieutenant Guilliame Bernard said. "I think this demonstrates the fact that there is a place for secular policework in our society." The Royal Gendarmerie has come under fire since it was reported that the Inquisition's new "War On Crime" initiative was aimed at least in part at uprooting secular police corruption.

Inquisition officials made a stunning announcement yesterday about arrests of a number of high-ranking Gendarmerie officers for charges including racketeering, bribery and extortion.

Secular police forces are often criticized as lax and inefficient because they are privately funded by feudal lords, or in the case of Paris, by the King himself.

"It really depends on where you go," a member of the Hall of the Robe, who spoke on the condition of anonymity, said. "If the local lord is a good man, his constabulary force will be as well. If he's venal and cruel, chances are his law enforcement officials will be the same."

Inquisition officials claim they are not out to tarnish the reputation of the Royal Gendarmerie or any secular law enforcement agencies.

"We are very grateful to have

continued on page B8

AUSTRIAN EMPEROR REFUSES CONSIDERATION OF CONSTITUTIONAL MONARCHY

Rejects pleas from subjects regarding formation of semi-autonomous prefectures

Holy Roman Emperor Karl-Josef has dismissed a constitution drafted by a Hungarian assembly earlier this year and recently ratified by a Galician legislative body.

The constitution has also received support in the Italian hinterlands of the Austrian Empire. It calls for a limit to the emperor's authority, and for greater legislative control in outlying provinces by local elected assemblies.

In spite of the proposed constitution's popular support, the Emperor was dismissive.

"The power of a king is derived from God, not the will of the people" said Felix von Schwartzenberg, a spokesman for the Monarchy. "Emperor Karl Josef reserves His right to govern His subjects as He sees fit."

Many worry that this perceived inflexibility will de-stabilize the Habsburg territories. Russia, a long-time ally of Austria, is beginning to show impatience over the question of Serbian independence. Russia has long supported Serbian claims for independence, and has indicated she may not intervene on the behalf

continued on page A21

INSIDE

AN INTERVIEW WITH THE DUKE OF LORRAINE, SPEAKER OF THE SWORD

Next to His Majesty Louis XXII, the Hall of the Sword is the most powerful legislative body in France. Following the Restoration of the French Monarchy, the French aristocracy imposed a constitution on the king limiting the power of the crown with a parliament consisting of two bodies, the Hall of the Robe and the Hall of the Sword. Only nobles who can trace their titles to the First Crusade may join the ranks of the Sword. Few men have risen so meteorically and with so much panache among the Sword's ranks as David-Louis Plantard, the forty-ninth Duke of Lorraine. His bid to become Speaker of the Sword earlier this year went virtually unchallenged, and he has rallied a large coalition to the cause of French nationalism. The Duke made space in his busy schedule to talk to Le Journal about the secret of his success, how he deals with rivals, and why he's not really a politician. Read on to discover some of the inner workings of this fascinating and complex man.

Our first line of defense: légionnaires on parade. Lorraine first made a name for himself as a légionnare battalion commander in Indochina.

LJdL: Thanks very much for your time, Your Excellency.

L: You're more than welcome.

LJdL: Let's get right down to the point. Many people in His Majesty Louis XXII's Court have called you an agitator and have said that your warlike position on foreign affairs only antagonizes others. How do you respond to this?

L: I think it's important, vitally important, to realize the old ways are rapidly deteriorating. As is being so patently demonstrated in the Holy Roman Empire, *nationalism* is becoming a very potent force in the world. For France to maintain its position of power, we must harness the power of French people with the spirit of nationalism. That is the purpose of my speeches, and that is the goal of what some people might call a "warlike" foreign agenda.

LJdL: Right, let's talk about your military experience for a bit. You feel your experience as a field commander in the colonies has been extremely important in making you who you are, and has contributed to your success in the Hall of the Sword.

L: There is no question about it.

LJdL: And why is that, exactly?

L: A politician can't be truly great unless he has had the experience of commanding an army. The might of Rome, of Sparta, of every great civilization, has been predicated on military power. Serving in France's military is the greatest thing a young French man can do with his life. I still feel uncomfortable in a civilian suit, and I probably always will. I don't and never have considered myself a politician. I'm a man of action, and I believe my actions speak much more eloquently than my words.

LJdL: It's hard to believe politics aren't a major consideration of yours. It must be important to court members of the Hall of the Robe, for example, since their approval is needed to pass legislature into law.

L: I suppose obsequiousness is one way of approaching a problem, but it's not the only way. The secret to my success is really quite simple. I've never been afraid to throw down my gloves to stand up for what I think is best for France. That's why the Hall of the Sword is mine, and I intend to keep it that way.

I fight for what I believe in, and And I think the members of the Hall of the Robe will see that my proposed policies can only enhance France's power and prestige.

LJdL: Well, let's talk about your policies for a moment. Some people have said that a "hard-line" stance towards France's neighbors runs a risk of two or more nations declaring war at once. You don't think that's dangerous?

L: Well, let's look at the situation objectively. Does placating tyrants make a country safer? Is France belligerent, or are our neighbors? I can tell you, as a lord with holdings on the Alsace border, it is France and her citizens that act in ways conducive to peace and harmony. In the face of the constant warmongering on the part of the Kaiser, it is only natural that any French patriot would be concerned with keeping the Prussians in check.

History has shown that the Germans are an aggressive, belligerent race. The only thing they respect is cold steel. And if that is what they desire, they shall have it.

LJdL: Do you have a similar point of view on issues further East and South? Are you concerned about our border with Islam on the Iberian Peninsula?

L: Of course. Who wouldn't be?

LJdL: So, my original question: what if a war opens up on two fronts? A war with Prussia in the East, and a war with the Cordovan Caliphate on the Spanish border?

L: The solution is perfectly simple. Some members of the Hall of the Robe have said we must show a conciliatory attitude towards our neighbors. But nothing could more harmful for France in the long run. I believe we must fortify ourselves, make France strong enough to fight on two fronts at once.

LJdL: You don't think that's an impossible task?

L: Not only do I think it's possible, I think it is absolutely vital for France's future. And let's not forget that the Holy Roman Empire is a shadow of its former self. So the Ottomans are another, unknown factor in the mix. The Balkans are a political tinderbox, and no one knows the real strength of the Sultan's forces. I cannot stress enough how important it is France be prepared for whatever the future holds.

LJdL: But your admittedly militaristic stance has incurred the displeasure of the King. Since he appoints positions on the Hall of the Robe, won't you always find yourself outvoted? What makes you think you can stand up to the Hall of the Robe and the King?

L: Well, that's a very good point: if both the King and the Robe vote against a bill it will not become law, even if the Sword approves it. Since the King appoints positions to the Hall of the Robe, the Robe will always be filled with his supporters and he will therefore always have a two-thirds majority over the Sword.

LJdL: Isn't that true?

L: Absolutely not. I think you're taking certain things for granted. For instance, until I entered the the Hall of the Sword, it was divided twenty different ways due to petty feuds amongst the great houses of France. Political analysts thought it was completely impossible for the ancient houses of France to organize ourselves into a force to be reckoned with.

LJdL: That's true.

L: And it's true that the King appoints the members of the Hall of the Robe. Even so, the Robe is not necessarily a rubber stamp for the King. The members of the Robe have a right, a duty, to make their own choices and to vote with their consciences. That's exactly what I'm hoping will happen. The King has enjoyed virtual despotism since the Restoration, but I think all that is about to change.

LJdL: Our time is just about up, Your Excellency. Any closing remarks?

L: Just that French culture is very precious to me, as it is to all of my countrymen, and I fervently hope our nation can come together and meet the storm that's coming head on.

> **"Not only do I think it's possible, I think it is absolutely vital for France's future."**

CHAPTER FIVE
SHADOWS BENEATH THE CITY

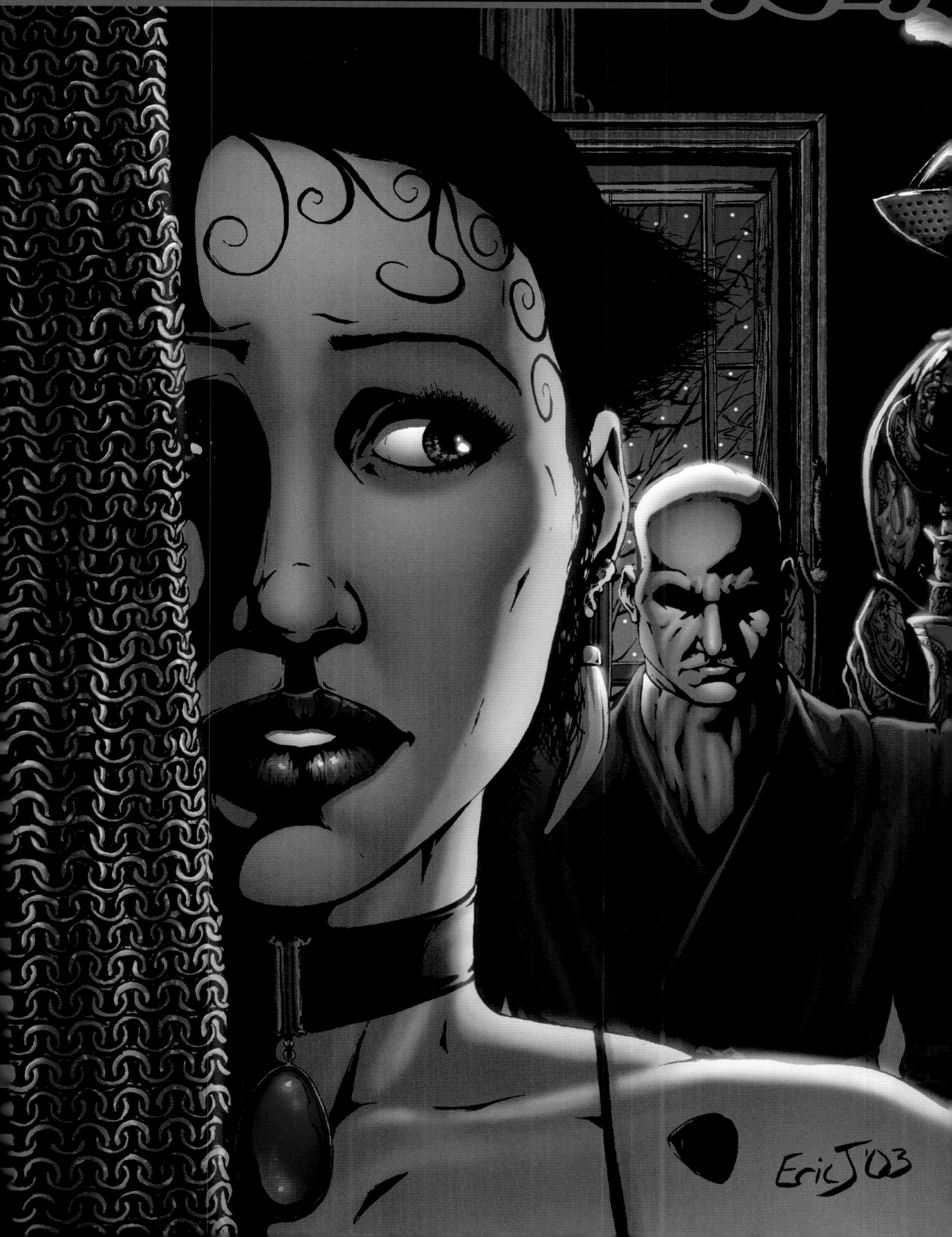
EricJ'03

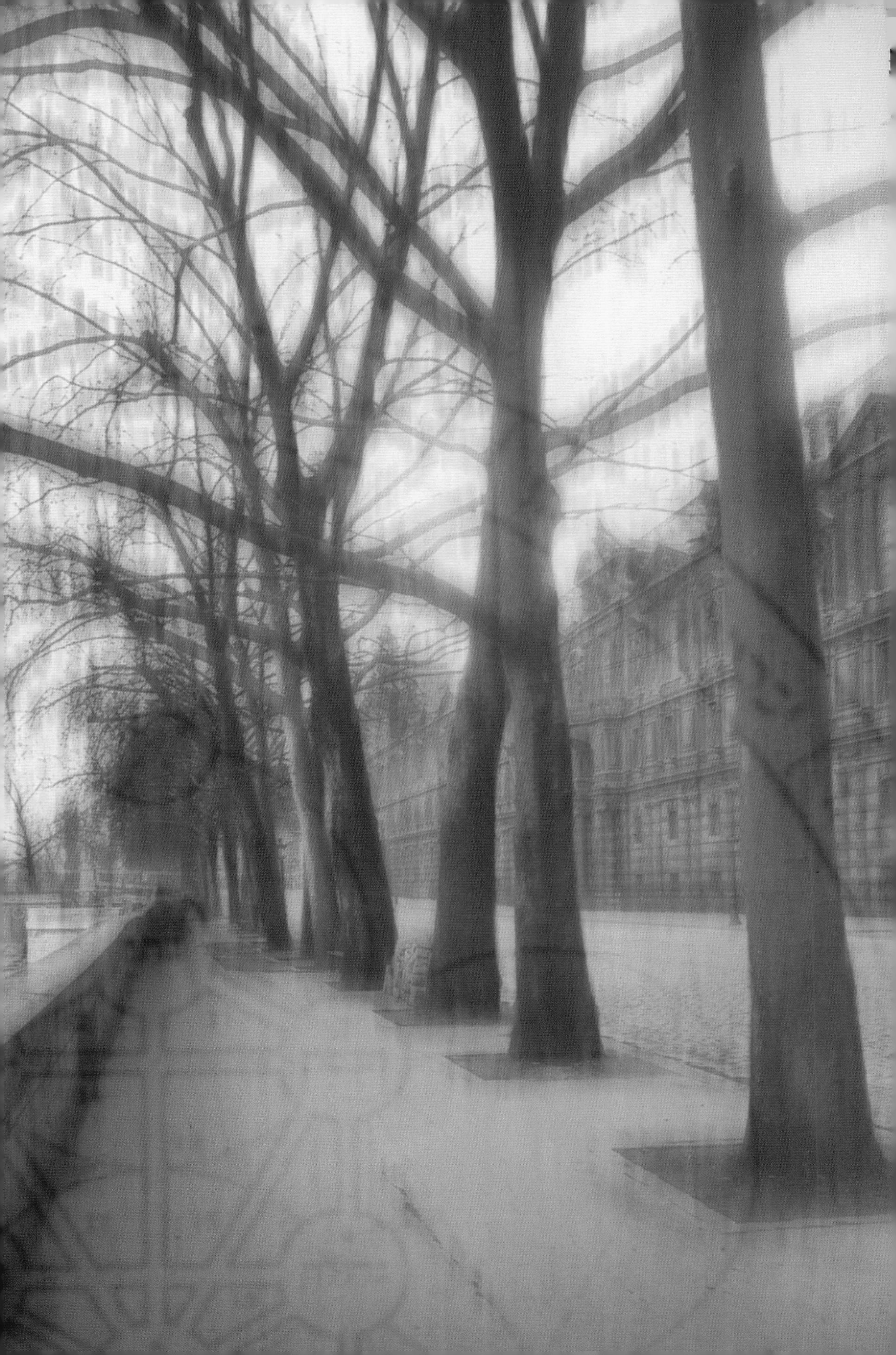

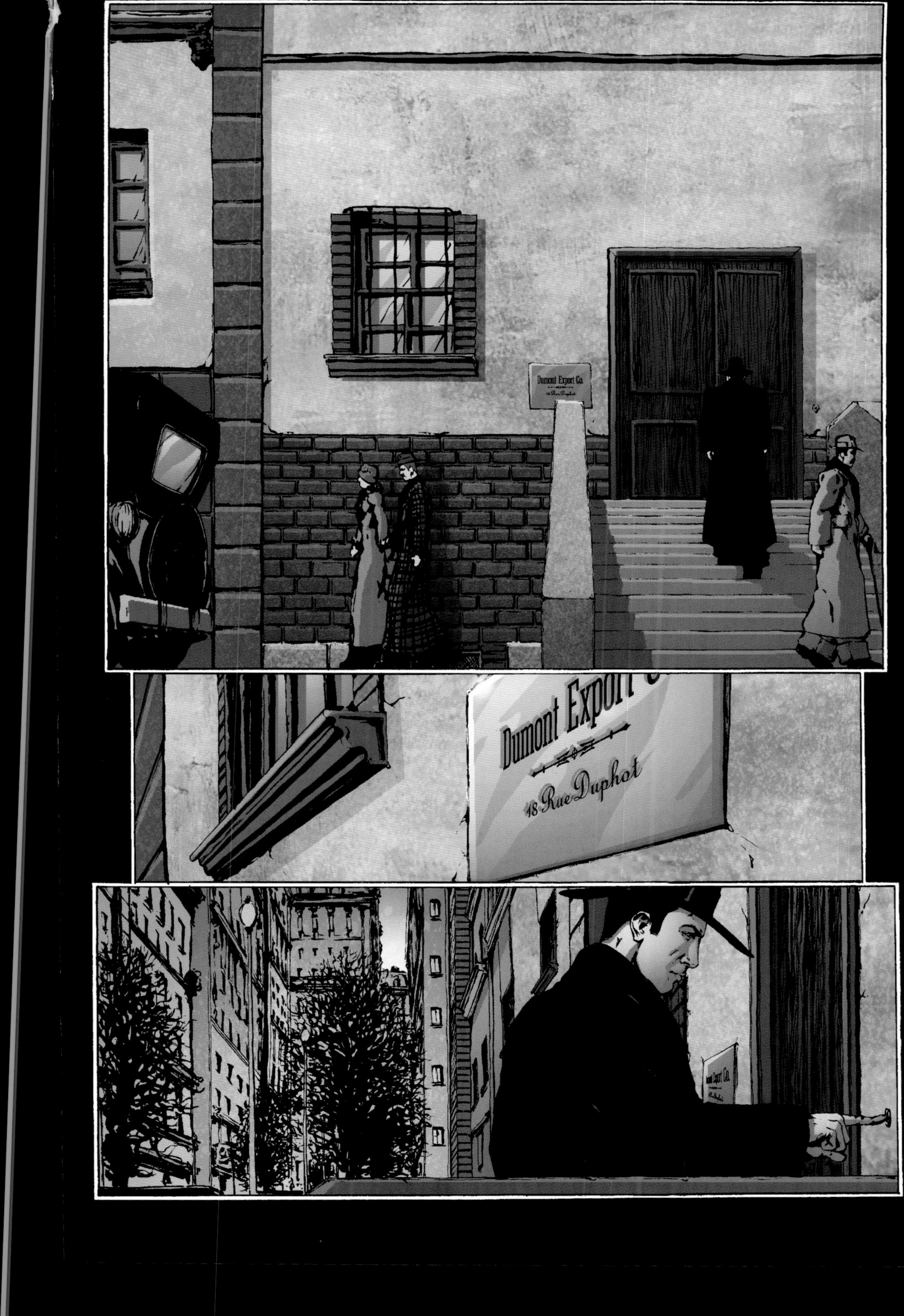
Dumont Export Co.
18 Rue Duphot
Dumont Export
18 Rue Duphot
Dumont Export Co.

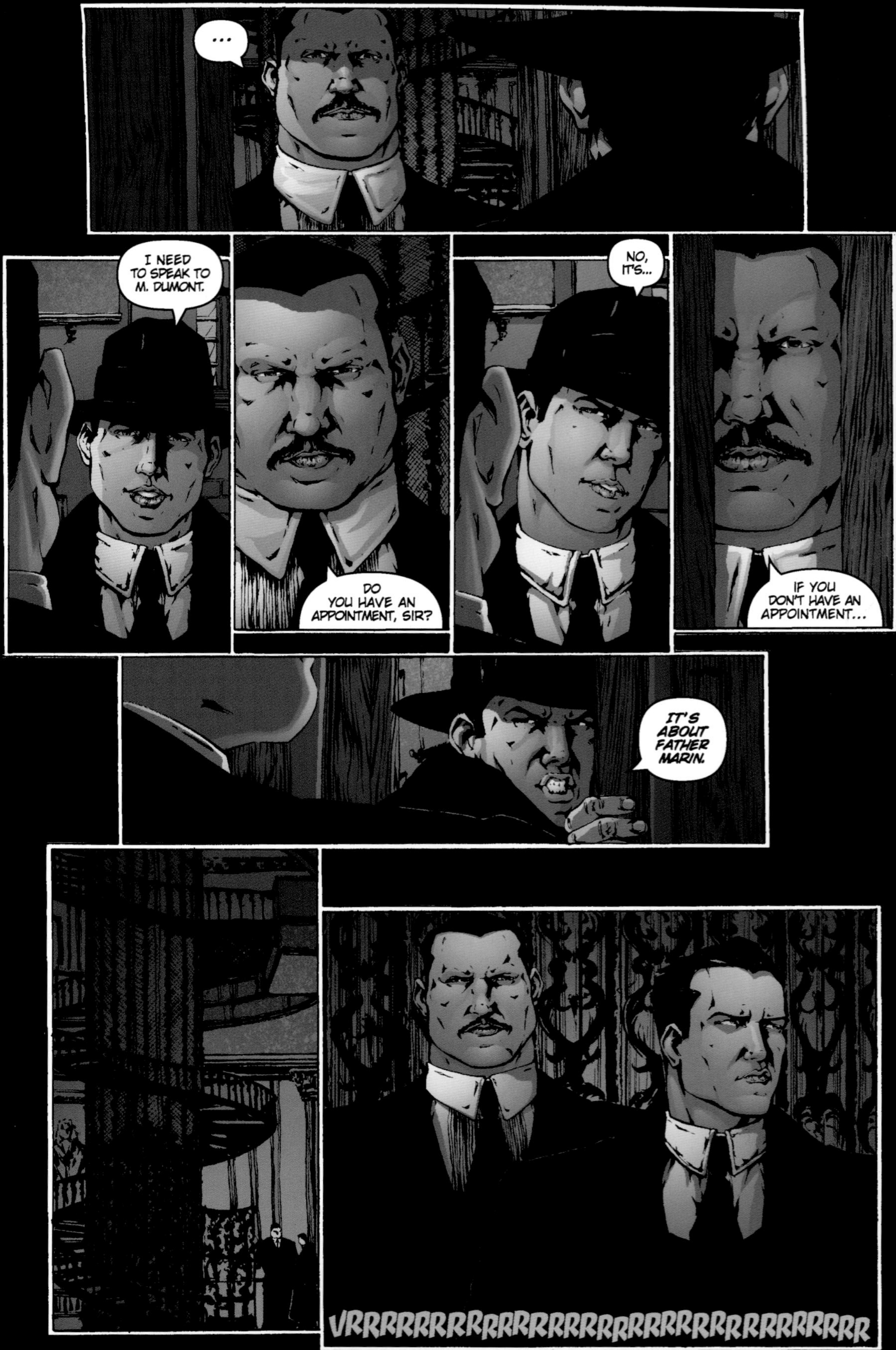
...
I NEED TO SPEAK TO M. DUMONT.
DO YOU HAVE AN APPOINTMENT, SIR?
NO, IT'S...
IF YOU DON'T HAVE AN APPOINTMENT...
IT'S ABOUT FATHER MARIN.
VRRRRRRRRRRRRRRRRRRRRRRRRRRRRRRRRRRRR

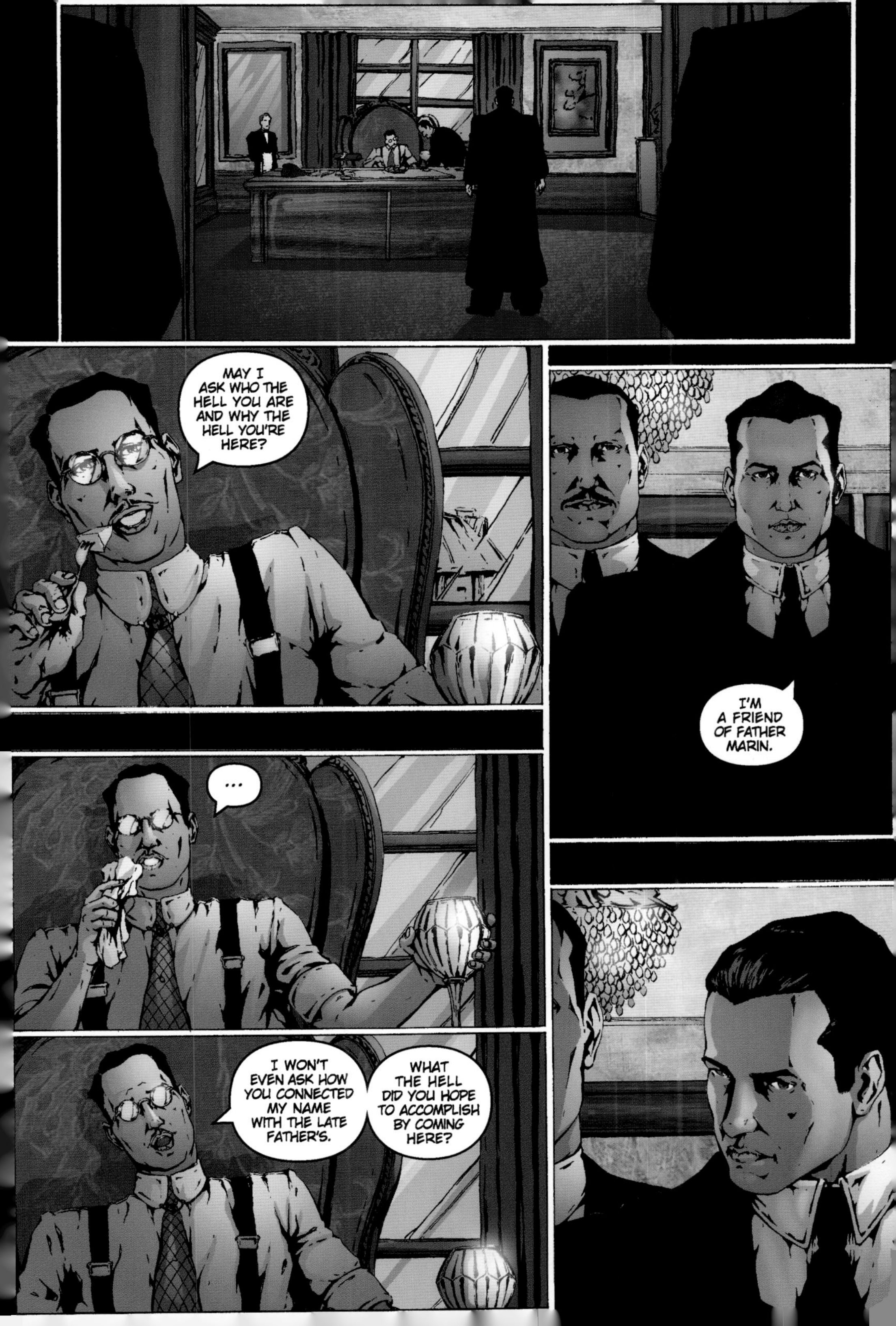
MAY I ASK WHO THE HELL YOU ARE AND WHY THE HELL YOU'RE HERE?
I'M A FRIEND OF FATHER MARIN.
...
I WON'T EVEN ASK HOW YOU CONNECTED MY NAME WITH THE LATE FATHER'S.
WHAT THE HELL DID YOU HOPE TO ACCOMPLISH BY COMING HERE?

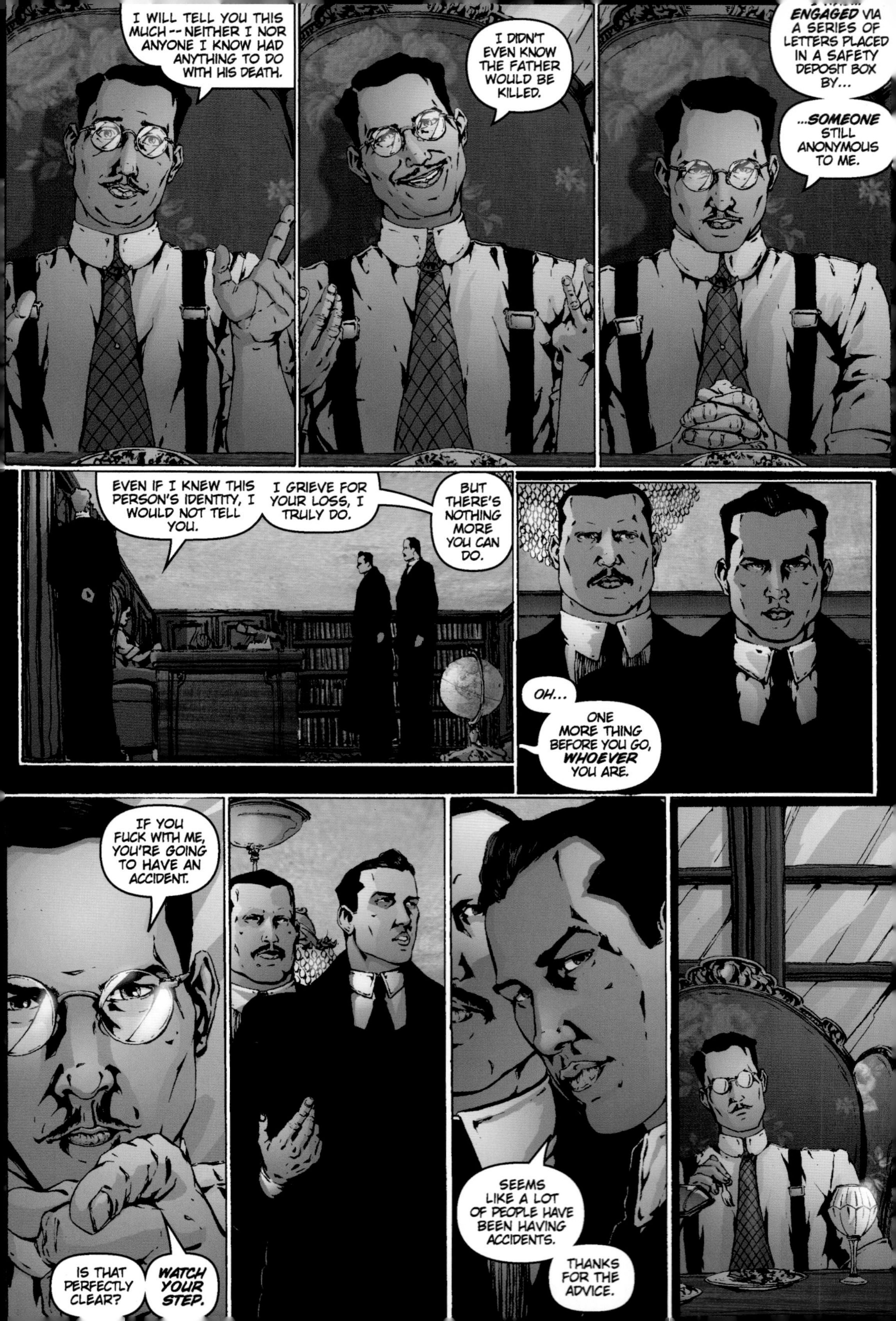
I WILL TELL YOU THIS MUCH -- NEITHER I NOR ANYONE I KNOW HAD ANYTHING TO DO WITH HIS DEATH.
I DIDN'T EVEN KNOW THE FATHER WOULD BE KILLED.
ENGAGED VIA A SERIES OF LETTERS PLACED IN A SAFETY DEPOSIT BOX BY...
...SOMEONE STILL ANONYMOUS TO ME.
EVEN IF I KNEW THIS PERSON'S IDENTITY, I WOULD NOT TELL YOU.
I GRIEVE FOR YOUR LOSS, I TRULY DO.
BUT THERE'S NOTHING MORE YOU CAN DO.
OH...
ONE MORE THING BEFORE YOU GO, WHOEVER YOU ARE.
IF YOU FUCK WITH ME, YOU'RE GOING TO HAVE AN ACCIDENT.
IS THAT PERFECTLY CLEAR?
WATCH YOUR STEP.
SEEMS LIKE A LOT OF PEOPLE HAVE BEEN HAVING ACCIDENTS.
THANKS FOR THE ADVICE.

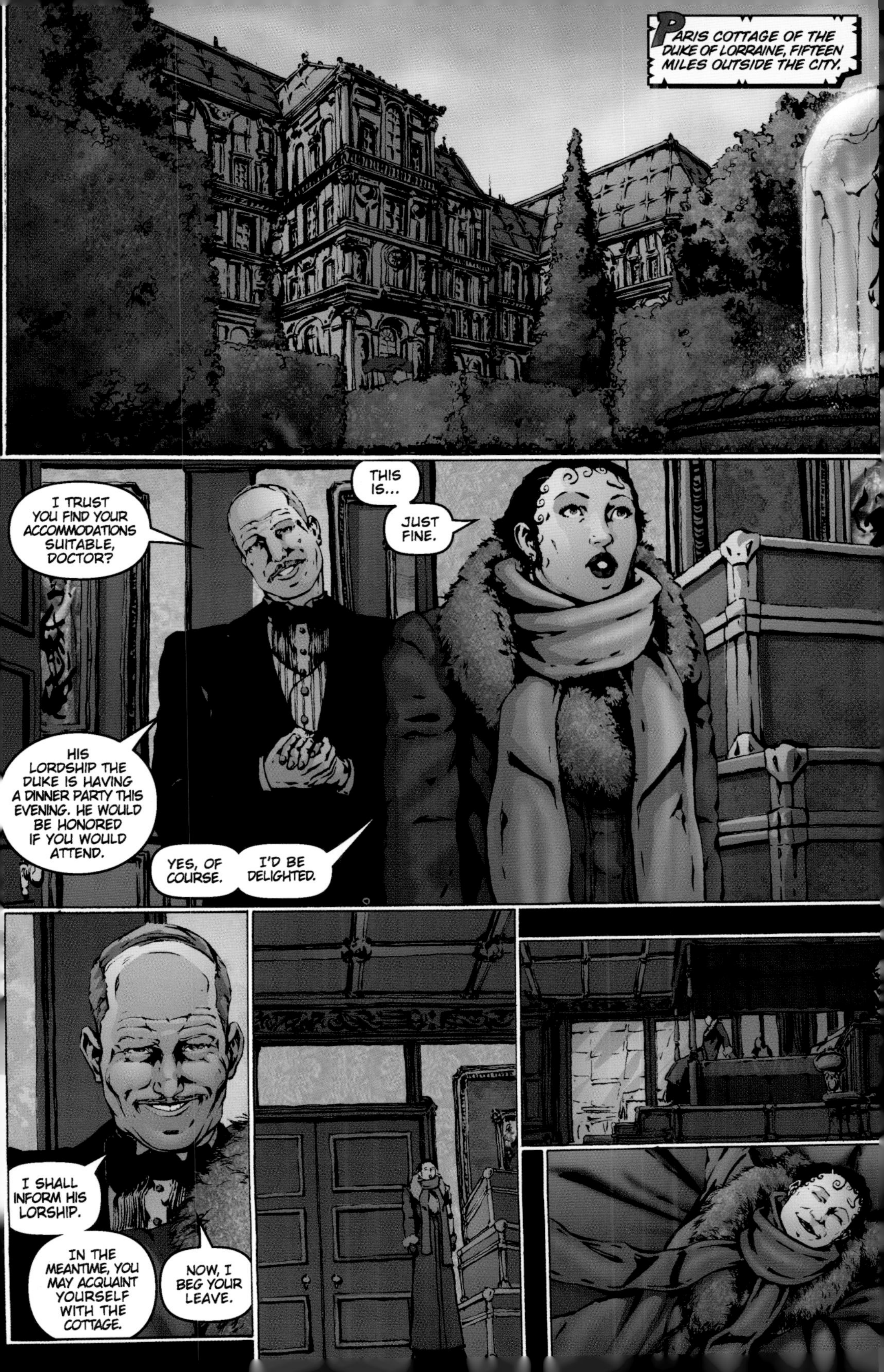
PARIS COTTAGE OF THE DUKE OF LORRAINE, FIFTEEN MILES OUTSIDE THE CITY.
I TRUST YOU FIND YOUR ACCOMMODATIONS SUITABLE, DOCTOR?
THIS IS...
JUST FINE.
HIS LORDSHIP THE DUKE IS HAVING A DINNER PARTY THIS EVENING. HE WOULD BE HONORED IF YOU WOULD ATTEND.
YES, OF COURSE.
I'D BE DELIGHTED.
I SHALL INFORM HIS LORSHIP.
IN THE MEANTIME, YOU MAY ACQUAINT YOURSELF WITH THE COTTAGE.
NOW, I BEG YOUR LEAVE.

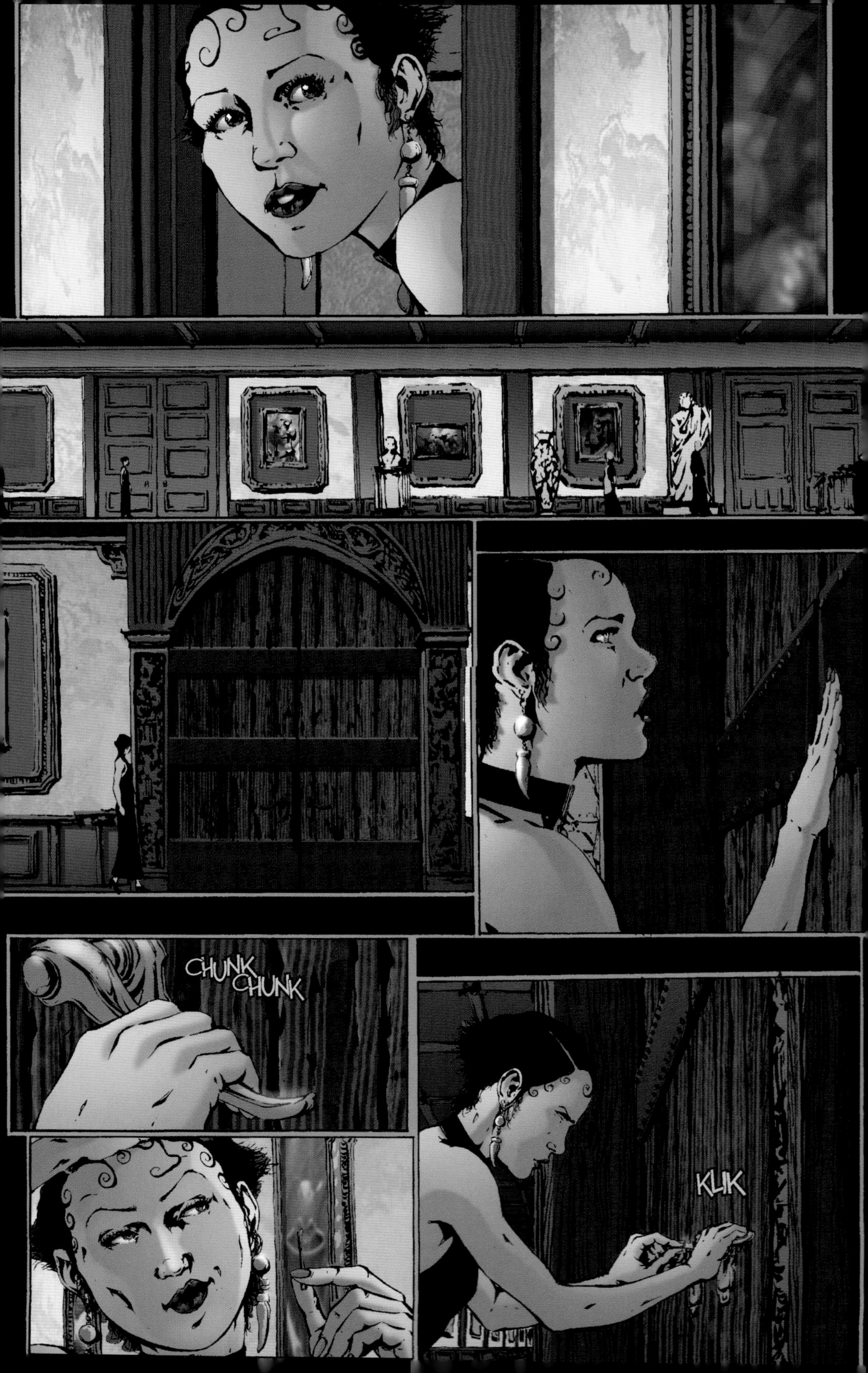
CHUNK
CHUNK
KLIK

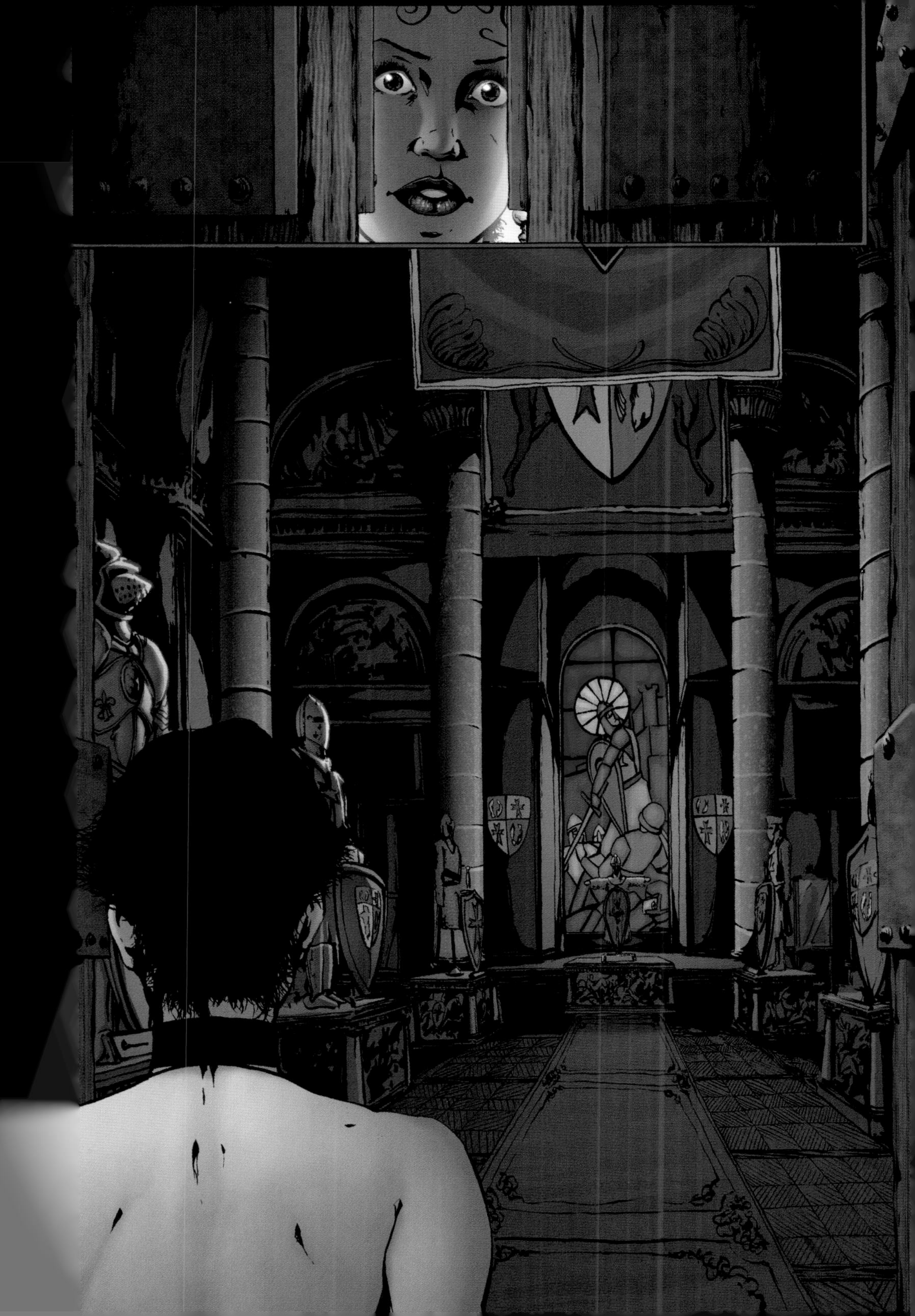

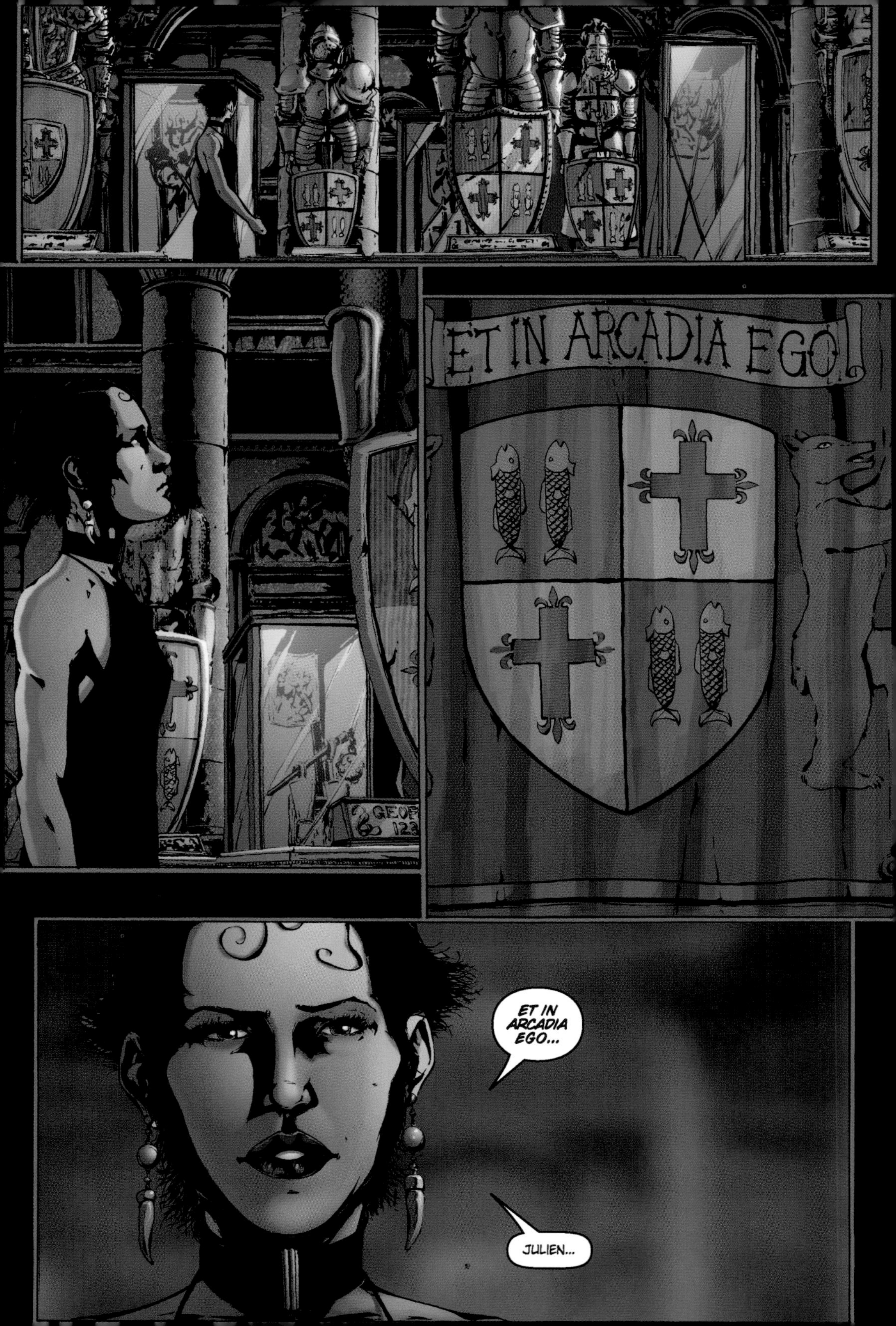
ET IN ARCADIA EGO
GEOR
123
ET IN ARCADIA EGO...
JULIEN...

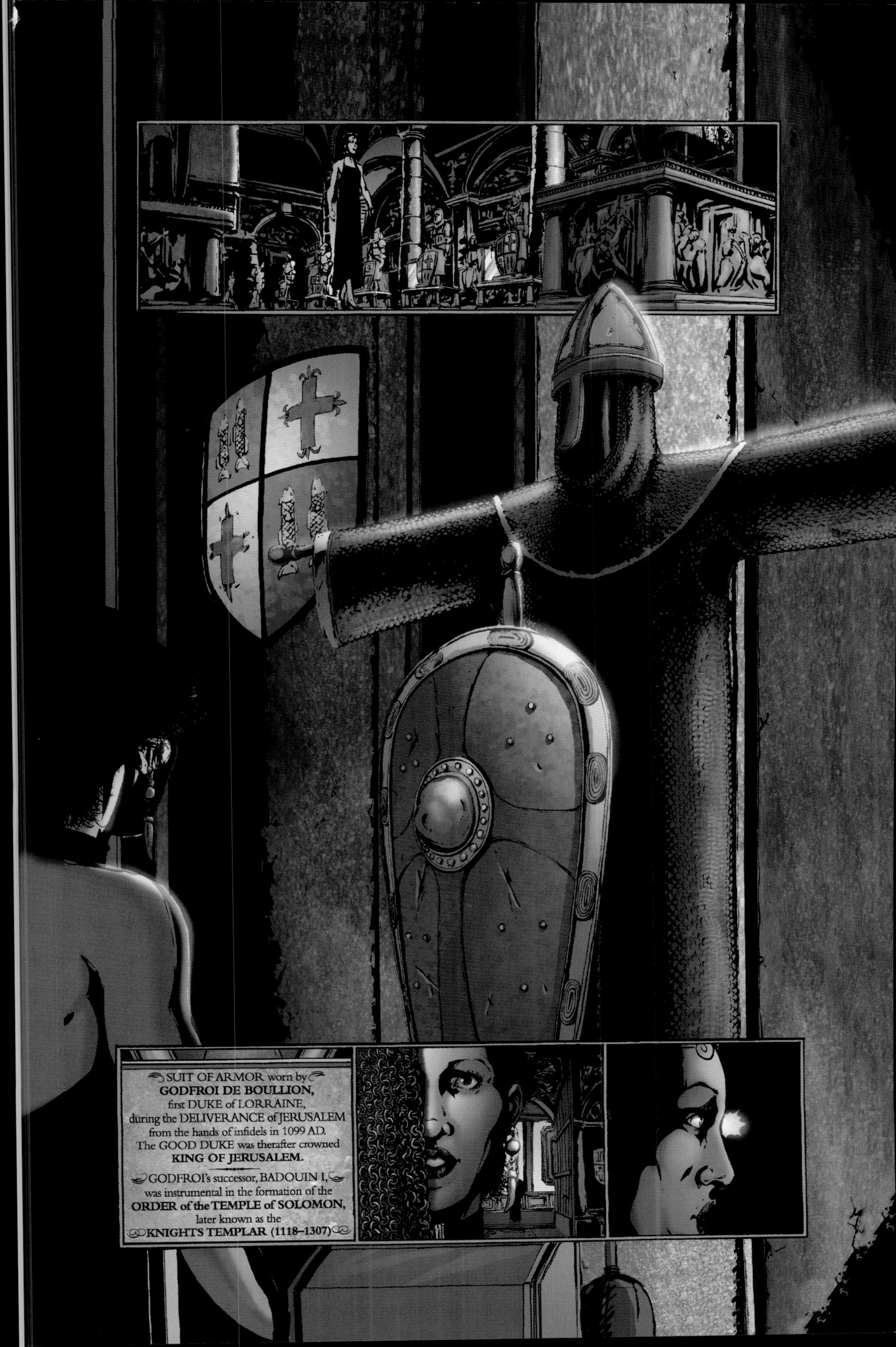
SUIT OF ARMOR worn by
GODFROI DE BOULLION,
first DUKE of LORRAINE,
during the DELIVERANCE of JERUSALEM
from the hands of infidels in 1099 AD.
The GOOD DUKE was therafter crowned
KING OF JERUSALEM.
GODFROI's successor, BADOUIN I,
was instrumental in the formation of the
ORDER of the TEMPLE of SOLOMON,
later known as the
KNIGHTS TEMPLAR (1118–1307)

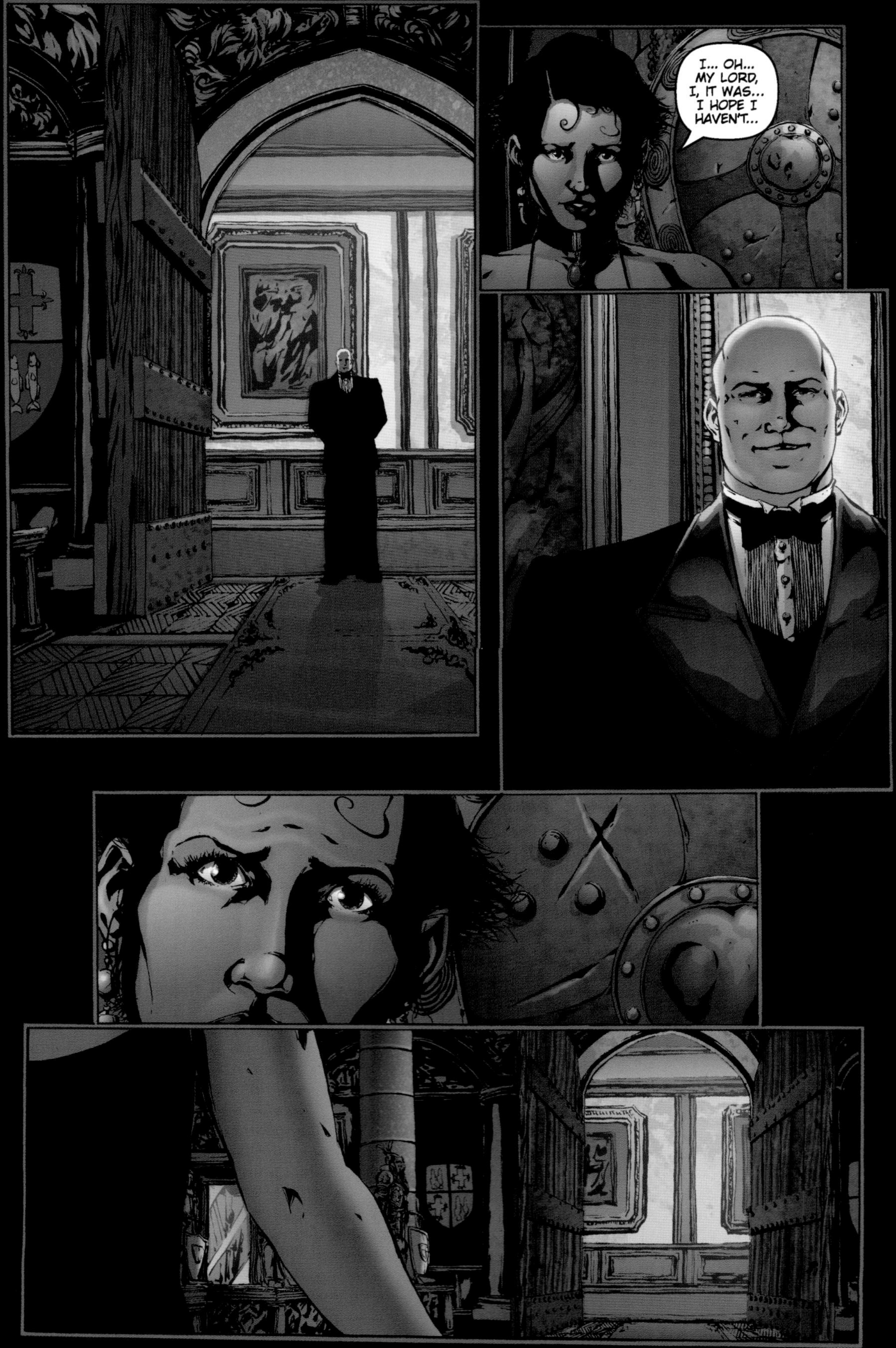
I... OH... MY LORD, I, IT WAS... I HOPE I HAVEN'T...

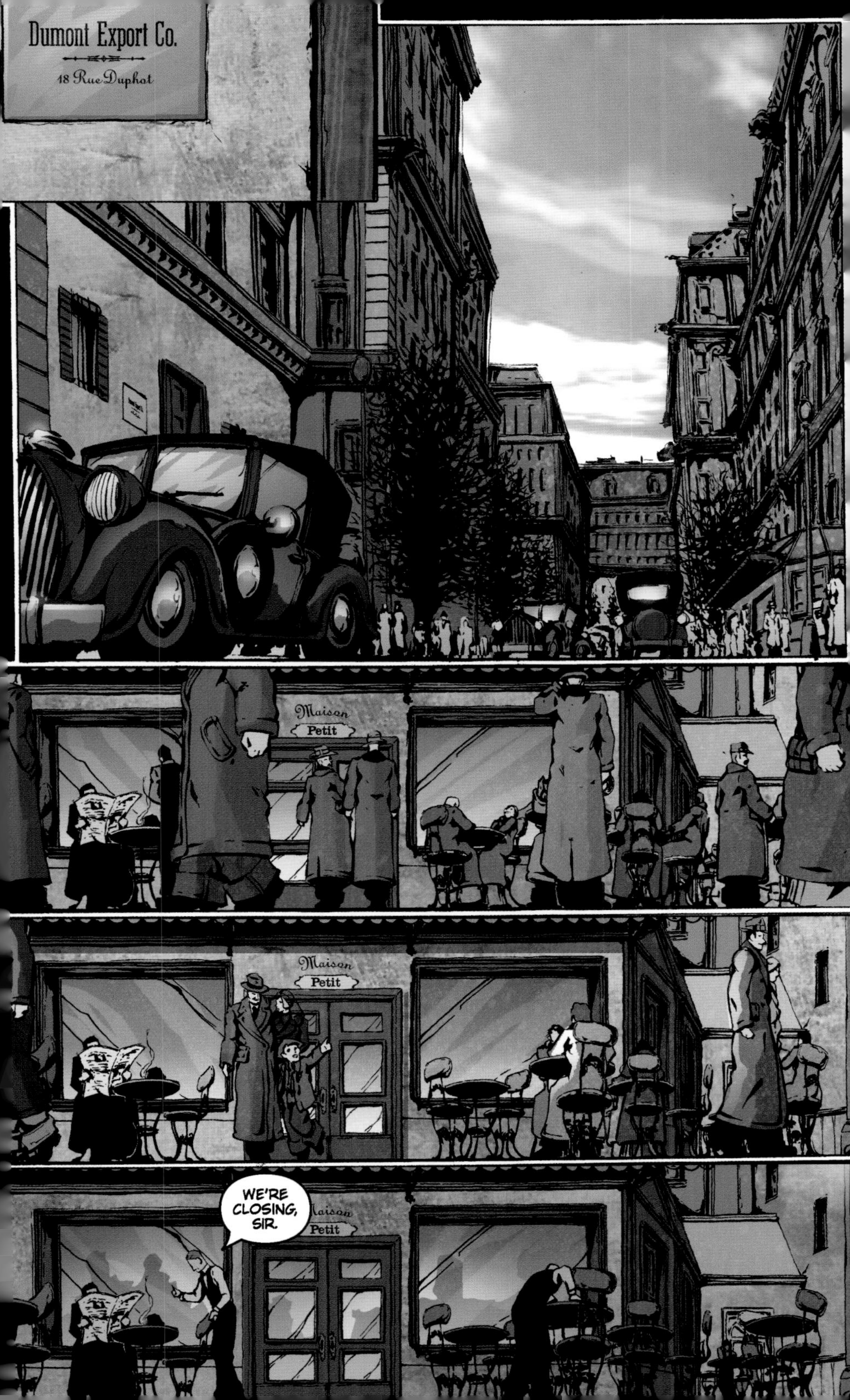
Dumont Export Co.
18 Rue Duphot
Maison
Petit
Maison
Petit
WE'RE CLOSING, SIR.
Maison
Petit

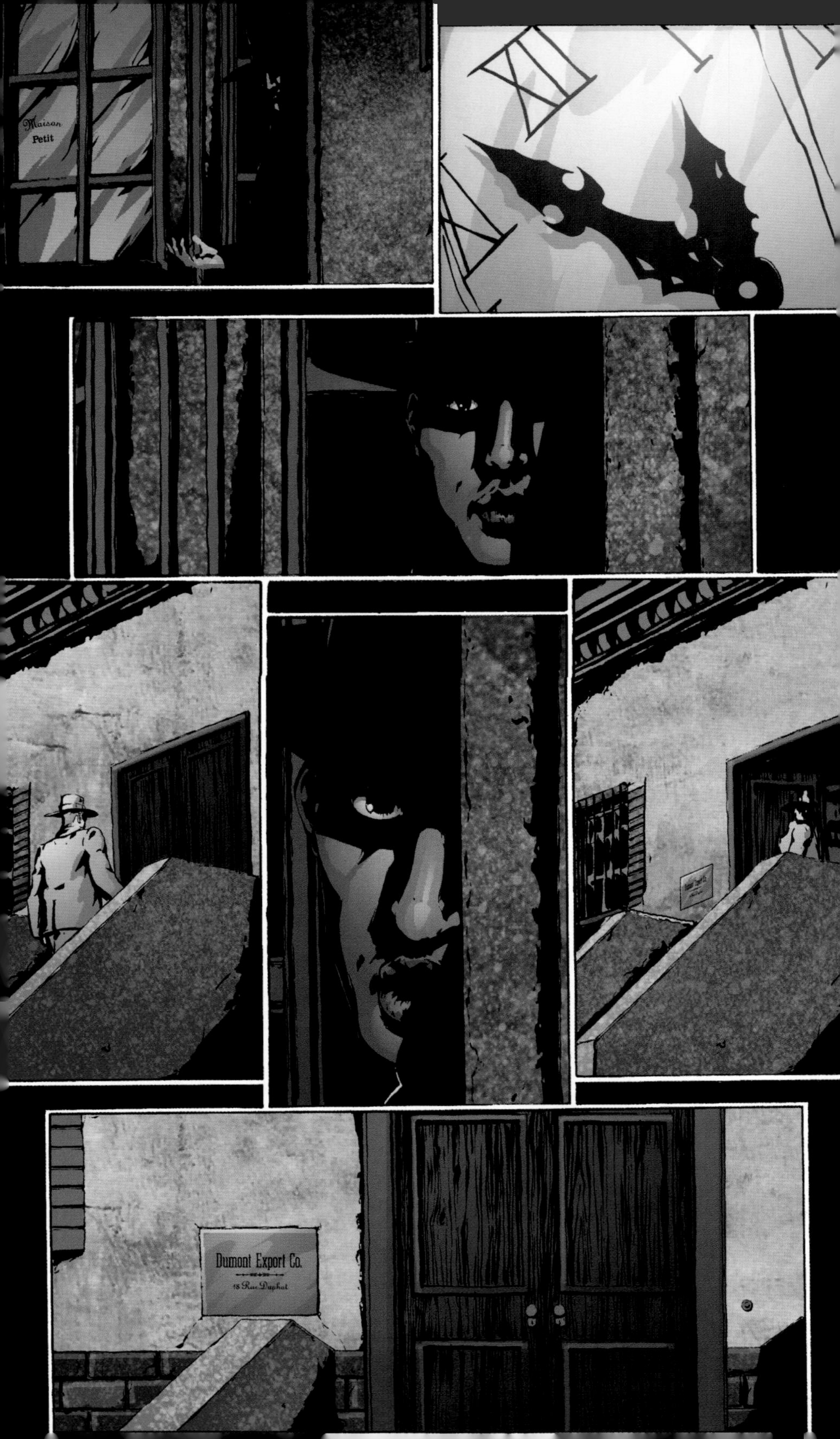
Maison
Petit
Dumont Export Co.
18 Rue Duphot

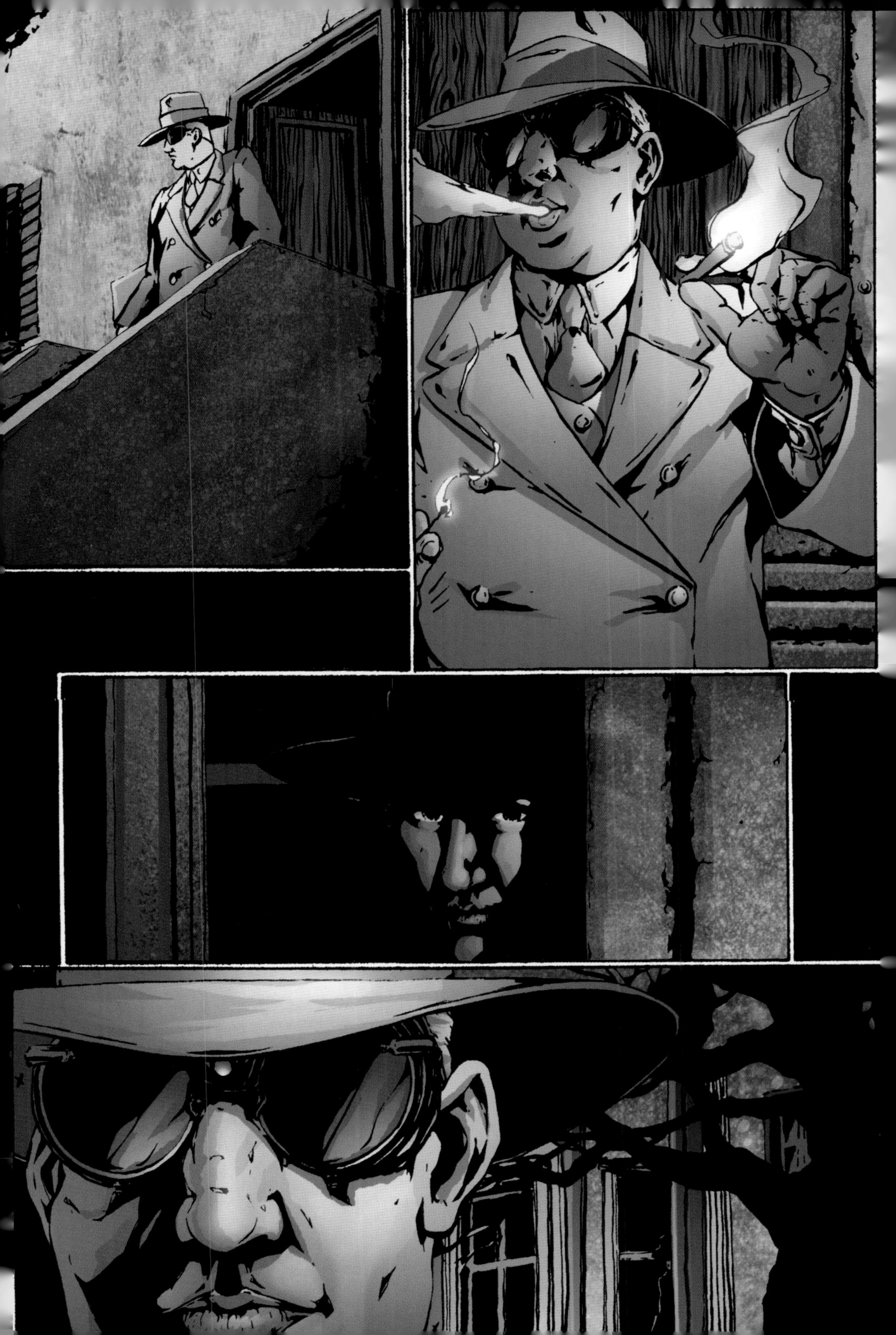

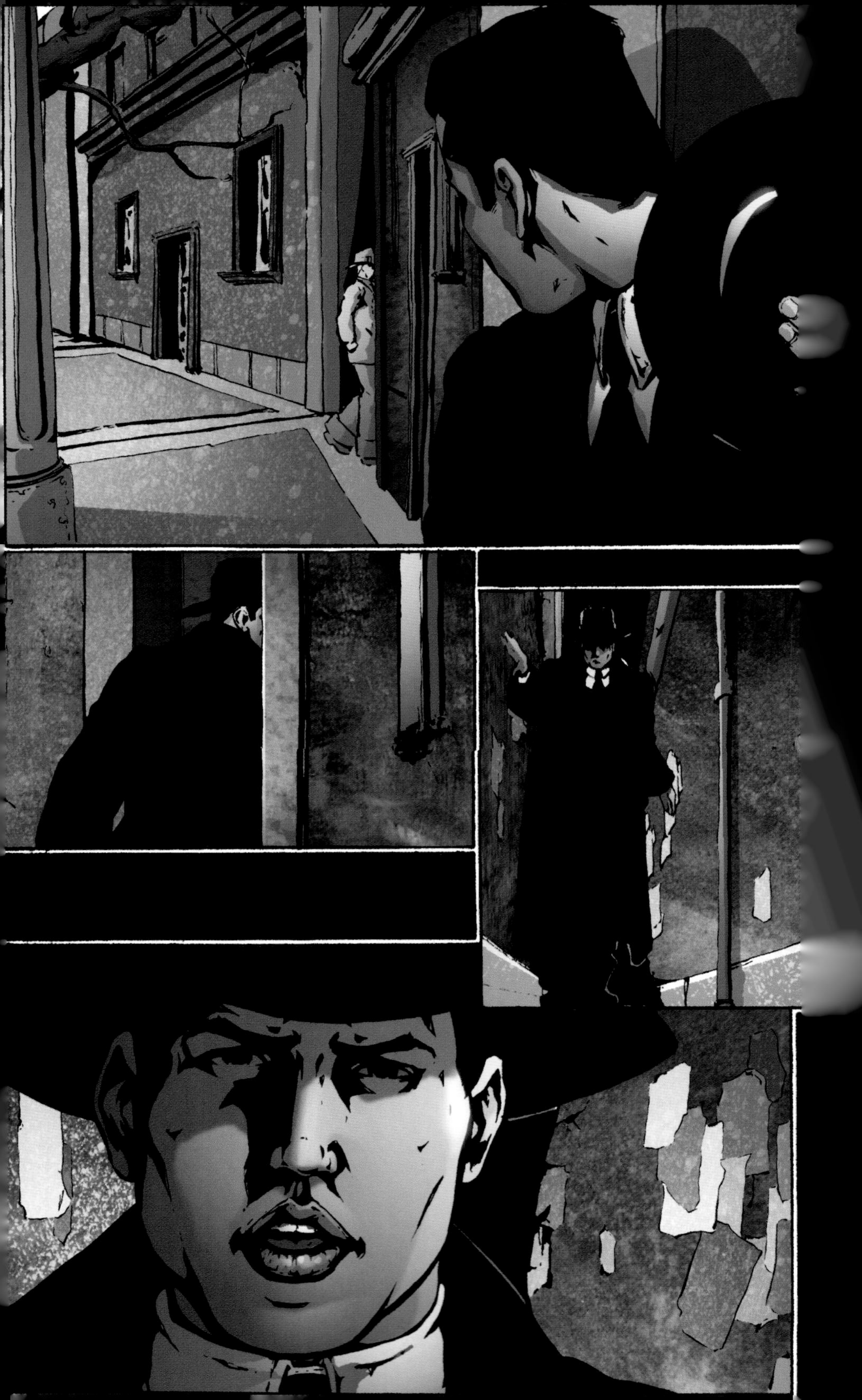

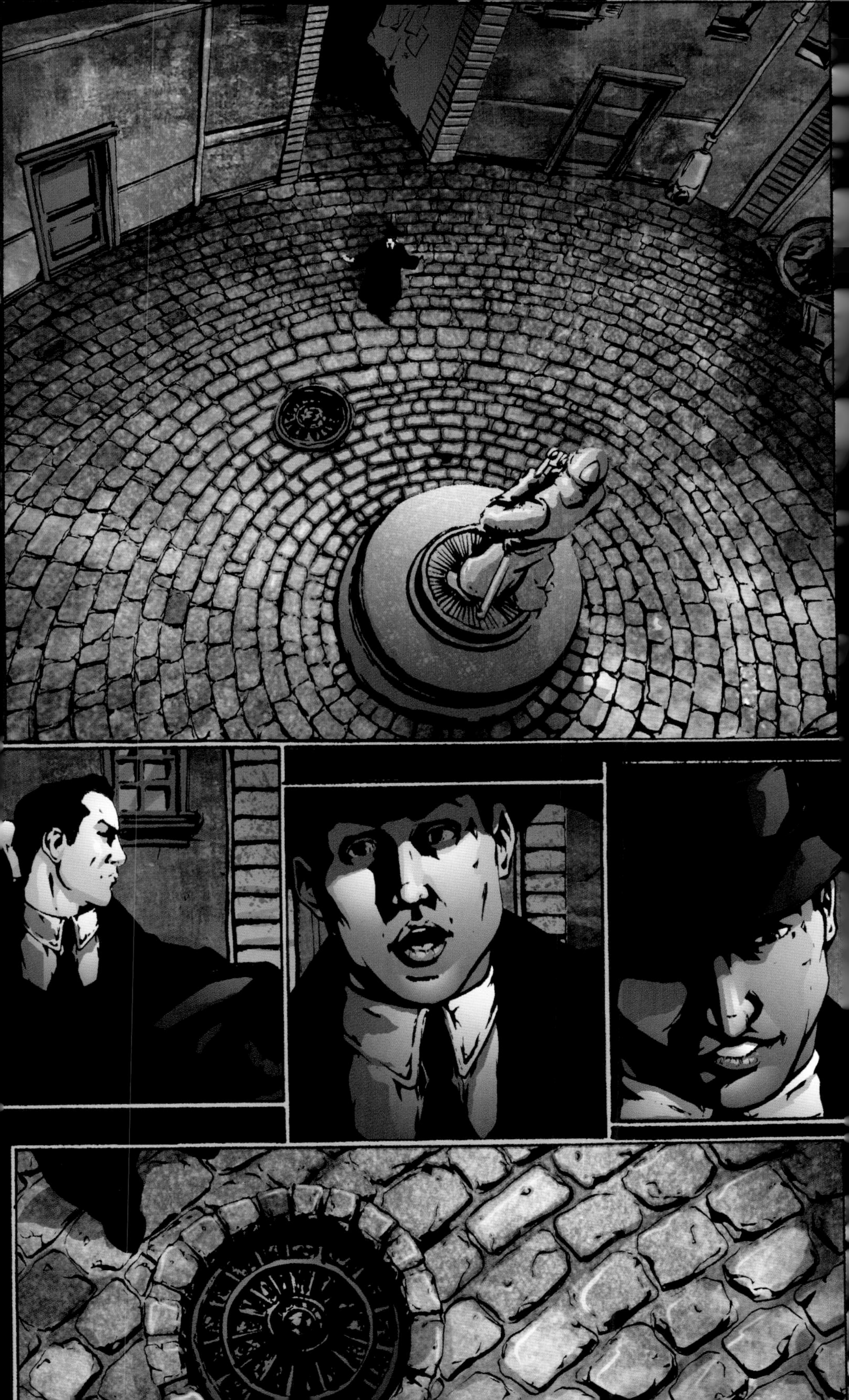

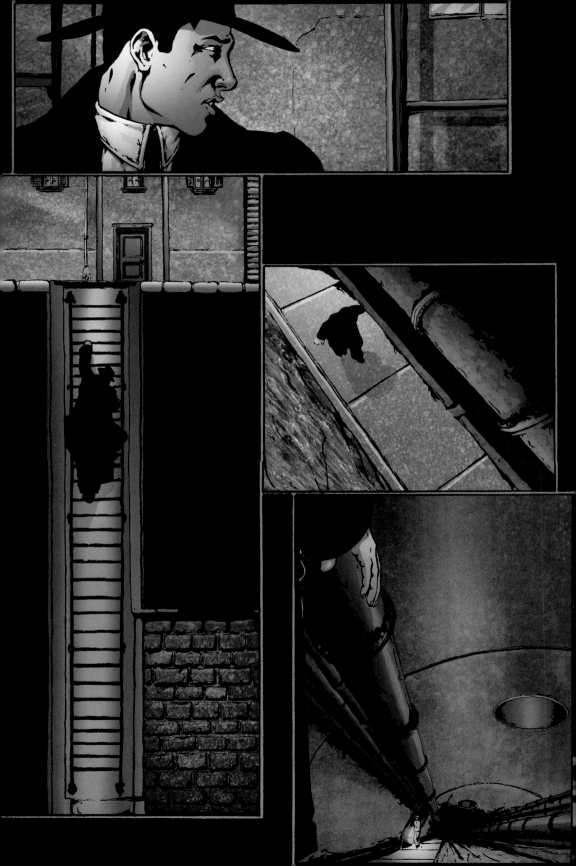

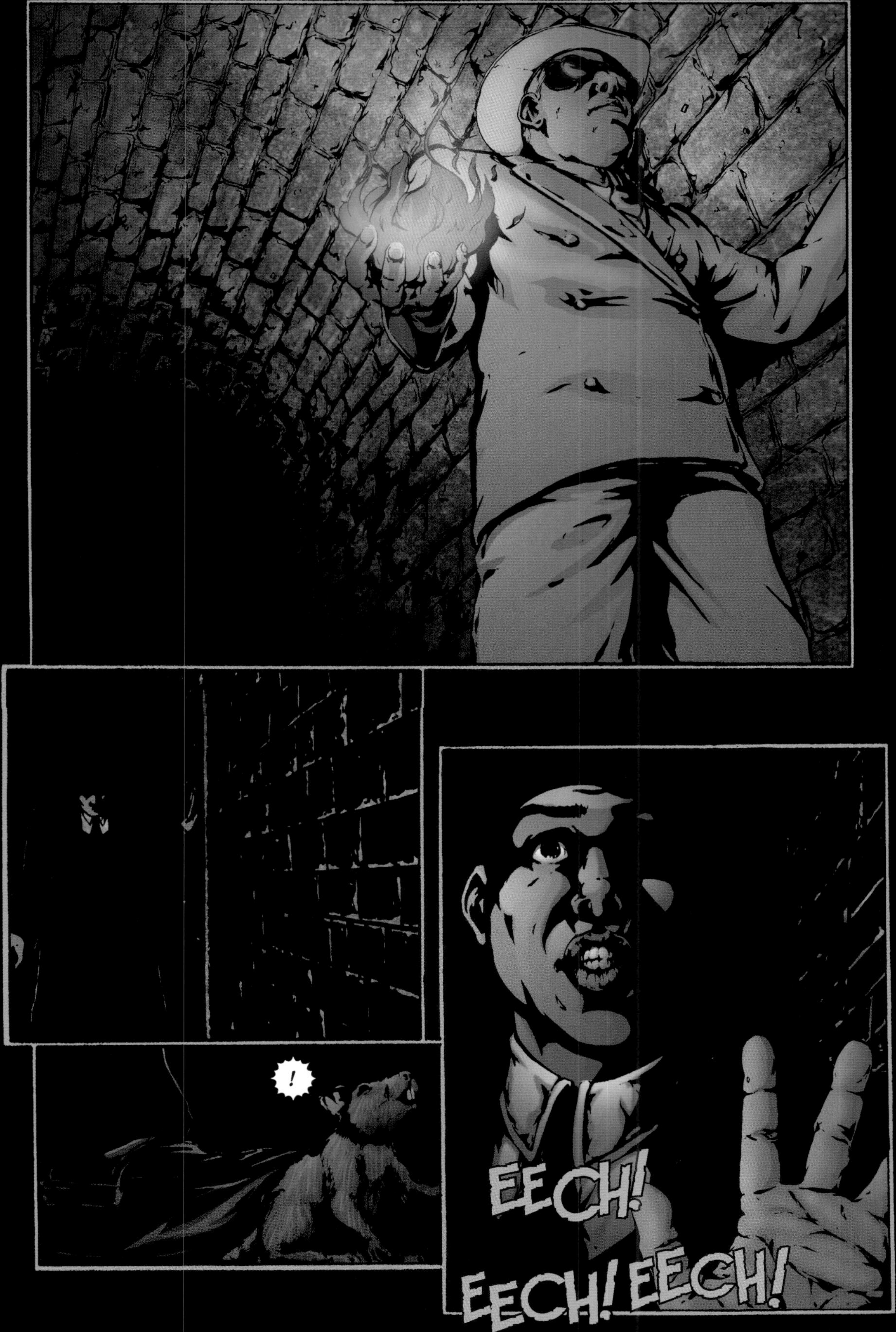
!
EECH!
EECH! EECH!

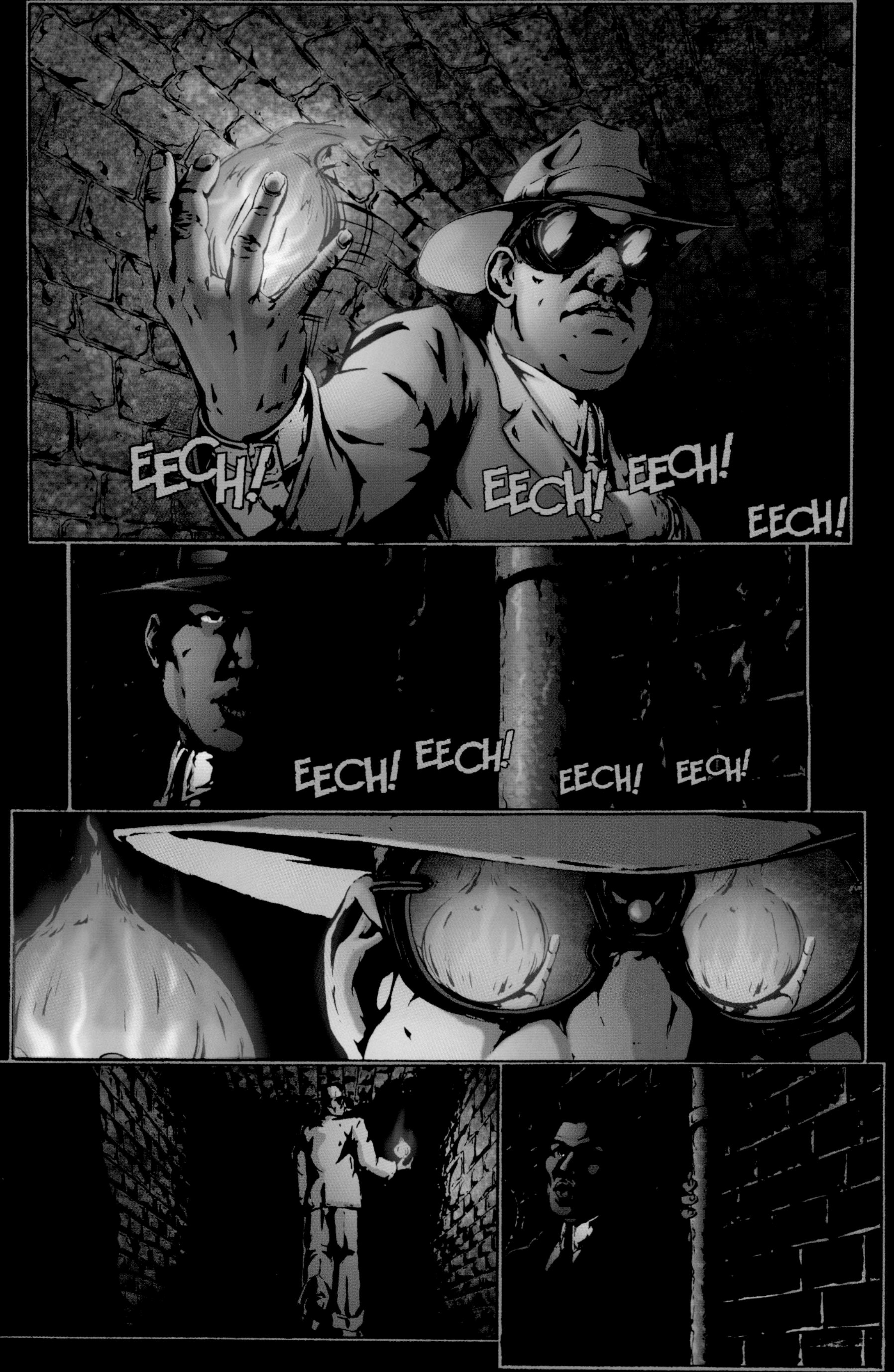
EECH!
EECH!
EECH!
EECH!
EECH!
EECH!
EECH!
EECH!

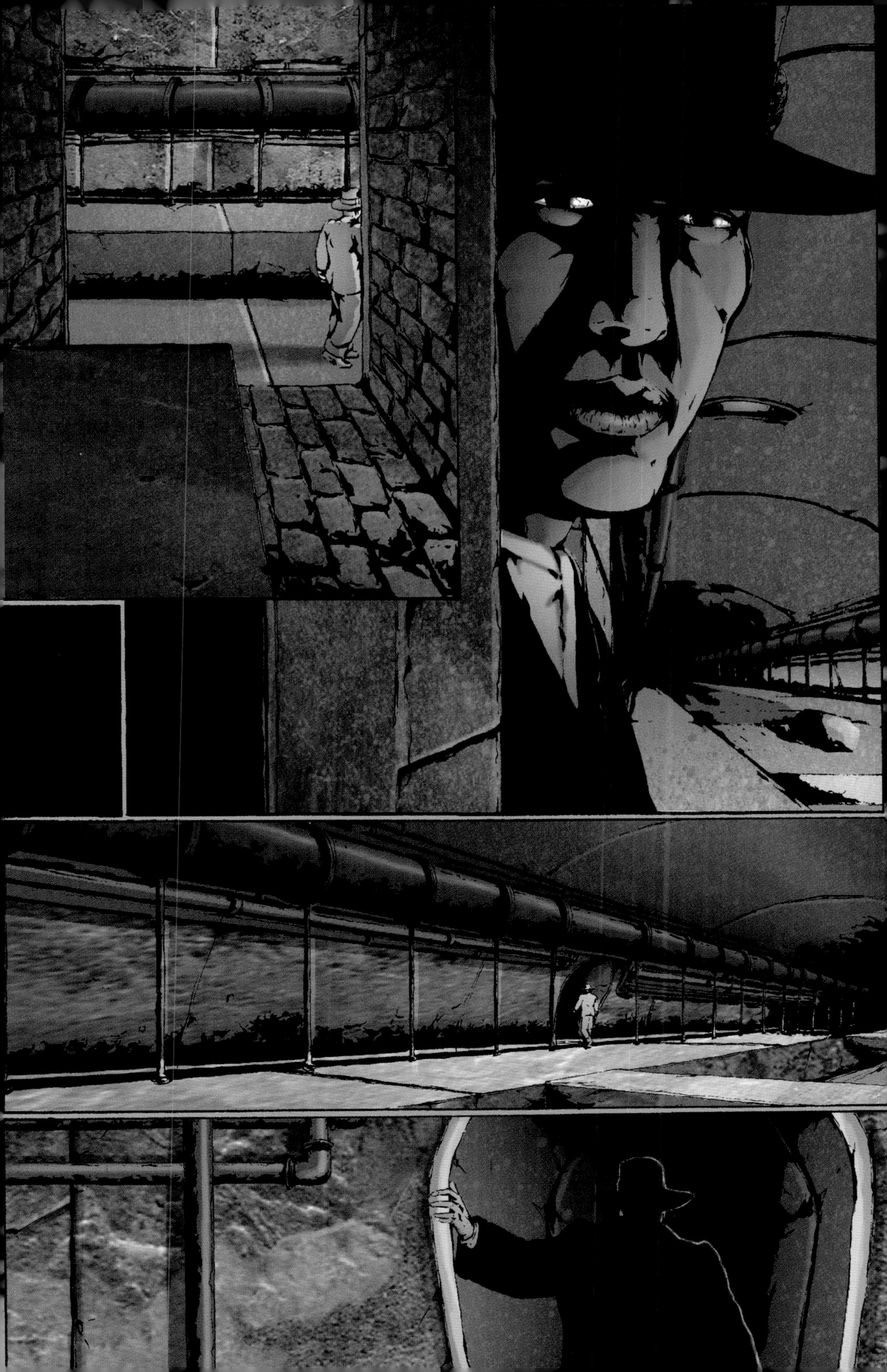

SHHHHHHHHHHHHHHHHHHHHHHHHHHHHHH

SHHHHHHHHHHHHHHHHHHHHHHHHHHHHHHHHHHHHHHHHH

HHHHHHHHHHHHHHHHHHHHHHHH

SHHHHHHHHHHHHHHHHHHHHHHHHH

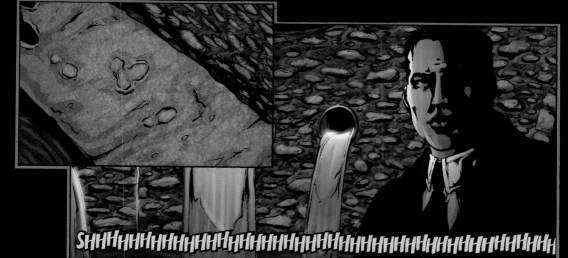

SHHHHHHHHHHHHHHHHHHHHHHHHHHHHHHHHHHHHHHHHH

SHHHHHHHHHHHHHHHHHHHHHH

SHHHHHHHHHHHHHHHHHHHHHHHHH

KLIK

SHHHHHHHHHHHHHHHHHHHHHHHHHHHHHHHHH

KKKKKK

SHHHHHHHHHHHHHHHH

SHHHHHHHHHHHHHHHHHHHHHHHHH

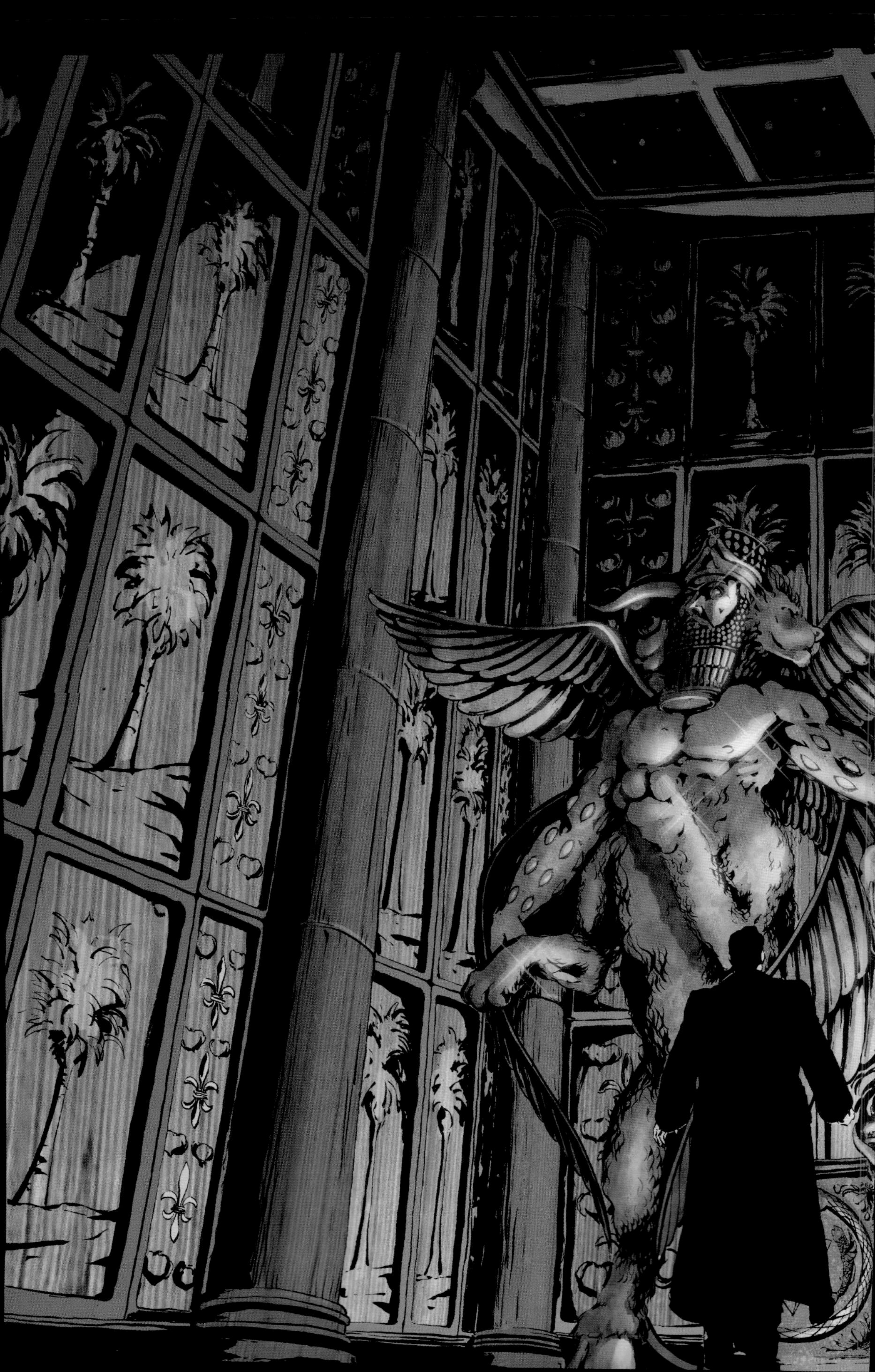

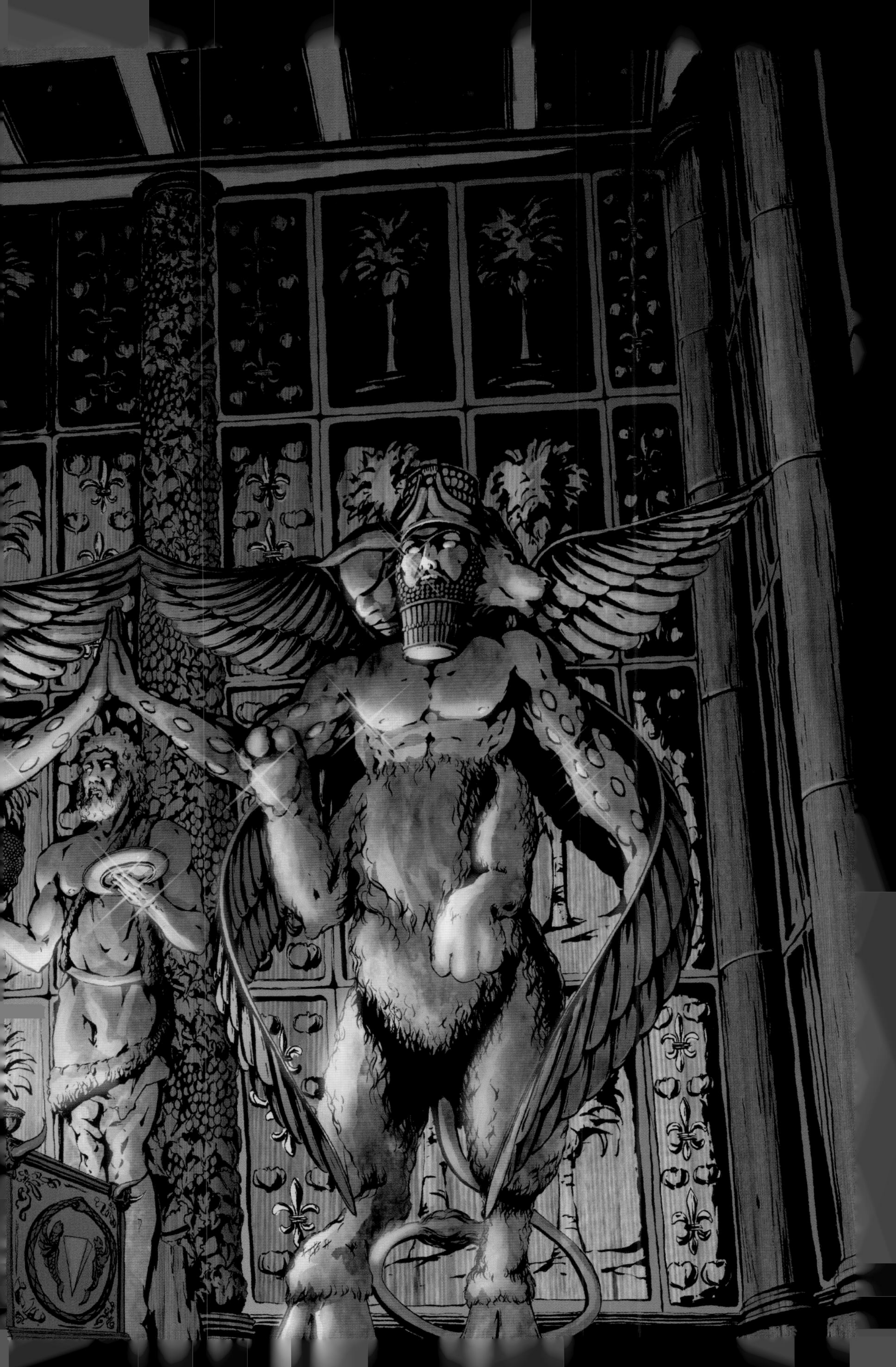

Le Journal de la Liberté

Paris's leading anglophone newspaper • vol. 205, no. 99 • Oct. 22, MCMXXXIII

Editors in Chief: M. Tait Bergstrom, M. Matthew Pasteris. **Story Editor:** M. Arvid Nelson. **Art Editors:** M. EricJ, M. Jeromy Cox. **Photography Editor:** M. Alexander Waldman. **Layout Supervisor:** M. William Kartalopoulos. **Editors Emeritus:** M. Clark A. Smith, M. Howard P. Lovecraft, M. Robert E. Howard. Redacted by the Holy Inquisition under the direction of His Excellency Archbishop Emile-Jean Ireneaux. Le Journal de Liberté is printed under the benign auspices of his most puissant majesty KING LOUIS XXII of FRANCE. GOD SAVE THE KING.

Papal Seal

of Approval

JUNIOR MEMBER OF THE HALL OF THE ROBE ARRESTED FOR WITCHCRAFT

Friends, Family Express Disbelief and Shock at Surprise Arrest, Crown Pledges Support

This ordinary-looking doorway hides an entrance to an illegal alchemical laboratory, according to Inquisition officials. Photo: Eugène Atget, staff photographer

Paris – Until his arrest late yesterday afternoon, Baron Marcel Brassac was a rising star in French politics. Inquisition officials shocked the French political world when they announced he had been charged with witchcraft and was being held in custody in an undisclosed location.

Brassac is one of the youngest people ever to become a member of the Hall of the Robe. At the age of 36 he was granted the title of Baron and formally invited to join the Robe. It is extremely unusual for appointments to the Robe to be granted at such a young age.

"He was a powerful voice for the Crown's policies," said a member of the Robe who spoke on condition of anonymity. "I just can't believe he'd get mixed up in something like sorcery."

Details about the arrest itself were not forthcoming. It is common practice for Inquisitors to seal off a magic-related crime scene from the public.

"It is best we do not disclose the details of the Baron's arrest," Inquisitor Gervase, assigned to the case, said. "Suffice it to say the evidence against the Baron is iron clad and more than circumstantial."

However, many of his colleagues and family immediately came to his support.

"We don't know where Marcel is right now, so we're a little bit frightened," his wife said. "But I have never known him to be interested in magic or the occult. I'm just in shock right now."

A spokesman for the King was also quick to stand behind the fallen Baron.

"The Crown will provide legal council for Baron Brassac's defense. Of course, if he is guilty he must accept the consequences, but it is the King's position that this is some kind of horrible mistake."

Brassac has often drawn praise from the King for his staunch support of Royal policy. Brassac and a coalition of the King's supporters clashed with the Duke of Lorraine and the Hall of the Sword on many issues, including the colonization of the Holy Land and the *Continued on page B2*

BILL DECLARING BASTILLE DAY "NATIONAL DAY OF MOURNING" PASSES HALL OF THE ROBE

Paris – The Hall of the Robe yesterday passed a bill declaring July 14th a "National Day of Mourning" in a move that surprised few people.

The bill is being reviewed by the Hall of the Sword and is expected to pass by a wide margin.

"Bastille Day," as July 14th has come to be known, marks the anniversary of the storming of Bastille Prison in 1789, an event which triggered the bloody French Revolution in which many aristocrats lost their lives to unruly mobs before Royalists consolidated their forces and crushed the rebellion, reinstalling the House of Bourbon to the throne.

While the day is considered a national catastrophe by most members of the nobility, the appeal of "liberty, equality and brotherhood," the ideals of the Revolution, still attract many people.

But not, it seems, the members of the Hall of the Robe.

"While many of us received *Continued on page B3*

⊱ INSIDE ⊰

Plus sanctimonious editorials by editors A. Nelson and EricJ

Three Virginia Farms Razed Under Cover of Darkness

Confederates Denounce "Guerrilla Border Raids"

Attacks Blamed on Radical Abolitionists

Falls Church, VA, Confederate States of America – Several Southern farms near the Federal Republic border were razed to the ground last night. Although no one was killed, Confederate officials say the attacks caused "tens of thousands of dollars" in property damage.

All the farms attacked were owned by slave holders, prompting officials on both sides to blame the attacks on radical abolitionist guerrillas. Southern officials said they suspected the raids were funded by the FRA.

"These attacks were too well organized to be a solitary group of outlaws acting on their own," Franklin DeWitt, mayor of Falls Church, said. "We wouldn't be surprised if the White House were directly responsible for this outrage."

Federal officials were quick to deny the charge.

"It is not and has never been this government's policy to settle differences through clandestine and lawless acts of destruction," White House spokesman Arnold Fleischer said.

The farm owners themselves were visibly shaken. *Continued on page A11*

Marketplace Blast kills Five and Wounds Fifteen in Sarajevo

More Turmoil for Troubled Holy Roman Empire Province

Sarajevo, Holy Roman Empire – The hustle of morning business hours in a crowded Sarajevo marketplace was thrown into bloody chaos when an explosion ripped open a busy storefront, sending broken glass and fragments of debris hurling into passersby.

One child and four adults were killed in the blast. The wounded were taken to a nearby hospital. Doctors said most victims were in critical condition and would likely not last the night.

Serbian separatists were blamed for the attack, although no group has claimed responsibility.

Ferdinand Beust, chancellor of the Holy Roman Empire, denounced the violence, which came a day after Emperor Karl Josef rejected multilateral pleas for a constitutional monarchy in the geographically and ethically far-flung empire.

"This is an outrage. An act of cowardice and terrorism, and we will punish those responsible in the strictest possible measures." *Continued on page A8*

CHAPTER SIX

THE HIDDEN PRIORY

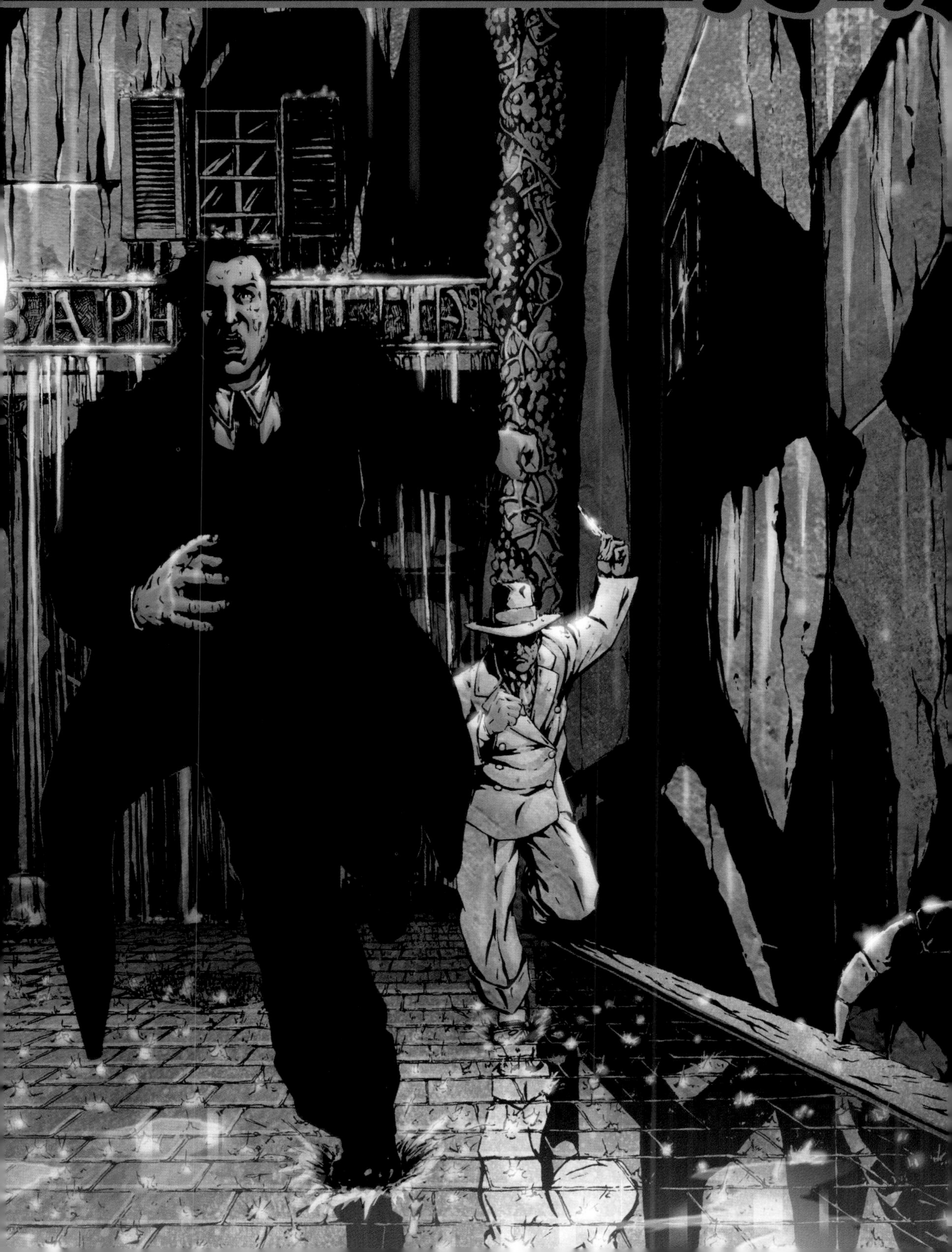

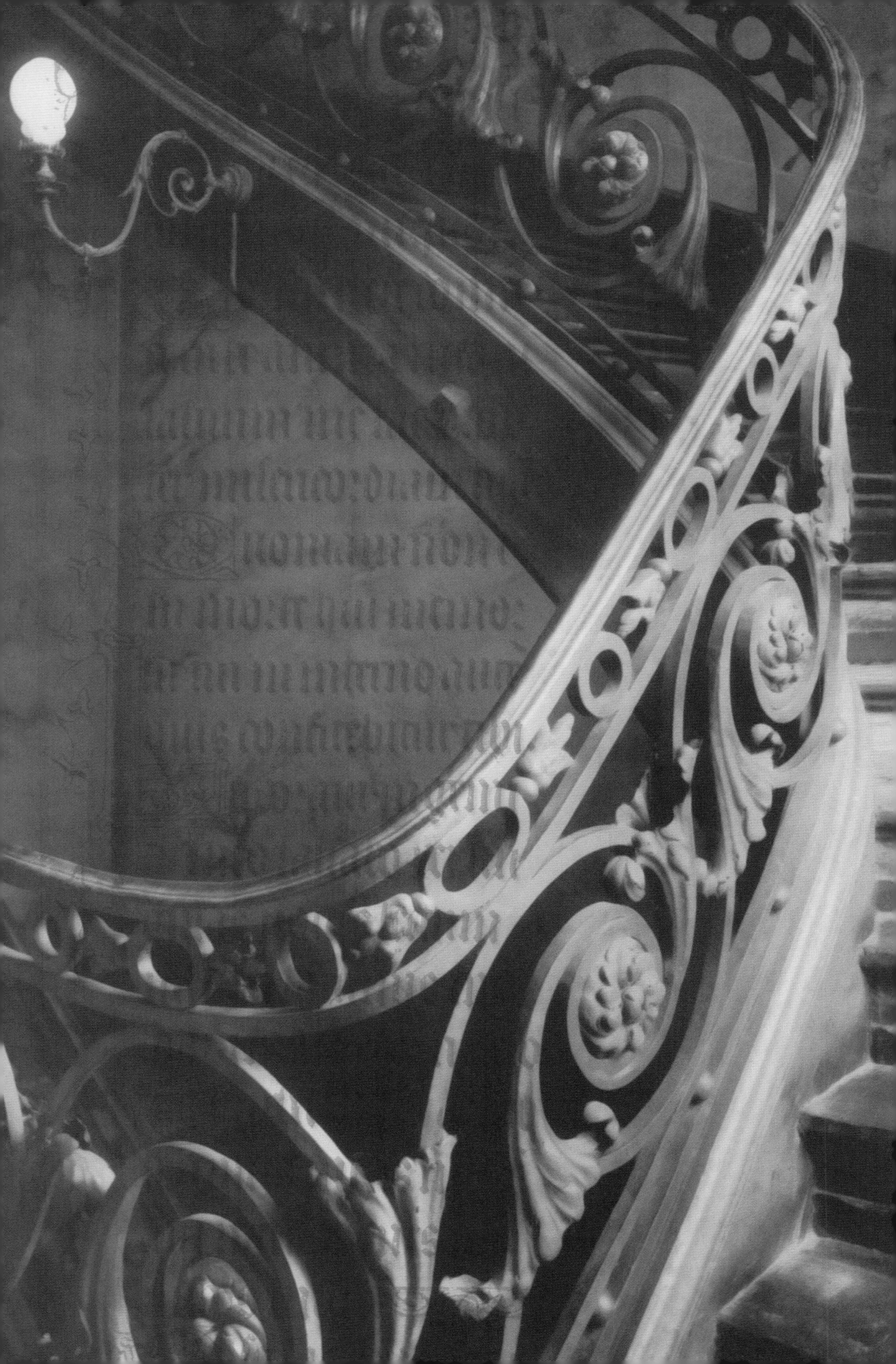

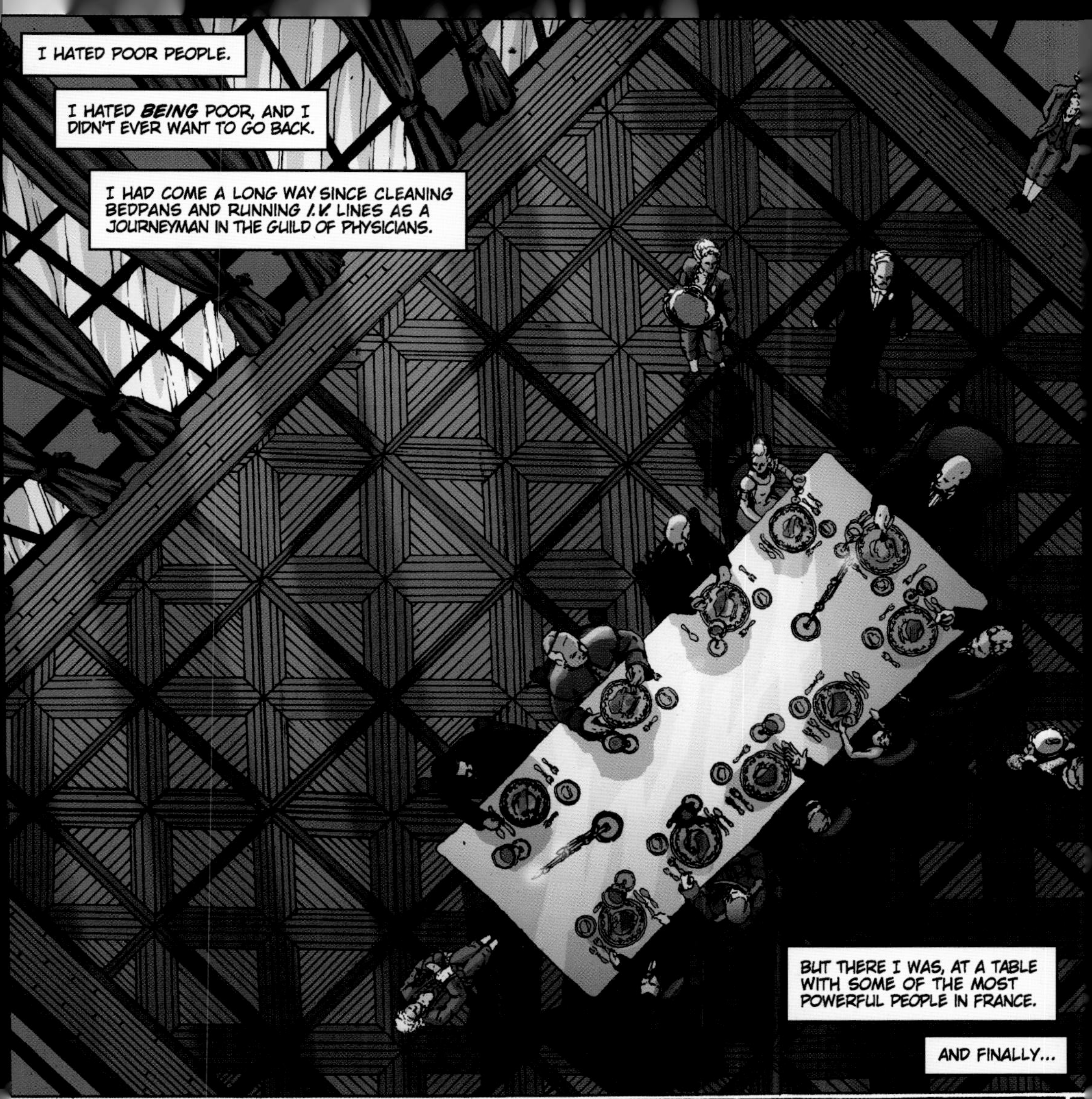
I HATED POOR PEOPLE.
I HATED BEING POOR, AND I DIDN'T EVER WANT TO GO BACK.
I HAD COME A LONG WAY SINCE CLEANING BEDPANS AND RUNNING I.V. LINES AS A JOURNEYMAN IN THE GUILD OF PHYSICIANS.
BUT THERE I WAS, AT A TABLE WITH SOME OF THE MOST POWERFUL PEOPLE IN FRANCE.
AND FINALLY...

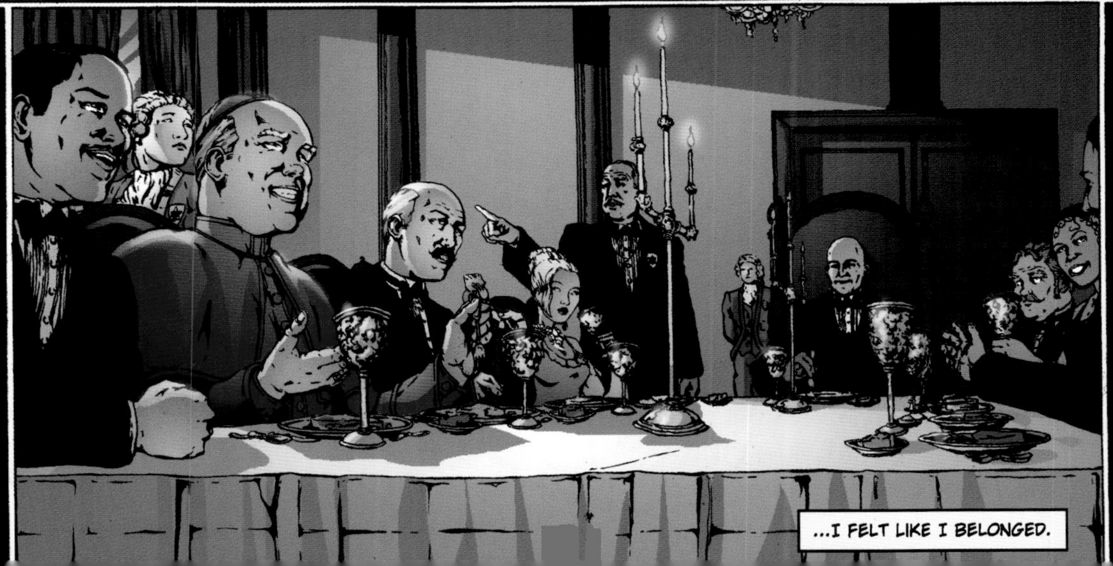
...I FELT LIKE I BELONGED.

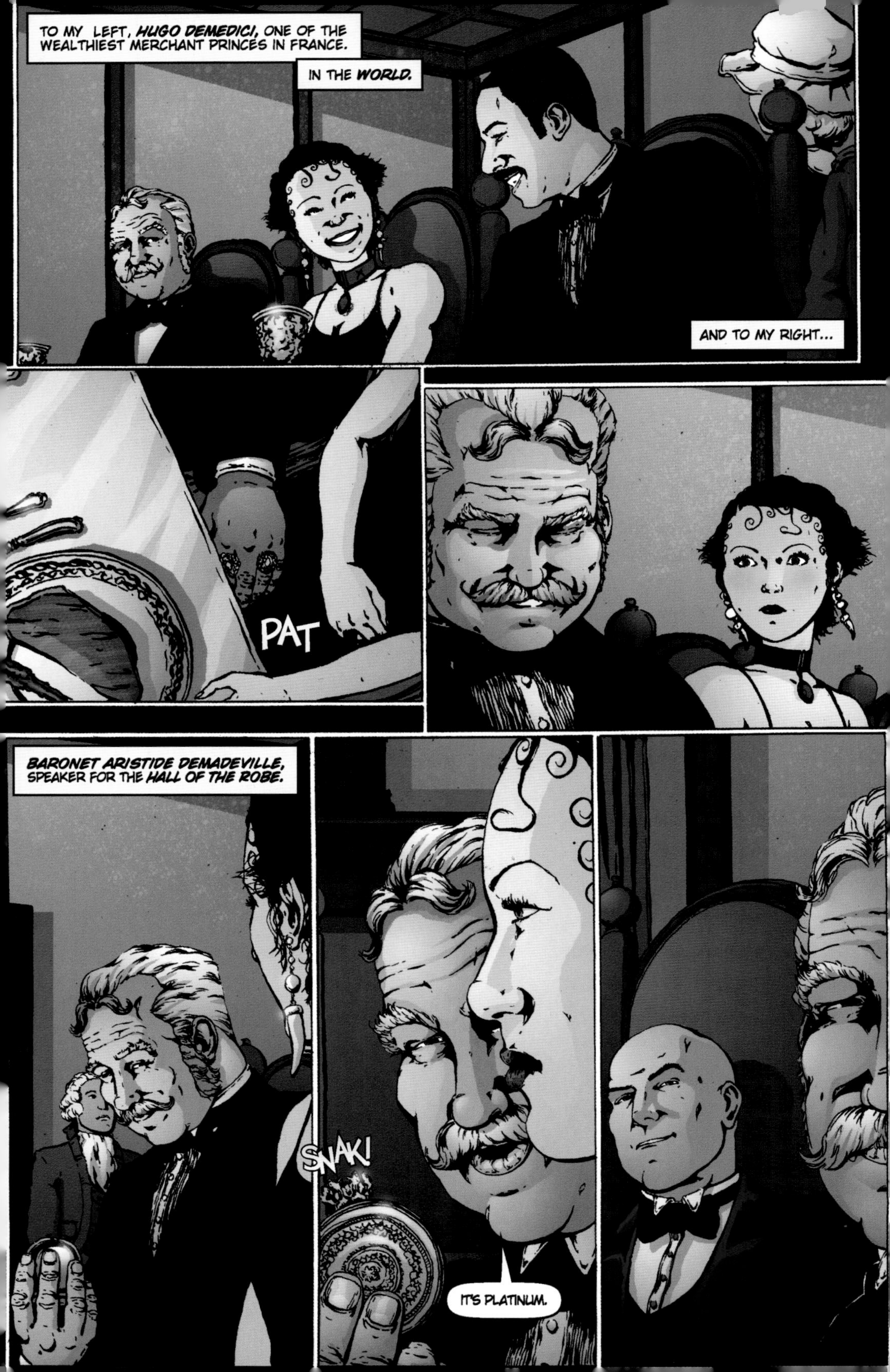
TO MY LEFT, HUGO DEMEDICI, ONE OF THE WEALTHIEST MERCHANT PRINCES IN FRANCE.
IN THE WORLD.
AND TO MY RIGHT...
PAT
BARONET ARISTIDE DEMADEVILLE, SPEAKER FOR THE HALL OF THE ROBE.
SNAK!
IT'S PLATINUM.

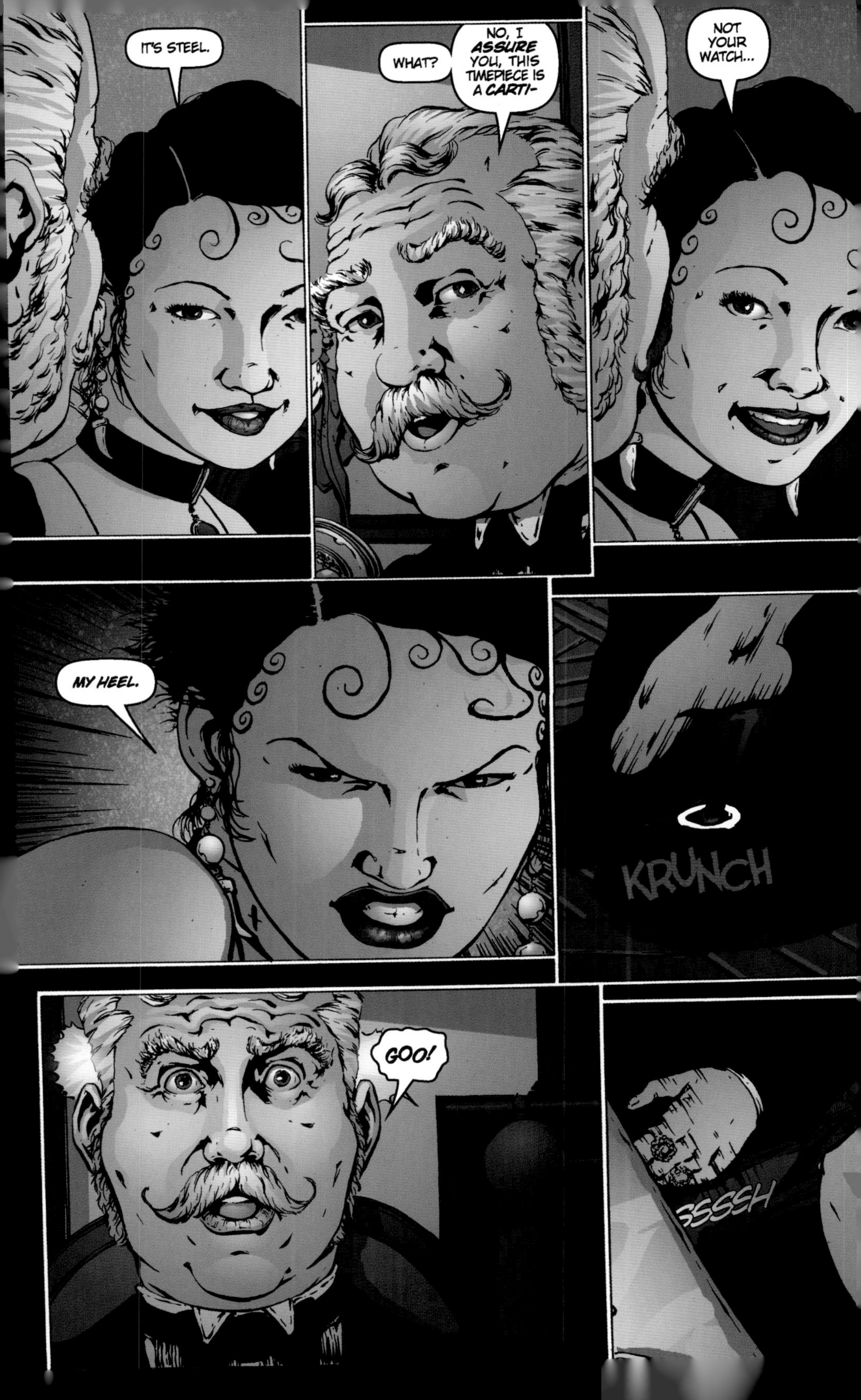

IT'S STEEL.
WHAT?
NO, I ASSURE YOU, THIS TIMEPIECE IS A CARTI-
NOT YOUR WATCH...
MY HEEL.
KRUNCH
GOO!
SSSSH

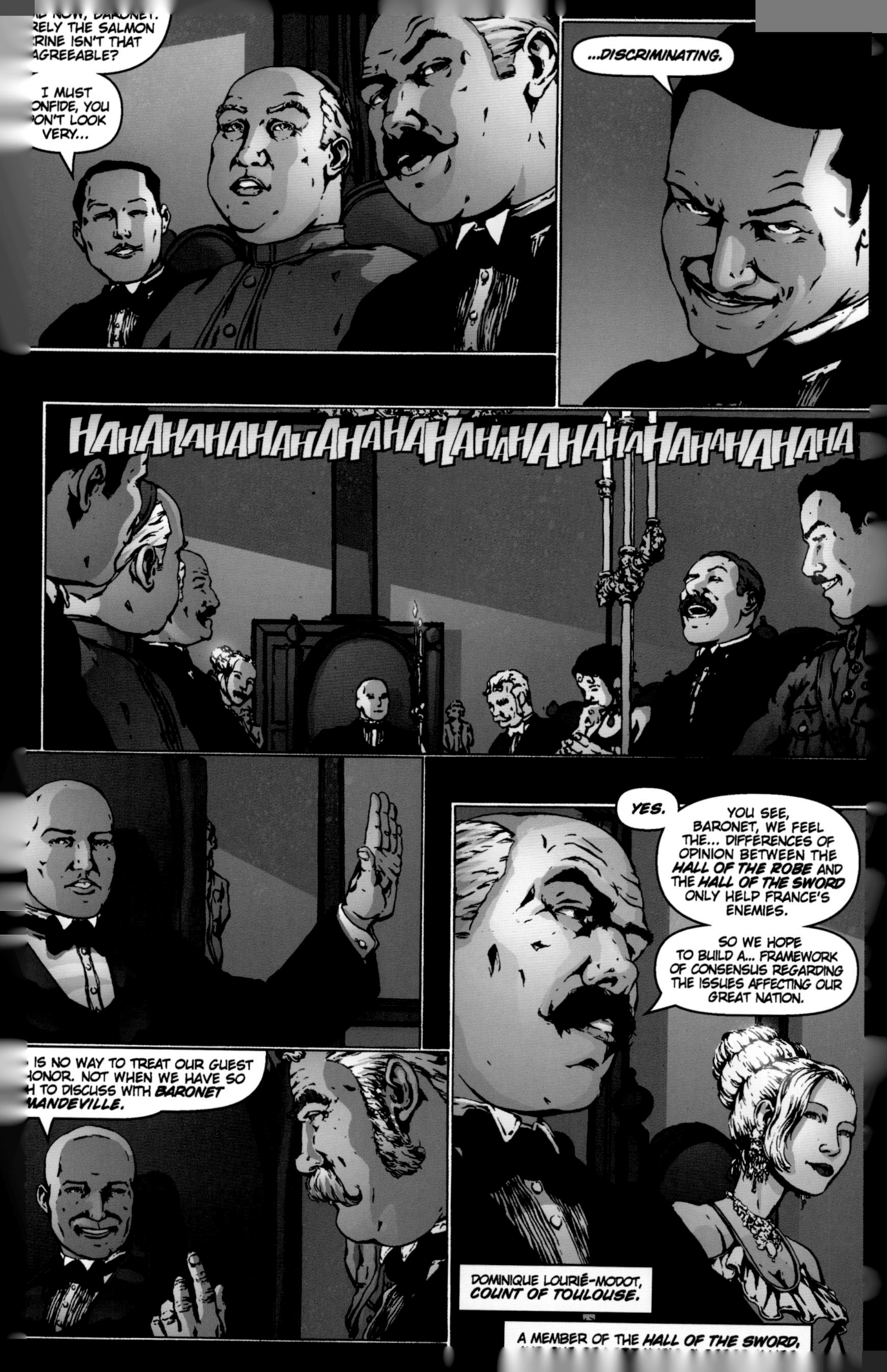

...ND NOW, BARONET. ...RELY THE SALMON ...RINE ISN'T THAT ...AGREEABLE?
I MUST ...ONFIDE, YOU ...ON'T LOOK VERY...
...DISCRIMINATING.
HAHAHAHAHAHAHAHAHAHAHAHAHAHAHAHAHAHAHAHAHA
...IS NO WAY TO TREAT OUR GUEST ...HONOR. NOT WHEN WE HAVE SO ...H TO DISCUSS WITH BARONET ...MANDEVILLE.
YES.
YOU SEE, BARONET, WE FEEL THE... DIFFERENCES OF OPINION BETWEEN THE HALL OF THE ROBE AND THE HALL OF THE SWORD ONLY HELP FRANCE'S ENEMIES.
SO WE HOPE TO BUILD A... FRAMEWORK OF CONSENSUS REGARDING THE ISSUES AFFECTING OUR GREAT NATION.
DOMINIQUE LOURIÉ-MODOT, COUNT OF TOULOUSE.
A MEMBER OF THE HALL OF THE SWORD,

ISSUES.

THAT'S RIGHT.

THE DE MEDICI FAMILY HAS SENT GEOGRAPHICAL SURVEILLANCE EXPEDITIONS TO PALESTINE. IT SEEMS THERE ARE...

...SIGNIFICANT RESERVES OF LIQUID PETROCARBON BENEATH ALL THAT SAND.

OIL.

IMAGINE...

IMAGINE WHAT, MR. DEMEDICI?

IMAGINE IF WE COULD TAP THOSE RESERVES! IT WOULD TRANSFORM FRANCE'S ECONOMY, PUT IT FAR AHEAD OF THE ENGLISH AND THE PRUSSIANS.

THE DEMEDICI FAMILY BELIEVES IT'S POSSIBLE, AND WE WOULD...

...AND THE DEMEDICIS WOULD BE MORE THAN HAPPY TO UNDERWRITE THE VENTURE.

I'M SURE.

ONE CAN'T SIMPLY... REDUCE FOREIGN POLICY TO A BALANCE SHEET...

BUT WHAT ABOUT THE POLITICAL CONSEQUENCES? HOW WILL THE ENGLISH CROWN REACT TO

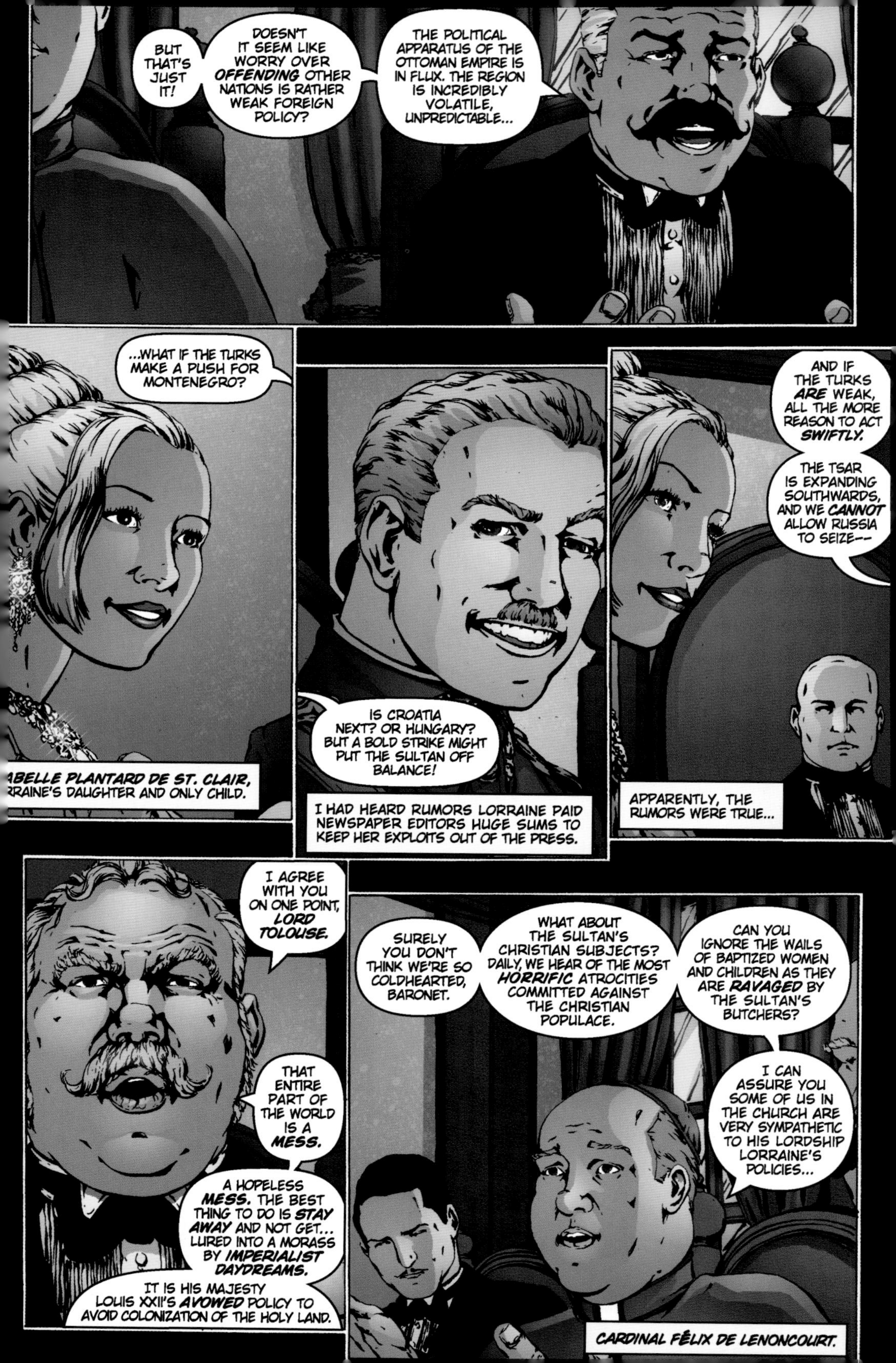
BUT THAT'S JUST IT!
DOESN'T IT SEEM LIKE WORRY OVER *OFFENDING* OTHER NATIONS IS RATHER WEAK FOREIGN POLICY?
THE POLITICAL APPARATUS OF THE OTTOMAN EMPIRE IS IN FLUX. THE REGION IS INCREDIBLY VOLATILE, UNPREDICTABLE...
...WHAT IF THE TURKS MAKE A PUSH FOR MONTENEGRO?
ABELLE PLANTARD DE ST. CLAIR, RRAINE'S DAUGHTER AND ONLY CHILD.
IS CROATIA NEXT? OR HUNGARY? BUT A BOLD STRIKE MIGHT PUT THE SULTAN OFF BALANCE!
I HAD HEARD RUMORS LORRAINE PAID NEWSPAPER EDITORS HUGE SUMS TO KEEP HER EXPLOITS OUT OF THE PRESS.
AND IF THE TURKS *ARE* WEAK, ALL THE MORE REASON TO ACT *SWIFTLY.*
THE TSAR IS EXPANDING SOUTHWARDS, AND WE *CANNOT* ALLOW RUSSIA TO SEIZE--
APPARENTLY, THE RUMORS WERE TRUE...
I AGREE WITH YOU ON ONE POINT, *LORD TOLOUSE.*
THAT ENTIRE PART OF THE WORLD IS A *MESS.*
A HOPELESS *MESS.* THE BEST THING TO DO IS *STAY AWAY* AND NOT GET... LURED INTO A MORASS BY *IMPERIALIST DAYDREAMS.*
IT IS HIS MAJESTY LOUIS XXII'S *AVOWED* POLICY TO AVOID COLONIZATION OF THE HOLY LAND.
SURELY YOU DON'T THINK WE'RE SO COLDHEARTED, BARONET.
WHAT ABOUT THE SULTAN'S CHRISTIAN SUBJECTS? DAILY, WE HEAR OF THE MOST *HORRIFIC* ATROCITIES COMMITTED AGAINST THE CHRISTIAN POPULACE.
CAN YOU IGNORE THE WAILS OF BAPTIZED WOMEN AND CHILDREN AS THEY ARE *RAVAGED* BY THE SULTAN'S BUTCHERS?
I CAN ASSURE YOU SOME OF US IN THE CHURCH ARE VERY SYMPATHETIC TO HIS LORDSHIP LORRAINE'S POLICIES...
CARDINAL FÉLIX DE LENONCOURT.

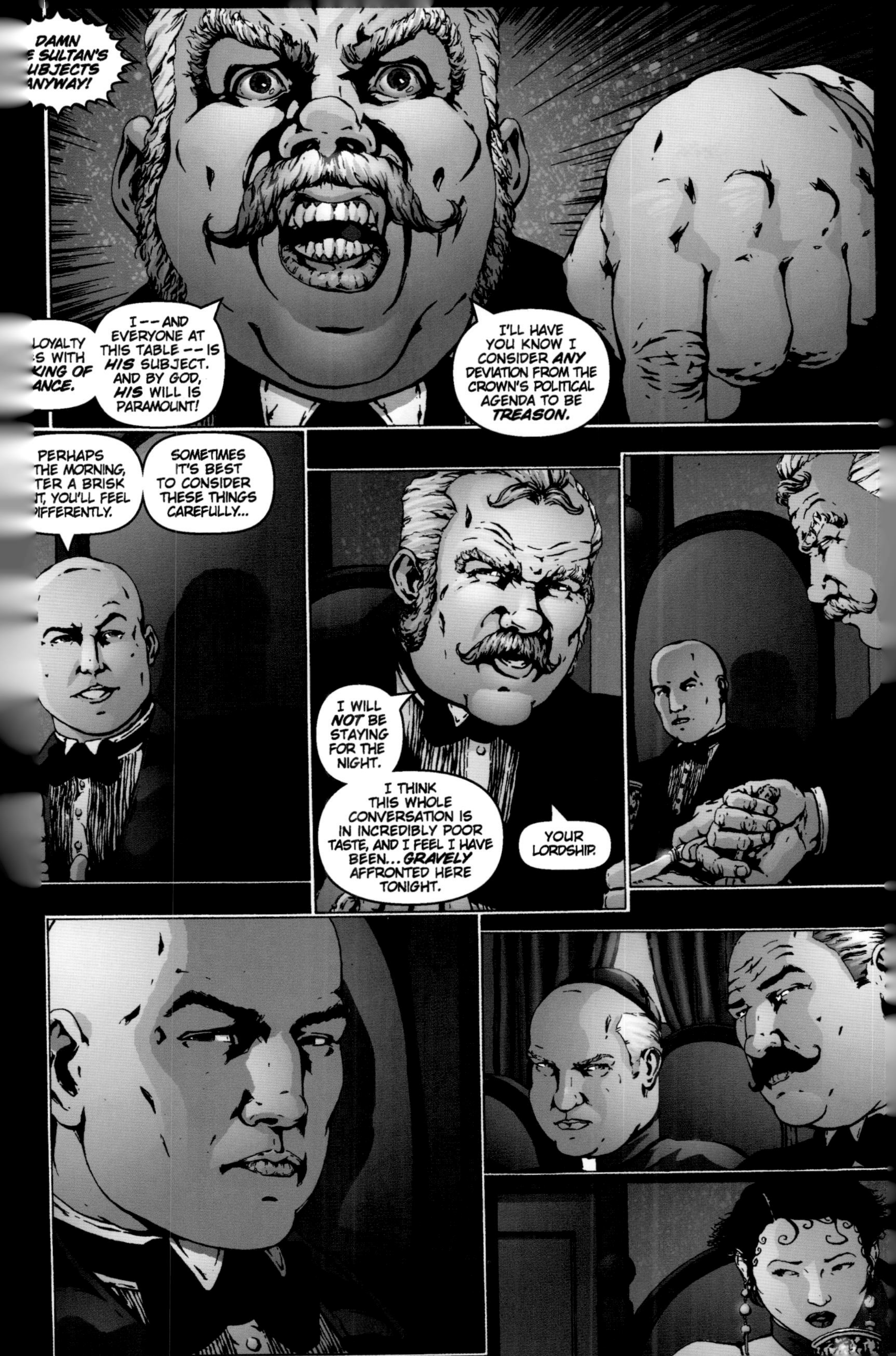
DAMN
E SULTAN'S
UBJECTS
ANYWAY!
LOYALTY
S WITH
KING OF
ANCE.
I -- AND EVERYONE AT THIS TABLE -- IS HIS SUBJECT. AND BY GOD, HIS WILL IS PARAMOUNT!
I'LL HAVE YOU KNOW I CONSIDER ANY DEVIATION FROM THE CROWN'S POLITICAL AGENDA TO BE TREASON.
PERHAPS
THE MORNING,
TER A BRISK
IT, YOU'LL FEEL
DIFFERENTLY.
SOMETIMES IT'S BEST TO CONSIDER THESE THINGS CAREFULLY...
I WILL NOT BE STAYING FOR THE NIGHT.
I THINK THIS WHOLE CONVERSATION IS IN INCREDIBLY POOR TASTE, AND I FEEL I HAVE BEEN... GRAVELY AFFRONTED HERE TONIGHT.
YOUR LORDSHIP.

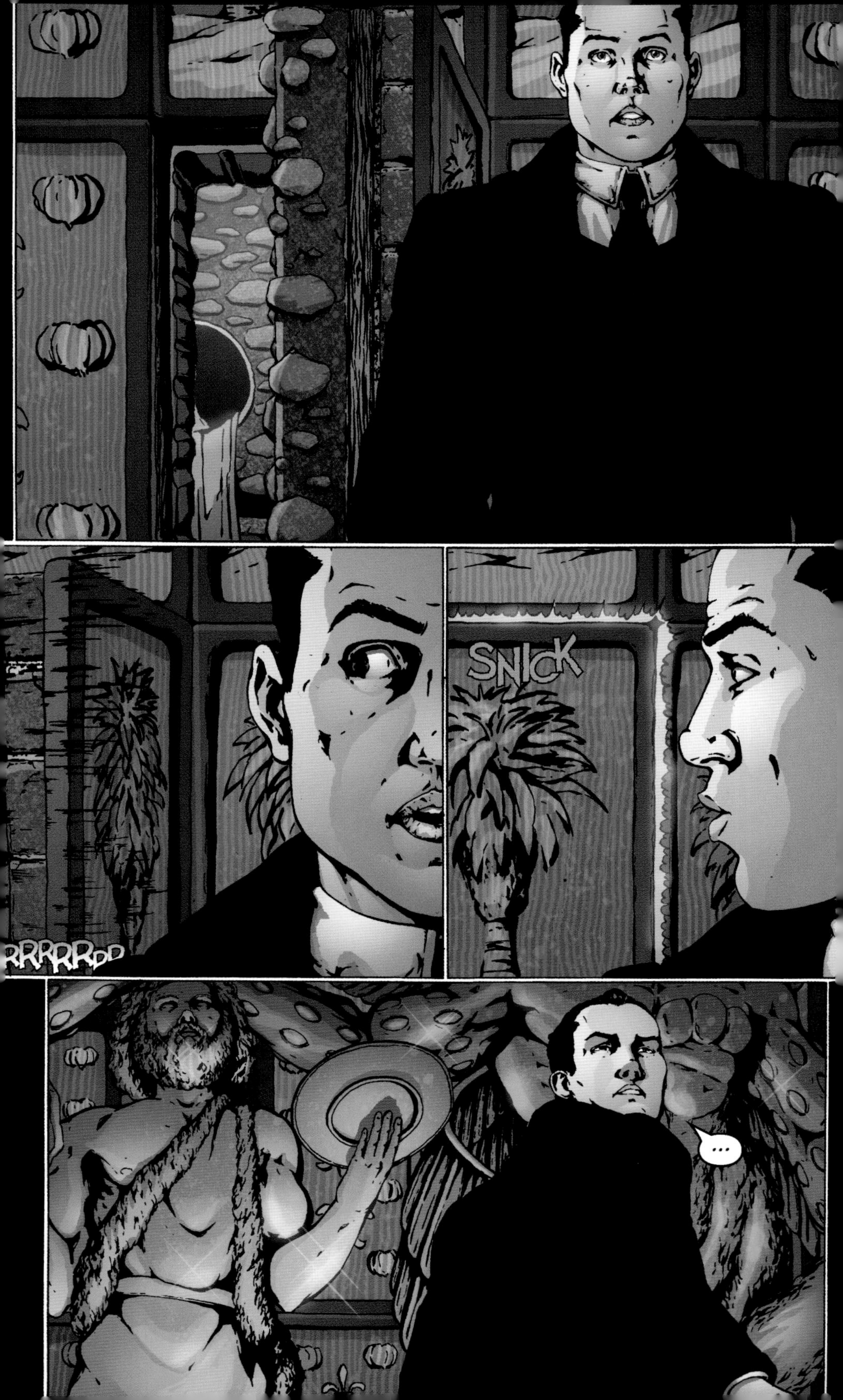
RRRRRDD
SNICK
...

I SEARCHED DUSTY MEMORIES OF GREEK MYTHS FROM LONG-AGO CLASSES, BUT I COULD NOT IDENTIFY THE STRANGE, MONSTROUS FIGURES.

DEMONS?

I RECOGNIZED SOME THINGS ON THE ALTAR:

THE SNAKE EATING ITS TAIL WAS *UROBOROS,* AN ANCIENT GREEK SYMBOL FOR THE WORLD.

BUT WHAT ABOUT THE INVERTED PYRAMID? THE WINGED FISH?

AND WHAT ABOUT THE STATUE IN THE CENTER?

ALMOST LIKE A SAINT, BUT...

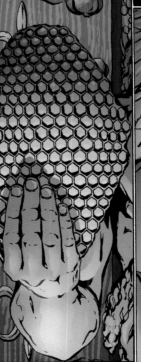

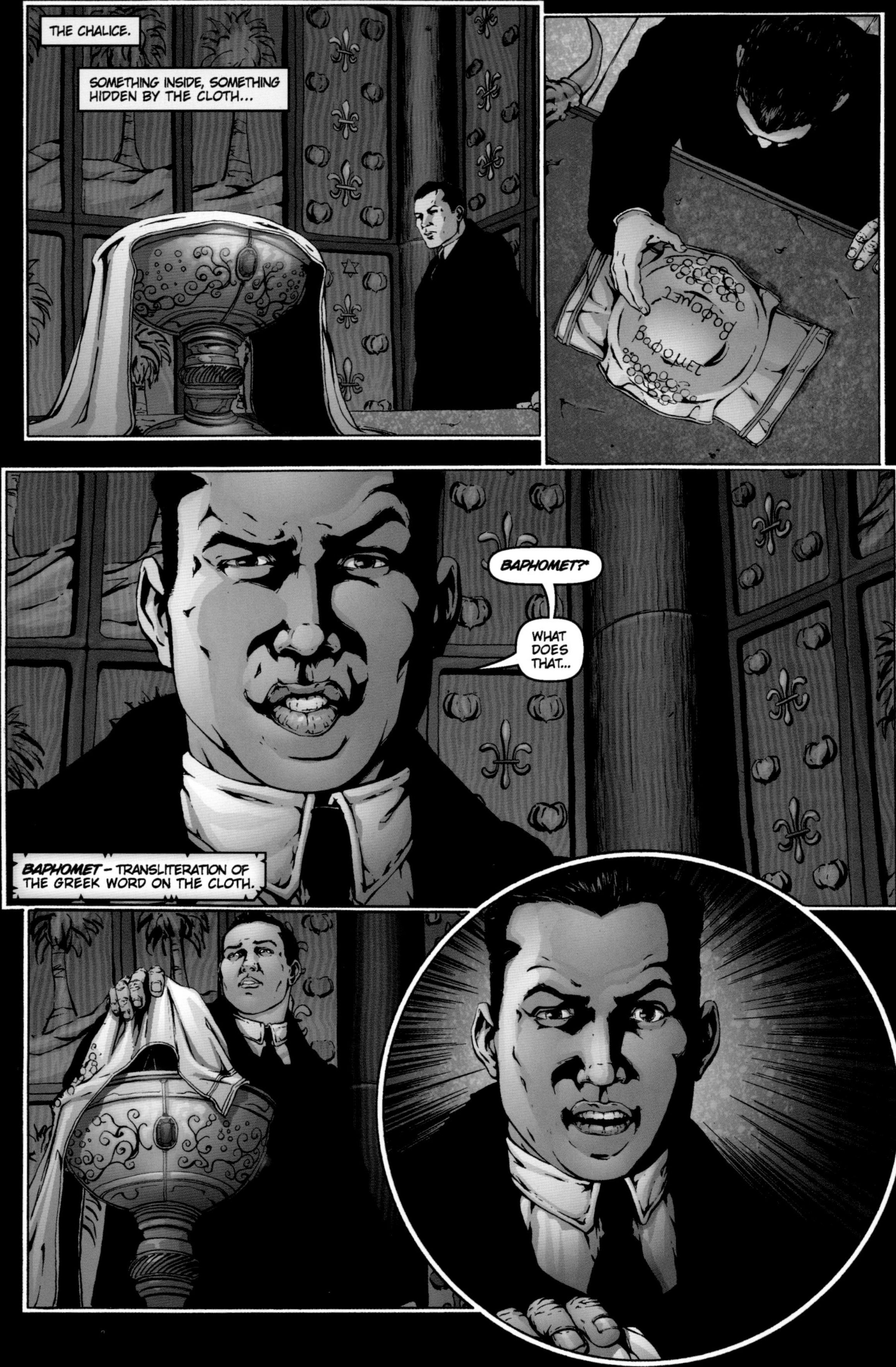
THE CHALICE.
SOMETHING INSIDE, SOMETHING HIDDEN BY THE CLOTH...
BAPHOMET?*
WHAT DOES THAT...
BAPHOMET – TRANSLITERATION OF THE GREEK WORD ON THE CLOTH.

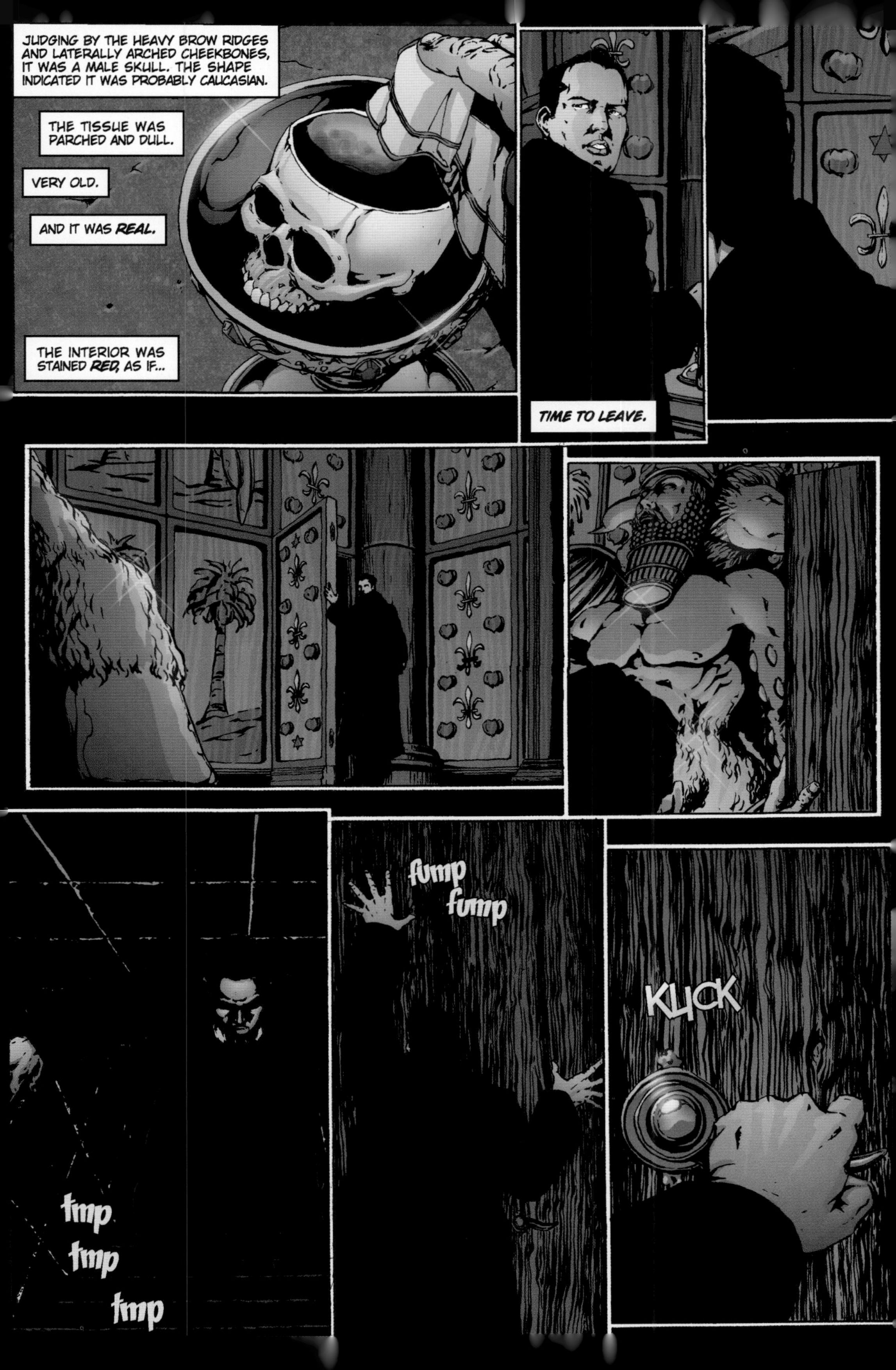
JUDGING BY THE HEAVY BROW RIDGES AND LATERALLY ARCHED CHEEKBONES, IT WAS A MALE SKULL. THE SHAPE INDICATED IT WAS PROBABLY CAUCASIAN.
THE TISSUE WAS PARCHED AND DULL.
VERY OLD.
AND IT WAS *REAL.*
THE INTERIOR WAS STAINED *RED,* AS IF...
TIME TO LEAVE.
tmp
tmp
tmp
fump
fump
KLICK

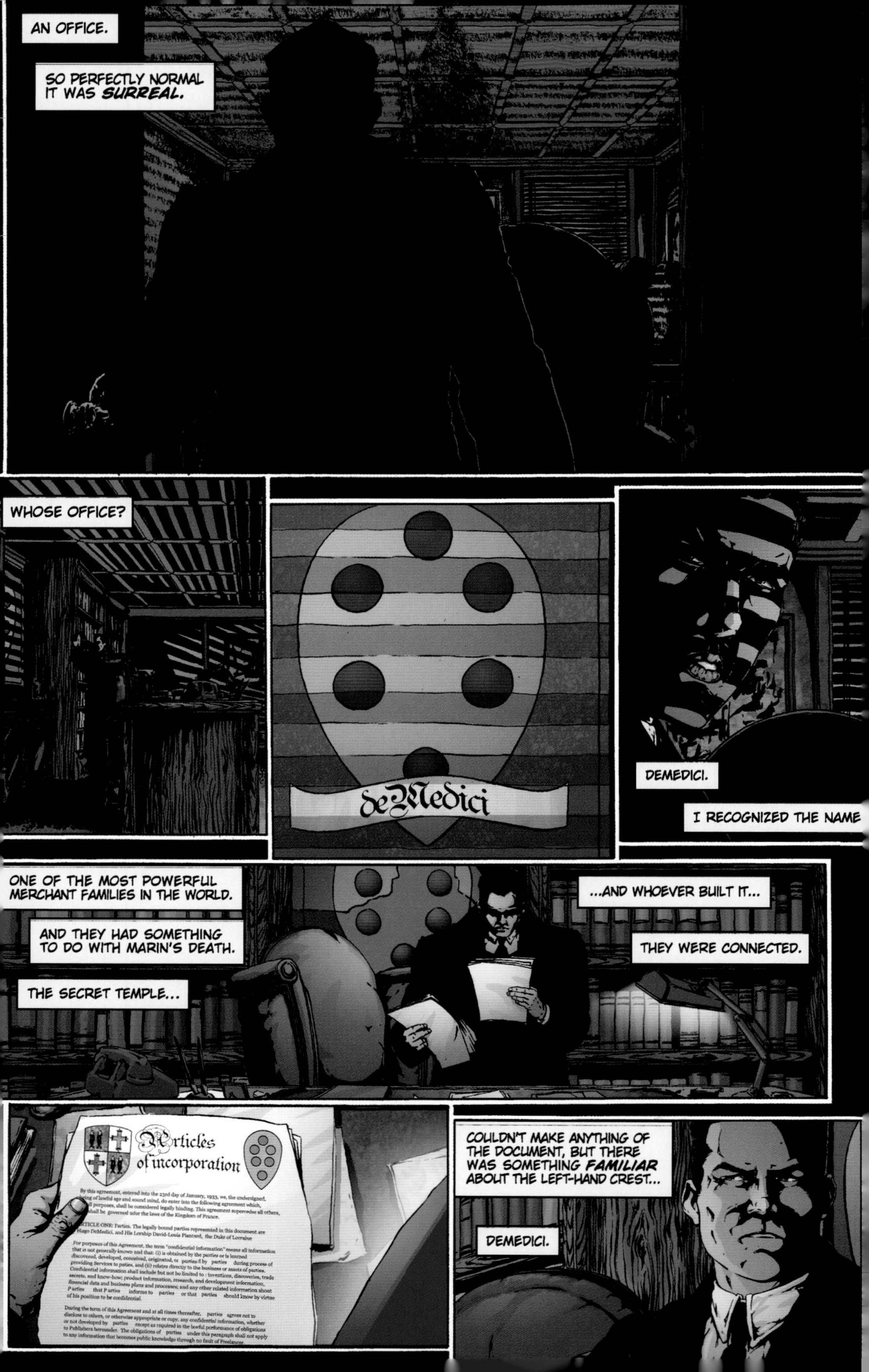
AN OFFICE.
SO PERFECTLY NORMAL IT WAS *SURREAL.*
WHOSE OFFICE?
deMedici
DEMEDICI.
I RECOGNIZED THE NAME
ONE OF THE MOST POWERFUL MERCHANT FAMILIES IN THE WORLD.
AND THEY HAD SOMETHING TO DO WITH MARIN'S DEATH.
THE SECRET TEMPLE...
...AND WHOEVER BUILT IT...
THEY WERE CONNECTED.
Articles of incorporation
By this agreement, entered into the 23rd day of January, 1933, we, the undersigned, being of lawful age and sound mind, do enter into the following agreement which, ll purposes, shall be considered legally binding. This agreement supercedes all others, shall be governed udor the laws of the Kingdom of France.
RTICLE ONE: Parties. The legally bound parties represented in this document are Hugo DeMedici, and His Lorship David-Louis Plantard, the Duke of Lorraine
For purposes of this Agreement, the term "confidential information" means all information that is not generally known and that: (i) is obtained by the parties or is learned discovered, developed, conceived, originated, or partiesd by parties during process of providing Services to paties, and (ii) relates directly to the business or assets of parties. Confidential information shall include but not be limited to : inventions, discoveries, trade secrets, and know-how; product information, research, and development information, financial data and business plans and processes; and any other related information about Parties that Parties informs to parties or that parties should know by virtue of his position to be confidential.
During the term of this Agreement and at all times thereafter, parties agrees not to disclose to others, or otherwise appropriate or copy, any confidential information, whether or not developed by parties except as required in the lawful performance of obligations to Publishers hereunder. The obligations of parties under this paragraph shall not apply to any information that becomes public knowledge through no fault of Freelancer.
COULDN'T MAKE ANYTHING OF THE DOCUMENT, BUT THERE WAS SOMETHING *FAMILIAR* ABOUT THE LEFT-HAND CREST...
DEMEDICI.

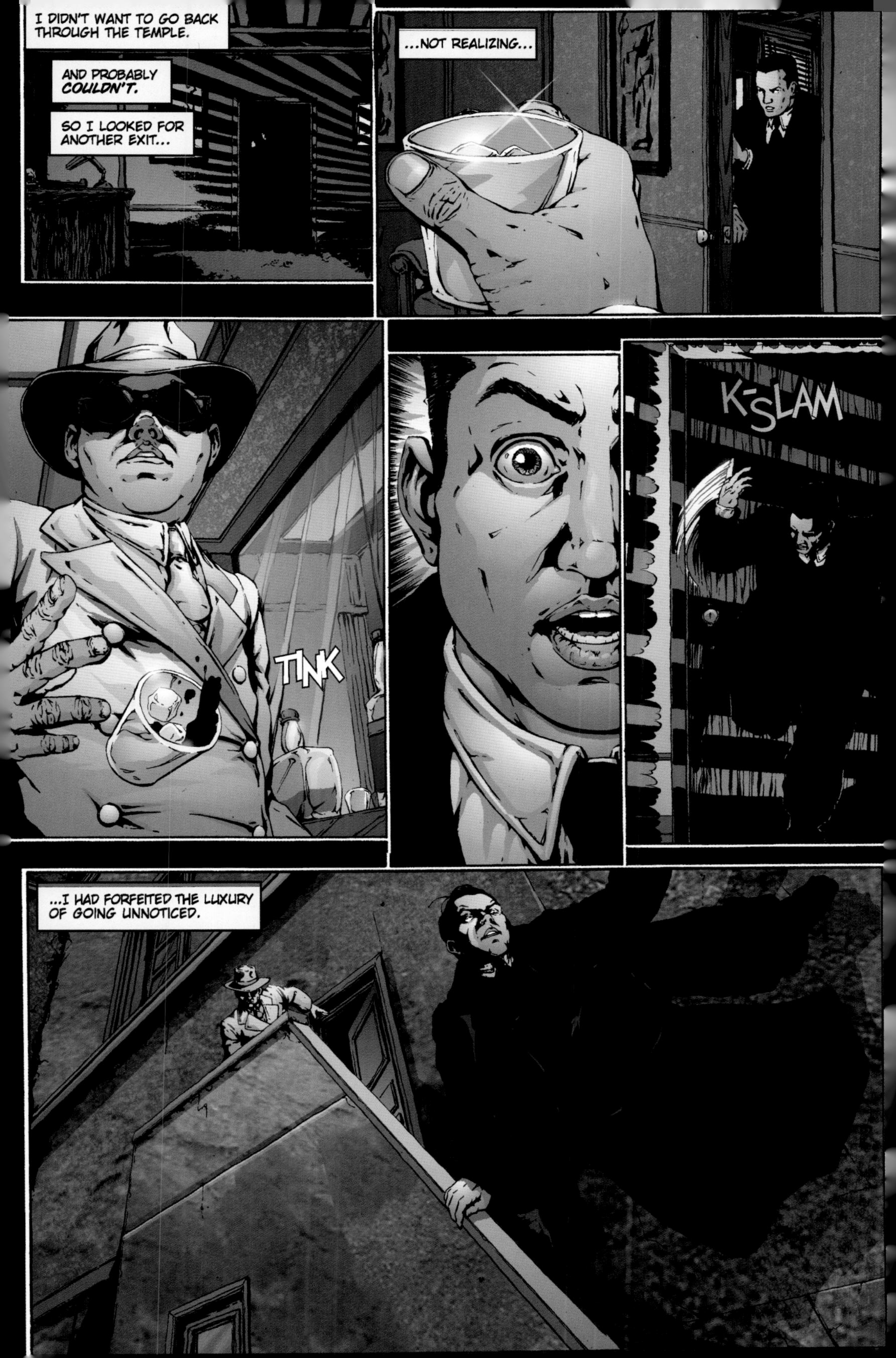
I DIDN'T WANT TO GO BACK THROUGH THE TEMPLE.
AND PROBABLY *COULDN'T.*
SO I LOOKED FOR ANOTHER EXIT...
...NOT REALIZING...
TINK
K-SLAM
...I HAD FORFEITED THE LUXURY OF GOING UNNOTICED.

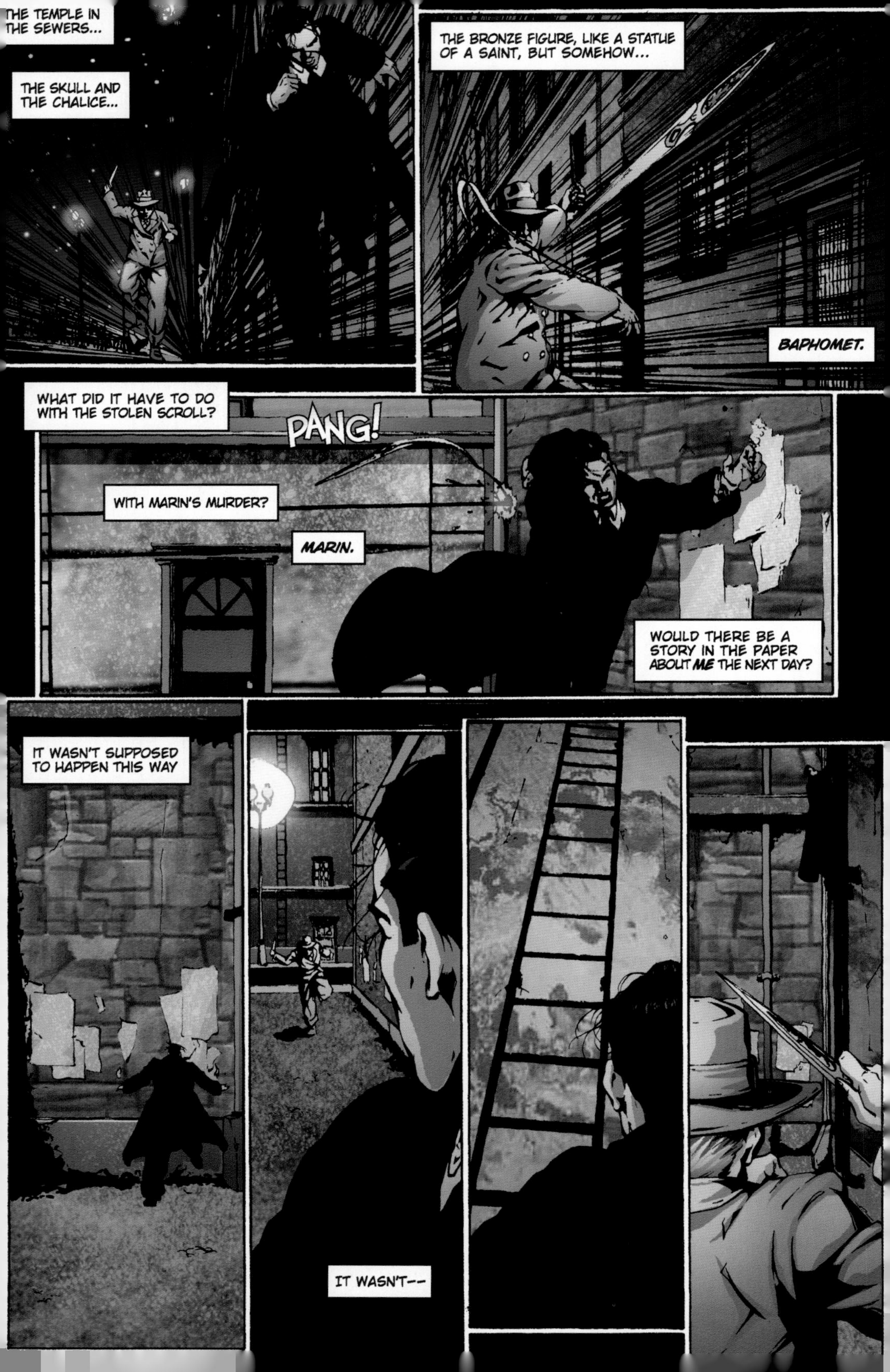
THE TEMPLE IN THE SEWERS...
THE SKULL AND THE CHALICE...
THE BRONZE FIGURE, LIKE A STATUE OF A SAINT, BUT SOMEHOW...
BAPHOMET.
WHAT DID IT HAVE TO DO WITH THE STOLEN SCROLL?
PANG!
WITH MARIN'S MURDER?
MARIN.
WOULD THERE BE A STORY IN THE PAPER ABOUT ME THE NEXT DAY?
IT WASN'T SUPPOSED TO HAPPEN THIS WAY
IT WASN'T--

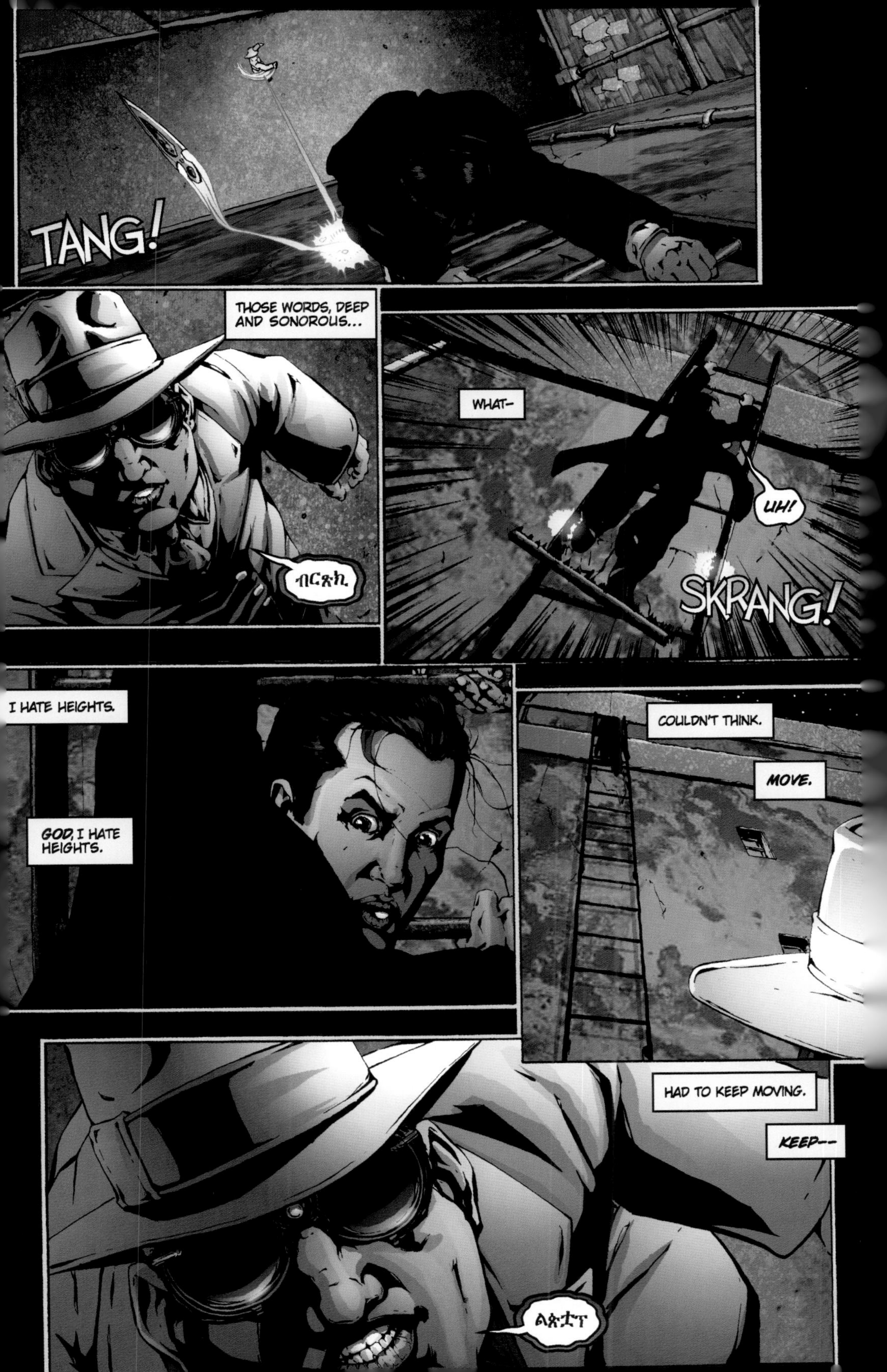
TANG!
THOSE WORDS, DEEP AND SONOROUS...
ብርጽኪ
WHAT-
UH!
SKRANG!
I HATE HEIGHTS.
GOD, I HATE HEIGHTS.
COULDN'T THINK.
MOVE.
HAD TO KEEP MOVING.
KEEP--

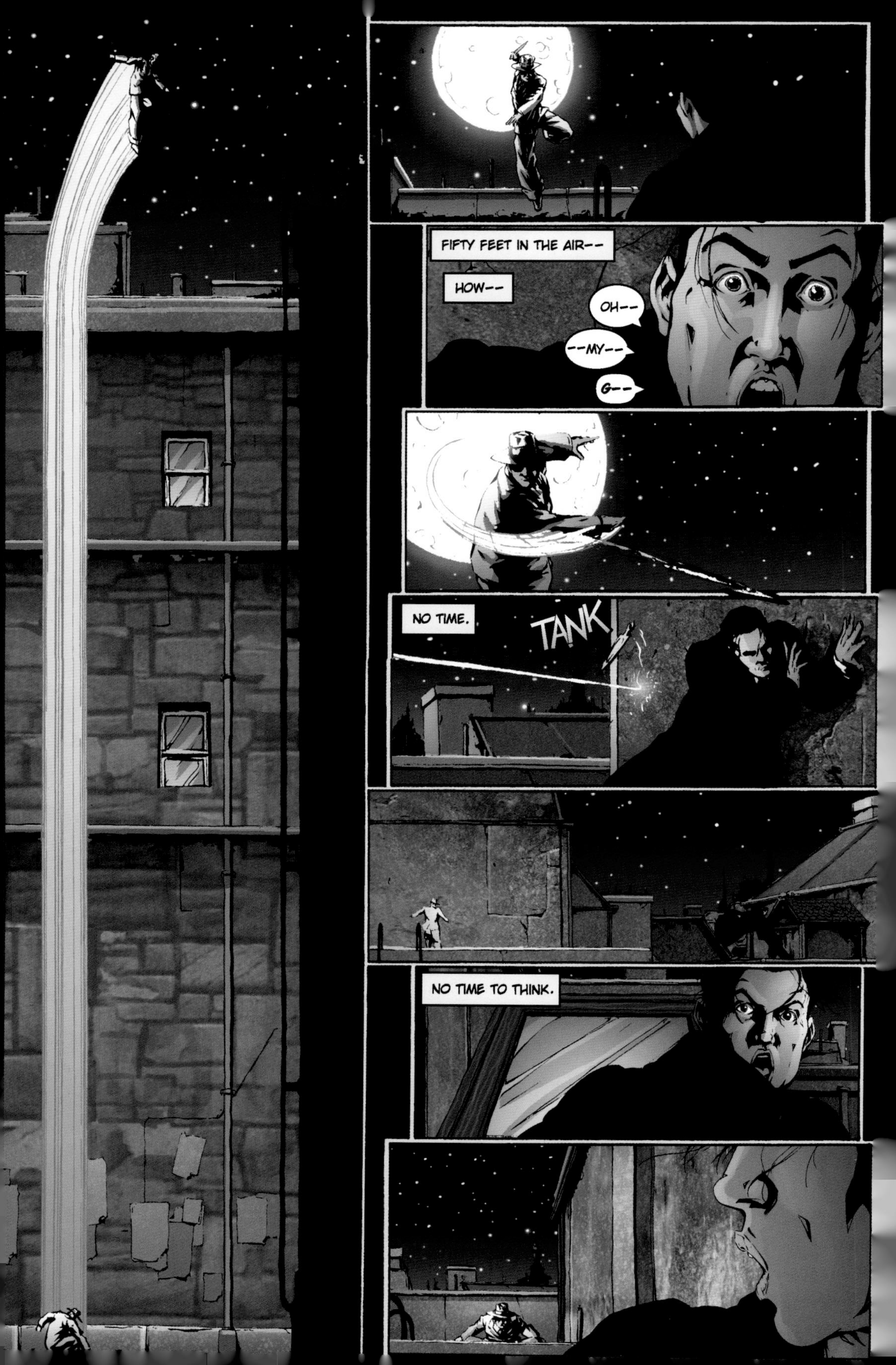
FIFTY FEET IN THE AIR--
HOW--
OH--
--MY--
G--
NO TIME.
TANK
NO TIME TO THINK.

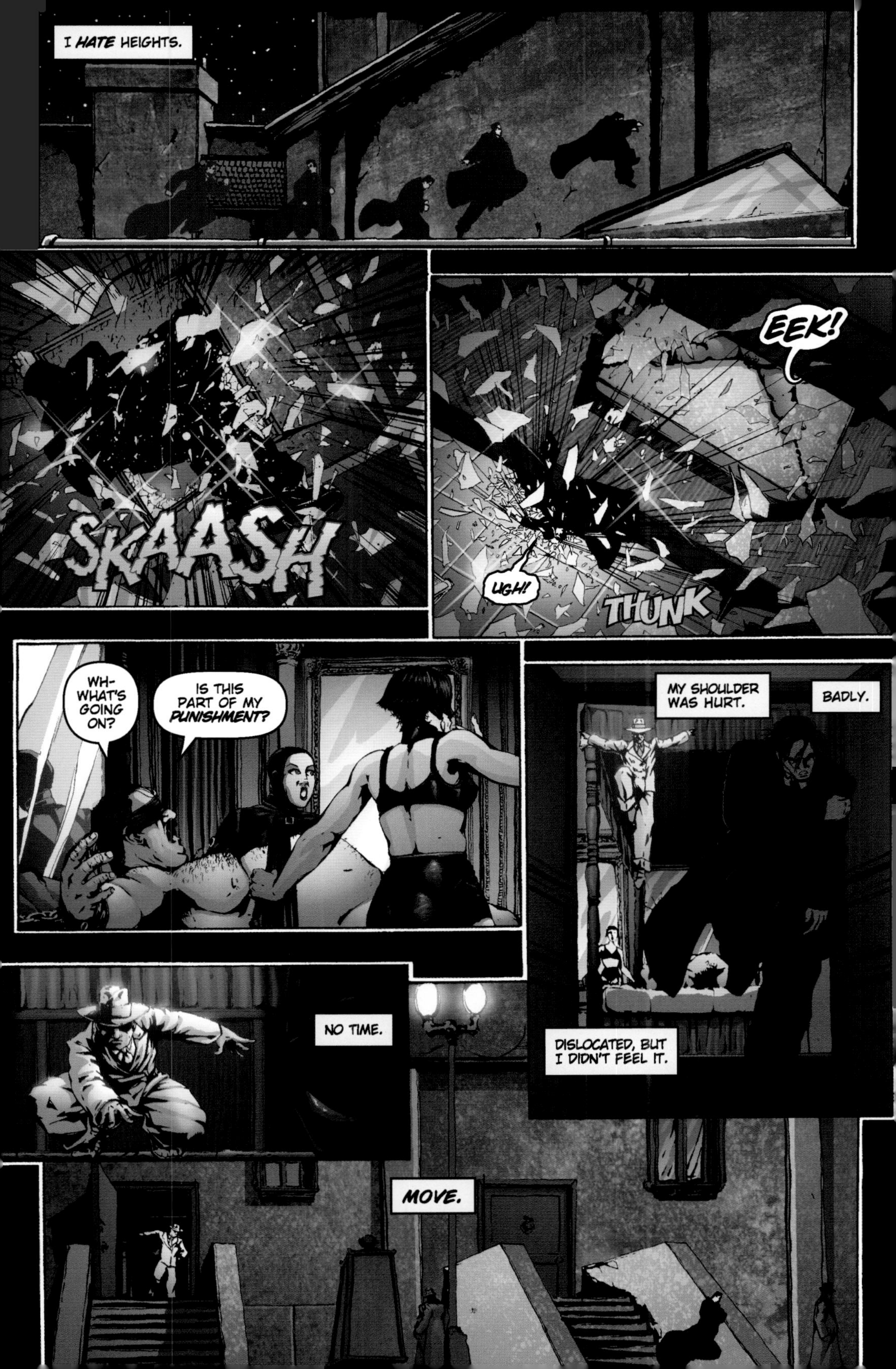
I HATE HEIGHTS.
SKAASH
EEK!
UGH!
THUNK
WH-WHAT'S GOING ON?
IS THIS PART OF MY PUNISHMENT?
MY SHOULDER WAS HURT.
BADLY.
DISLOCATED, BUT I DIDN'T FEEL IT.
NO TIME.
MOVE.

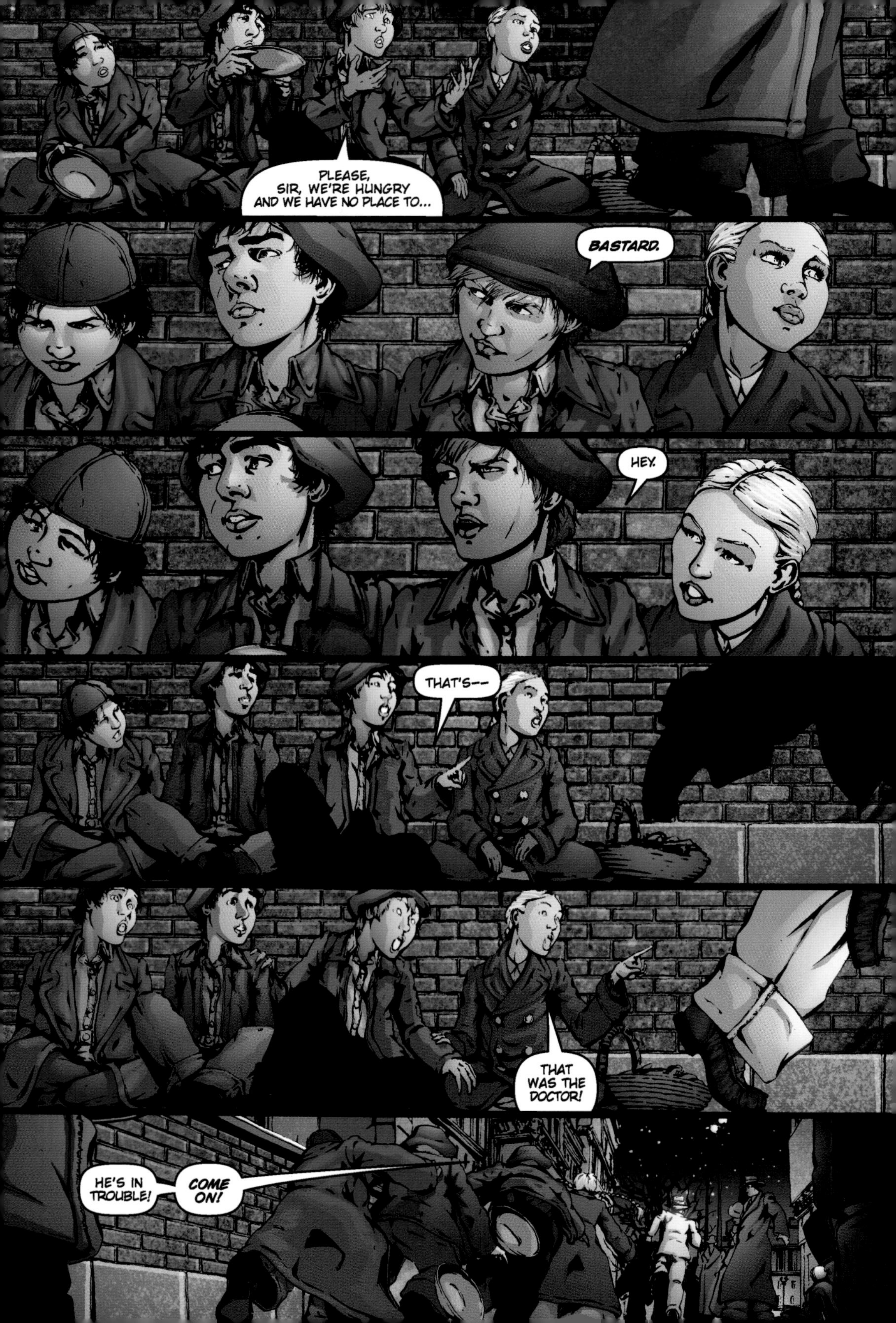
PLEASE, SIR, WE'RE HUNGRY AND WE HAVE NO PLACE TO...
BASTARD.
HEY.
THAT'S--
THAT WAS THE DOCTOR!
HE'S IN TROUBLE!
COME ON!

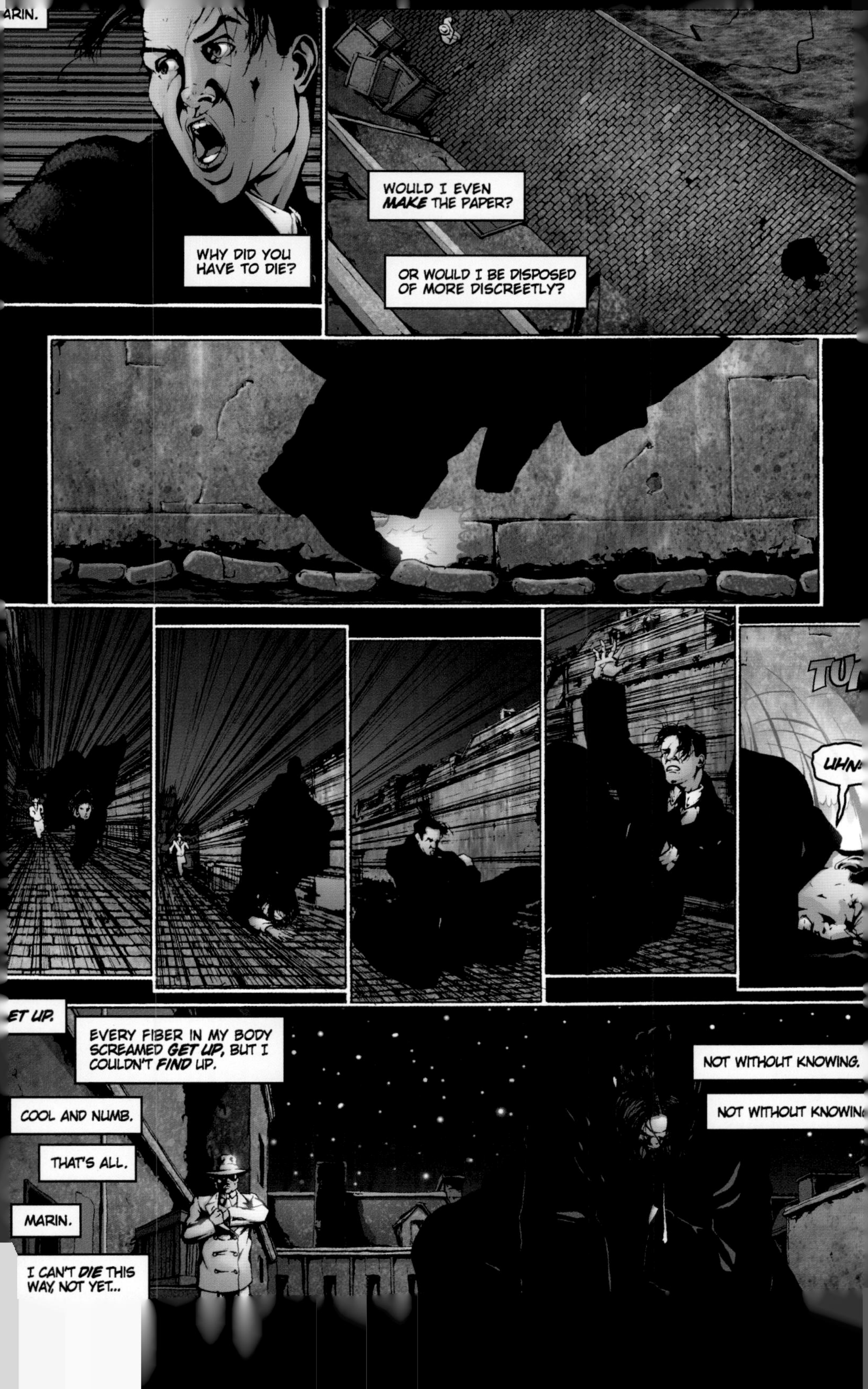
ARIN.
WHY DID YOU HAVE TO DIE?
WOULD I EVEN MAKE THE PAPER?
OR WOULD I BE DISPOSED OF MORE DISCREETLY?
TU
UHN
ET UP.
EVERY FIBER IN MY BODY SCREAMED GET UP, BUT I COULDN'T FIND UP.
COOL AND NUMB.
THAT'S ALL.
MARIN.
I CAN'T DIE THIS WAY, NOT YET...
NOT WITHOUT KNOWING.
NOT WITHOUT KNOWIN

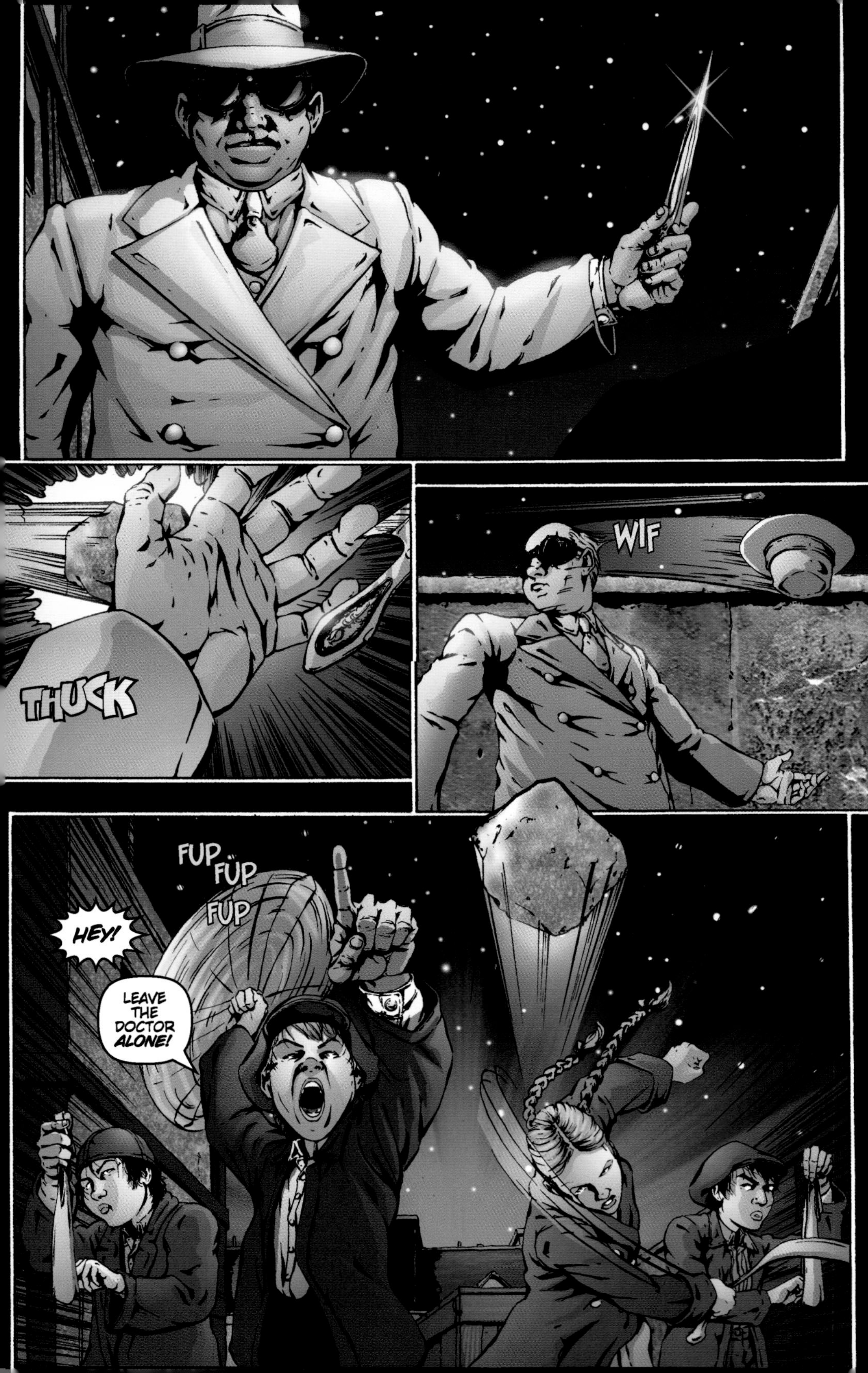
THUCK
WIF
FUP
FUP
FUP
HEY!
LEAVE THE DOCTOR ALONE!

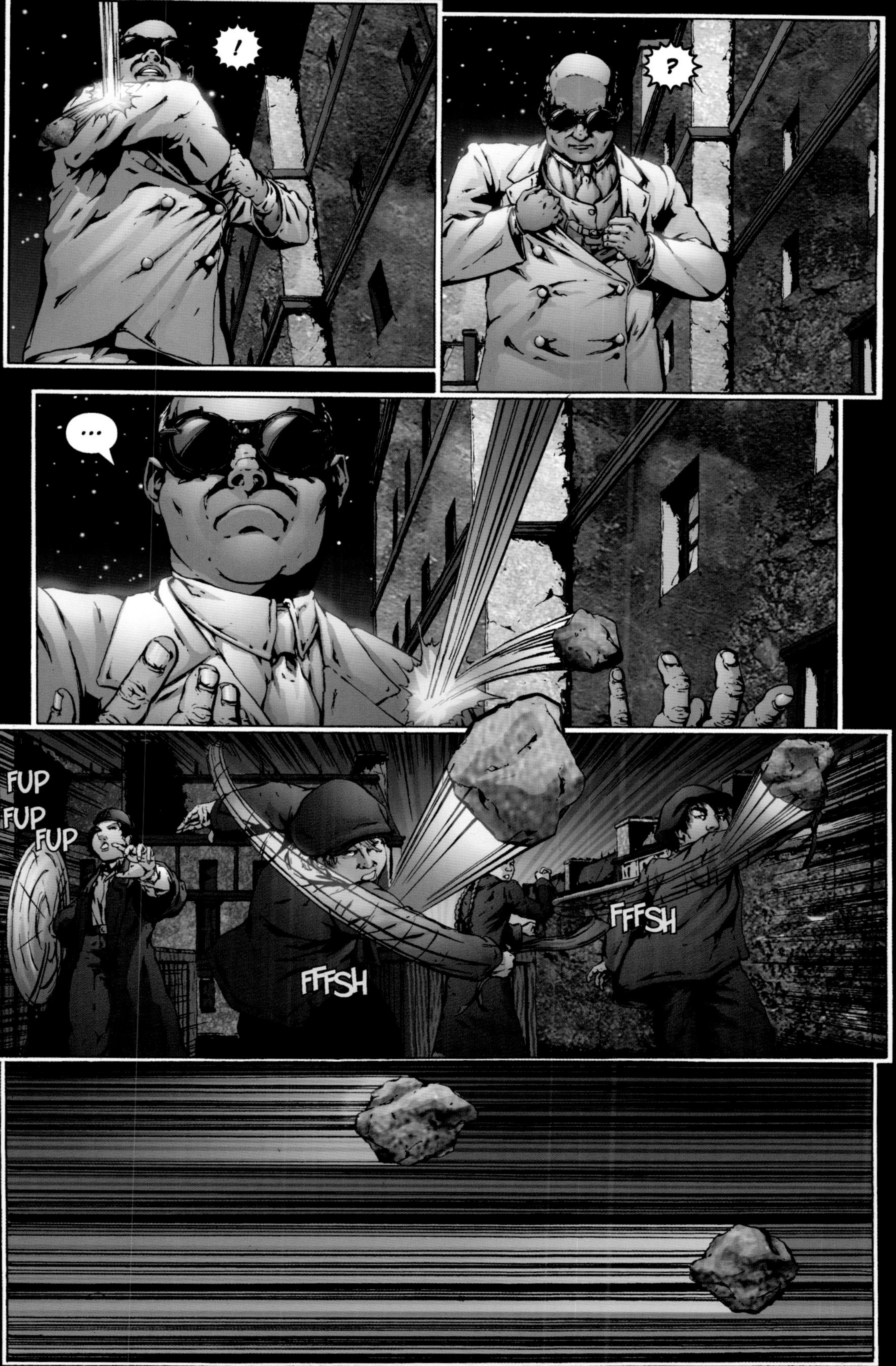
!
?
...
FUP
FUP
FUP
FFFSH
FFFSH

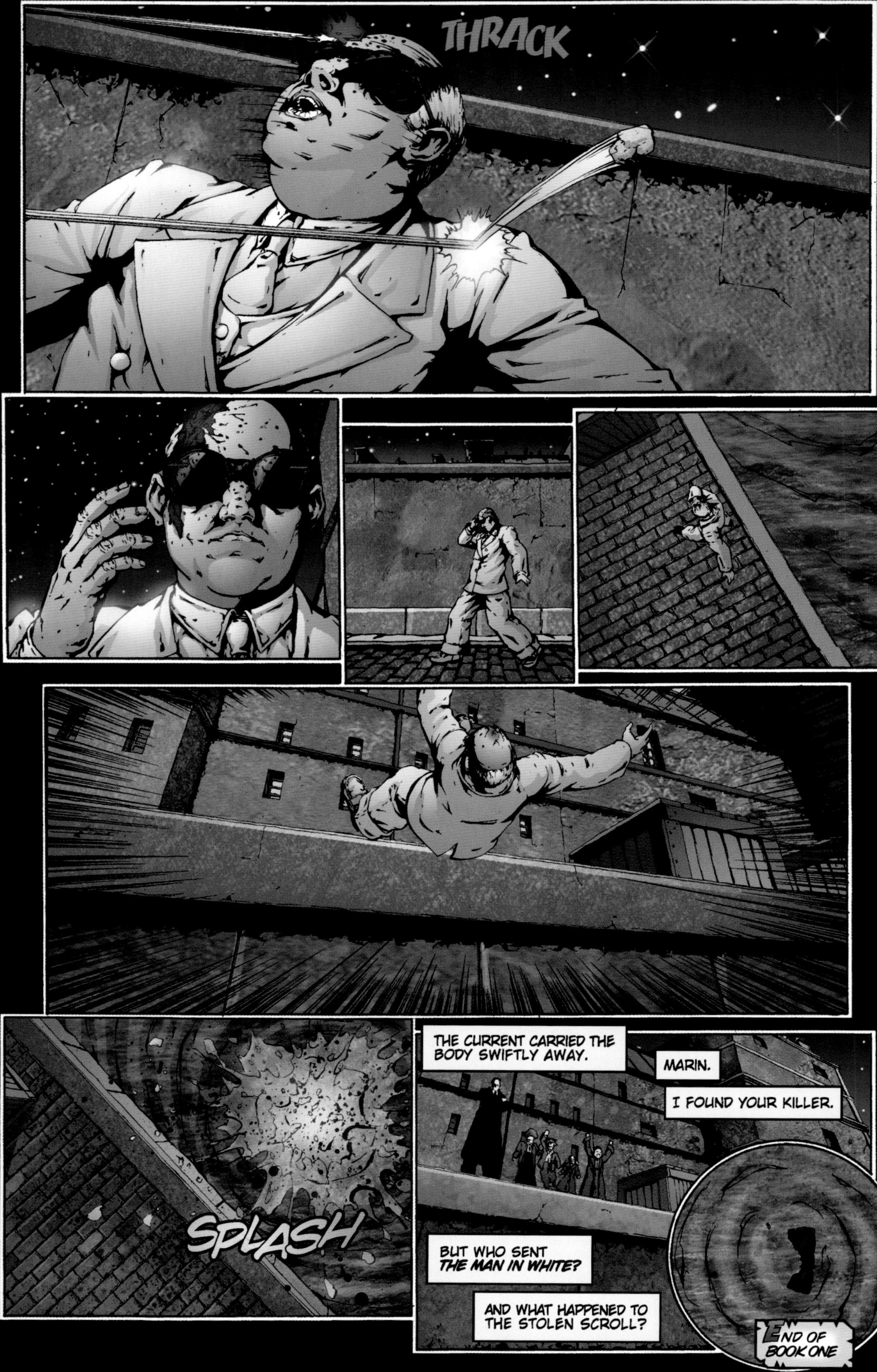
THRACK
SPLASH
THE CURRENT CARRIED THE BODY SWIFTLY AWAY.
MARIN.
I FOUND YOUR KILLER.
BUT WHO SENT *THE MAN IN WHITE?*
AND WHAT HAPPENED TO THE STOLEN SCROLL?
END OF BOOK ONE

Le Journal de la Liberté

Paris's leading anglophone newspaper • vol. 205, no. 100 • Oct. 23, MCMXXXIII

Editors in Chief: M. Tait Bergstrom, M. Matthew Pasteris. **Story Editor:** M. Arvid Nelson. **Art Editors:** M. EricJ, M. Jeromy Cox. **Photography Editor:** M. Alexander Waldman. **Layout Supervisor:** M. William Kartalopoulos. **Editors Emeritus:** M. Clark A. Smith, M. Howard P. Lovecraft, M. Robert E. Howard. Redacted by the Holy Inquisition under the direction of His Excellency Archbishop Emile-Jean Ireneaux. Le Journal de Liberté is printed under the benign auspices of his most puissant majesty KING LOUIS XXII of FRANCE. GOD SAVE THE KING.

Papal Seal

of Approval

King Grants Noble Titles to Two Influential Advisors

Paris, France — King Louis XXII granted titles of nobility to two trusted advisors yesterday. The move is widely seen as a step towards filling two vacant seats on the Hall of the Robe.

Noble entitlement, which can only be granted by the King, is a prerequisite for membership in the Hall of the Robe.

Because the King also has the exclusive right to appoint members to the Hall of the Robe under French law, the Robe is a virtual mouthpiece for Royal policies.

Many members of France's other parliamentary house, the Hall of the Sword, are critical of this system.

"We always find ourselves out-maneuvered," said one Sword member, who spoke on condition of anonymity. "The King is virtually assured a majority vote on any bill."

The King, the Hall of the Sword, and the Hall of the Robe each have one vote on proposed legislation. A measure requires a two-thirds majority to pass either house, while the King casts a vote alone. Two of three parties must vote for a bill for it to pass.

Historically, the Hall of the Robe has always sided with the King over the Sword, without exception.

"We are indeed chosen for our loyalty to the King, amongst other things," said Aristide deMandeville, Speaker for the Robe. "Every member of the Robe owes a great deal to His Majesty."

Yet it is possible for the Robe
continued on page A4

WEALTHY PARIS BUSINESSMAN SLAIN

Paris, France — Wealthy Parisian importer Baptiste Dumont was found murdered early today in his townhouse. Dumont was 38 years old.

Inquisition officials were quick to seal off the area, and an investigation into the death is underway.

Sophie Bigune, the housekeeper who found the corpse, described the horrific nature of the crime.

"I never saw anything that bad before. He was all cut up, all over his body, like someone was carving some kind of magical pattern into him. It wasn't Christian," she said.

Inquisitors dismissed her story. "The wounds in no way point to a ritualistic murder," Inquisitor LeGris, assigned to the case, said. He said her story was the "hysteria of an old woman."

Jean-Maurice Lefevre, a forensic attaché from the Guild of Physicians, corroborated LeGris' story. "He sustained many puncture and slashing wounds," Lefevre said. "No one of them was fatal, but the combination produced severe blood loss, to which he succumbed."

The attack occurred sometime early in the morning, according to him.

Dumont escaped an impoverished youth to become a successful importer of Italian goods. He

Rue Duphot, scene of the carnage. Photo: Eugene Atget, staff photographer

had many connections with the deMedici family.

The late businessman's associates strongly denied accusations Dumont had been involved in organized crime.

"He was a fierce competitor," Charles Maréchal, a business acquaintance, said. "That's all I have to say."

However, Dumont was arraigned several times over his life on charges of racketeering, assault, and pandering. All charges were eventually dropped.

"Just because a man makes something of himself, just because he comes from humble origins, he has to endure outra-

geous slander," Pierre Modot, Dumont's solicitor, said. "My client struggled his whole life against unfounded charges engineered specifically to damage his reputation."

Inquisitors expressed doubt.

"Pierre Modot is an iniquitous slime who protects criminals and reprobates from the judgment of the Lord," LeGris said. "Dumont was no different. St. Peter will cast all his kind into the Lake of Fire."

LeGris declined to comment if Dumont's death was related to his alleged underground activities.

No further details were available.

Excavators Discover Catacombs

Paris, France — A group of Paris workers digging a metro line have uncovered a medieval catacomb filled with the remains of our city's medieval denizens.

"It's really creepy to think of all of those bones just lying there in the darkness for so long," Gérard DuChamp, the workers' foreman, said.

Huge piles of stacked bones were discovered in a tunnel carved out of the city's bedrock.

According to Professor Devereaux of the Sorbonne, there's no mystery to the discovery.

"A lot of medieval graveyards had to be dug up and relocated in underground vaults as Paris grew," he said. "A grisly necessity."

MISSING MISSIONARIES' HEADLESS BODIES FOUND IN AMAZONIA

Amazonia — The slain bodies of two dozen missionaries were found yesterday in a small Amazonian settlement. The discovery confirmed fears the missionaries had been killed by indigenous peoples.

The corpses bore wounds attesting to a savage assault. Several of the corpses were headless.

"The savages have a beastly tradition of shrinking the head of their enemies and wearing them as jewelry," said Bishop Cornelius Navarro, who oversees many missionary expeditions to South America.

The expedition began several months ago, and was headed by Father Samson O'Malley, who

led a group of the faithful from the British Isles into the darkest forests of the Amazon, hoping to win souls for Christ among the heathen.

Tragically, O'Malley's corpse was missing its head. Who knows? At this very moment it is probably swinging from a shaman's neck.

Navarro expressed concern and regret over the incident.

"This only demonstrates the need for more missionary activity in Amazon," he said.

Other Church members were not so sympathetic.

"These forest-folk are savages and the spawn of Satan, and they should be exterminated with ex-
continued on page B11

LE JOURNAL SPECIAL: "THE INVISIBLE EMPIRE"

Ah, Venice. Widely considered the birthplace of the great mercantile empires, Venice has changed little since the 1500s. Detail of a painting by Canaletto.

"The new class of mercantilist entrepreneurs is the single greatest reason for the advancement of European society in modern times. It is also the single greatest threat to our cherished Christian values." Thus spoke Pope John XIV in a papal bull issued last year. The supreme pontiff's words perfectly sum up the generally held attitude towards the new class of "self-made men" who have come into prominence in the space of a few short generations, the *merchant princes*. These men earn their living not from inherited property or physical toil, but from the buying, selling and distribution of goods. This new elite of the middle class has built vast empires based on the ephemeral flow of goods and money throughout the world. This "invisible empire" of trade is a fascinating and controversial element of our society and had become inextricably intertwined with the economies of the Christian world.

"I make nothing, I do not practice a trade and I have no noble title," says Edmund Upshire, reclining in the burgundy leather chair of his cavernous London office. "But without people like me, economies would cease to function."

It may sound like a riddle, but it's not. Upshire is a member of the elite echelons of the middle class. His family rules a vast empire, but it's not an empire you can quantify in military might or expanse of land. The Upshire domains exist in the cargo holds of hundreds of merchant marine vessels, in the bowels of hundreds of factories and locked away in dozens of bank vaults.

Over the course of several generations, Upshire's family has built an empire of banking and commerce.

"I buy things from one place and sell them at another. I analyze markets, assess risks, and determine how to best make a profit," he says.

He and a small group of elite businessmen are often called "merchant princes." The nobility first applied this term derisively, but as the power of the merchant princes grew, it became clear the joke was on the aristocratic establishment.

There is no exact definition of the term merchant prince, but it is only applicable to a handful of powerful merchant families

throughout Europe.

Upshire's trade empire is based in London, one of the largest centers of finance in the world. Britain and the Netherlands were the first countries to liberalize money lending laws, and many academics believe this led to the rise of their economies while giving birth to the merchant princes themselves.

"Lending money at interest is an absolute necessity for an entrepreneur to do business," Secondino deMedici, of the deMedici family, said. "It's foolish to call it a sin, to call it usury, because it's neither. It's impossible to start a business without borrowing capital. Much prosperity has been generated through moneylending."

The deMedicis originated as the ruling elite of Florence. They expanded to Venice where they have created an enormous economic empire. Venice is widely considered to be the first great economic capital of Europe, and it thrives today.

Secondino deMedici, a senior executive of the family, explains more about how a merchant prince operates. "We don't own any ships or factories. Instead we contract services on a for-hire basis and buy and sell goods depending on where market conditions are best. It helps spread risk."

However, it is exactly this attitude that has earned the mer-

Lovely Copenhagen, the Jewel of the North. "Everyone really should see Copenhagen at least once in their lives," merchant prince Hans Richter confides.

chant princes the stigma of being lawless opportunists.

"They're more 'pirate princes' than merchant princes," said a Prussian finance minister, who choose to speak anonymously. "They owe allegiance to neither Church nor king."

"Christ simply isn't part of their money-making equation," Papal Nuncio Artyom Swiatek said. "They will engage in any activity, even African slave trading, so long as it is profitable"

Upshire declined to comment on any involvement in the slave trade, as did deMedici. But deMedici is dismissive of Swiatek's concerns.

"Some people are under the impression that the 'stateless' quality of our business, as it is called, necessarily entails lawlessness and profiteering. In fact, nothing could be further from the truth. Our multinational trade networks favor stability and prosperity for all," he said.

"War, famine and poverty are bad for business; they make it harder to sell goods, harder to make money," Upshire added. "We have an absolute vested interest in peace and widespread wealth."

But no group is more critical of the Merchant Princes than the Guilds.

"They talk a lot about spreading peace and prosperity, but it's all nonsense," Christoph deProvence,

a member of the High Guild Council, said. "They thrive on instability, and they have enormous leverage when it comes to manipulating the marketplace. The end result is that ordinary guild artisans end up earning barely enough to live on for the sake of someone's crystal chandelier in Venice or London."

Hans Richter, a merchant prince based in Copenhagen, the economic nexus of the Baltic and Scandinavian countries, rejects this claim.

"If anything, we have helped the guilds, help them compete and offer better services. The net result is entirely positive for people of every social class."

But Richter does not dispute the fact that merchant princes have an enormous amount of power.

"One must remember, it's not just about trade," he said. "It's about other things, like banking and insurance and trading in corporate stock. The term 'invisible empire' really is accurate."

Whatever the case, influence of the merchant princes seems here to stay: last week Upshire bought the ancestral home of the Earls of Warwick from the recently impoverished noble family for an undisclosed sum.

He has already replaced the Warwick shield on the estate's front gates with his own newly minted crest. ⚜

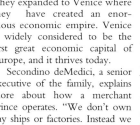

London has come into international pre-eminence because of its concentration of finance interests. Lloyd's, the city's most renown bank, began as a coffee house.

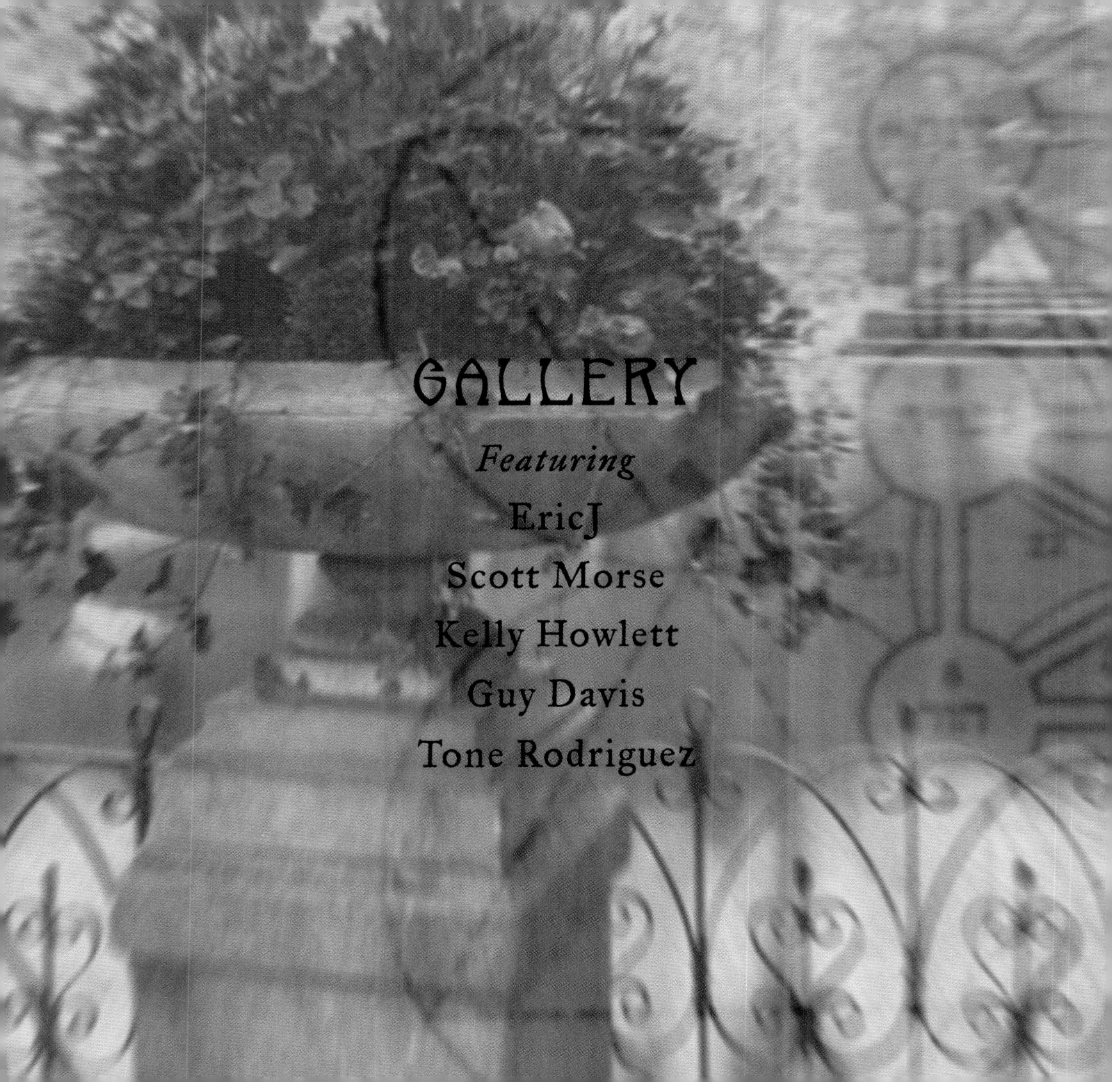

GALLERY

Featuring

EricJ

Scott Morse

Kelly Howlett

Guy Davis

Tone Rodriguez

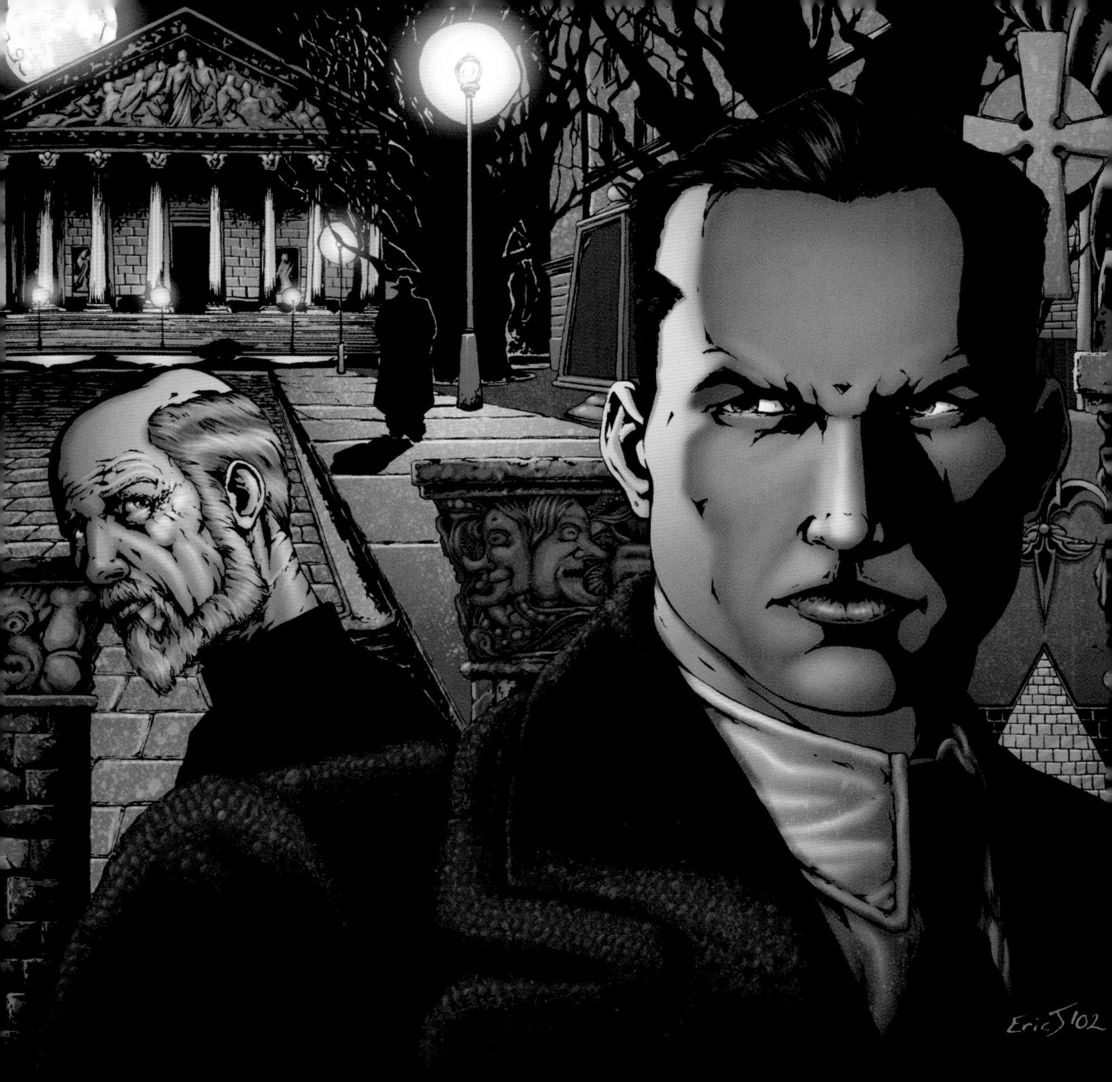
EricJ '02

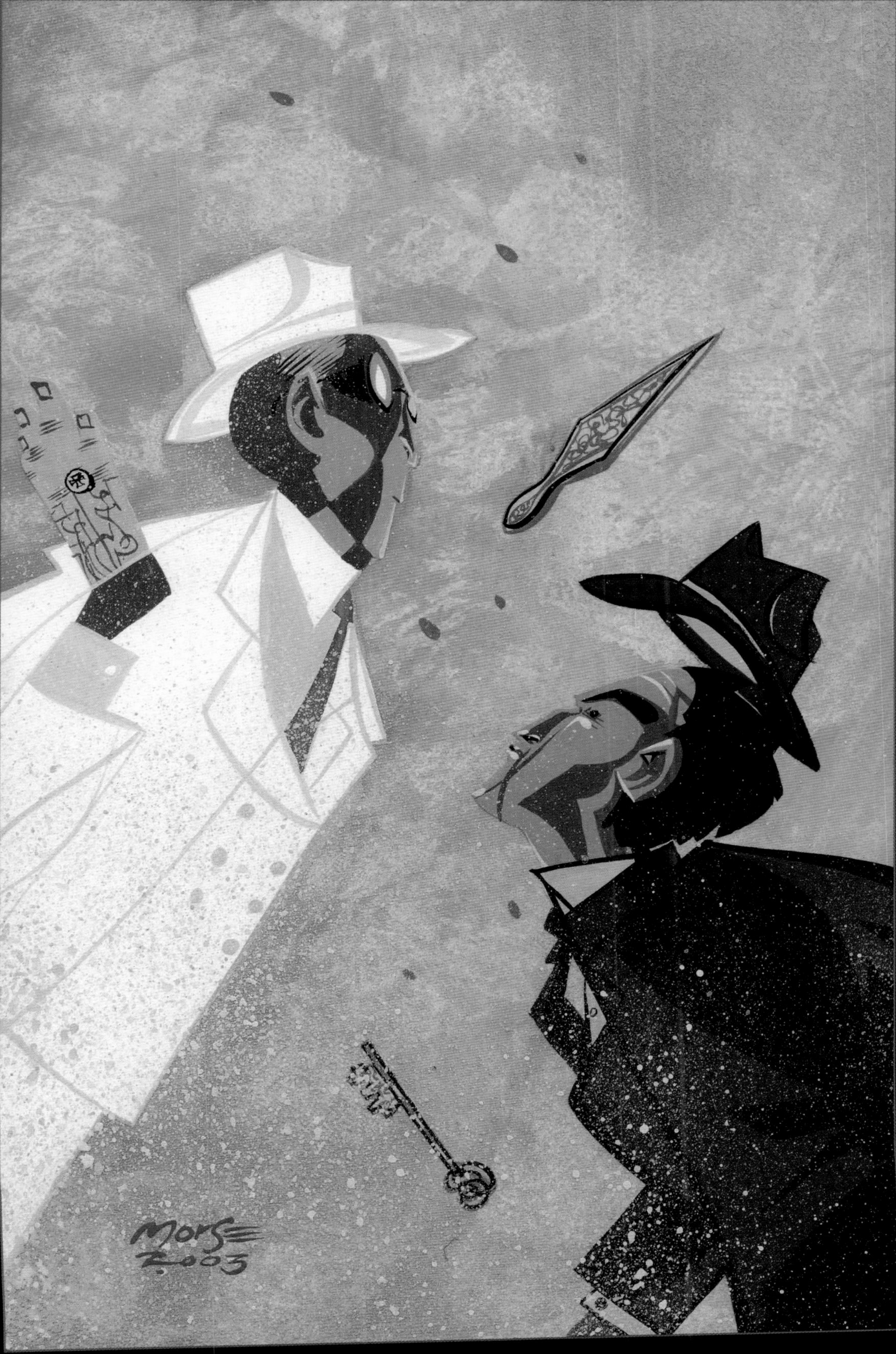

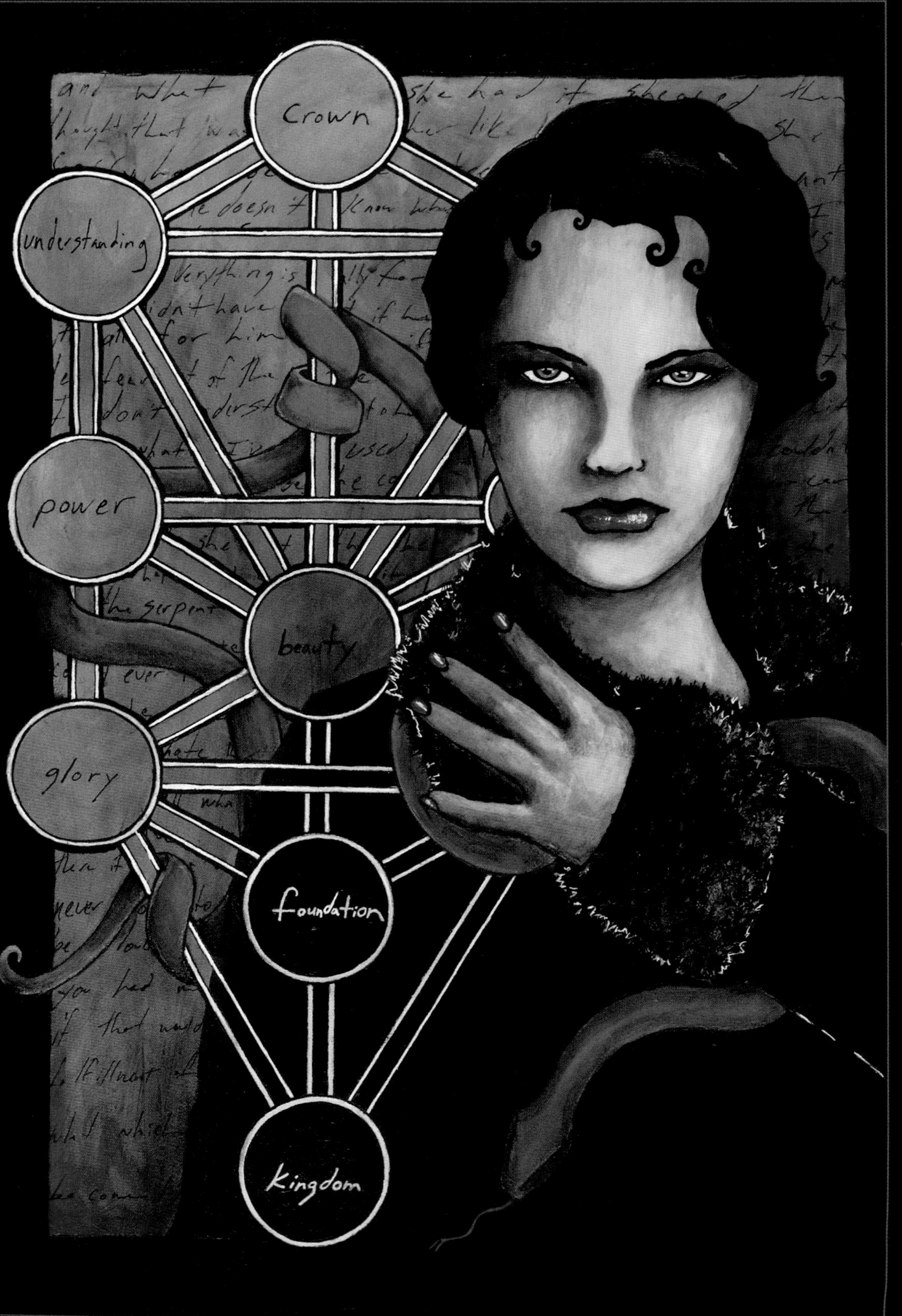
Crown
understanding
power
beauty
glory
foundation
kingdom

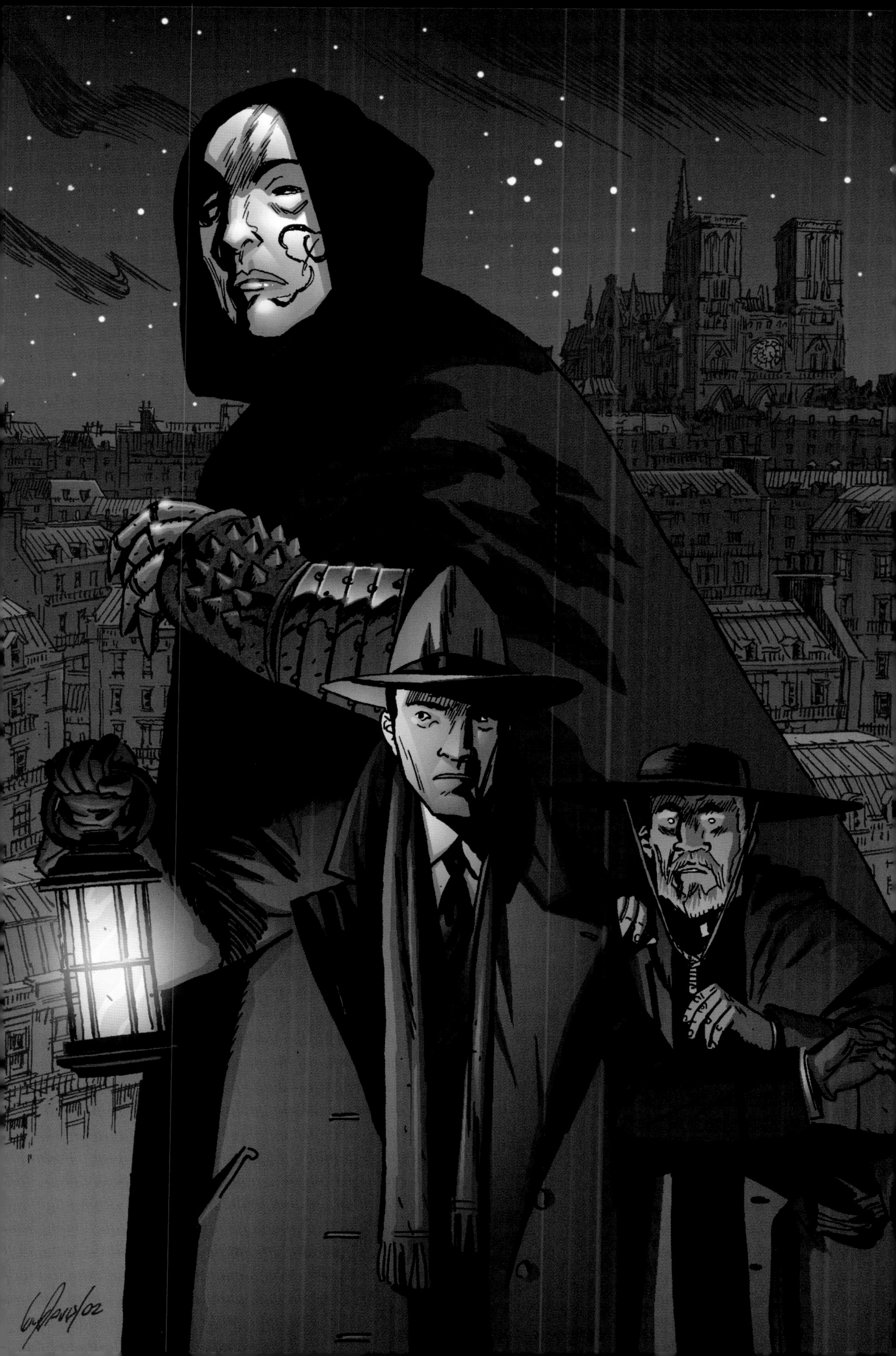

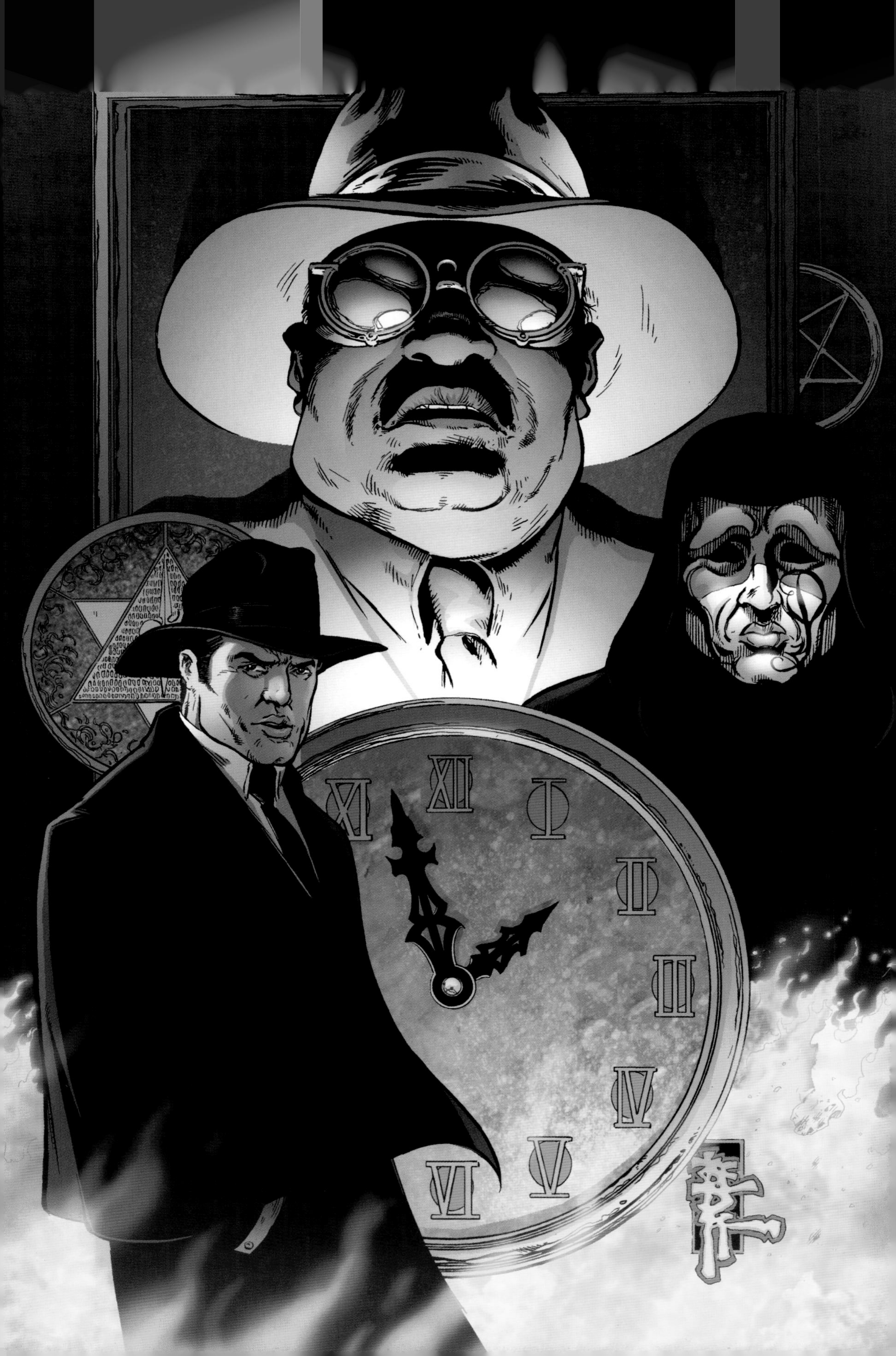

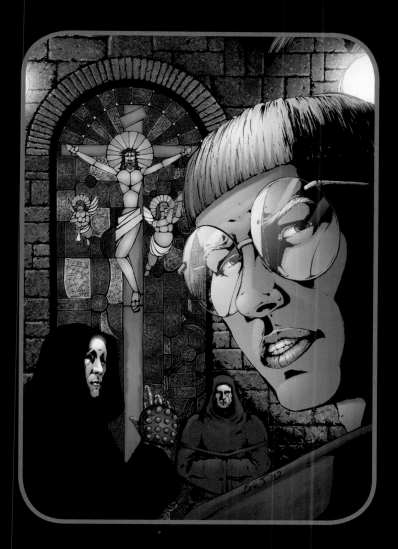

BROTHER MATTHEW
BLESSED ARE THE MEEK

BROTHER MATTHEW:
Blessed Are the Meek

an introduction by Arvid Nelson

IMAGE COMICS DECIDED TO publish *Rex Mundi* #0 as a one-shot in 2001. No one knew if there was a readership for an alternate history noir thriller about . . . Jesus.

So EricJ and I cooked up *Brother Matthew* as a web comic to promote *Rex Mundi* before it hit the shelves. *Brother Matthew* is set in the world of *Rex Mundi*, and, like its big brother, it's a mystery series. But that's where the similarities end.

Rex Mundi borrows from classic Hollywood noir: the detective, Julien, walks a precarious line between the cops—the Inquisitors—and the robbers, the secret society members. There are no "good guys." Everyone is out to protect themselves. The hero is always changed profoundly at the end of his quest because the biggest mystery he's solving is himself.

Brother Matthew, on the other hand, takes from classic English mystery serials like *Sherlock Holmes* or G. K. Chesterton's *Father Brown* stories. The cops are bumbling idiots—well-meaning, but they're always missing the size-twelve footprints outside the window or the bloodstained handkerchief. Evil is always exposed and overcome at the end. The stories are episodic, and don't change the main character very much.

Eric and I also wanted to follow the format of daily newspaper strips from the 1930s and '40s. That's why we did *Brother Matthew* in horizontal, three-panel strips. We debuted a new episode every Friday on the Rex Mundi website.

Brother Matthew is special to me because it's my first published work. Before *Rex Mundi* ever came out, *Brother Matthew* saw print in the pages of *Comics International,* a UK comics magazine. Dez Skinn, the editor of *CI,* even devoted a front cover to us. It's one of the main reasons *Rex Mundi* #0 sold out initially and why it continues to do so well in the UK. Go' bless ya, Dez.

And so, here is the complete *Brother Matthew* as it appeared on the web and in the pages of *Comics International*. I hope you enjoy reading it as much as I enjoyed writing and lettering it.

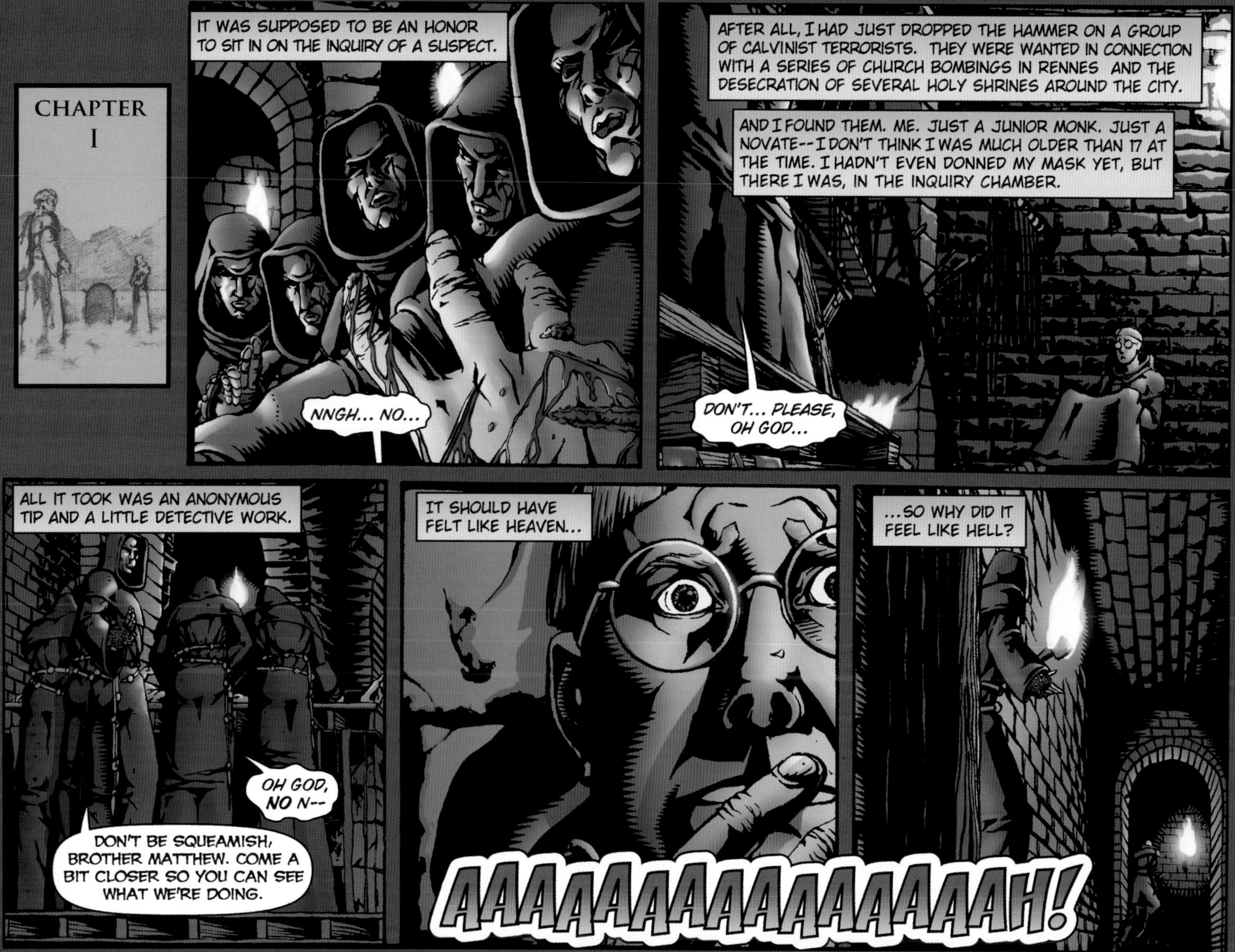
CHAPTER
I
IT WAS SUPPOSED TO BE AN HONOR TO SIT IN ON THE INQUIRY OF A SUSPECT.
NNGH... NO...
AFTER ALL, I HAD JUST DROPPED THE HAMMER ON A GROUP OF CALVINIST TERRORISTS. THEY WERE WANTED IN CONNECTION WITH A SERIES OF CHURCH BOMBINGS IN RENNES AND THE DESECRATION OF SEVERAL HOLY SHRINES AROUND THE CITY.
AND I FOUND THEM. ME. JUST A JUNIOR MONK. JUST A NOVATE--I DON'T THINK I WAS MUCH OLDER THAN 17 AT THE TIME. I HADN'T EVEN DONNED MY MASK YET, BUT THERE I WAS, IN THE INQUIRY CHAMBER.
DON'T... PLEASE, OH GOD...
ALL IT TOOK WAS AN ANONYMOUS TIP AND A LITTLE DETECTIVE WORK.
OH GOD, NO N--
DON'T BE SQUEAMISH, BROTHER MATTHEW. COME A BIT CLOSER SO YOU CAN SEE WHAT WE'RE DOING.
IT SHOULD HAVE FELT LIKE HEAVEN...
...SO WHY DID IT FEEL LIKE HELL?
AAAAAAAAAAAAAAAH!

CHAPTER
II
THERE WAS AN EMPTY HOLE IN MY STOMACH WHERE MY DINNER HAD BEEN. BUT ALREADY THE TORTURE OF THE CALVINIST SEEMED SO UNREAL, LIKE A BAD DREAM.
PATER NOSTER, QUI EST IN COELIS...
...SANTIFICETUR NOMEN TUUM AD VENIAT...
I HAD NO IDEA WHAT WOULD HAPPEN -- I THOUGHT I MIGHT EVEN BE EXPELLED FROM THE INQUISITION, AND THE IDEA WASN'T TOTALLY UNAPPEALING TO ME.
BUT I WAS WRONG.
REGNUM TUUM...
FRERÉ MATTHEW...
YES, BROTHER?
...YOU'RE GOING TO PARIS.
P... PAR...
ARCHBISHOP IRENEAUX HAS PERSONALLY REQUESTED YOU BE ASSIGNED TO THE PARISIAN INQUISITION.
A COURIER FROM HIS DIOCESE JUST ARRIVED A FEW MOMENTS AGO. I'M TOLD YOU'RE TO LEAVE TOMORROW AT DAWN.
HIS EXCELLENCY IRENEAUX IS A BUSY MAN. YOU'VE TURNED A LOT OF HEADS...
...BROTHER.
...T-TUUM FIAT VOLUNTAS TUA SICUT...
KSLAM!
Eric J. '01

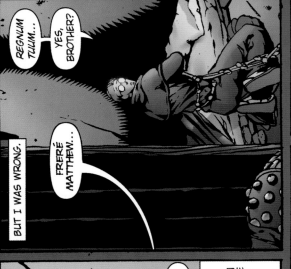

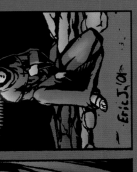

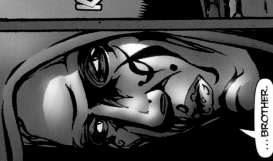

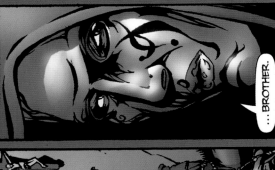

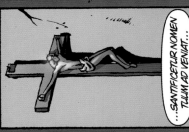

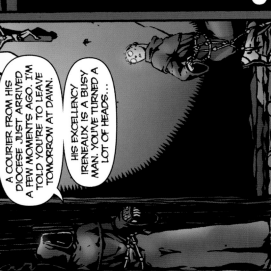

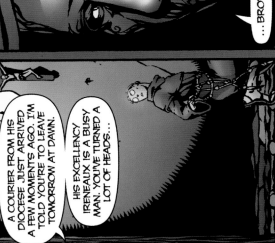

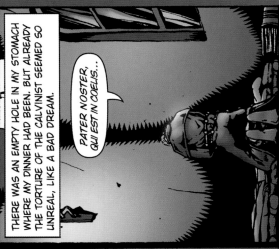

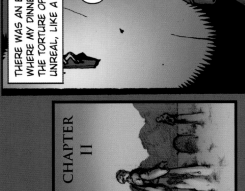

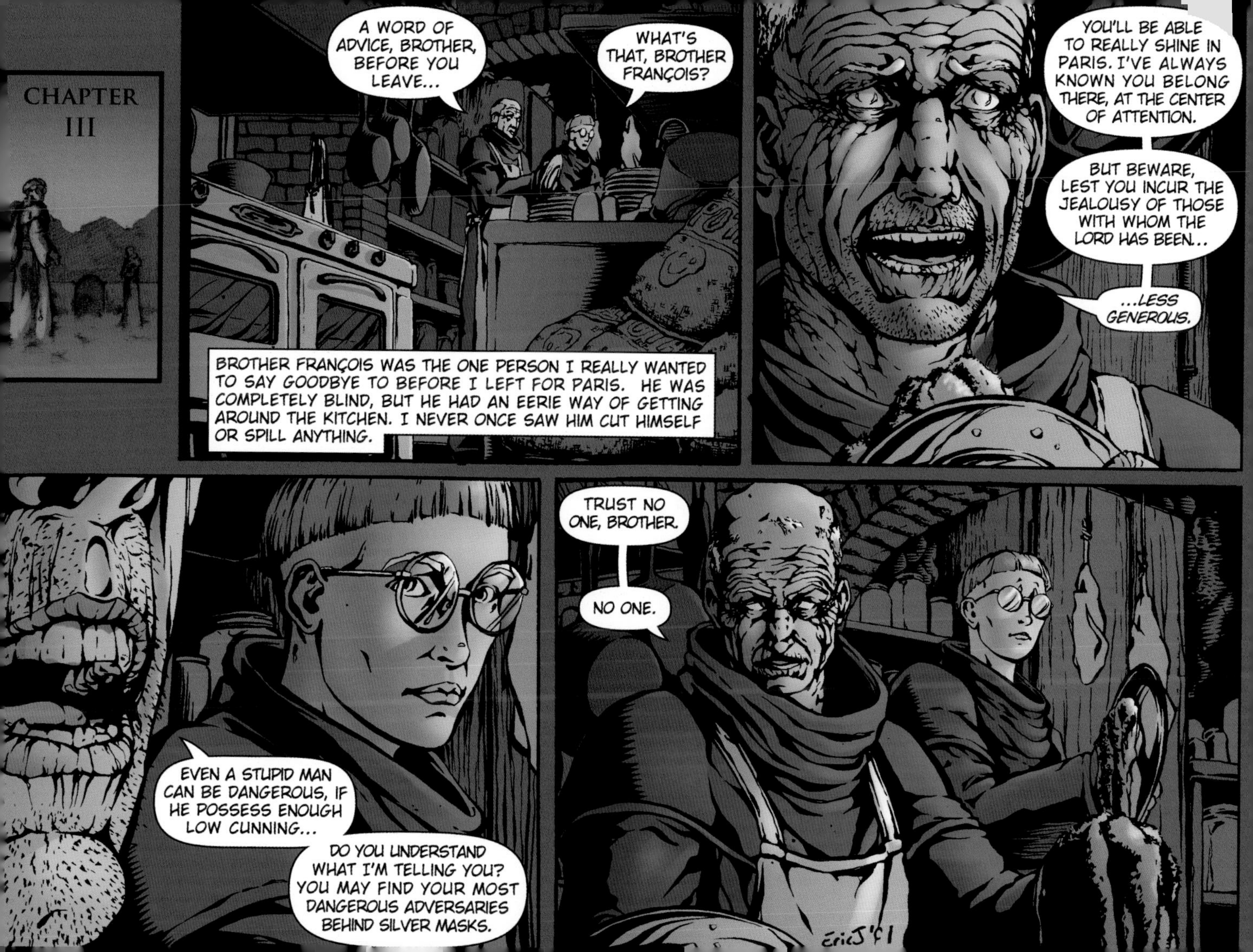
CHAPTER III
A WORD OF ADVICE, BROTHER, BEFORE YOU LEAVE...
WHAT'S THAT, BROTHER FRANÇOIS?
BROTHER FRANÇOIS WAS THE ONE PERSON I REALLY WANTED TO SAY GOODBYE TO BEFORE I LEFT FOR PARIS. HE WAS COMPLETELY BLIND, BUT HE HAD AN EERIE WAY OF GETTING AROUND THE KITCHEN. I NEVER ONCE SAW HIM CUT HIMSELF OR SPILL ANYTHING.
YOU'LL BE ABLE TO REALLY SHINE IN PARIS. I'VE ALWAYS KNOWN YOU BELONG THERE, AT THE CENTER OF ATTENTION.
BUT BEWARE, LEST YOU INCUR THE JEALOUSY OF THOSE WITH WHOM THE LORD HAS BEEN...
...LESS GENEROUS.
EVEN A STUPID MAN CAN BE DANGEROUS, IF HE POSSESS ENOUGH LOW CUNNING...
DO YOU UNDERSTAND WHAT I'M TELLING YOU? YOU MAY FIND YOUR MOST DANGEROUS ADVERSARIES BEHIND SILVER MASKS.
TRUST NO ONE, BROTHER.
NO ONE.
EricJ'01

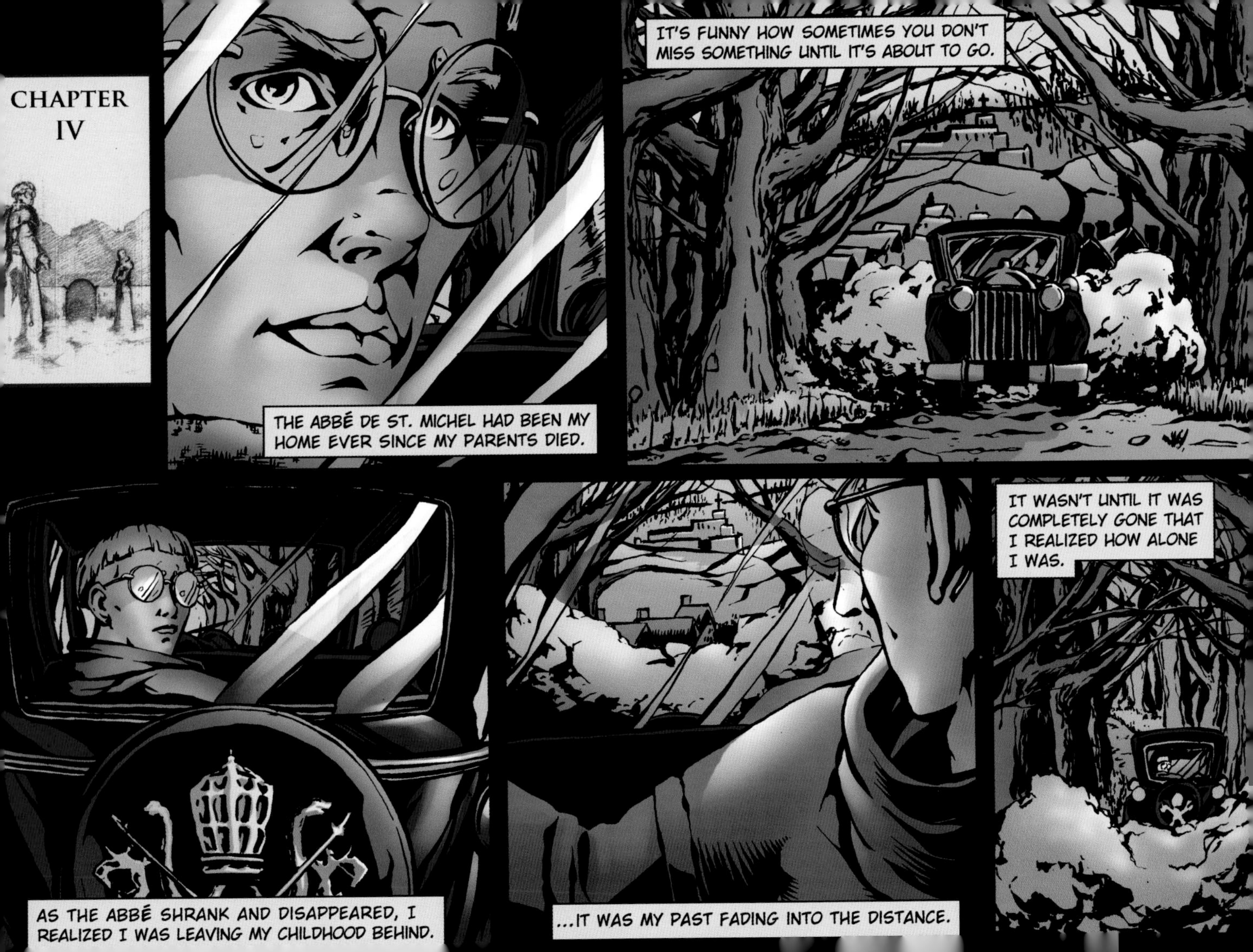
CHAPTER IV
THE ABBÉ DE ST. MICHEL HAD BEEN MY HOME EVER SINCE MY PARENTS DIED.
IT'S FUNNY HOW SOMETIMES YOU DON'T MISS SOMETHING UNTIL IT'S ABOUT TO GO.
AS THE ABBÉ SHRANK AND DISAPPEARED, I REALIZED I WAS LEAVING MY CHILDHOOD BEHIND.
...IT WAS MY PAST FADING INTO THE DISTANCE.
IT WASN'T UNTIL IT WAS COMPLETELY GONE THAT I REALIZED HOW ALONE I WAS.

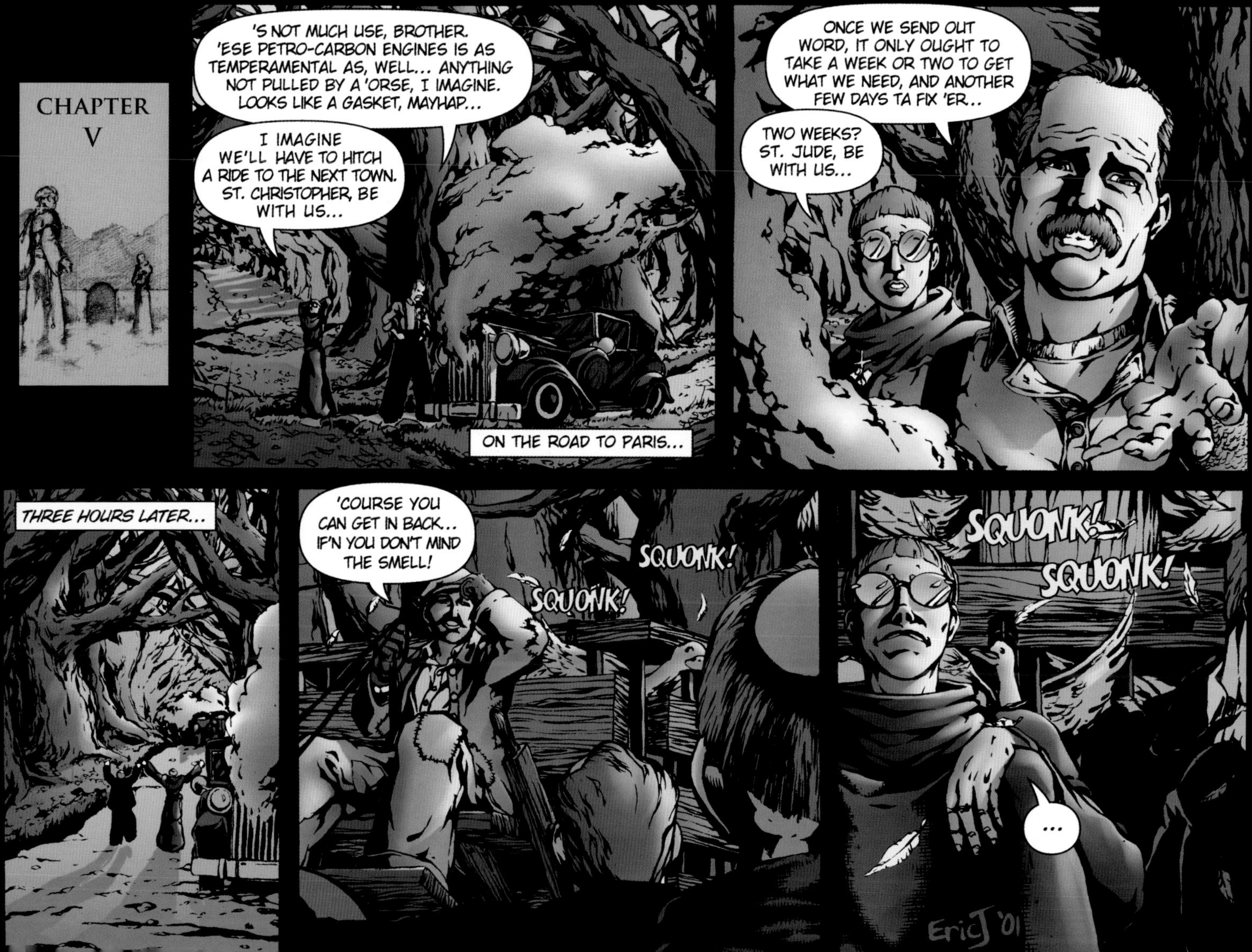
CHAPTER
V
'S NOT MUCH USE, BROTHER. 'ESE PETRO-CARBON ENGINES IS AS TEMPERAMENTAL AS, WELL... ANYTHING NOT PULLED BY A 'ORSE, I IMAGINE. LOOKS LIKE A GASKET, MAYHAP...
I IMAGINE WE'LL HAVE TO HITCH A RIDE TO THE NEXT TOWN. ST. CHRISTOPHER, BE WITH US...
ON THE ROAD TO PARIS...
ONCE WE SEND OUT WORD, IT ONLY OUGHT TO TAKE A WEEK OR TWO TO GET WHAT WE NEED, AND ANOTHER FEW DAYS TA FIX 'ER...
TWO WEEKS? ST. JUDE, BE WITH US...
THREE HOURS LATER...
'COURSE YOU CAN GET IN BACK... IF'N YOU DON'T MIND THE SMELL!
SQUONK!
SQUONK!
SQUONK!
SQUONK!
...
EricJ '01

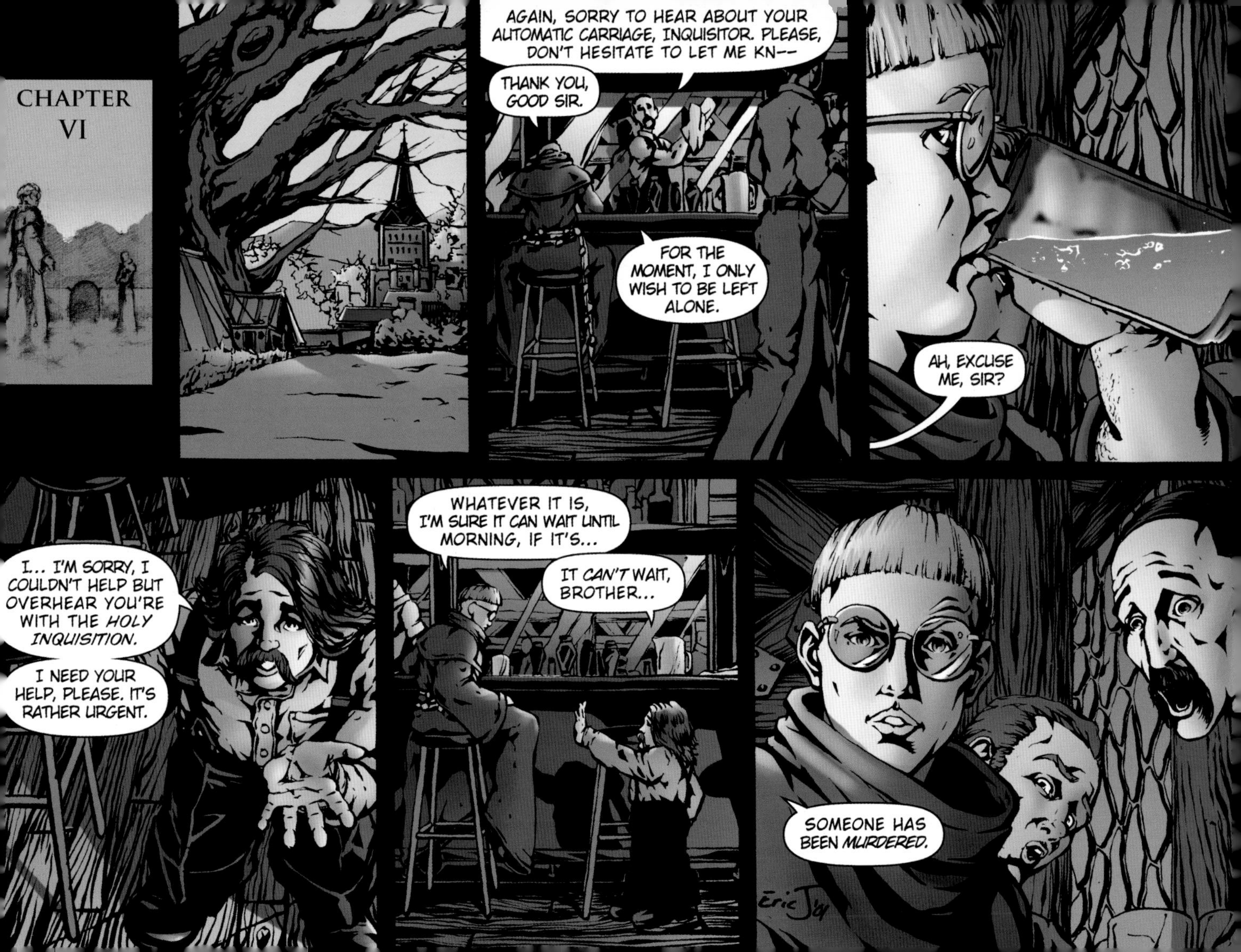
CHAPTER
VI
AGAIN, SORRY TO HEAR ABOUT YOUR AUTOMATIC CARRIAGE, INQUISITOR. PLEASE, DON'T HESITATE TO LET ME KN--
THANK YOU, GOOD SIR.
FOR THE MOMENT, I ONLY WISH TO BE LEFT ALONE.
AH, EXCUSE ME, SIR?
I... I'M SORRY, I COULDN'T HELP BUT OVERHEAR YOU'RE WITH THE *HOLY INQUISITION*.
I NEED YOUR HELP, PLEASE. IT'S RATHER URGENT.
WHATEVER IT IS, I'M SURE IT CAN WAIT UNTIL MORNING, IF IT'S...
IT *CAN'T* WAIT, BROTHER...
SOMEONE HAS BEEN *MURDERED*.
Eric J '04

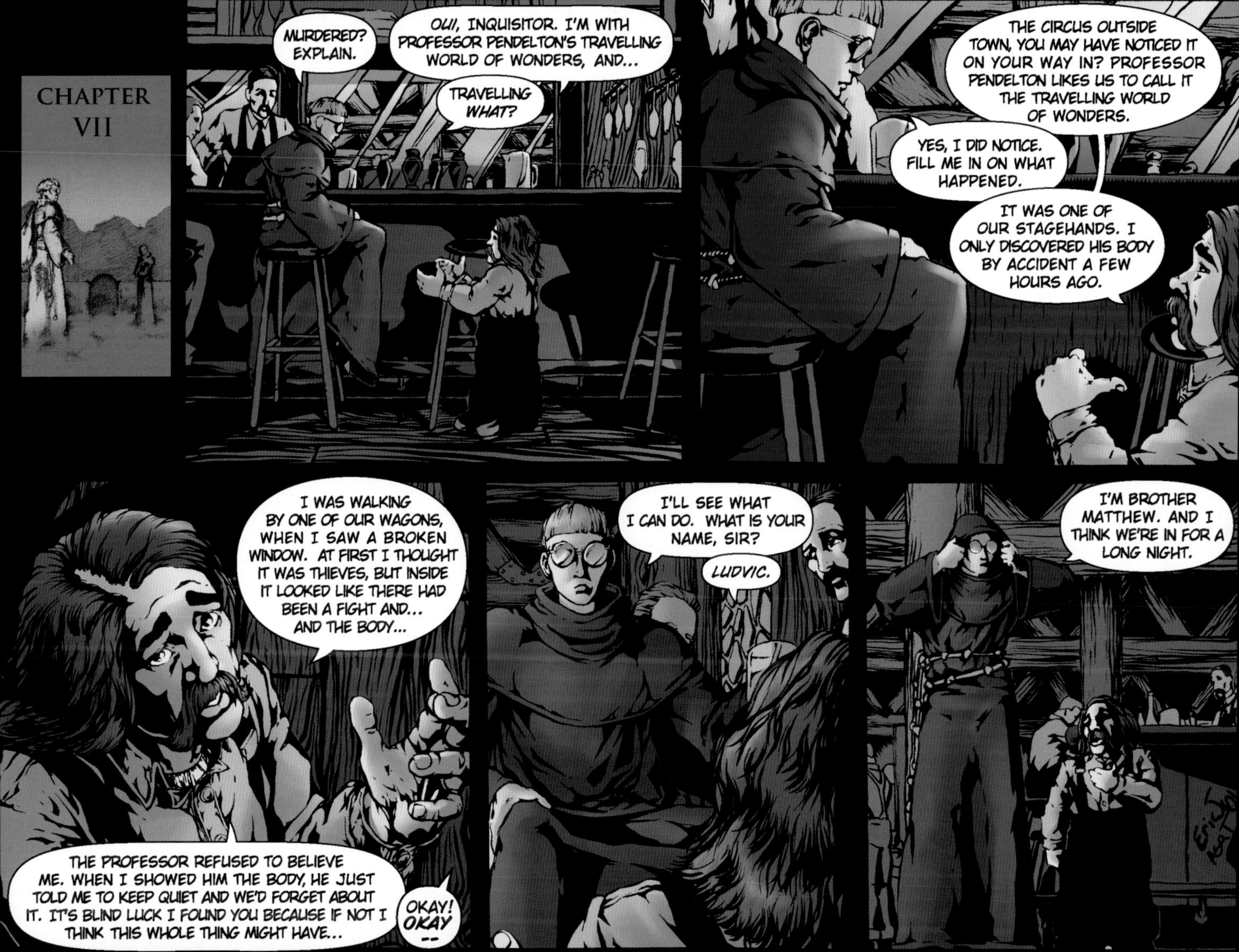
CHAPTER
VII
MURDERED? EXPLAIN.
OUI, INQUISITOR. I'M WITH PROFESSOR PENDELTON'S TRAVELLING WORLD OF WONDERS, AND...
TRAVELLING WHAT?
THE CIRCUS OUTSIDE TOWN, YOU MAY HAVE NOTICED IT ON YOUR WAY IN? PROFESSOR PENDELTON LIKES US TO CALL IT THE TRAVELLING WORLD OF WONDERS.
YES, I DID NOTICE. FILL ME IN ON WHAT HAPPENED.
IT WAS ONE OF OUR STAGEHANDS. I ONLY DISCOVERED HIS BODY BY ACCIDENT A FEW HOURS AGO.
I WAS WALKING BY ONE OF OUR WAGONS, WHEN I SAW A BROKEN WINDOW. AT FIRST I THOUGHT IT WAS THIEVES, BUT INSIDE IT LOOKED LIKE THERE HAD BEEN A FIGHT AND... AND THE BODY...
THE PROFESSOR REFUSED TO BELIEVE ME. WHEN I SHOWED HIM THE BODY, HE JUST TOLD ME TO KEEP QUIET AND WE'D FORGET ABOUT IT. IT'S BLIND LUCK I FOUND YOU BECAUSE IF NOT I THINK THIS WHOLE THING MIGHT HAVE...
OKAY! OKAY --
I'LL SEE WHAT I CAN DO. WHAT IS YOUR NAME, SIR?
LUDVIC.
I'M BROTHER MATTHEW. AND I THINK WE'RE IN FOR A LONG NIGHT.

CHAPTER VIII

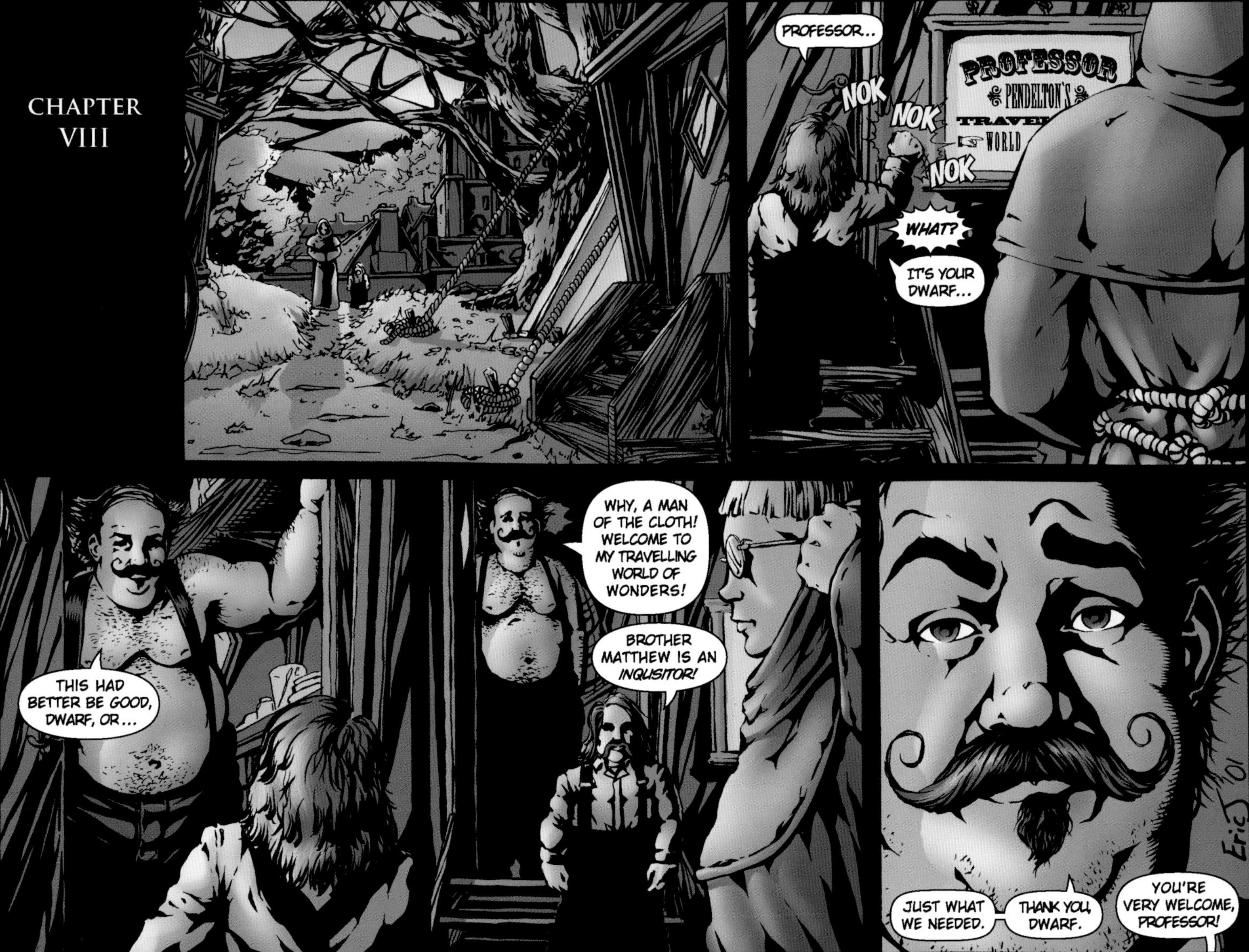
PROFESSOR...
NOK
NOK
NOK
PROFESSOR
PENDELTON'S
WORLD
WHAT?
IT'S YOUR DWARF...
THIS HAD BETTER BE GOOD, DWARF, OR...
WHY, A MAN OF THE CLOTH! WELCOME TO MY TRAVELLING WORLD OF WONDERS!
BROTHER MATTHEW IS AN *INQUSITOR!*
JUST WHAT WE NEEDED.
THANK YOU, DWARF.
YOU'RE VERY WELCOME, PROFESSOR!
Eric J '01

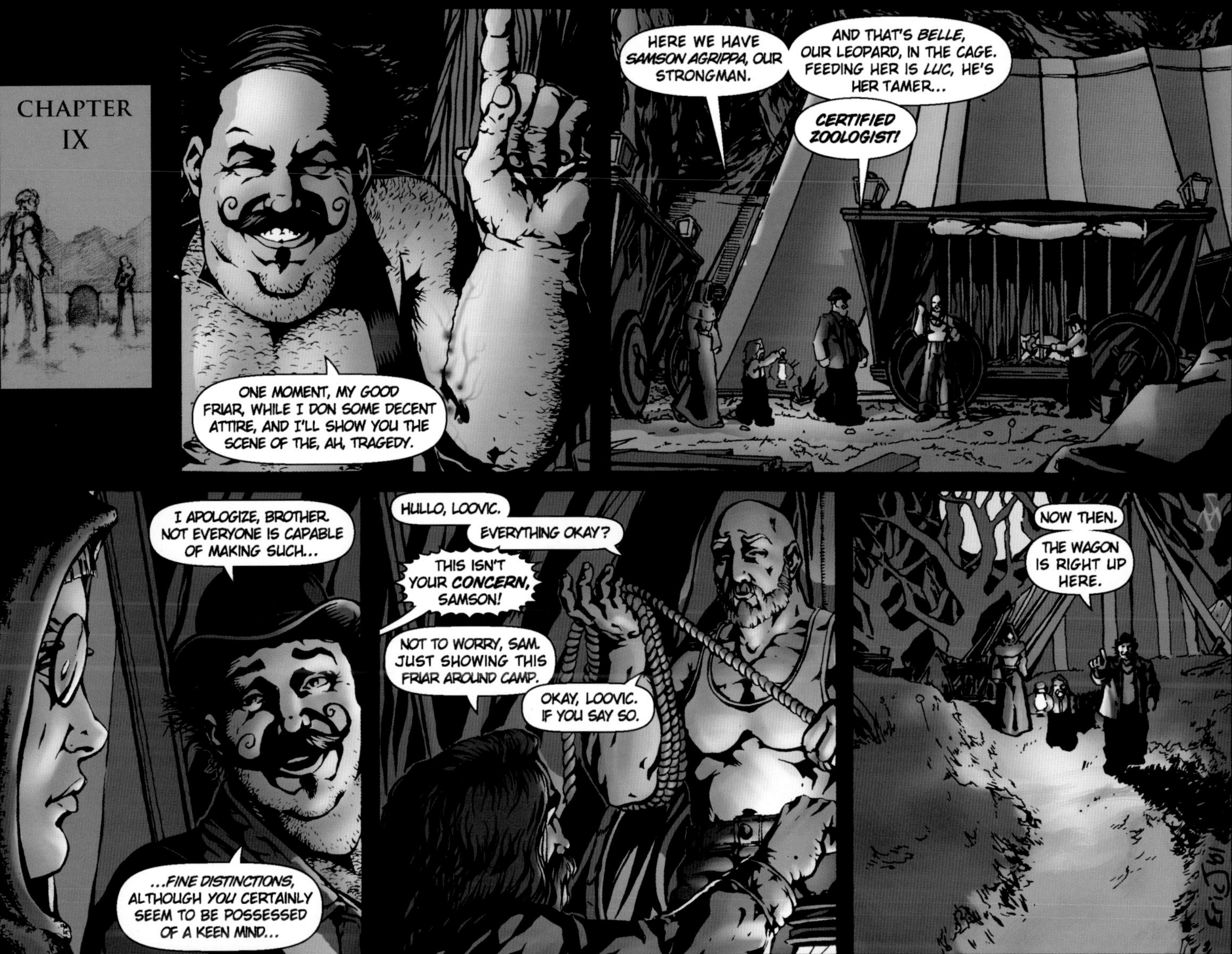
CHAPTER IX
ONE MOMENT, MY GOOD FRIAR, WHILE I DON SOME DECENT ATTIRE, AND I'LL SHOW YOU THE SCENE OF THE, AH, TRAGEDY.
HERE WE HAVE SAMSON AGRIPPA, OUR STRONGMAN.
AND THAT'S BELLE, OUR LEOPARD, IN THE CAGE. FEEDING HER IS LUC, HE'S HER TAMER...
CERTIFIED ZOOLOGIST!
I APOLOGIZE, BROTHER. NOT EVERYONE IS CAPABLE OF MAKING SUCH...
...FINE DISTINCTIONS, ALTHOUGH YOU CERTAINLY SEEM TO BE POSSESSED OF A KEEN MIND...
HULLO, LOOVIC.
EVERYTHING OKAY?
THIS ISN'T YOUR CONCERN, SAMSON!
NOT TO WORRY, SAM. JUST SHOWING THIS FRIAR AROUND CAMP.
OKAY, LOOVIC. IF YOU SAY SO.
NOW THEN.
THE WAGON IS RIGHT UP HERE.

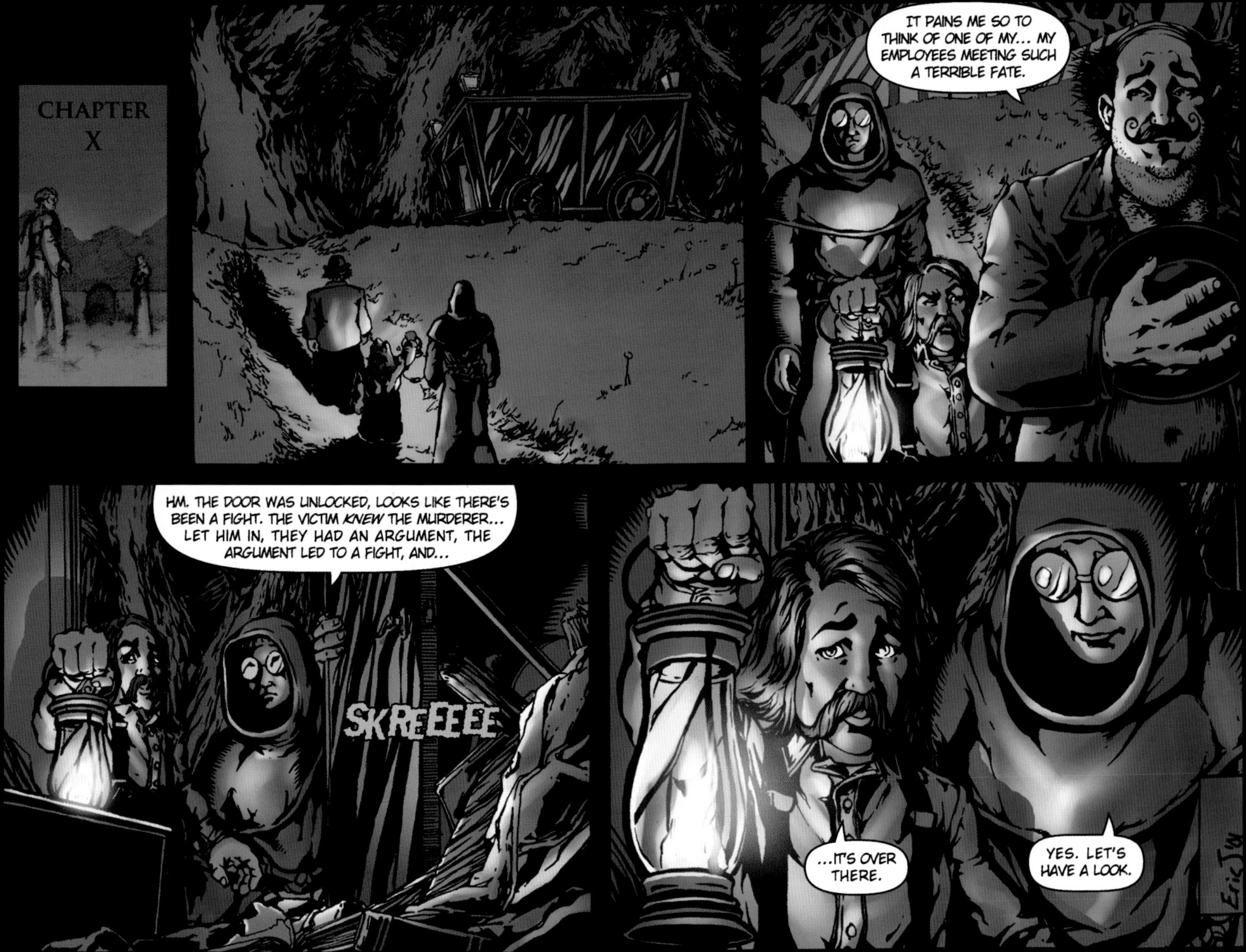
CHAPTER
X
IT PAINS ME SO TO THINK OF ONE OF MY... MY EMPLOYEES MEETING SUCH A TERRIBLE FATE.
HM. THE DOOR WAS UNLOCKED, LOOKS LIKE THERE'S BEEN A FIGHT. THE VICTIM *KNEW* THE MURDERER... LET HIM IN, THEY HAD AN ARGUMENT, THE ARGUMENT LED TO A FIGHT, AND...
SKREEEEE
...IT'S OVER THERE.
YES. LET'S HAVE A LOOK.

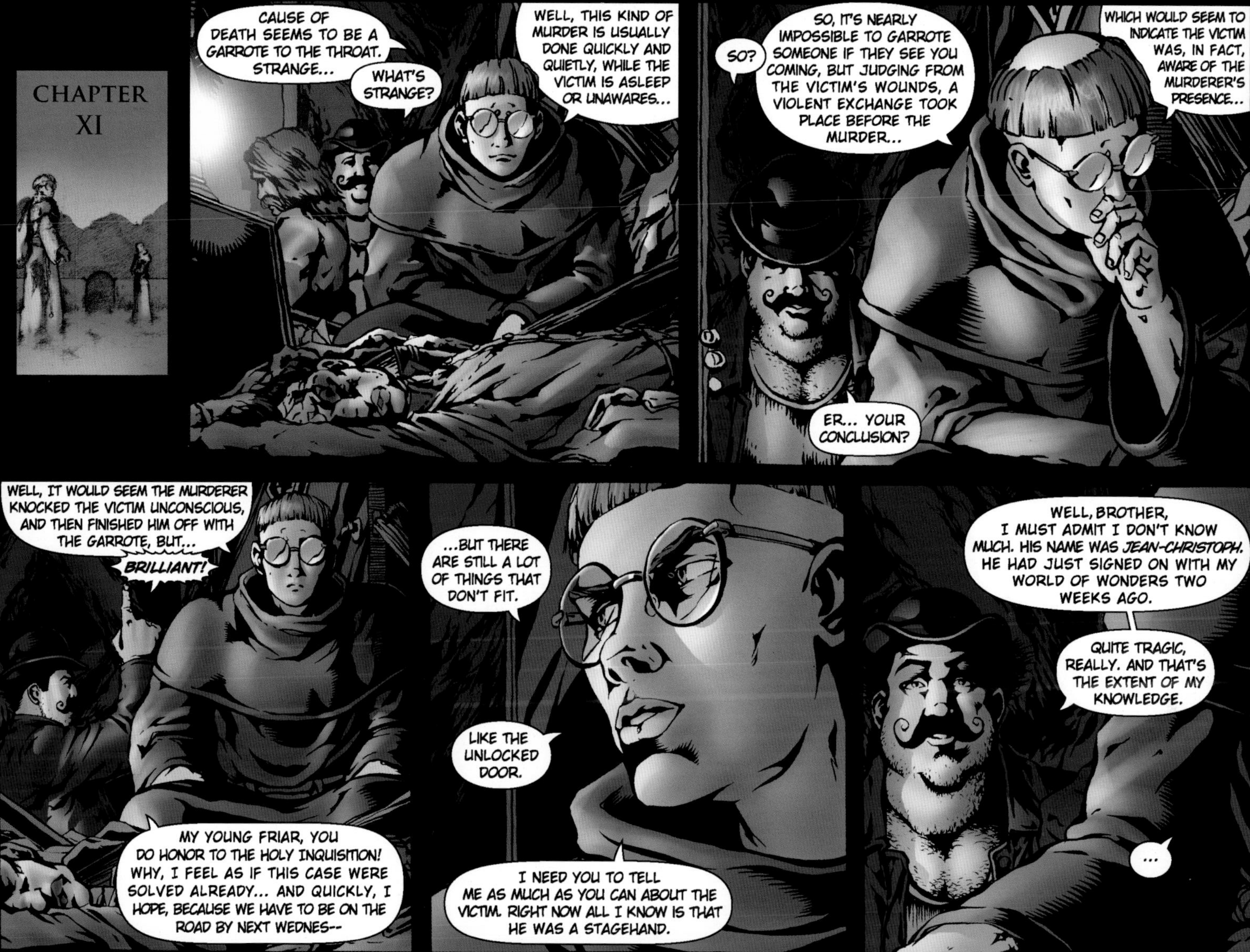
CHAPTER XI
CAUSE OF DEATH SEEMS TO BE A GARROTE TO THE THROAT. STRANGE...
WHAT'S STRANGE?
WELL, THIS KIND OF MURDER IS USUALLY DONE QUICKLY AND QUIETLY, WHILE THE VICTIM IS ASLEEP OR UNAWARES...
SO, IT'S NEARLY IMPOSSIBLE TO GARROTE SOMEONE IF THEY SEE YOU COMING, BUT JUDGING FROM THE VICTIM'S WOUNDS, A VIOLENT EXCHANGE TOOK PLACE BEFORE THE MURDER...
SO?
WHICH WOULD SEEM TO INDICATE THE VICTIM WAS, IN FACT, AWARE OF THE MURDERER'S PRESENCE...
ER... YOUR CONCLUSION?
WELL, IT WOULD SEEM THE MURDERER KNOCKED THE VICTIM UNCONSCIOUS, AND THEN FINISHED HIM OFF WITH THE GARROTE, BUT...
BRILLIANT!
MY YOUNG FRIAR, YOU DO HONOR TO THE HOLY INQUISITION! WHY, I FEEL AS IF THIS CASE WERE SOLVED ALREADY... AND QUICKLY, I HOPE, BECAUSE WE HAVE TO BE ON THE ROAD BY NEXT WEDNES--
...BUT THERE ARE STILL A LOT OF THINGS THAT DON'T FIT.
LIKE THE UNLOCKED DOOR.
I NEED YOU TO TELL ME AS MUCH AS YOU CAN ABOUT THE VICTIM. RIGHT NOW ALL I KNOW IS THAT HE WAS A STAGEHAND.
WELL, BROTHER, I MUST ADMIT I DON'T KNOW MUCH. HIS NAME WAS JEAN-CHRISTOPH. HE HAD JUST SIGNED ON WITH MY WORLD OF WONDERS TWO WEEKS AGO.
QUITE TRAGIC, REALLY. AND THAT'S THE EXTENT OF MY KNOWLEDGE.
...

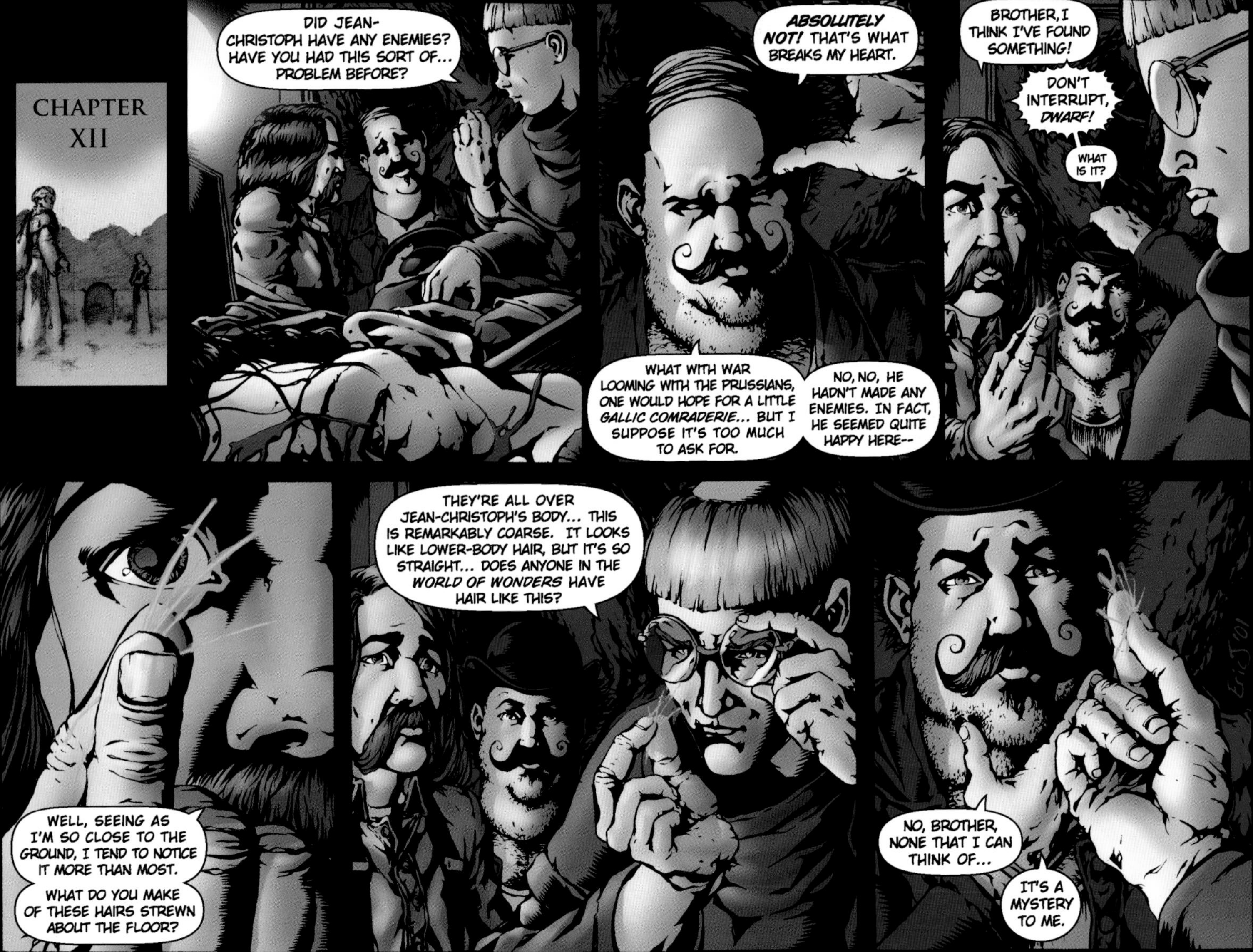
CHAPTER XII
DID JEAN-CHRISTOPH HAVE ANY ENEMIES? HAVE YOU HAD THIS SORT OF... PROBLEM BEFORE?
ABSOLUTELY NOT! THAT'S WHAT BREAKS MY HEART.
WHAT WITH WAR LOOMING WITH THE PRUSSIANS, ONE WOULD HOPE FOR A LITTLE GALLIC COMRADERIE... BUT I SUPPOSE IT'S TOO MUCH TO ASK FOR.
NO, NO, HE HADN'T MADE ANY ENEMIES. IN FACT, HE SEEMED QUITE HAPPY HERE--
BROTHER, I THINK I'VE FOUND SOMETHING!
DON'T INTERRUPT, DWARF!
WHAT IS IT?
WELL, SEEING AS I'M SO CLOSE TO THE GROUND, I TEND TO NOTICE IT MORE THAN MOST.
WHAT DO YOU MAKE OF THESE HAIRS STREWN ABOUT THE FLOOR?
THEY'RE ALL OVER JEAN-CHRISTOPH'S BODY... THIS IS REMARKABLY COARSE. IT LOOKS LIKE LOWER-BODY HAIR, BUT IT'S SO STRAIGHT... DOES ANYONE IN THE WORLD OF WONDERS HAVE HAIR LIKE THIS?
NO, BROTHER, NONE THAT I CAN THINK OF...
IT'S A MYSTERY TO ME.

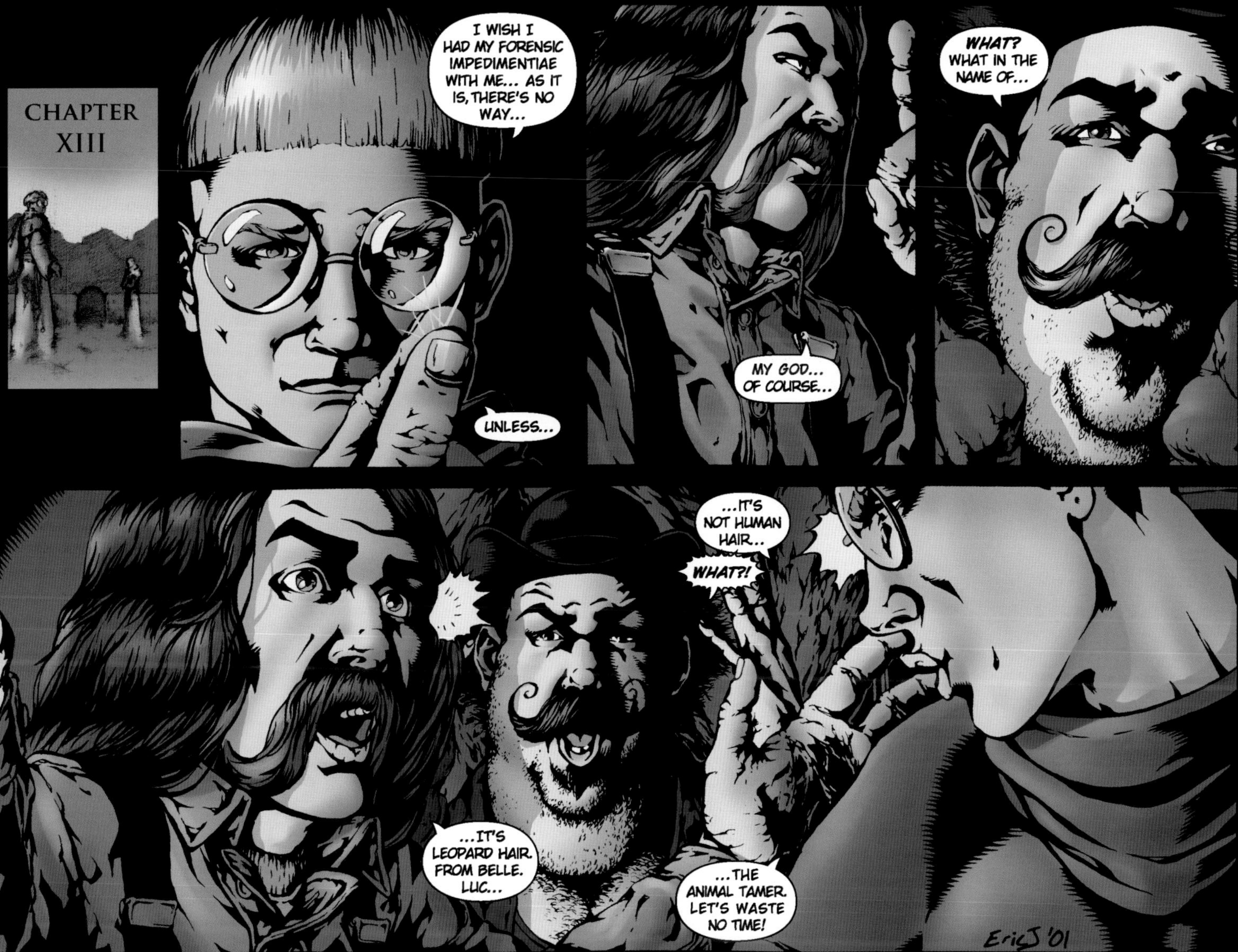
CHAPTER XIII
I WISH I HAD MY FORENSIC IMPEDIMENTIAE WITH ME... AS IT IS, THERE'S NO WAY...
UNLESS...
MY GOD... OF COURSE...
WHAT? WHAT IN THE NAME OF...
...IT'S NOT HUMAN HAIR...
WHAT?!
...IT'S LEOPARD HAIR. FROM BELLE. LUC...
...THE ANIMAL TAMER. LET'S WASTE NO TIME!
EricJ '01

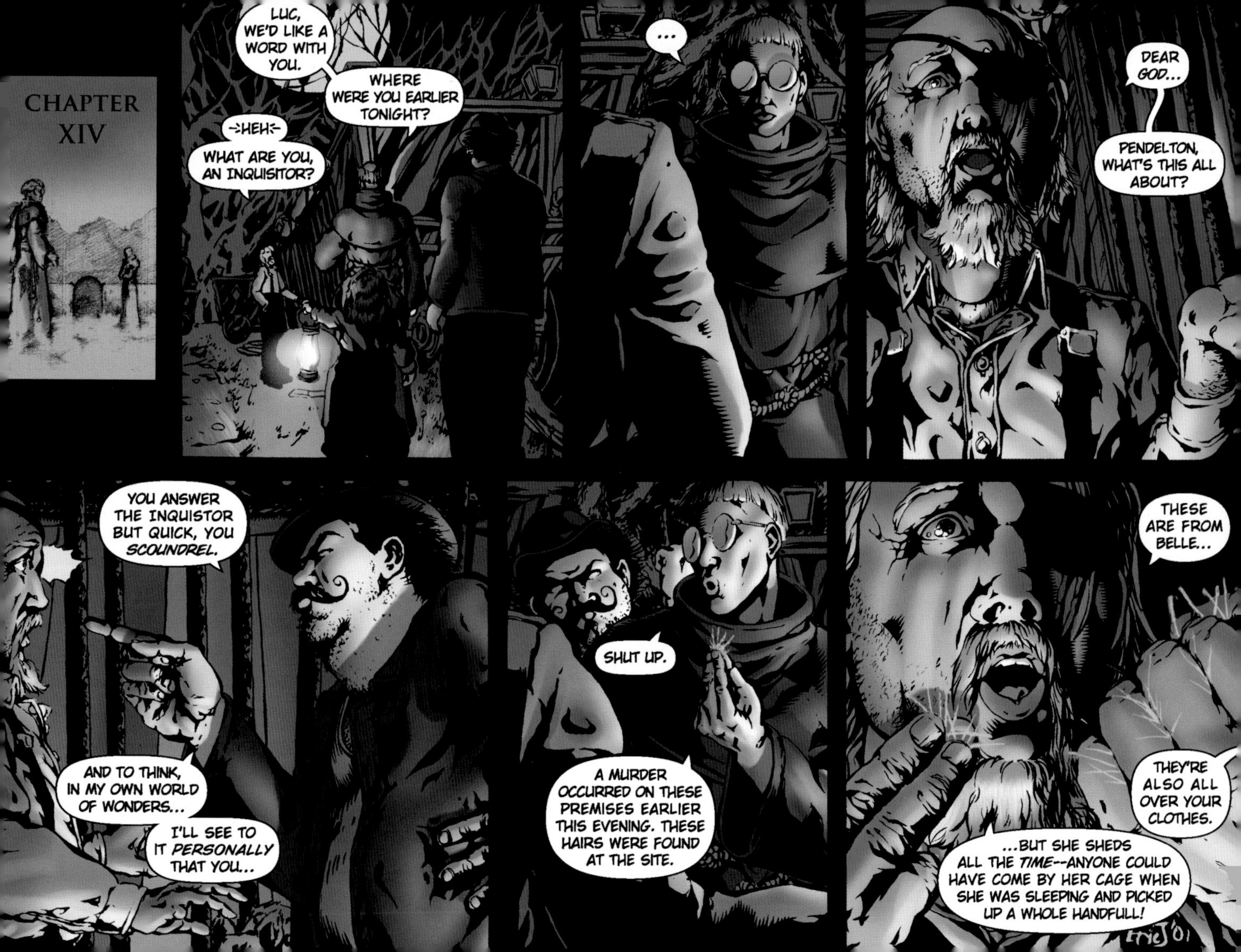
CHAPTER XIV
LUC, WE'D LIKE A WORD WITH YOU.
WHERE WERE YOU EARLIER TONIGHT?
-:HEH:-
WHAT ARE YOU, AN INQUISITOR?
...
DEAR GOD...
PENDELTON, WHAT'S THIS ALL ABOUT?
YOU ANSWER THE INQUISTOR BUT QUICK, YOU SCOUNDREL.
AND TO THINK, IN MY OWN WORLD OF WONDERS...
I'LL SEE TO IT PERSONALLY THAT YOU...
SHUT UP.
A MURDER OCCURRED ON THESE PREMISES EARLIER THIS EVENING. THESE HAIRS WERE FOUND AT THE SITE.
THESE ARE FROM BELLE...
THEY'RE ALSO ALL OVER YOUR CLOTHES.
...BUT SHE SHEDS ALL THE TIME--ANYONE COULD HAVE COME BY HER CAGE WHEN SHE WAS SLEEPING AND PICKED UP A WHOLE HANDFULL!

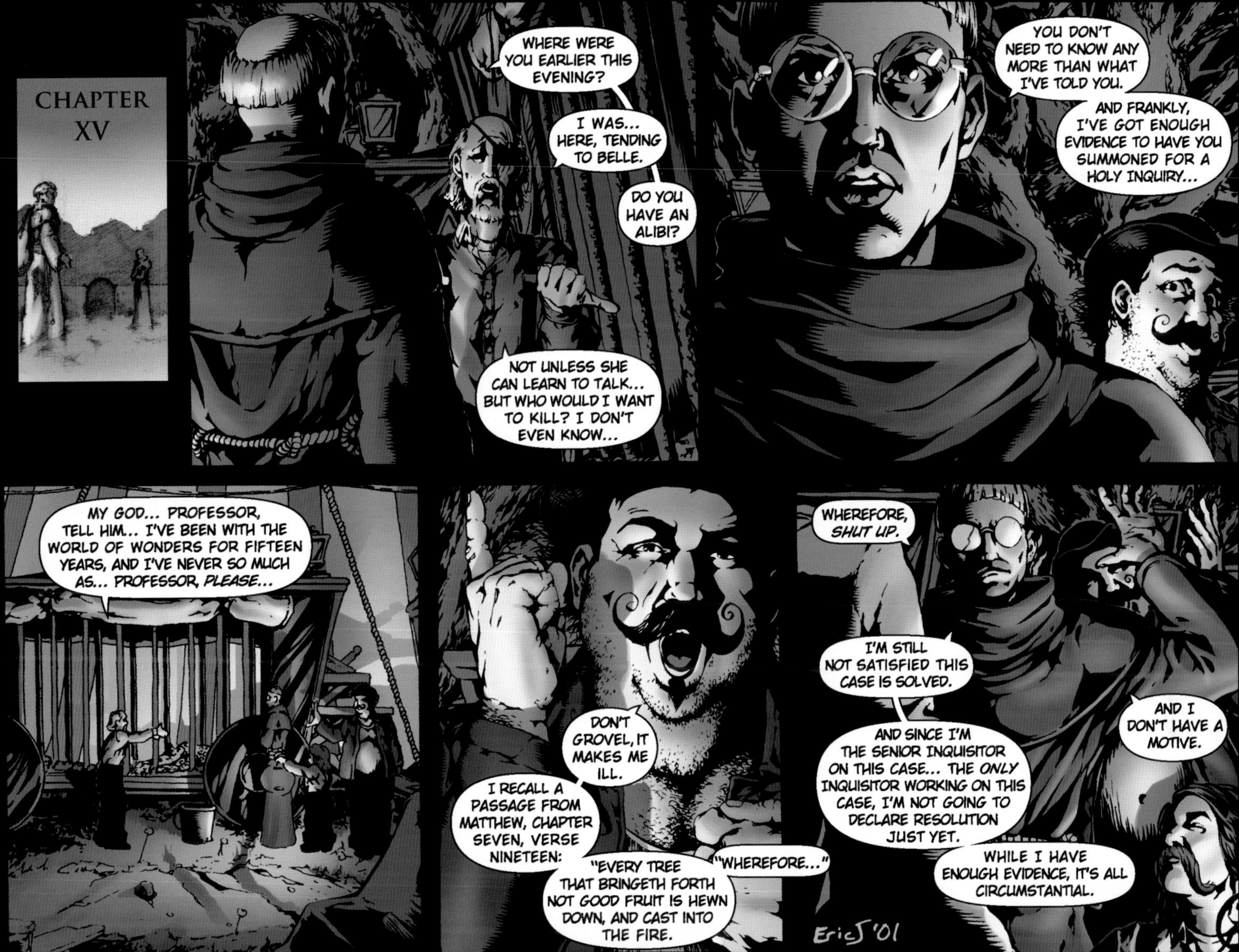
CHAPTER XV
WHERE WERE YOU EARLIER THIS EVENING?
I WAS... HERE, TENDING TO BELLE.
DO YOU HAVE AN ALIBI?
NOT UNLESS SHE CAN LEARN TO TALK... BUT WHO WOULD I WANT TO KILL? I DON'T EVEN KNOW...
YOU DON'T NEED TO KNOW ANY MORE THAN WHAT I'VE TOLD YOU.
AND FRANKLY, I'VE GOT ENOUGH EVIDENCE TO HAVE YOU SUMMONED FOR A HOLY INQUIRY...
MY GOD... PROFESSOR, TELL HIM... I'VE BEEN WITH THE WORLD OF WONDERS FOR FIFTEEN YEARS, AND I'VE NEVER SO MUCH AS... PROFESSOR, *PLEASE*...
DON'T GROVEL, IT MAKES ME ILL.
I RECALL A PASSAGE FROM MATTHEW, CHAPTER SEVEN, VERSE NINETEEN:
"EVERY TREE THAT BRINGETH FORTH NOT GOOD FRUIT IS HEWN DOWN, AND CAST INTO THE FIRE.
"WHEREFORE..."
WHEREFORE, *SHUT UP*.
I'M STILL NOT SATISFIED THIS CASE IS SOLVED.
AND SINCE I'M THE SENIOR INQUISITOR ON THIS CASE... THE *ONLY* INQUISITOR WORKING ON THIS CASE, I'M NOT GOING TO DECLARE RESOLUTION JUST YET.
WHILE I HAVE ENOUGH EVIDENCE, IT'S ALL CIRCUMSTANTIAL.
AND I DON'T HAVE A MOTIVE.
EricJ '01

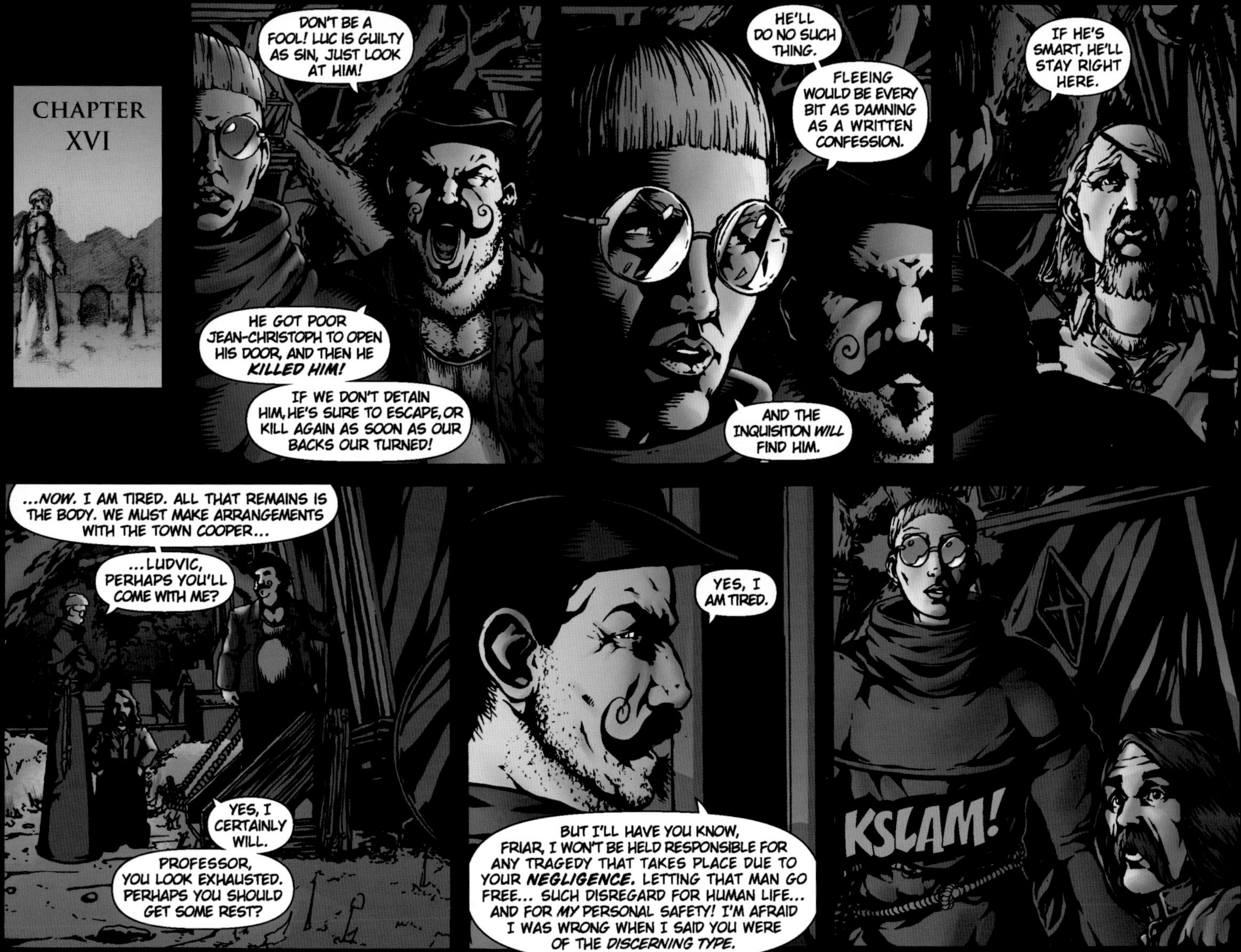
CHAPTER XVI
DON'T BE A FOOL! LUC IS GUILTY AS SIN, JUST LOOK AT HIM!
HE GOT POOR JEAN-CHRISTOPH TO OPEN HIS DOOR, AND THEN HE *KILLED HIM!*
IF WE DON'T DETAIN HIM, HE'S SURE TO ESCAPE, OR KILL AGAIN AS SOON AS OUR BACKS OUR TURNED!
HE'LL DO NO SUCH THING.
FLEEING WOULD BE EVERY BIT AS DAMNING AS A WRITTEN CONFESSION.
AND THE INQUISITION *WILL* FIND HIM.
IF HE'S SMART, HE'LL STAY RIGHT HERE.
...*NOW.* I AM TIRED. ALL THAT REMAINS IS THE BODY. WE MUST MAKE ARRANGEMENTS WITH THE TOWN COOPER...
...LUDVIC, PERHAPS YOU'LL COME WITH ME?
YES, I CERTAINLY WILL.
PROFESSOR, YOU LOOK EXHAUSTED. PERHAPS YOU SHOULD GET SOME REST?
YES, I AM TIRED.
BUT I'LL HAVE YOU KNOW, FRIAR, I WON'T BE HELD RESPONSIBLE FOR ANY TRAGEDY THAT TAKES PLACE DUE TO YOUR ***NEGLIGENCE.*** LETTING THAT MAN GO FREE... SUCH DISREGARD FOR HUMAN LIFE... AND FOR *MY* PERSONAL SAFETY! I'M AFRAID I WAS WRONG WHEN I SAID YOU WERE OF THE *DISCERNING TYPE.*
KSLAM!

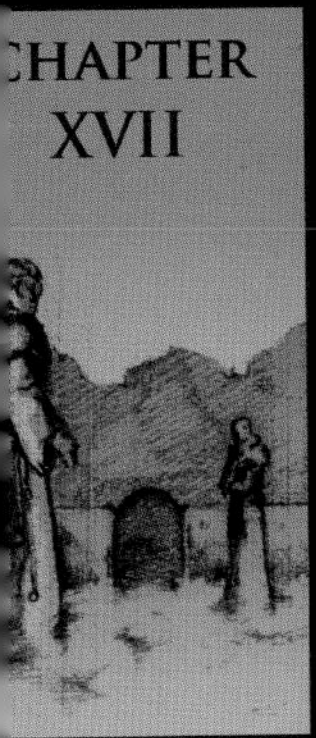
CHAPTER XVII

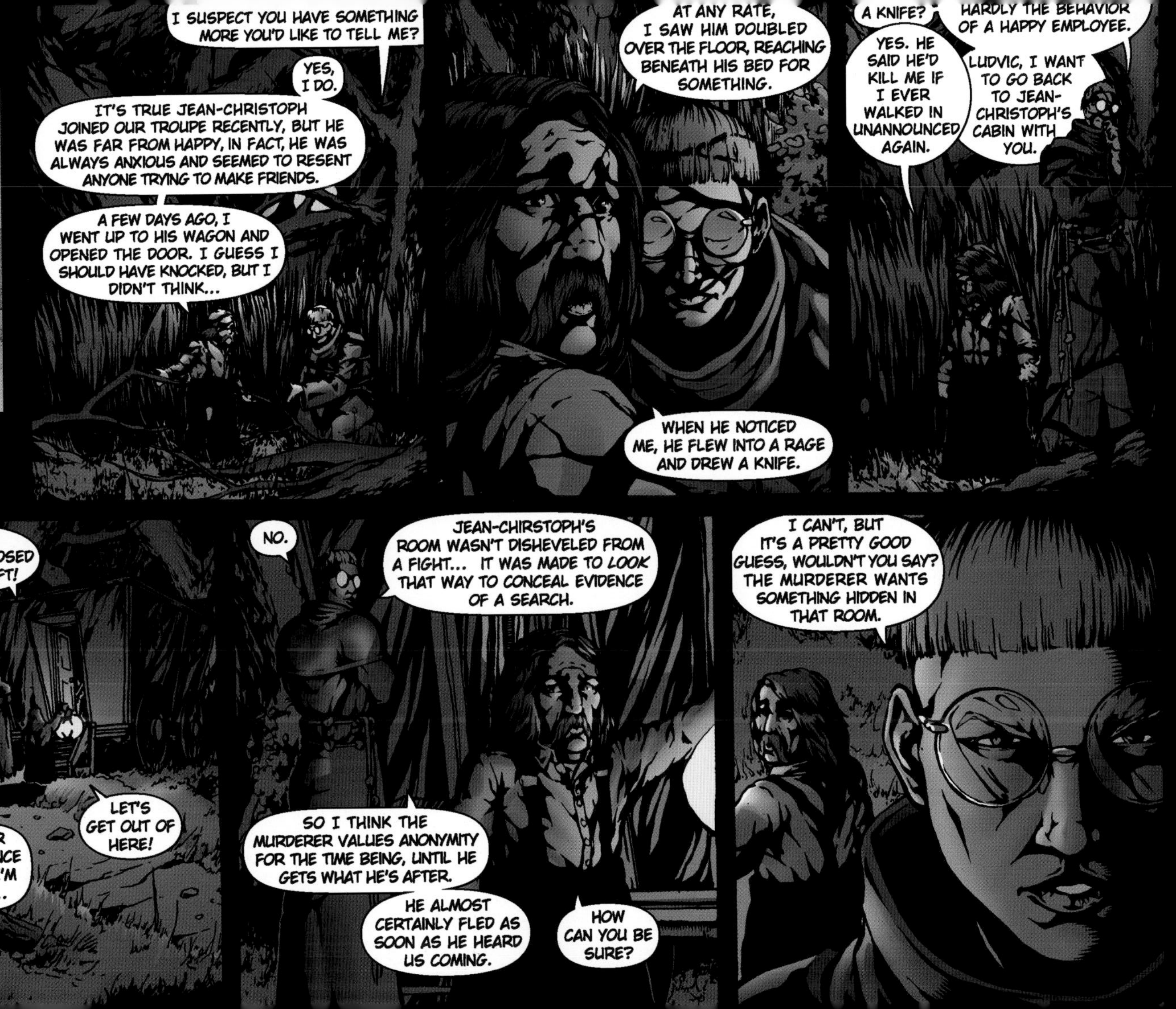
I SUSPECT YOU HAVE SOMETHING MORE YOU'D LIKE TO TELL ME?
YES, I DO.
IT'S TRUE JEAN-CHRISTOPH JOINED OUR TROUPE RECENTLY, BUT HE WAS FAR FROM HAPPY, IN FACT, HE WAS ALWAYS ANXIOUS AND SEEMED TO RESENT ANYONE TRYING TO MAKE FRIENDS.
A FEW DAYS AGO, I WENT UP TO HIS WAGON AND OPENED THE DOOR. I GUESS I SHOULD HAVE KNOCKED, BUT I DIDN'T THINK...
AT ANY RATE, I SAW HIM DOUBLED OVER THE FLOOR, REACHING BENEATH HIS BED FOR SOMETHING.
WHEN HE NOTICED ME, HE FLEW INTO A RAGE AND DREW A KNIFE.
A KNIFE?
YES. HE SAID HE'D KILL ME IF I EVER WALKED IN UNANNOUNCED AGAIN.
HARDLY THE BEHAVIOR OF A HAPPY EMPLOYEE.
LUDVIC, I WANT TO GO BACK TO JEAN-CHRISTOPH'S CABIN WITH YOU.
TH... THE DOOR WAS CLOSED WHEN WE LEFT!
LET'S GET OUT OF HERE!
YES... THE KILLER HAS RETURNED SINCE WE WERE HERE. I'M NOT SURPRISED...
NO.
JEAN-CHIRSTOPH'S ROOM WASN'T DISHEVELED FROM A FIGHT... IT WAS MADE TO LOOK THAT WAY TO CONCEAL EVIDENCE OF A SEARCH.
SO I THINK THE MURDERER VALUES ANONYMITY FOR THE TIME BEING, UNTIL HE GETS WHAT HE'S AFTER.
HE ALMOST CERTAINLY FLED AS SOON AS HE HEARD US COMING.
HOW CAN YOU BE SURE?
I CAN'T, BUT IT'S A PRETTY GOOD GUESS, WOULDN'T YOU SAY? THE MURDERER WANTS SOMETHING HIDDEN IN THAT ROOM.

CHAPTER XVIII

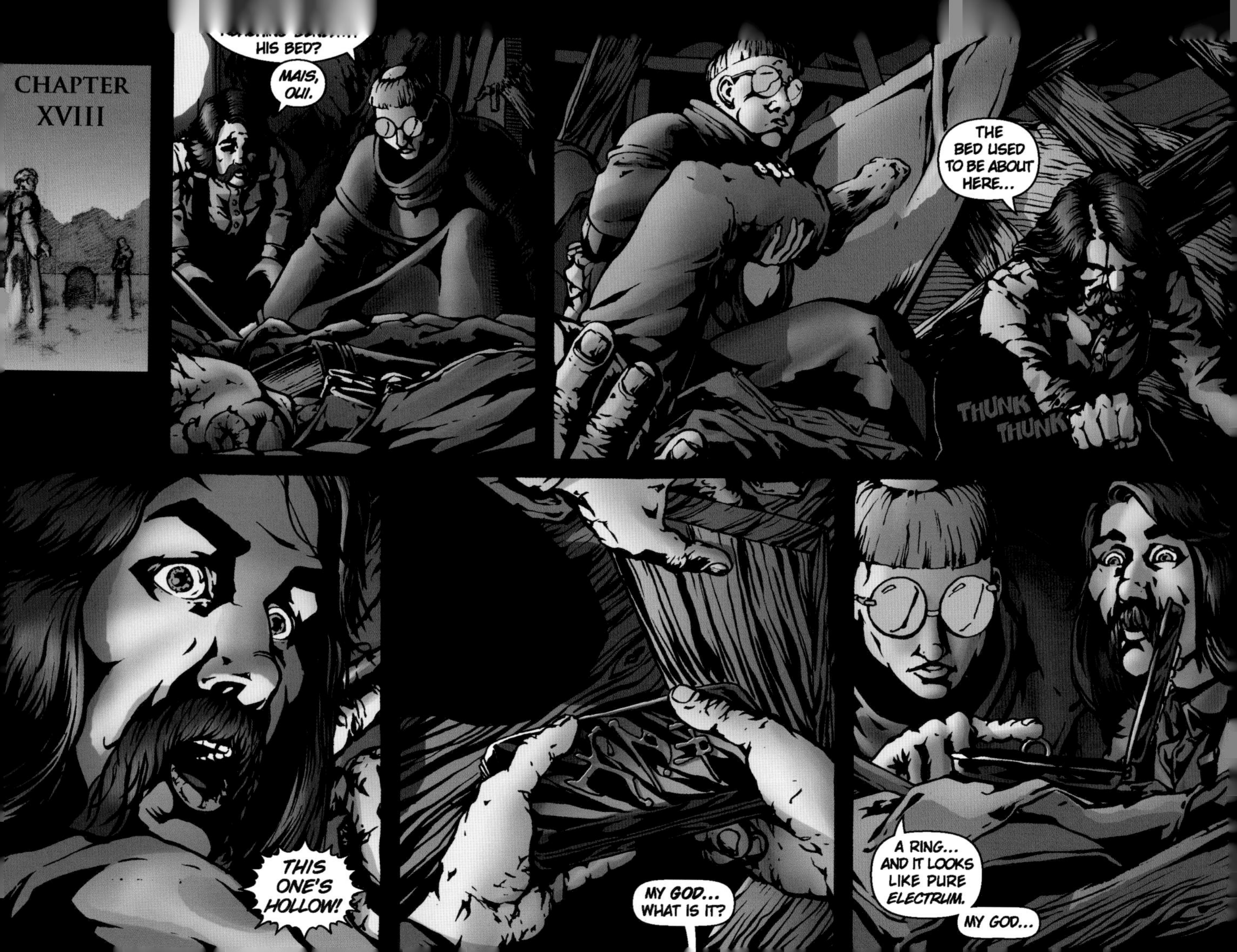
HIS BED?
MAIS, OUI.
THE BED USED TO BE ABOUT HERE...
THUNK THUNK
THIS ONE'S HOLLOW!
MY GOD... WHAT IS IT?
A RING... AND IT LOOKS LIKE PURE ELECTRUM.
MY GOD...

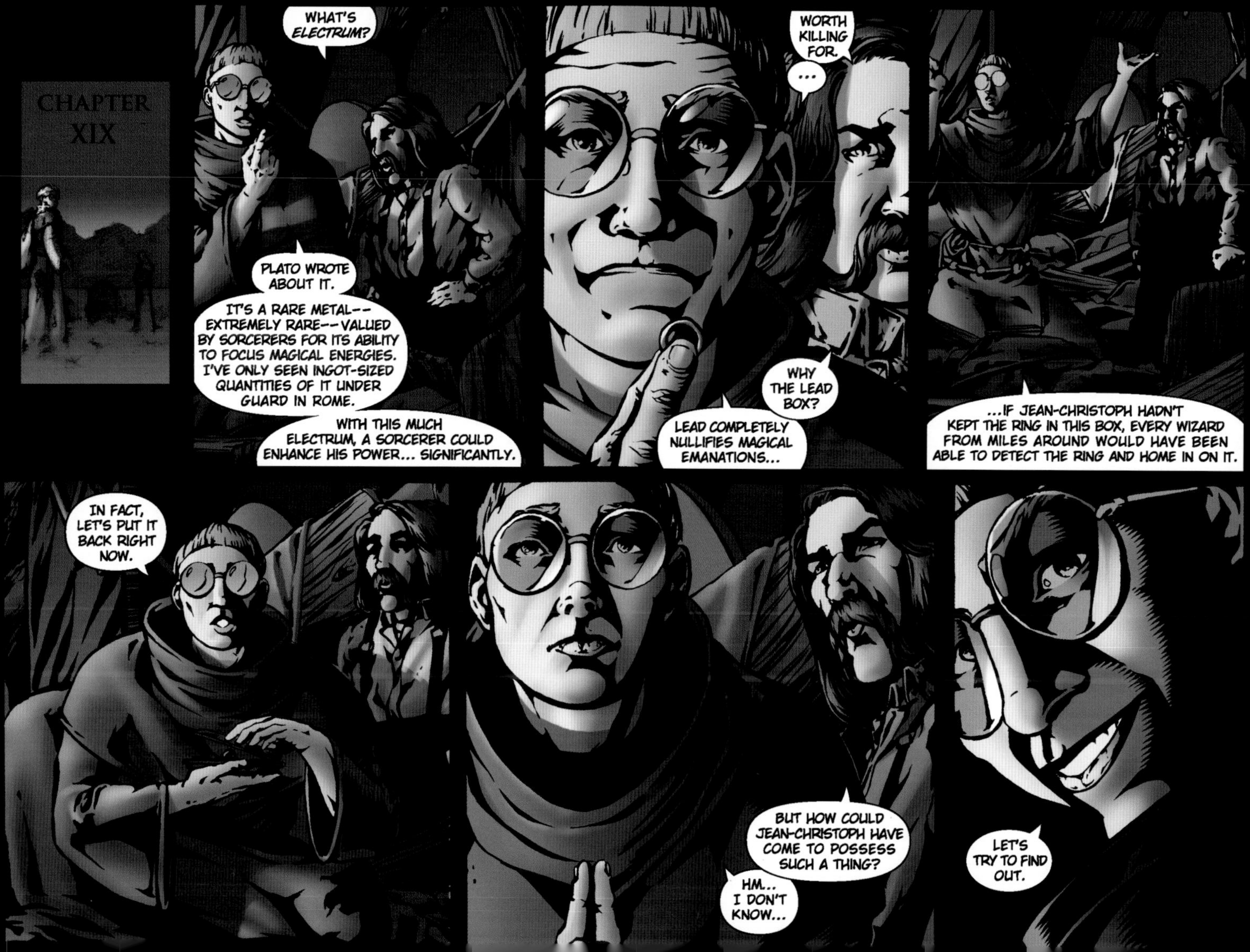
CHAPTER XIX
WHAT'S ELECTRUM?
PLATO WROTE ABOUT IT.
IT'S A RARE METAL--EXTREMELY RARE--VALUED BY SORCERERS FOR ITS ABILITY TO FOCUS MAGICAL ENERGIES. I'VE ONLY SEEN INGOT-SIZED QUANTITIES OF IT UNDER GUARD IN ROME.
WITH THIS MUCH ELECTRUM, A SORCERER COULD ENHANCE HIS POWER... SIGNIFICANTLY.
WORTH KILLING FOR.
...
WHY THE LEAD BOX?
LEAD COMPLETELY NULLIFIES MAGICAL EMANATIONS...
...IF JEAN-CHRISTOPH HADN'T KEPT THE RING IN THIS BOX, EVERY WIZARD FROM MILES AROUND WOULD HAVE BEEN ABLE TO DETECT THE RING AND HOME IN ON IT.
IN FACT, LET'S PUT IT BACK RIGHT NOW.
BUT HOW COULD JEAN-CHRISTOPH HAVE COME TO POSSESS SUCH A THING?
HM... I DON'T KNOW...
LET'S TRY TO FIND OUT.

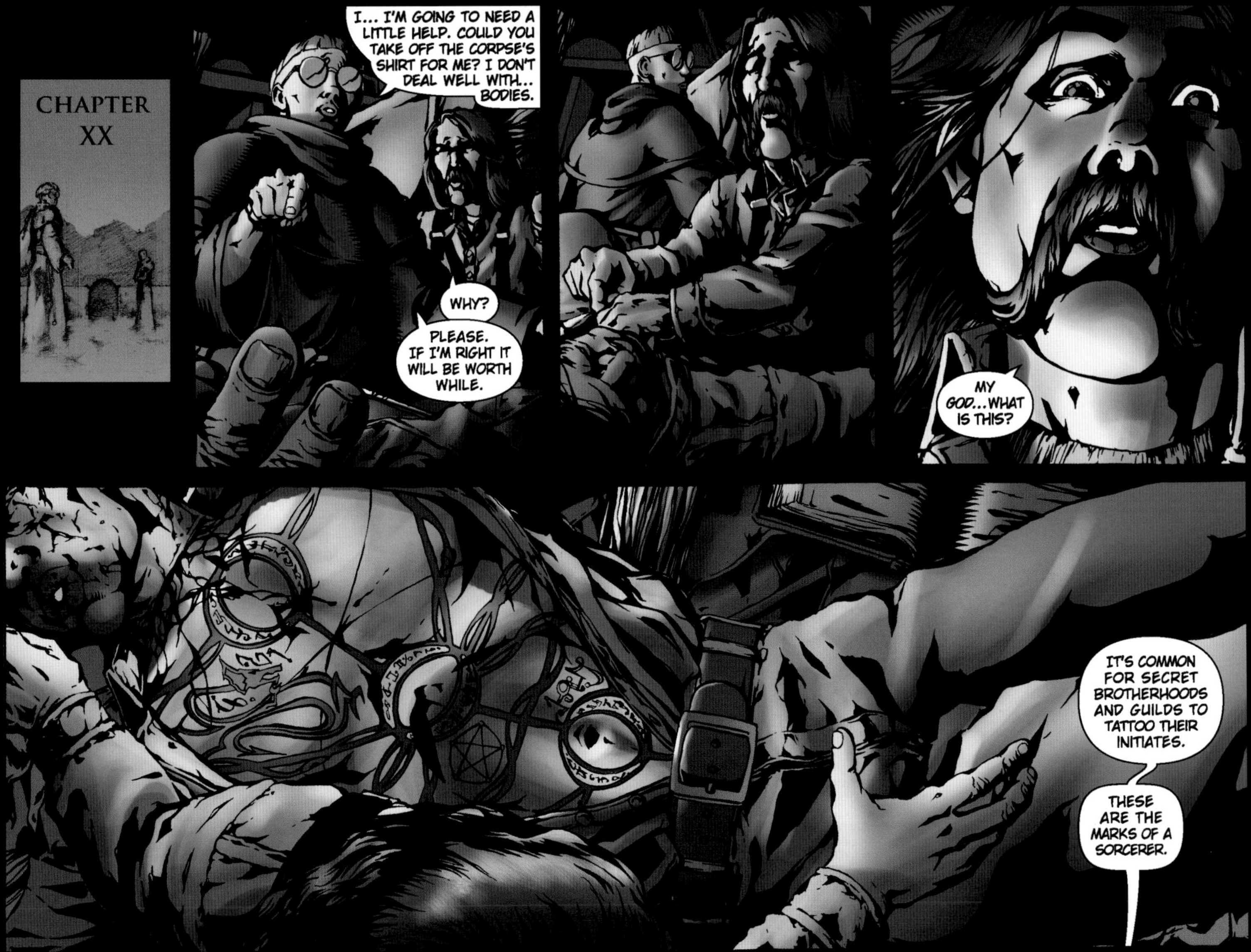
CHAPTER XX
I... I'M GOING TO NEED A LITTLE HELP. COULD YOU TAKE OFF THE CORPSE'S SHIRT FOR ME? I DON'T DEAL WELL WITH... BODIES.
WHY?
PLEASE. IF I'M RIGHT IT WILL BE WORTH WHILE.
MY GOD...WHAT IS THIS?
IT'S COMMON FOR SECRET BROTHERHOODS AND GUILDS TO TATTOO THEIR INITIATES.
THESE ARE THE MARKS OF A SORCERER.

CHAPTER XXI

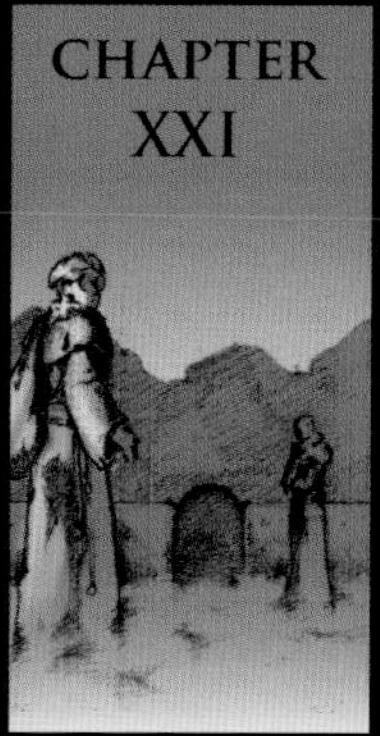

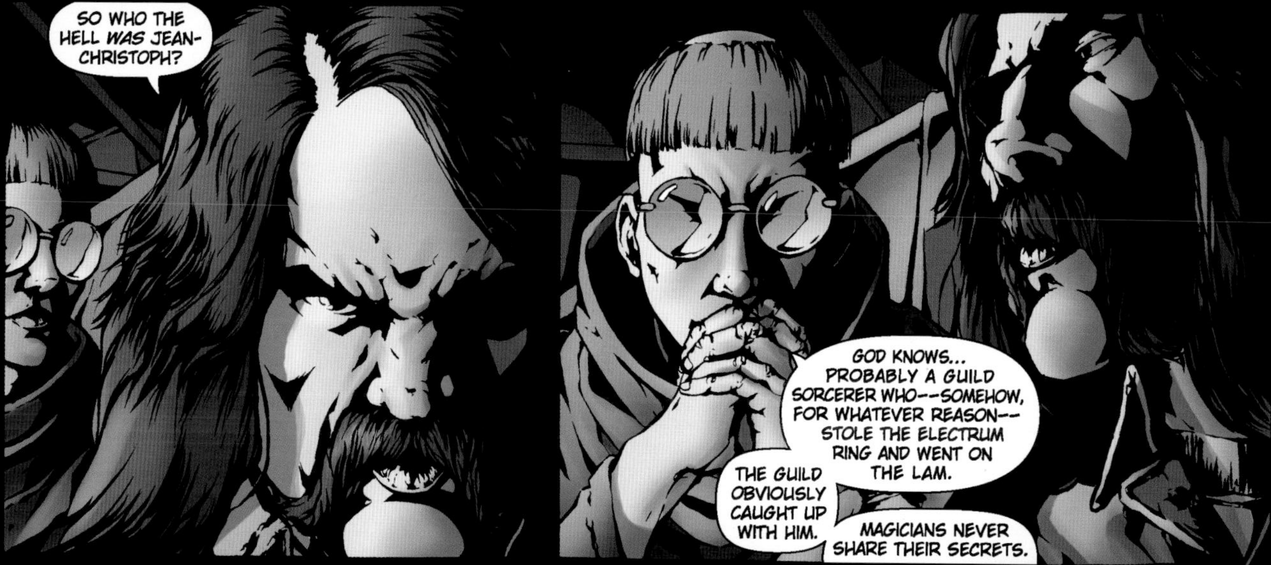
SO WHO THE HELL WAS JEAN-CHRISTOPH?
GOD KNOWS... PROBABLY A GUILD SORCERER WHO--SOMEHOW, FOR WHATEVER REASON--STOLE THE ELECTRUM RING AND WENT ON THE LAM.
THE GUILD OBVIOUSLY CAUGHT UP WITH HIM.
MAGICIANS NEVER SHARE THEIR SECRETS.

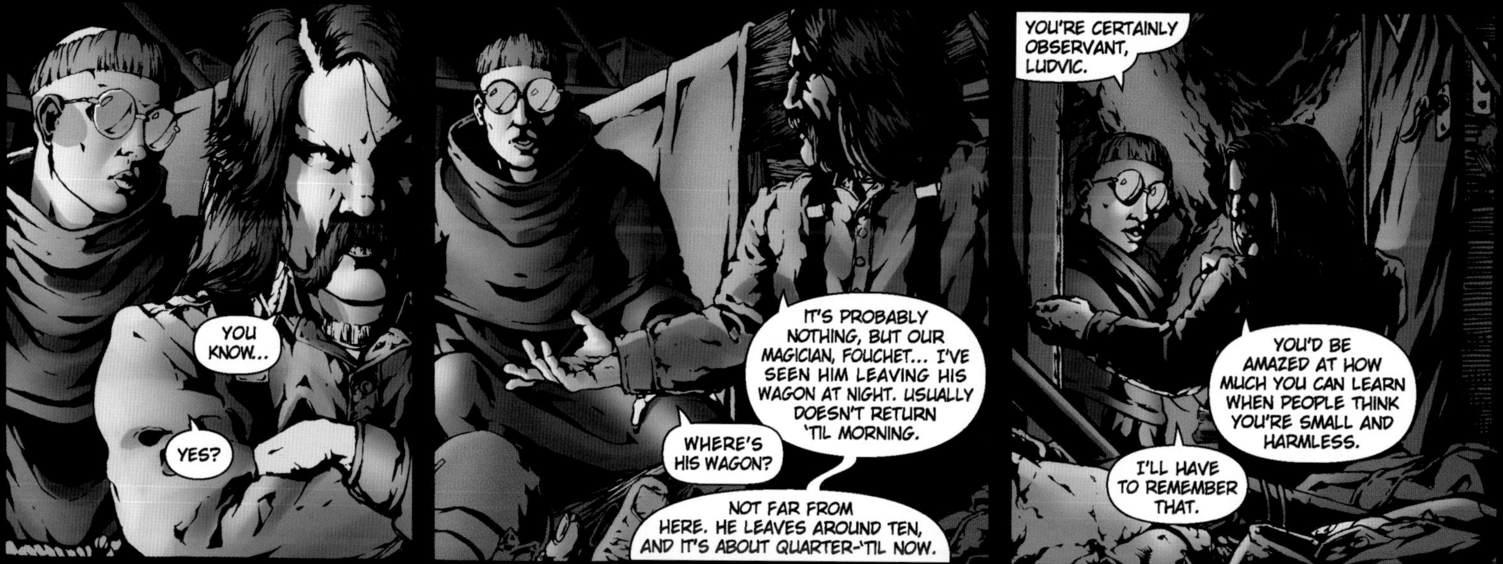
YOU KNOW...
YES?
IT'S PROBABLY NOTHING, BUT OUR MAGICIAN, FOUCHET... I'VE SEEN HIM LEAVING HIS WAGON AT NIGHT. USUALLY DOESN'T RETURN 'TIL MORNING.
WHERE'S HIS WAGON?
NOT FAR FROM HERE. HE LEAVES AROUND TEN, AND IT'S ABOUT QUARTER-'TIL NOW.
YOU'RE CERTAINLY OBSERVANT, LUDVIC.
YOU'D BE AMAZED AT HOW MUCH YOU CAN LEARN WHEN PEOPLE THINK YOU'RE SMALL AND HARMLESS.
I'LL HAVE TO REMEMBER THAT.

CHAPTER XXII

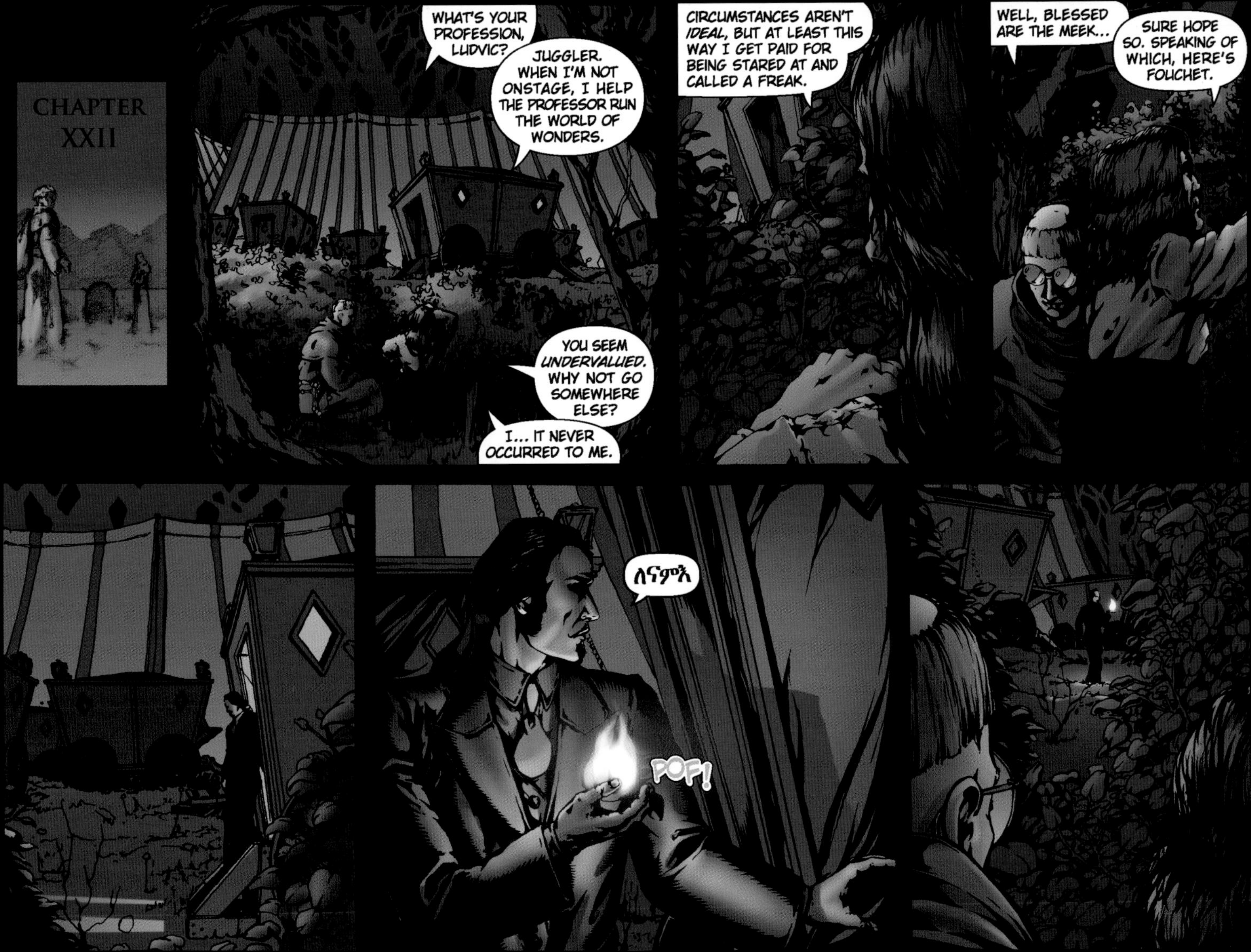
WHAT'S YOUR PROFESSION, LUDVIC?
JUGGLER. WHEN I'M NOT ONSTAGE, I HELP THE PROFESSOR RUN THE WORLD OF WONDERS.
YOU SEEM UNDERVALUED. WHY NOT GO SOMEWHERE ELSE?
I... IT NEVER OCCURRED TO ME.
CIRCUMSTANCES AREN'T IDEAL, BUT AT LEAST THIS WAY I GET PAID FOR BEING STARED AT AND CALLED A FREAK.
WELL, BLESSED ARE THE MEEK...
SURE HOPE SO. SPEAKING OF WHICH, HERE'S FOUCHET.
ለናምእ
POF!

CHAPTER XXIII

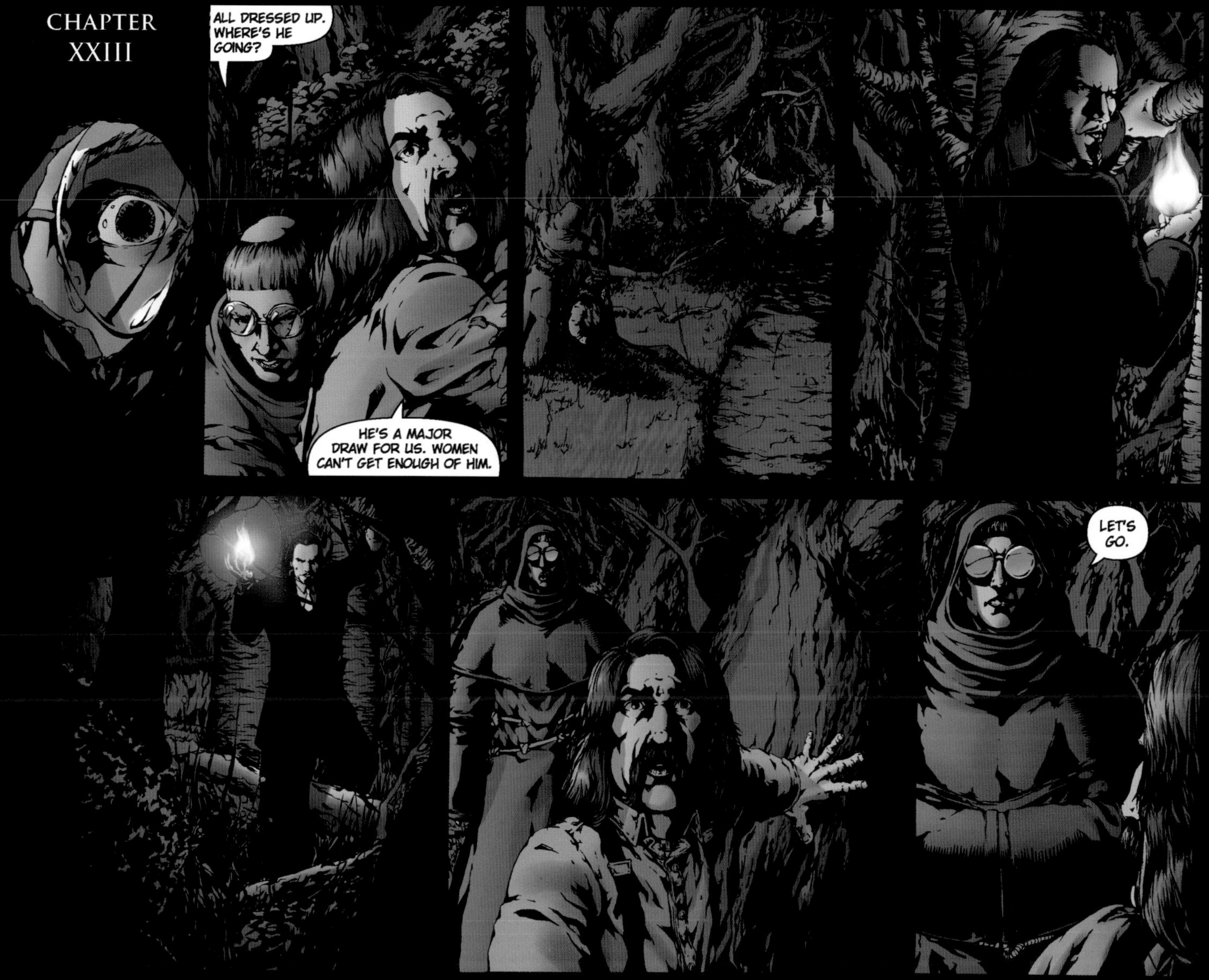
ALL DRESSED UP. WHERE'S HE GOING?
HE'S A MAJOR DRAW FOR US. WOMEN CAN'T GET ENOUGH OF HIM.
LET'S GO.

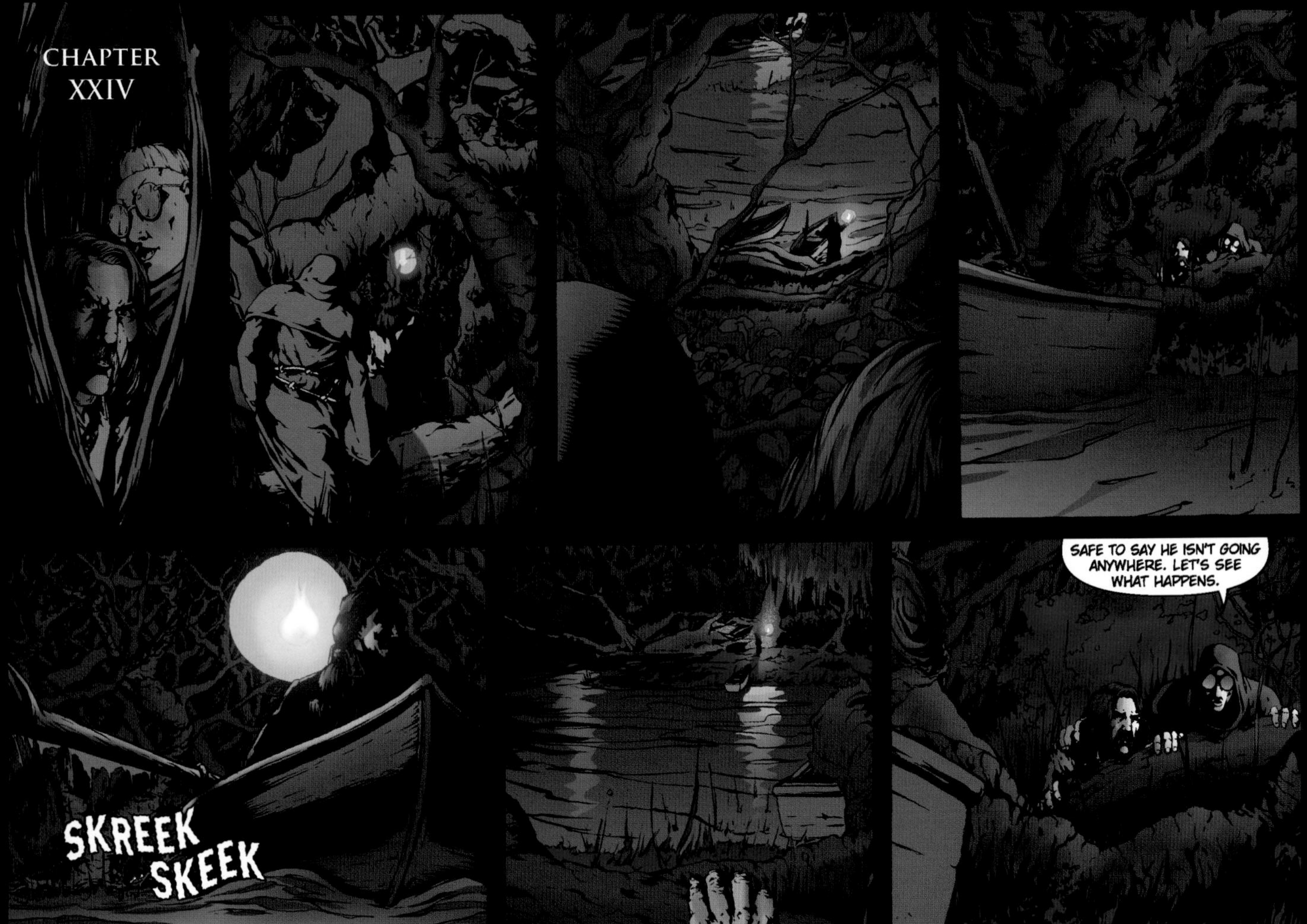
CHAPTER
XXIV
SKREEK
SKEEK
SAFE TO SAY HE ISN'T GOING ANYWHERE. LET'S SEE WHAT HAPPENS.

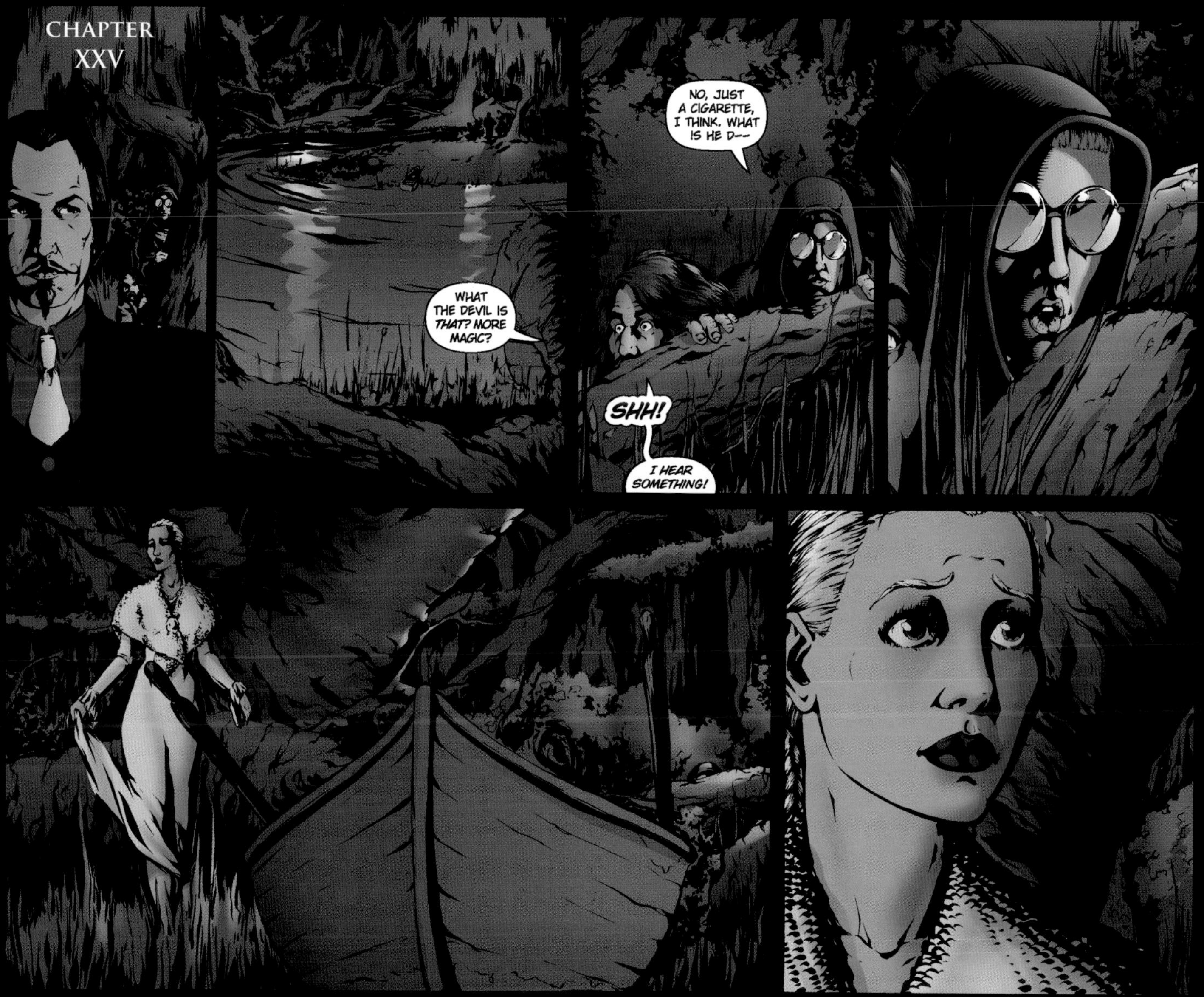
CHAPTER XXV
WHAT THE DEVIL IS THAT? MORE MAGIC?
NO, JUST A CIGARETTE, I THINK. WHAT IS HE D--
SHH!
I HEAR SOMETHING!

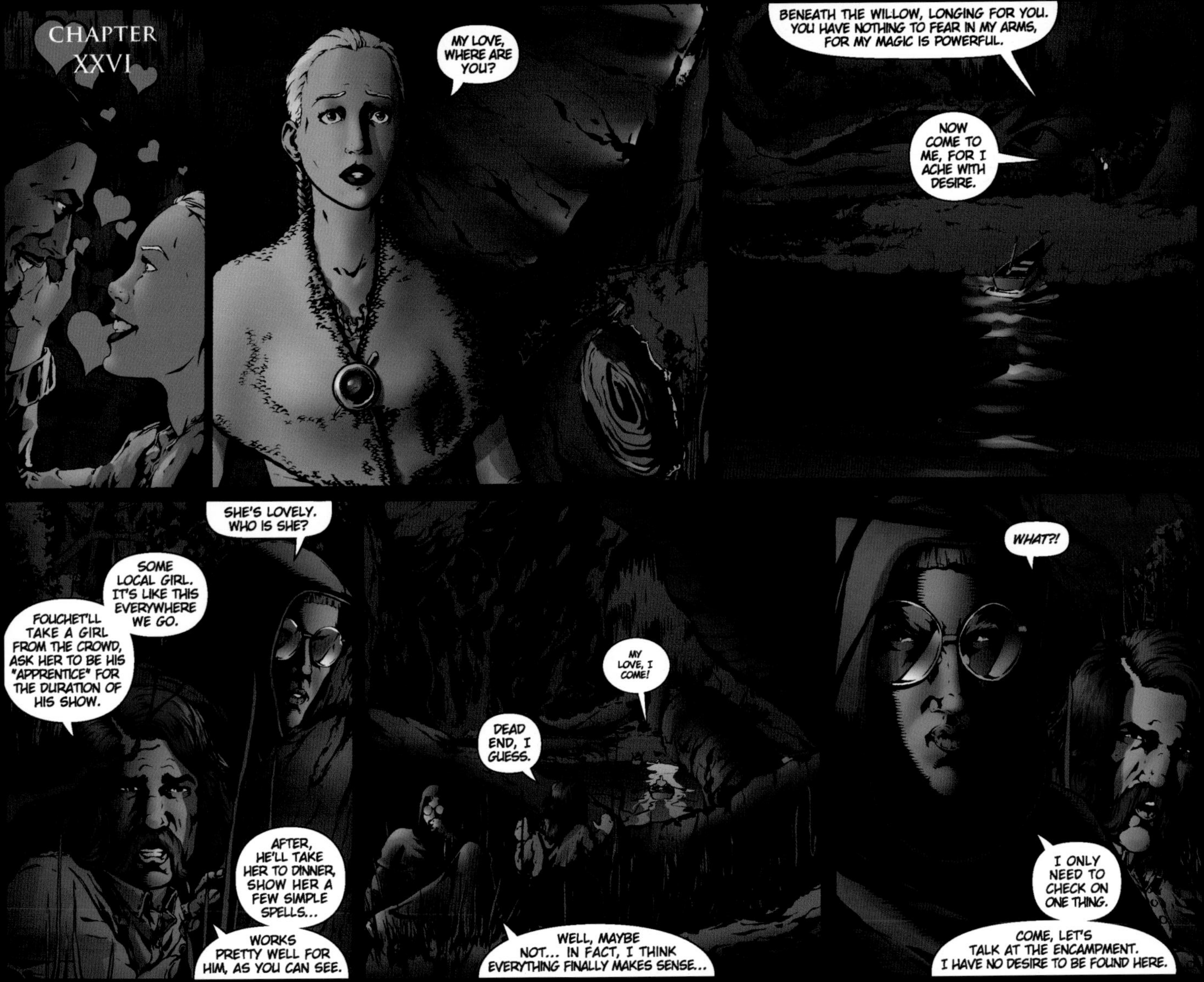
CHAPTER XXVI
MY LOVE, WHERE ARE YOU?
BENEATH THE WILLOW, LONGING FOR YOU. YOU HAVE NOTHING TO FEAR IN MY ARMS, FOR MY MAGIC IS POWERFUL.
NOW COME TO ME, FOR I ACHE WITH DESIRE.
SHE'S LOVELY. WHO IS SHE?
SOME LOCAL GIRL. IT'S LIKE THIS EVERYWHERE WE GO.
FOUCHET'LL TAKE A GIRL FROM THE CROWD, ASK HER TO BE HIS "APPRENTICE" FOR THE DURATION OF HIS SHOW.
AFTER, HE'LL TAKE HER TO DINNER, SHOW HER A FEW SIMPLE SPELLS...
WORKS PRETTY WELL FOR HIM, AS YOU CAN SEE.
MY LOVE, I COME!
DEAD END, I GUESS.
WELL, MAYBE NOT... IN FACT, I THINK EVERYTHING FINALLY MAKES SENSE...
WHAT?!
I ONLY NEED TO CHECK ON ONE THING.
COME, LET'S TALK AT THE ENCAMPMENT. I HAVE NO DESIRE TO BE FOUND HERE.

CHAPTER XXVII

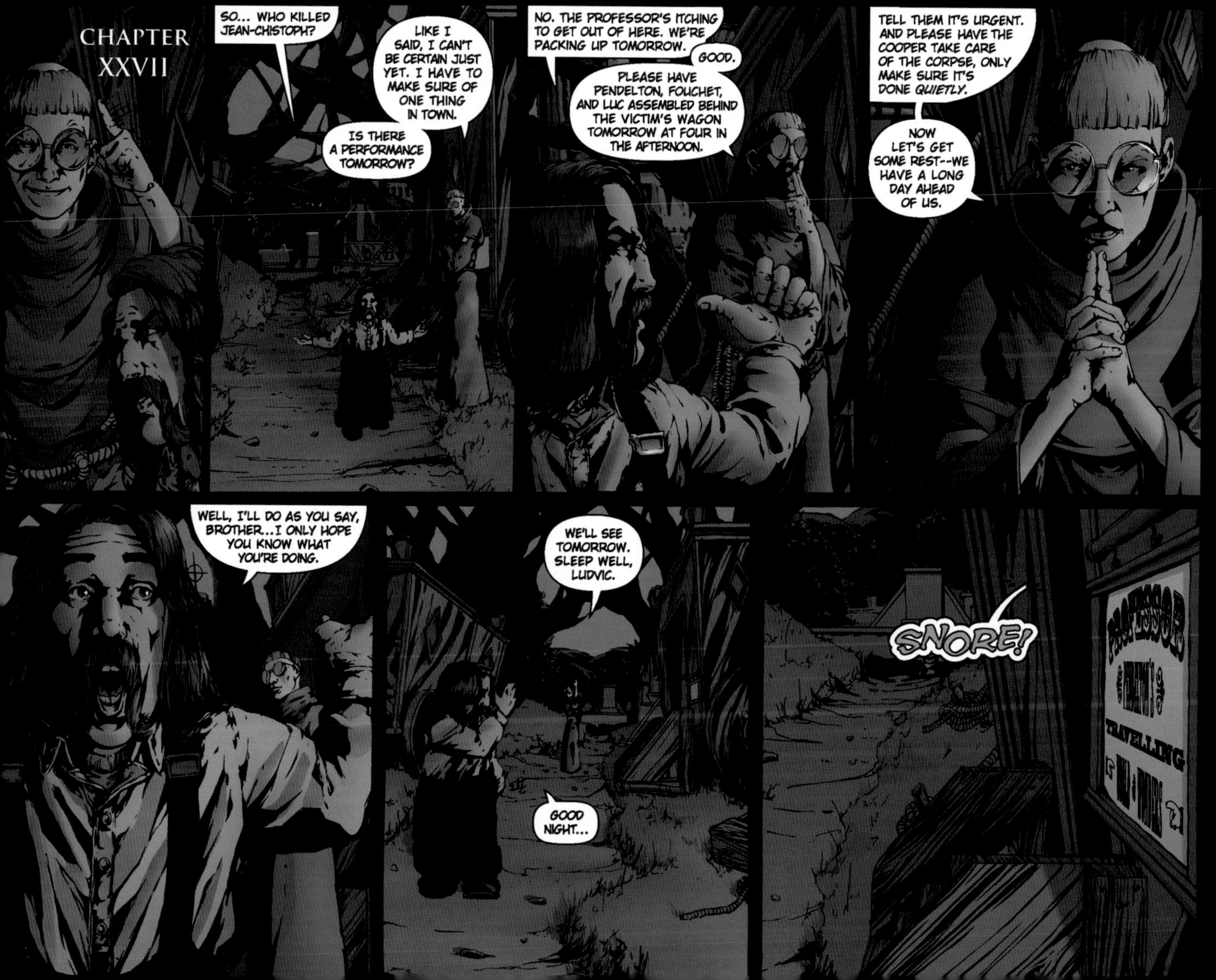

SO... WHO KILLED JEAN-CHISTOPH?
LIKE I SAID, I CAN'T BE CERTAIN JUST YET. I HAVE TO MAKE SURE OF ONE THING IN TOWN.
IS THERE A PERFORMANCE TOMORROW?
NO. THE PROFESSOR'S ITCHING TO GET OUT OF HERE. WE'RE PACKING UP TOMORROW.
GOOD.
PLEASE HAVE PENDELTON, FOUCHET, AND LUC ASSEMBLED BEHIND THE VICTIM'S WAGON TOMORROW AT FOUR IN THE AFTERNOON.
TELL THEM IT'S URGENT. AND PLEASE HAVE THE COOPER TAKE CARE OF THE CORPSE, ONLY MAKE SURE IT'S DONE QUIETLY.
NOW LET'S GET SOME REST--WE HAVE A LONG DAY AHEAD OF US.
WELL, I'LL DO AS YOU SAY, BROTHER...I ONLY HOPE YOU KNOW WHAT YOU'RE DOING.
WE'LL SEE TOMORROW. SLEEP WELL, LUDVIC.
GOOD NIGHT...
SNORE!
TRAVELLING

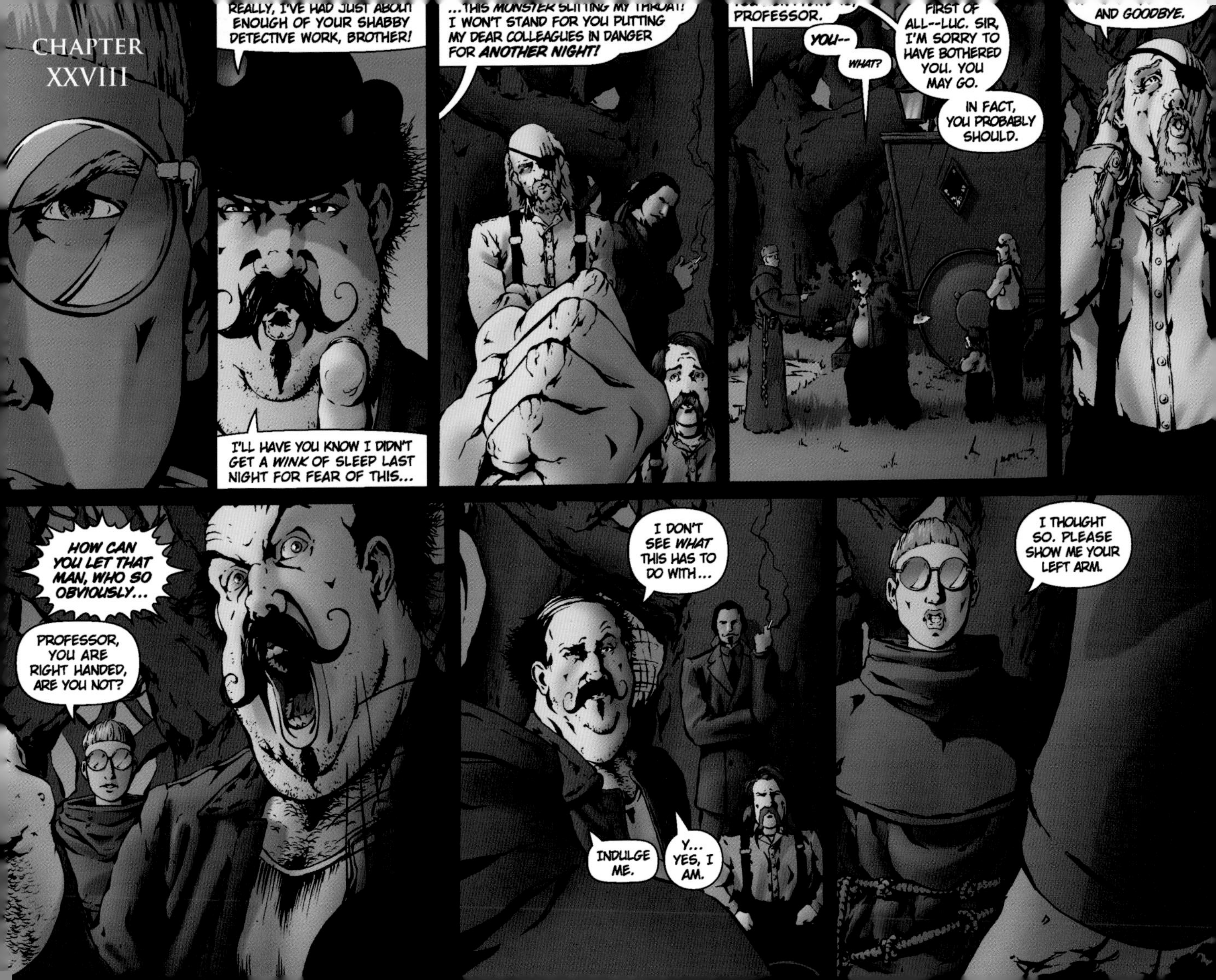
CHAPTER XXVIII
ENOUGH OF YOUR SHABBY DETECTIVE WORK, BROTHER!
I'LL HAVE YOU KNOW I DIDN'T GET A WINK OF SLEEP LAST NIGHT FOR FEAR OF THIS...
I WON'T STAND FOR YOU PUTTING MY DEAR COLLEAGUES IN DANGER FOR ANOTHER NIGHT!
PROFESSOR.
YOU--
WHAT?
FIRST OF ALL--LUC. SIR, I'M SORRY TO HAVE BOTHERED YOU. YOU MAY GO.
IN FACT, YOU PROBABLY SHOULD.
AND GOODBYE.
HOW CAN YOU LET THAT MAN, WHO SO OBVIOUSLY...
PROFESSOR, YOU ARE RIGHT HANDED, ARE YOU NOT?
I DON'T SEE WHAT THIS HAS TO DO WITH...
INDULGE ME.
Y... YES, I AM.
I THOUGHT SO. PLEASE SHOW ME YOUR LEFT ARM.

CHAPTER XXIX

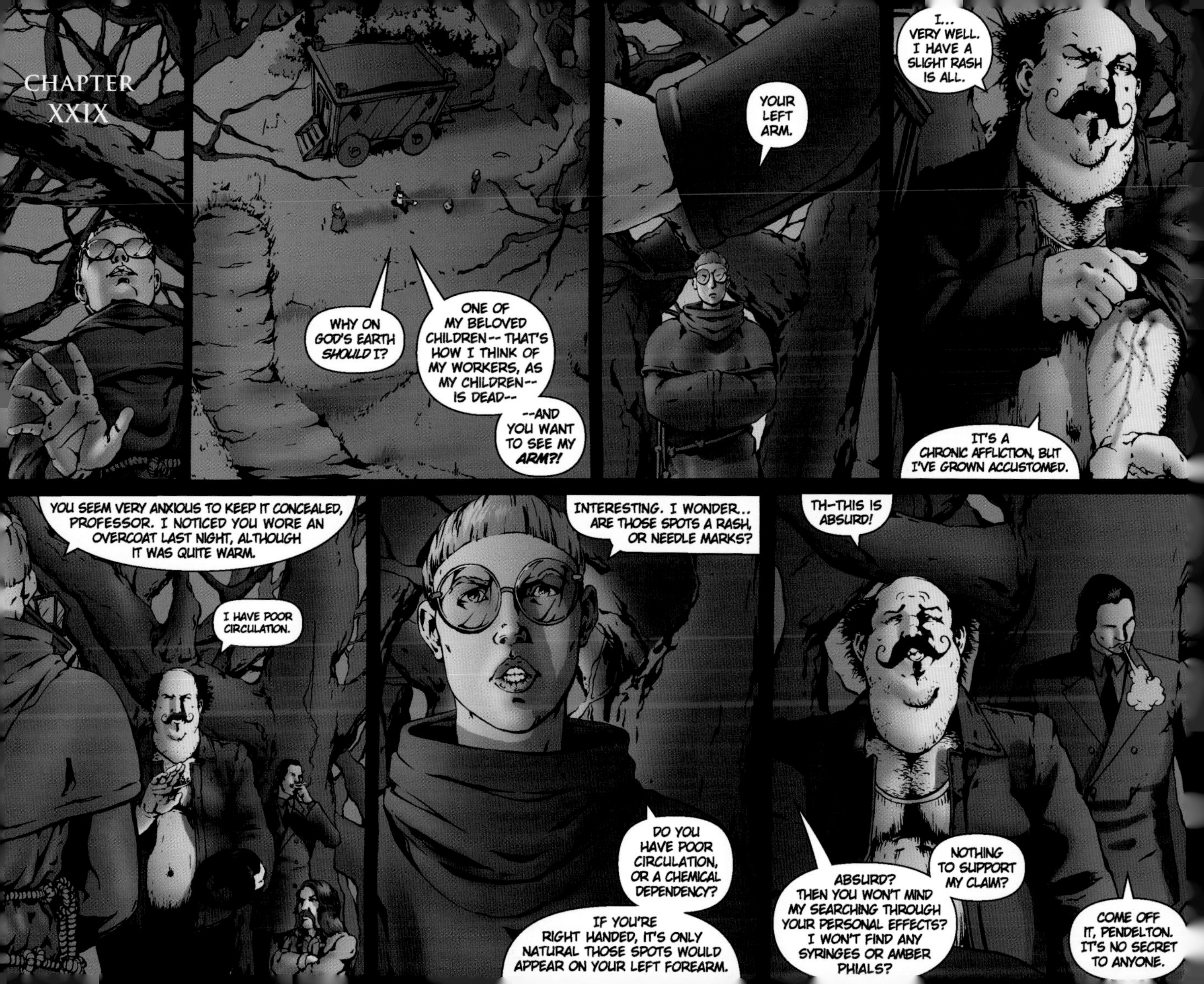

WHY ON GOD'S EARTH *SHOULD* I?
ONE OF MY BELOVED CHILDREN-- THAT'S HOW I THINK OF MY WORKERS, AS MY CHILDREN-- IS DEAD--
--AND YOU WANT TO SEE MY ***ARM?!***
YOUR LEFT ARM.
I... VERY WELL. I HAVE A SLIGHT RASH IS ALL.
IT'S A CHRONIC AFFLICTION, BUT I'VE GROWN ACCUSTOMED.
YOU SEEM VERY ANXIOUS TO KEEP IT CONCEALED, PROFESSOR. I NOTICED YOU WORE AN OVERCOAT LAST NIGHT, ALTHOUGH IT WAS QUITE WARM.
I HAVE POOR CIRCULATION.
INTERESTING. I WONDER... ARE THOSE SPOTS A RASH, OR NEEDLE MARKS?
DO YOU HAVE POOR CIRCULATION, OR A CHEMICAL DEPENDENCY?
IF YOU'RE RIGHT HANDED, IT'S ONLY NATURAL THOSE SPOTS WOULD APPEAR ON YOUR LEFT FOREARM.
TH-THIS IS ABSURD!
ABSURD? THEN YOU WON'T MIND MY SEARCHING THROUGH YOUR PERSONAL EFFECTS? I WON'T FIND ANY SYRINGES OR AMBER PHIALS?
NOTHING TO SUPPORT MY CLAIM?
COME OFF IT, PENDELTON. IT'S NO SECRET TO ANYONE.

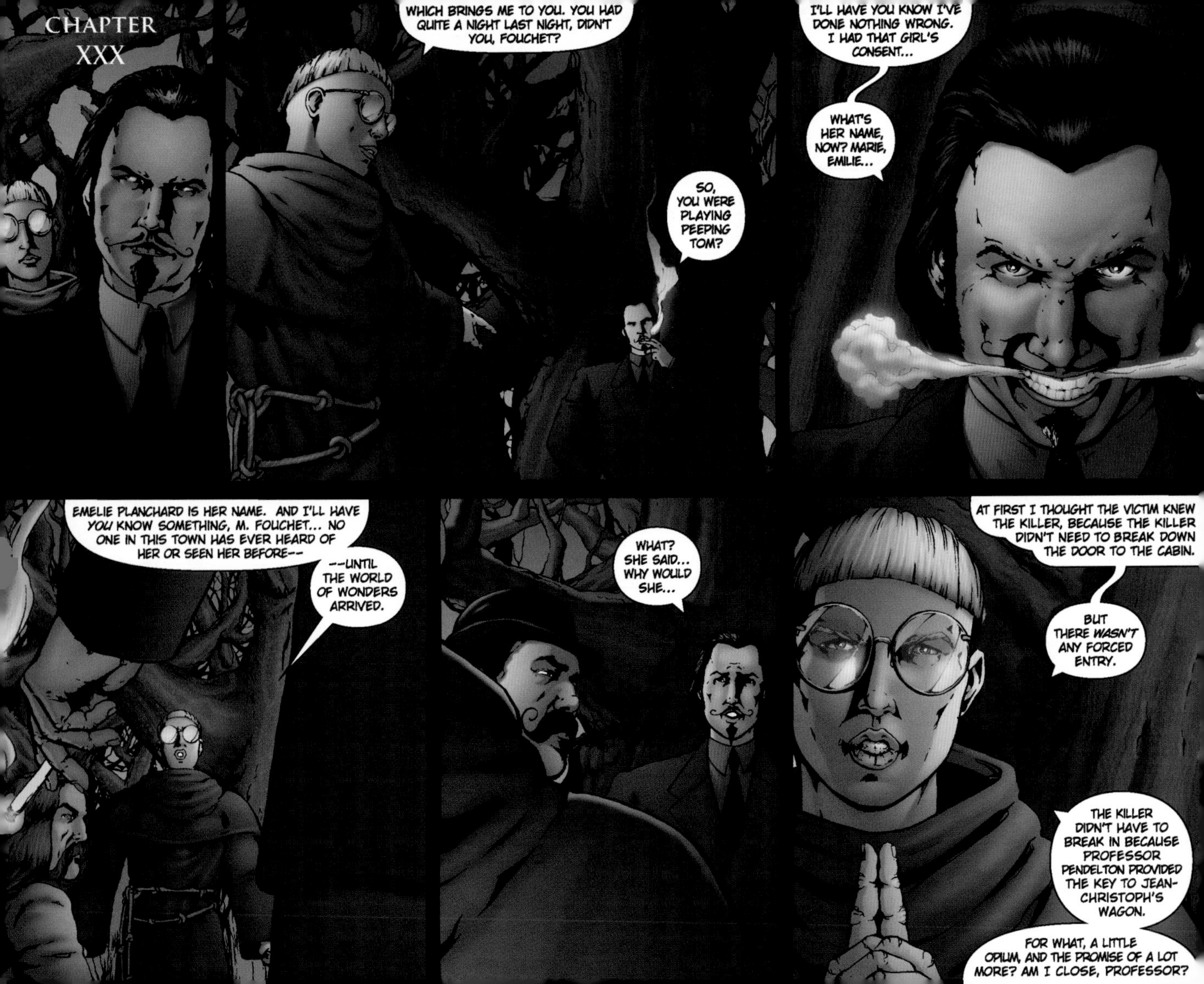
CHAPTER XXX
WHICH BRINGS ME TO YOU. YOU HAD QUITE A NIGHT LAST NIGHT, DIDN'T YOU, FOUCHET?
SO, YOU WERE PLAYING PEEPING TOM?
I'LL HAVE YOU KNOW I'VE DONE NOTHING WRONG. I HAD THAT GIRL'S CONSENT...
WHAT'S HER NAME, NOW? MARIE, EMILIE...
EMELIE PLANCHARD IS HER NAME. AND I'LL HAVE YOU KNOW SOMETHING, M. FOUCHET... NO ONE IN THIS TOWN HAS EVER HEARD OF HER OR SEEN HER BEFORE--
--UNTIL THE WORLD OF WONDERS ARRIVED.
WHAT? SHE SAID... WHY WOULD SHE...
AT FIRST I THOUGHT THE VICTIM KNEW THE KILLER, BECAUSE THE KILLER DIDN'T NEED TO BREAK DOWN THE DOOR TO THE CABIN.
BUT THERE WASN'T ANY FORCED ENTRY.
THE KILLER DIDN'T HAVE TO BREAK IN BECAUSE PROFESSOR PENDELTON PROVIDED THE KEY TO JEAN-CHRISTOPH'S WAGON.
FOR WHAT, A LITTLE OPIUM, AND THE PROMISE OF A LOT MORE? AM I CLOSE, PROFESSOR?

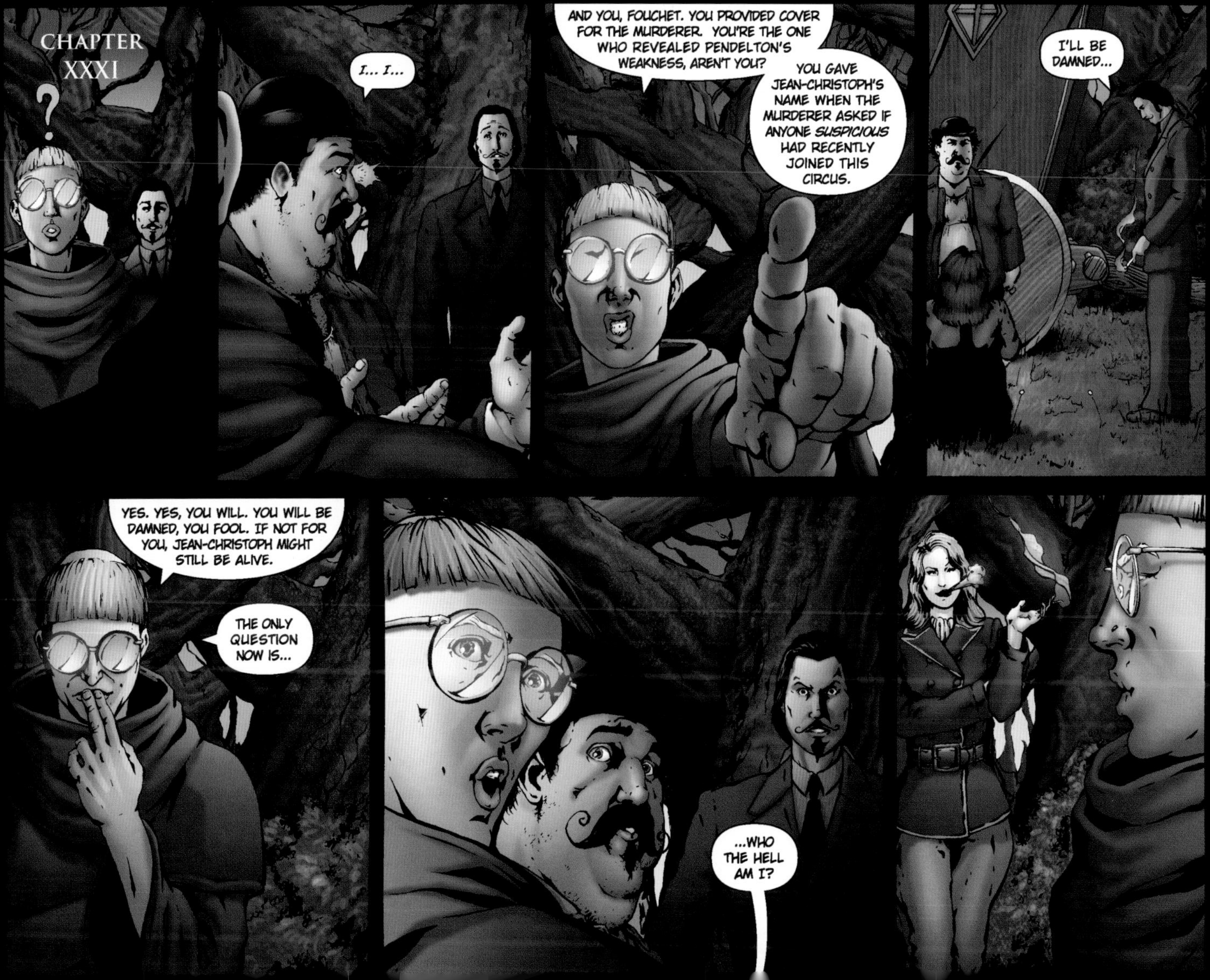
CHAPTER XXXI
?
I... I...
AND YOU, FOUCHET. YOU PROVIDED COVER FOR THE MURDERER. YOU'RE THE ONE WHO REVEALED PENDELTON'S WEAKNESS, AREN'T YOU?
YOU GAVE JEAN-CHRISTOPH'S NAME WHEN THE MURDERER ASKED IF ANYONE *SUSPICIOUS* HAD RECENTLY JOINED THIS CIRCUS.
I'LL BE DAMNED...
YES. YES, YOU WILL. YOU WILL BE DAMNED, YOU FOOL. IF NOT FOR YOU, JEAN-CHRISTOPH MIGHT STILL BE ALIVE.
THE ONLY QUESTION NOW IS...
...WHO THE HELL AM I?

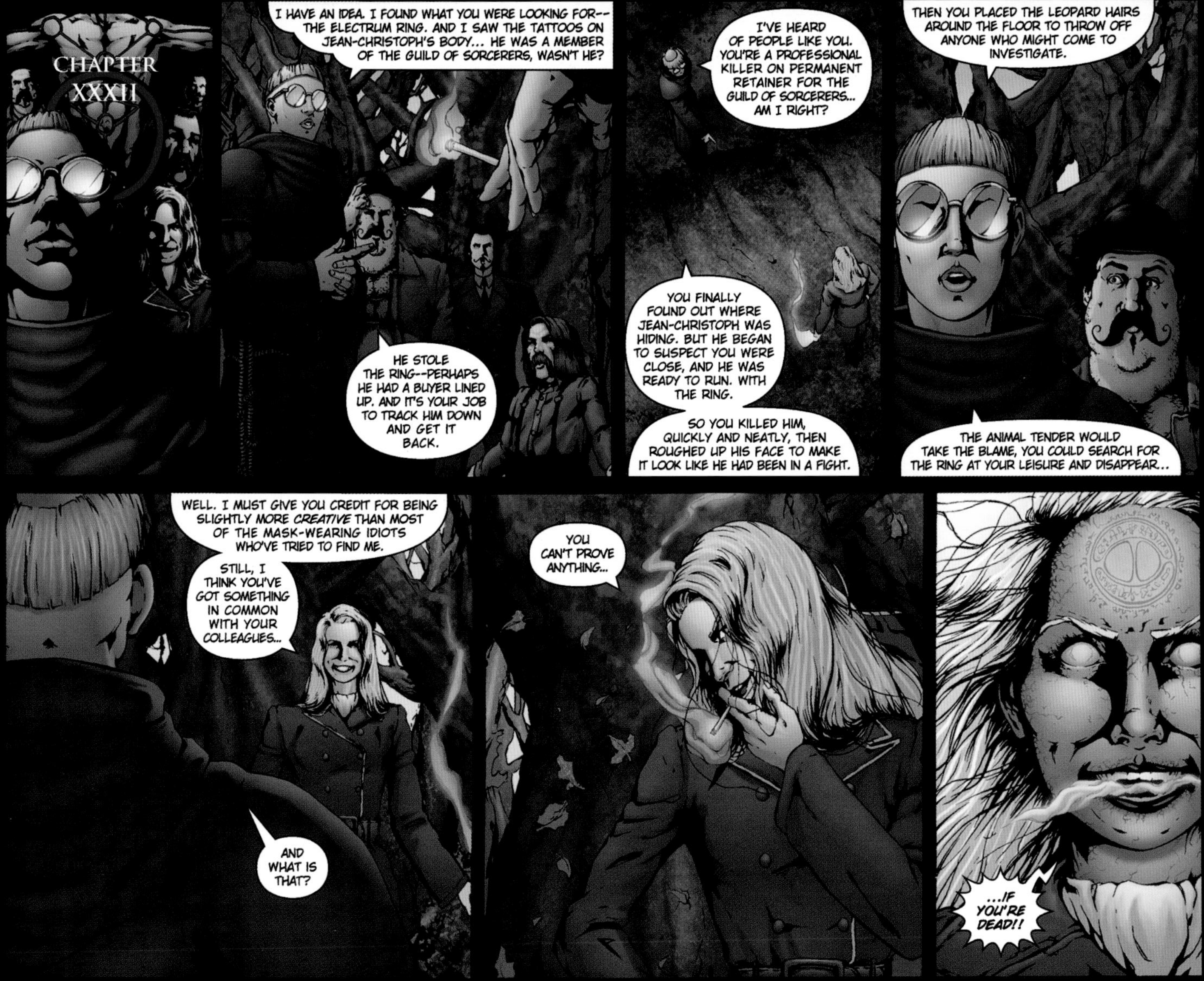
CHAPTER XXXII
I HAVE AN IDEA. I FOUND WHAT YOU WERE LOOKING FOR--THE ELECTRUM RING. AND I SAW THE TATTOOS ON JEAN-CHRISTOPH'S BODY... HE WAS A MEMBER OF THE GUILD OF SORCERERS, WASN'T HE?
HE STOLE THE RING--PERHAPS HE HAD A BUYER LINED UP. AND IT'S YOUR JOB TO TRACK HIM DOWN AND GET IT BACK.
I'VE HEARD OF PEOPLE LIKE YOU. YOU'RE A PROFESSIONAL KILLER ON PERMANENT RETAINER FOR THE GUILD OF SORCERERS... AM I RIGHT?
YOU FINALLY FOUND OUT WHERE JEAN-CHRISTOPH WAS HIDING. BUT HE BEGAN TO SUSPECT YOU WERE CLOSE, AND HE WAS READY TO RUN. WITH THE RING.
SO YOU KILLED HIM, QUICKLY AND NEATLY, THEN ROUGHED UP HIS FACE TO MAKE IT LOOK LIKE HE HAD BEEN IN A FIGHT.
THEN YOU PLACED THE LEOPARD HAIRS AROUND THE FLOOR TO THROW OFF ANYONE WHO MIGHT COME TO INVESTIGATE.
THE ANIMAL TENDER WOULD TAKE THE BLAME, YOU COULD SEARCH FOR THE RING AT YOUR LEISURE AND DISAPPEAR...
WELL. I MUST GIVE YOU CREDIT FOR BEING SLIGHTLY MORE CREATIVE THAN MOST OF THE MASK-WEARING IDIOTS WHO'VE TRIED TO FIND ME.
STILL, I THINK YOU'VE GOT SOMETHING IN COMMON WITH YOUR COLLEAGUES...
AND WHAT IS THAT?
YOU CAN'T PROVE ANYTHING...
...IF YOU'RE DEAD!!

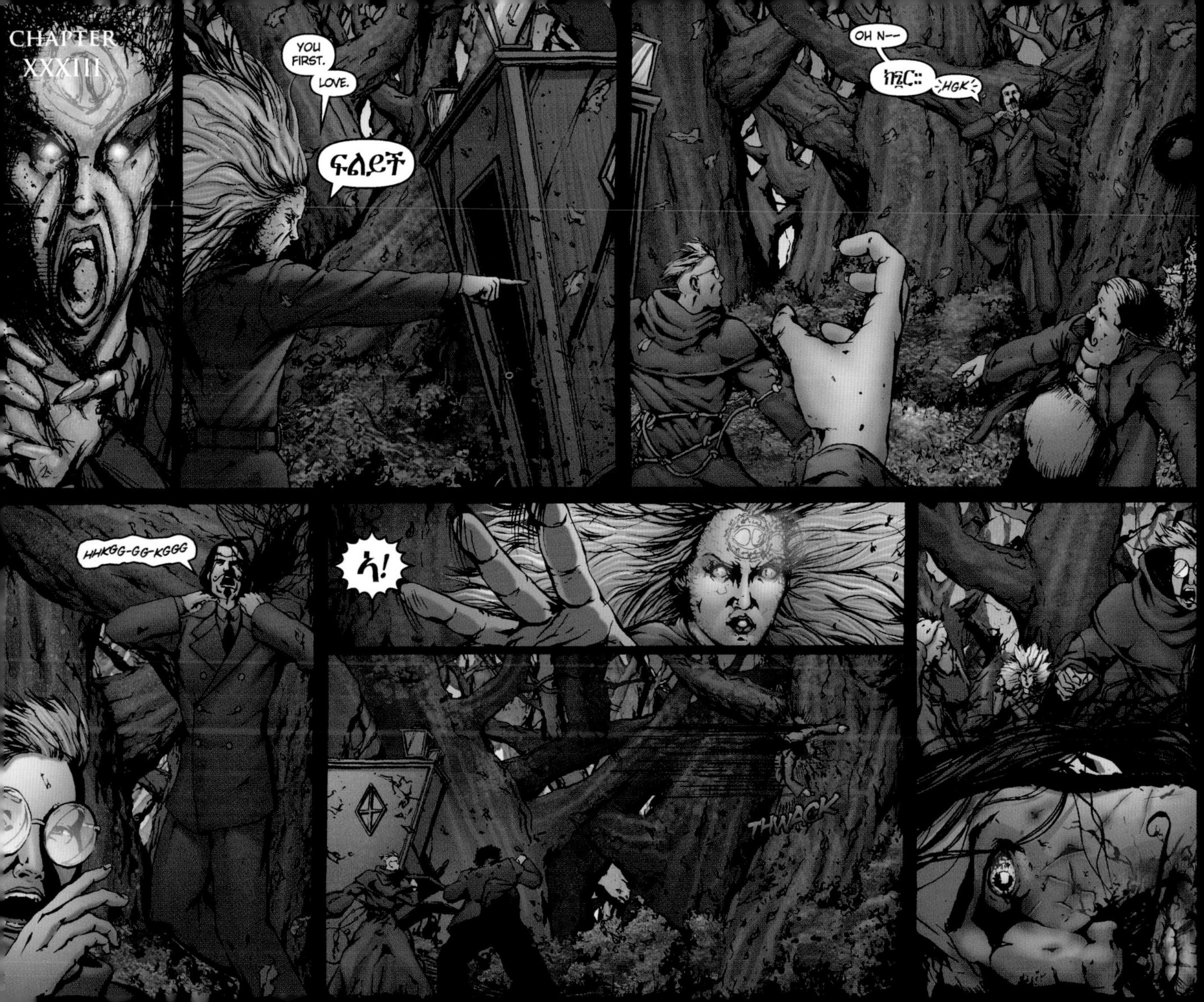
CHAPTER
XXXIII
YOU FIRST.
LOVE.
ፍሊይች
OH N--
ክሿር::
HGK
HHKGG-GG-KGGG
ኣ!
THWACK

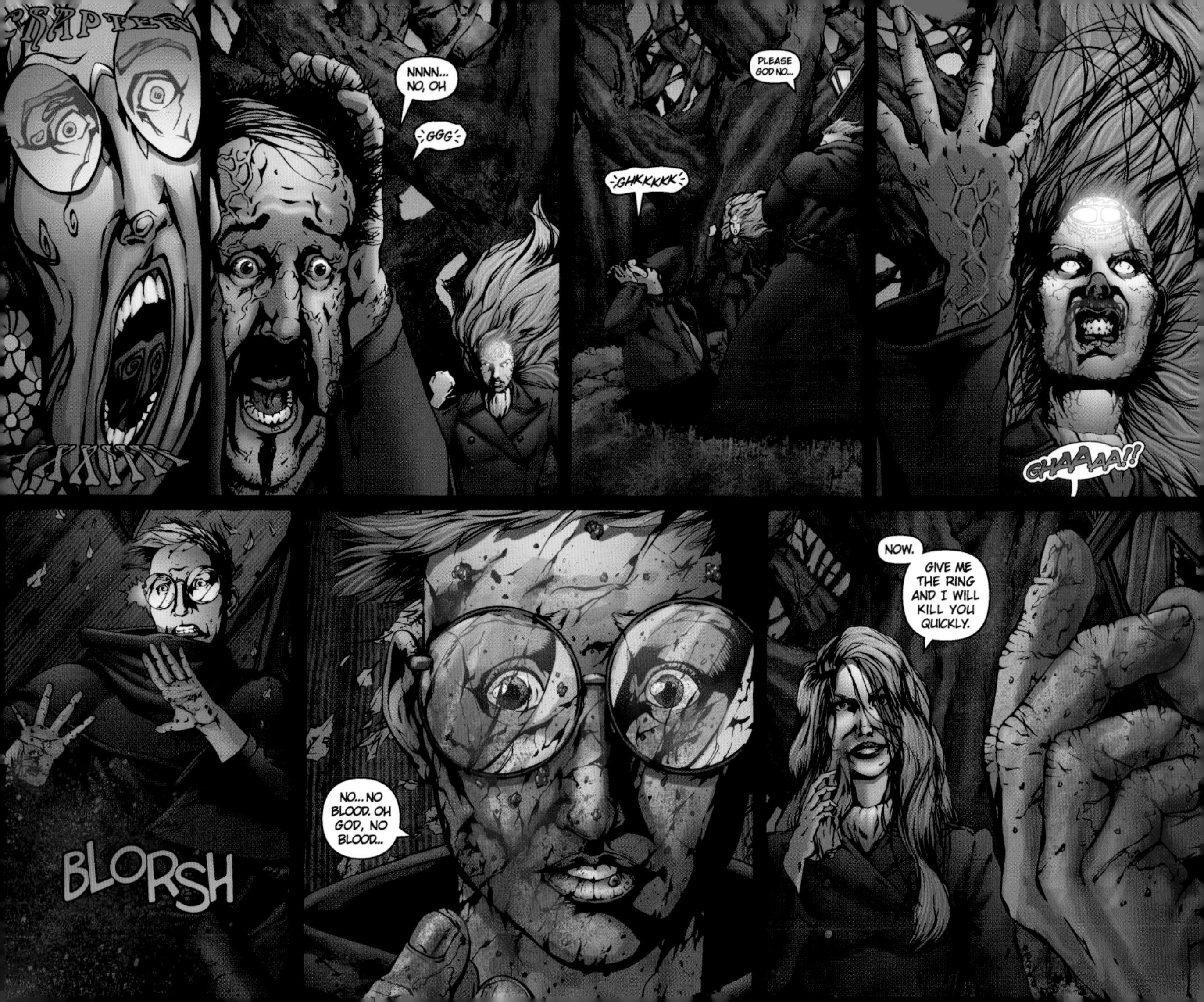
CHAPTER
NNNN... NO, OH
GGG
PLEASE GOD NO...
GHKKKKK
GHAAAA!!
BLORSH
NO... NO BLOOD. OH GOD, NO BLOOD...
NOW.
GIVE ME THE RING AND I WILL KILL YOU QUICKLY.

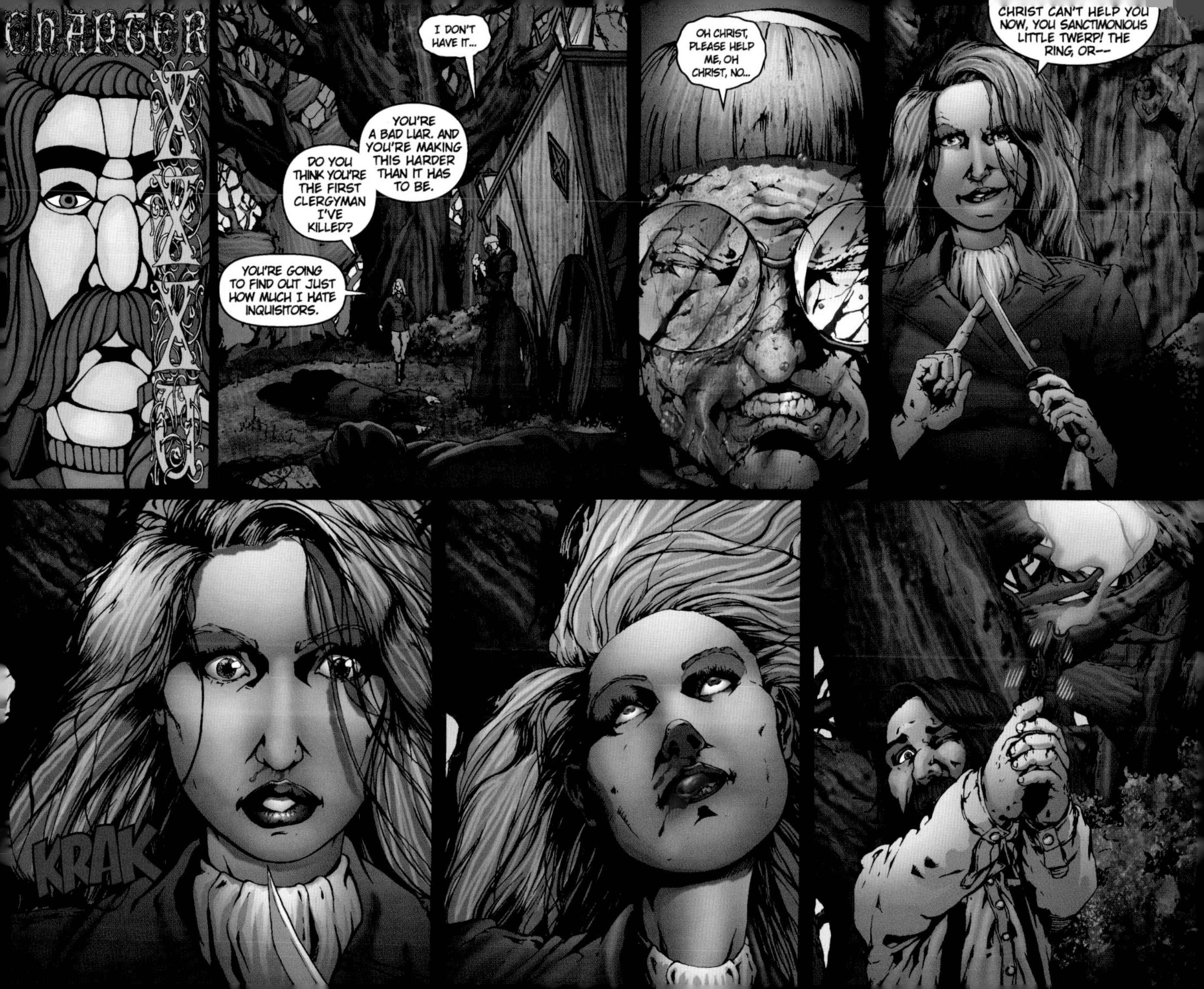
CHAPTER
I DON'T HAVE IT...
YOU'RE A BAD LIAR. AND YOU'RE MAKING THIS HARDER THAN IT HAS TO BE.
DO YOU THINK YOU'RE THE FIRST CLERGYMAN I'VE KILLED?
YOU'RE GOING TO FIND OUT JUST HOW MUCH I HATE INQUISITORS.
OH CHRIST, PLEASE HELP ME, OH CHRIST, NO...
CHRIST CAN'T HELP YOU NOW, YOU SANCTIMONIOUS LITTLE TWERP! THE RING, OR--
KRAK

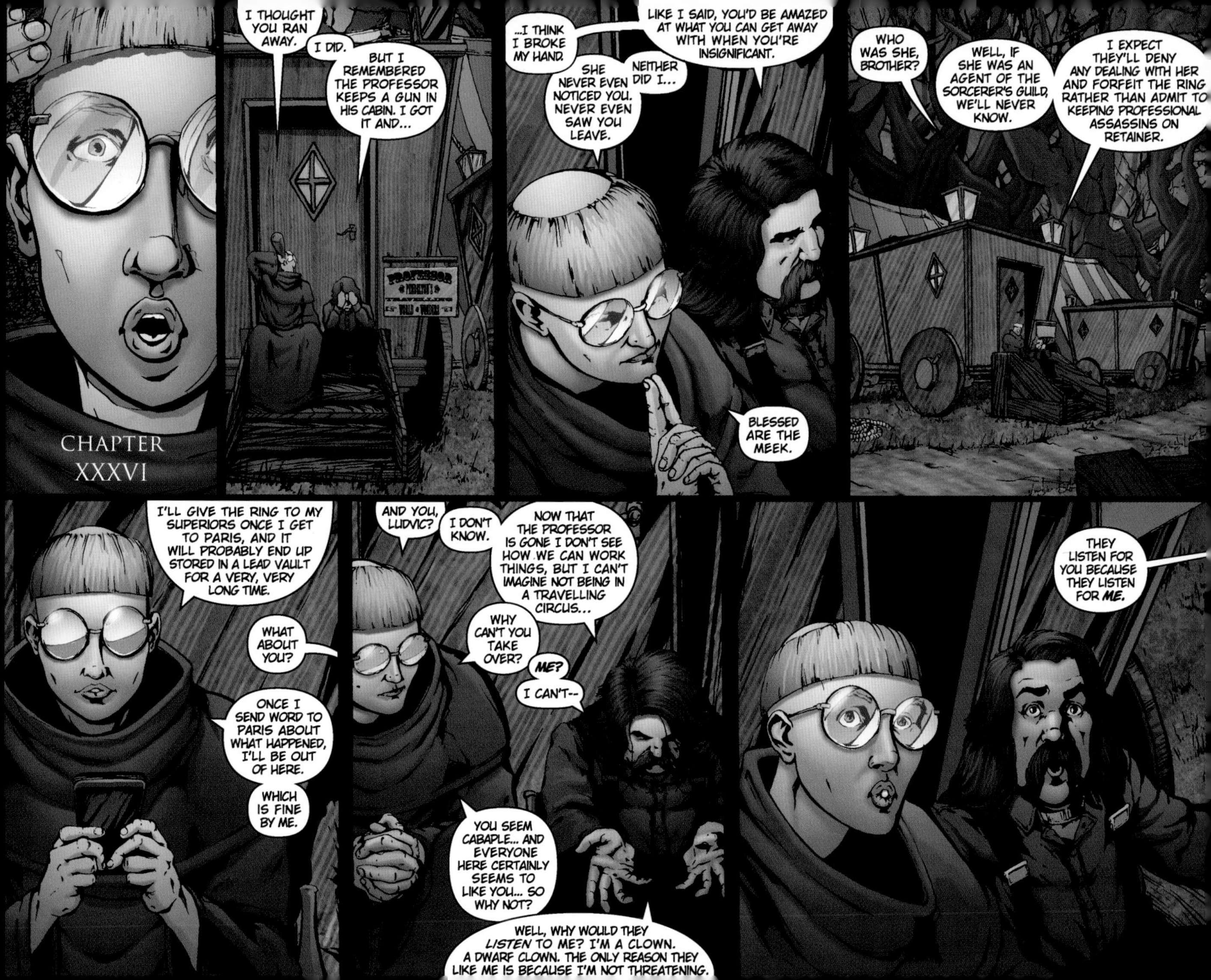
CHAPTER
XXXVI
I THOUGHT YOU RAN AWAY.
I DID.
BUT I REMEMBERED THE PROFESSOR KEEPS A GUN IN HIS CABIN. I GOT IT AND...
...I THINK I BROKE MY HAND.
LIKE I SAID, YOU'D BE AMAZED AT WHAT YOU CAN GET AWAY WITH WHEN YOU'RE INSIGNIFICANT.
NEITHER DID I...
SHE NEVER EVEN NOTICED YOU. NEVER EVEN SAW YOU LEAVE.
BLESSED ARE THE MEEK.
WHO WAS SHE, BROTHER?
WELL, IF SHE WAS AN AGENT OF THE SORCERER'S GUILD, WE'LL NEVER KNOW.
I EXPECT THEY'LL DENY ANY DEALING WITH HER AND FORFEIT THE RING RATHER THAN ADMIT TO KEEPING PROFESSIONAL ASSASSINS ON RETAINER.
I'LL GIVE THE RING TO MY SUPERIORS ONCE I GET TO PARIS, AND IT WILL PROBABLY END UP STORED IN A LEAD VAULT FOR A VERY, VERY LONG TIME.
WHAT ABOUT YOU?
ONCE I SEND WORD TO PARIS ABOUT WHAT HAPPENED, I'LL BE OUT OF HERE.
WHICH IS FINE BY ME.
AND YOU, LUDVIC?
I DON'T KNOW.
NOW THAT THE PROFESSOR IS GONE I DON'T SEE HOW WE CAN WORK THINGS, BUT I CAN'T IMAGINE NOT BEING IN A TRAVELLING CIRCUS...
WHY CAN'T YOU TAKE OVER?
ME?
I CAN'T--
YOU SEEM CABAPLE... AND EVERYONE HERE CERTAINLY SEEMS TO LIKE YOU... SO WHY NOT?
WELL, WHY WOULD THEY LISTEN TO ME? I'M A CLOWN. A DWARF CLOWN. THE ONLY REASON THEY LIKE ME IS BECAUSE I'M NOT THREATENING.
THEY LISTEN FOR YOU BECAUSE THEY LISTEN FOR ME.

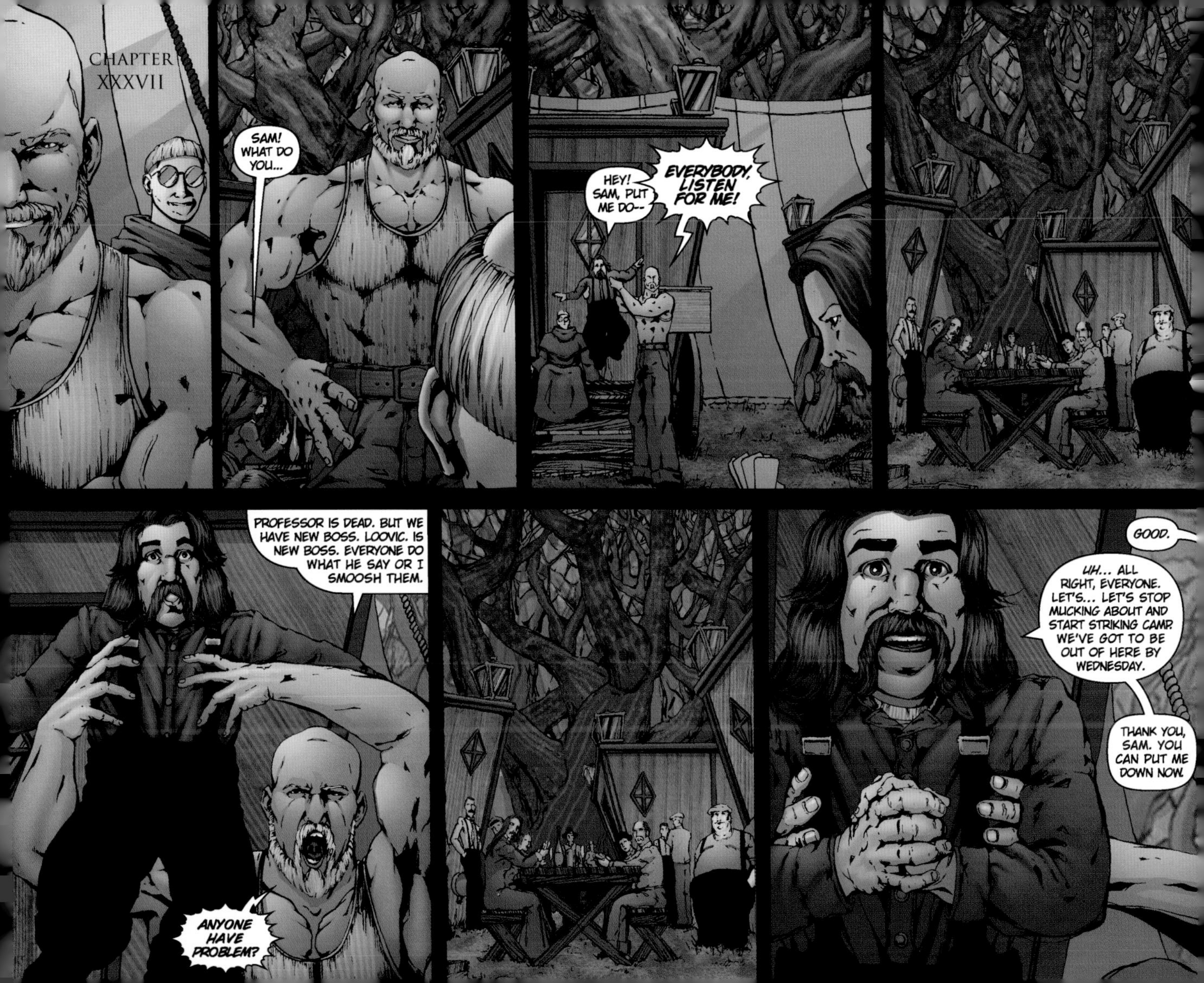
CHAPTER XXXVII
SAM! WHAT DO YOU...
HEY! SAM, PUT ME DO--
EVERYBODY, LISTEN FOR ME!
PROFESSOR IS DEAD. BUT WE HAVE NEW BOSS. LOOVIC. IS NEW BOSS. EVERYONE DO WHAT HE SAY OR I SMOOSH THEM.
ANYONE HAVE PROBLEM?
GOOD.
UH... ALL RIGHT, EVERYONE. LET'S... LET'S STOP MUCKING ABOUT AND START STRIKING CAMP. WE'VE GOT TO BE OUT OF HERE BY WEDNESDAY.
THANK YOU, SAM. YOU CAN PUT ME DOWN NOW.

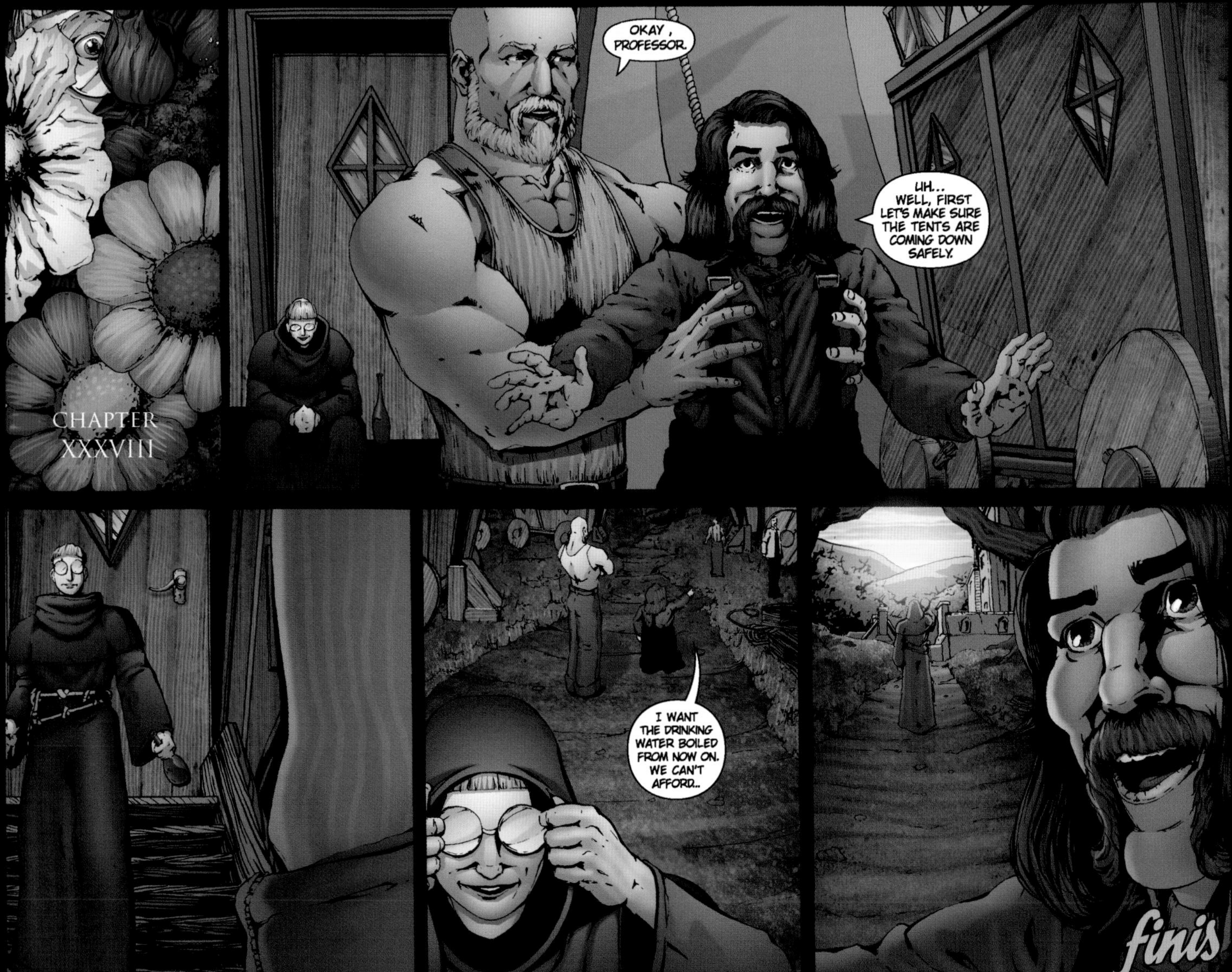
CHAPTER XXXVIII
OKAY, PROFESSOR.
UH... WELL, FIRST LET'S MAKE SURE THE TENTS ARE COMING DOWN SAFELY.
I WANT THE DRINKING WATER BOILED FROM NOW ON. WE CAN'T AFFORD...
finis

ALSO FROM DARK HORSE BOOKS!

ARVID NELSON
ERIC J
JEROMY COX
JIM DI BARTOLO
JUAN FERREYRA
REX MUNDI
BOOK THREE
The Lost Kings

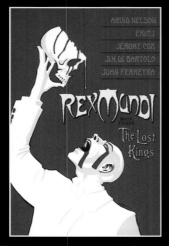

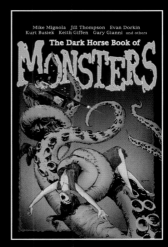

CHAPTER XXXIII

REX MUNDI VOLUME 3: THE LOST KINGS

Arvid Nelson, EricJ, Jim DiBartolo, and Juan Ferreyra

Julien furthers his investigation, only dimly aware of the forces tugging him down the trail of clues that lead to the doorstep, literally, of the Duke of Lorraine—a powerful man who seeks to provoke a massive, globe-spanning war that will soak the world in blood.

$16.95, ISBN: 1-59307-651-7

Mike Mignola Jill Thompson Evan Dorkin
Kurt Busiek Keith Giffen Gary Gianni and others
The Dark Horse Book of
MONSTERS

DARK HORSE BOOK OF MONSTERS

Mike Mignola, Gary Gianni, Evan Dorkin, Jill Thompson, Kurt Busiek, Keith Giffen, Arvid Nelson, Juan Ferreyra, and more.
Cover by Gary Gianni.

Mike Mignola takes Hellboy on a monster-crunching mission, Arvid Nelson and Juan Ferreyra reveal deadly secrets in a *Rex Mundi* story, and many more of the most talented folks in comics tell terrifying tales in this fourth addition to Dark Horse's Eisner-nominated books of *Hauntings, Witchcraft,* and *The Dead*.

$15.95, ISBN: 1-59307-656-8

HELLBOY
THE CHAINED COFFIN
and OTHERS
MIKE MIGNOLA

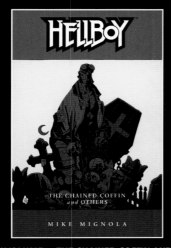

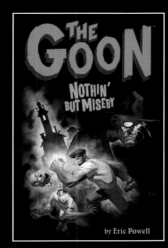

HELLBOY VOLUME 3: THE CHAINED COFFIN AND OTHERS

Mike Mignola

In this collection of short stories, Hellboy gets a terrible glimpse of his own origins in the ruined church where he was first brought to earth, Roger the Homunculus fights a giant made of human fat who happens to be his brother, and a grouchy corpse helps Hellboy find a missing baby.

$17.95, ISBN: 1-59307-091-8

THE GOON
NOTHIN' BUT MISERY
by Eric Powell

THE GOON VOLUME 1: NOTHIN' BUT MISERY

Eric Powell

The Zombie Priest is building himself an army of undead, and there's only one man who can put them in their place—the man they call Goon. This volume collects the impossible-to-find original series published by Albatross Exploding Funny Books in eye-popping full color for the first time ever!

$15.95, ISBN: 1-56971-998-5

AVAILABLE AT YOUR LOCAL COMICS SHOP OR BOOKSTORE
To find a comics shop in your area, call 1-888-266-4226
For more information or to order direct visit darkhorse.com or call 1-800-862-0052 • Mon.-Fri. 9 A.M. to 5 P.M. Pacific Time.
***Prices and availability subject to change without notice**

DARK HORSE COMICS *drawing on your nightmares*
darkhorse.com

ALSO FROM DARK HORSE BOOKS!

The DEVIL'S FOOTPRINTS
Scott Allie Paul Lee Brian Horton Dave Stewart

THE DEVIL'S FOOTPRINTS

Scott Allie, Paul Lee, Brian Horton, and Dave Stewart

Even after death, William Waite's foray into black magic continues to plague his heirs. Now it's up to his youngest son, Brandon, to protect his loved ones using the only means possible—witchcraft. But supernatural forces are unpredictable, and Brandon's good intentions just might destroy everything he's trying to save.

$14.95, ISBN: 1-56971-933-0

FREAKS of the HEARTLAND
STEVE NILES GREG RUTH

FREAKS OF THE HEARTLAND

Steve Niles and Greg Ruth

Under the weathered skies of America's heartland, and in the wounded hearts of every family in one tiny rural town, a terrible secret has been kept for too many years. Now, a young boy must try to keep his younger brother from falling victim to the tragic secret that binds the town's families together.

$17.95, ISBN: 1-59307-029-2

the BLACKBURNE COVENANT
fabian NICIEZA
stefano RAFFAELE

THE BLACKBURNE COVENANT

Fabian Nicieza and Stefano Raffaele

Someone is following Richard Kaine, someone interested in knowing how he came up with his best-selling historical-fantasy novel. How could he have written about an event that has been meticulously erased from every chronicle of human history? Who are the Blackburne Covenant, and why are they trying to kill Richard Kaine?

$12.95, ISBN: 1-56971-889-X

Revelations
PAUL JENKINS HUMBERTO RAMOS

REVELATIONS

Paul Jenkins & Humberto Ramos

When the cardinal next in line to succeed the ailing Pope turns up dead, Scotland Yard's finest detective, Charlie Northern, finds himself on a plane to Rome with little more than a full pack of cigarettes. With the help of a priest, a coroner, and one beautiful lawyer, Northern must uncover the facts in a place legendary for keeping its secrets.

$17.95, ISBN: 1-59307-239-2

AVAILABLE AT YOUR LOCAL COMICS SHOP OR BOOKSTORE

To find a comics shop in your area, call 1-888-266-4226

For more information or to order direct visit darkhorse.com or call 1-800-862-0052 • Mon.-Fri. 9 A.M. to 5 P.M. Pacific Time.

***Prices and availability subject to change without notice**

DARK HORSE COMICS *drawing on your nightmares*

darkhorse.com

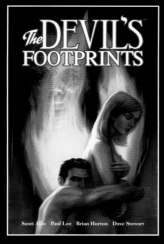